Bouchard

Child-Friendly Therapy

Biopsychosocial Innovations for Children and Families

Child-Friendly Therapy

Biopsychosocial Innovations for Children and Families

Marcia B. Stern, Psy.D.

W.W. Norton & Company
New York • London

The ambiguous figures on page 38 are by G. H. Fisher, "Seal/Donkey," "Rabbit/Indian," "Duck/Squirrel," from *Perception and Psychophysics*, volume 4, 1967. Used with permission of the Psychonomic Society of Publications.

The ambiguous figure on page 97 is by G. H. Fisher, "Mother, Father, and Daughter," from *American Journal of Psychology*, volume 81, copyright 1968 by the Board of Trustees of the University of Illinois. Used with the permission of the University of Illinois Press.

Screen Beans is a registered trademark of A Bit Better Corporation.

For information about permission to reproduce selections from this book, write to Permissions, W. W. Norton & Company, Inc., 500 Fifth Avenue, New York, NY 10110

The text of this book is composed in Goudy
with the display set in Coop Light.
Book Design and Composition by Publication Services, Inc.
Manufacturing by the Haddon Craftsmen, Inc.
Production Manager: Anna Oler

Library of Congress Cataloging-in-Publication Data
Stern, Marcia B.
  Child-friendly therapy: biopsychological innovations for children and families/
Marcia B. Stern
    p. cm.
  "A Norton professional book."
  Includes bibiographical references and index.
  ISBN 0-393-70355-X
    1. Child psychotherapy. 2. Family psychotherapy. I. Title.

RJ504 .S73 2002
618.92'8914--dc21

2002016646

W. W. Norton & Company, Inc., 500 Fifth Avenue, New York, N.Y. 10110
www.wwnorton.com

W. W. Norton & Company Ltd., Castle House, 75/76 Wells Street,
London W1T 3QT

1 2 3 4 5 6 7 8 9 0

With admiration and appreciation to Gillian Walker, friend, colleague, inspirer, mentor, motivator, scholar, and leader.

> Here's to the kids who are different,
> Kids who don't always get A's.
>   Kids who have ears
> Twice the size of their peers,
> And noses that go on for days.
> Here's to the kids who are different,
> Kids they call crazy or dumb.
>   Kids who don't fit,
> With the guts and the grit,
> Who dance to a different drum,
> Here's to the kids who are different,
> The kids with the mischievous streak,
>   For when they have grown,
> As history has shown,
> It's their difference that makes them unique.
>
> —Digby Wolfe

Contents

Acknowledgments

There were many people who supported this project. Without their help its completion would not have been possible. The ideas in this book developed from the collaborative thinking of my Unique Minds colleagues: Gillian Walker, Pat Heller, Anne Rivers, Martha Edwards, new member Angela Smith, former members Ana Escalante and Susan Shimmerlik, and the late Sondra Phelan. The synergy of our work together constantly drives my thinking in new ways. I am privileged to know and collaborate with these talented people. Our work together began at the Ackerman Institute for the Family and continues today at the NYU Child Study Center. Wonderful colleagues at both institutions are sources of support and provide the impetus for scholarly work. I am particularly grateful to Dr. Peter Steinglass, Executive Director of Ackerman, and to Dr. Harold Koplewicz, Director of the NYU Child Study Center.

My deepest appreciation goes to Lucy Aptekar, my dear friend and colleague whose editorial and reviewing assistance ensured that I expressed my ideas clearly. Your questions, wisdom, friendship, hand holding, unfailing support and advice from start to finish carried me through every step of the way.

Heartfelt gratitude and appreciation to:

The clients, the children, and the families, who generously shared their stories and artwork and taught me something new in every session.

Steve, my husband and steady anchor, helper, reader, assistant, friend, listener, reviewer, and chef extraordinaire. Thank you for always holding down the fort.

My loving son, Keith, for his abiding enthusiasm and optimism.

My mother, who taught me perseverance.

My sister and other family members, who cheered me on to the finish line.

Pat Heller, my wise and wonderful forever friend.

Rachel Schiller, who provided fresh eyes and editorial assistance at a critical juncture.

Menucha Stubenhaus, who skillfully helped manage the bibliography.

Daniela Jacobs, my frequent artistic collaborator, who made enchanting drawings for the jacket and book.

Catherine Rossi, who assisted me on the appendix, and Devan Aptekar, who helped tackle the proofs.

Dr. Keith Ditkowsky and Dr. Angela Smith, who read and made suggestions for the section on medication.

Special thanks to the Norton staff. Deborah Malmud embodies the important qualities of an editor, encouragement, warmth, sense of humor, skill, and availability, and Regina Dahlgren Ardini wields a skillful but gentle editorial pencil—I appreciated the notes that ended with "As always, call with any questions."

Thank you to those who read portions of the manuscript and gave feedback: Joan Hoffenberg, Lela Charney, Janice Josephson, Ilona Musen, Ray Wolfson, and Bruce Kessler.

Introduction

I had just finished a therapy session with Amelia. I smiled as I thought about how hard she was working and about the surprising insights she had into her current struggles. Amelia greeted her mom and brother in the waiting room. Then, in the time it took the three of them to reach the car in the driveway, I could hear the screams and shouts of yet another fight.

When I first started working with children it was largely within an individual model, with parents seen in collateral sessions. While I worked diligently, I sometimes felt that treatment wasn't "sticking." I noticed that too often our work together was "undone" a few minutes after the office door closed. It seemed that getting the results of our efforts out into the real world was like throwing spitballs at an elephant—I could hardly get anyone's attention.

Problems don't develop in a vacuum. Understanding the family context is crucial to change. Readings in family therapy had told me families operate as systems and each person's behavior influences how others behave. If family members succeed in changing a key behavior, then they may influence how other family members behave. With this in mind, I decided that the best way to help move things along for child clients was to bring in the family.

While family members can be the best resource the child has, how to engage the family and keep the child involved became the challenge. Family sessions would need to *include* and *involve* children—two different stories. To include children would mean having them in the office during sessions. To involve them would mean having their active participation—no solo block-building or coloring in the corner while the grown-ups talked.

As I moved from theory to practice, in my early family-centered sessions I felt like a newly married woman about to give a dinner party for her family and her in-laws. Would the "guests" talk to one another? (To add to this dilemma would be the referral group that presented particular challenges because of explosive behaviors, the clients whose difficulties often had biological under-pinnings.) What would it mean to bring a third or fourth person into the room—parent who has the same fiery passionate temperament as the referred child, a sibling whose inherited nature makes him more timid and withdrawn? There would be individuals with varying abilities and interests. How would I, as a therapist, make it all work?

There were other quandaries as well. Could I still get to know the child, separate from the family? Did family work mean leaving behind the individual work with the child? Could I find ways to make the treatment child-friendly and playful, highlight the child's voice, and help children and families take treatment home? While the child therapy literature offered a wealth of methods, there was an absence of techniques for those involved in family-centered work. Conversations with colleagues, additional training, reading, getting into the trenches and doing the work, and learning from clients helped move the process along.

And so I began. At first, sessions often felt unwieldy as I learned how to deal with more than one person at a time, varied energy and attention levels, differences in cognitive styles and abilities, varied difficulties in initiating and sustaining attention, and a wide range of communication skills. "Give up family-based work," I sometimes thought, "it has too many similarities to glassblowing—one false step and the fragile piece could lose its shape or crack." But on the other hand, I saw that it was working.

Over time, I was able to answer many of my own earlier questions. I discovered that everything I knew and learned had a place and was useful in a collaborative family-centered therapy: there was no need to leave behind the individual work with the child; child sessions have an important place; family inclusion and involvement certainly move the work along; there were ways to make the treatment child-friendly and playful, to highlight the child's voice, and to help children and families take treatment home.

What follows are the lessons I learned as I made my way on my child-friendly therapy journey. I have attempted to take up the quandaries I referred to earlier and present models and solutions for dealing with them. I have tried to bring together theory and utility and I hope I have accomplished that goal. This work is a continual learning experience and the challenge is ongoing. Software developers recognize the need to upgrade their software as they receive feedback from the users. I find that work with children and families also needs upgrades. The input from others helps to create new and improved user-friendly applications.

My teachers have been my clients; the inspiration has been these clients, the work, and the wisdom and legacy of clinicians and researchers such as Salvador Minuchin, David Epston, Michael White, Milton Erickson, Ellen Wachtel, and Beatrice (Betsy) Wood. In my work, every session is influenced by the synergy and group input of the Unique Minds Team I am part of at the Child Study Center at the NYU School of Medicine.

I always knew I wanted to work with children. For as long as I can remember I was lining up chairs and recruiting others to join my "class." I was always fascinated by how people felt about a particular event, no doubt a consequence of my own temperament and nature. That I felt deeply was surely shaped by an early tragedy that left me without a father or extended family. I learned courage from my mother as I watched her pull together the threads of hope that were left and build anew. I was to call on these lessons later as my own journey on life's highway had many challenging curves and turns. Now, after almost 30 years of working with them, children still fascinate me. I love to spend time with them and see the world through their eyes. They are the best teachers and collaborators in the world.

Child-Friendly Therapy

Biopsychosocial Innovations for Children and Families

PART I

Words Are Not Enough

A Biopsychosocial Approach

CHAPTER I

Child-Friendly Therapy

An Overview

TODAY'S KIDS AND FAMILIES

Jonah was entering school and needed to have a psychological evaluation. He reported to the testing site with his mom, Shelly, and his brother, Ezra. While Shelly and I talked, Ezra and Jonah played quietly. As I walked off with Jonah, Ezra looked at me longingly and asked me if I had anything that he could do. I reached into my closet and pulled out a large bag of small wooden figures. These figures had given my now-grown son hours of joy each day as his imagination brought them to life in battle, sports competition, or some other important activity. Ezra smiled broadly, and eagerly took them from my hand. A few minutes later there was a knock at the door of my testing room. It was Ezra and he appeared to be distressed. He looked up at me seriously and said, "Dr. Marcia, you forgot to give me the batteries."

In many respects we are dealing with a changed society of children. As clinicians, we often find them more difficult to engage in traditional talking therapy. Why? Today's kids are different than they were before the advent of VCRs, fax machines, video games, and computers. Video games may have had the most dramatic impact on the development of young children's brains; the adrenaline rush to the brain that occurs as kids run after pocket monsters whose names adults can't even pronounce, trains the brain to respond to high levels of stimulation. The more children play hand-held computer games, the more the reward circuitry of the brain gets reinforced. As a result we see a more passive generation with weak attention skills and little tolerance for boredom.[1] Children, whose parents may have been couch potatoes, sit for hours in front of the computer and are "mouse potatoes." This physical inactivity, combined with fast food and high-fat diets, is causing them to be overweight.[2]

The impact of information technology, where "snail-mail" brains give way to "e-mail" brains, along with the American love affair with visual stimulation, has systematically reinforced the need of today's kids for immediate gratification of their desires. The forces of American consumerism help to entrench this need. Today's kids are shoppers and mall-dwellers. Advertisers are aware of children's habits and increasingly target the huge and growing number of customers in the children's market. It is estimated that $2 billion is spent annually on marketing and advertising aimed at children. These efforts are successful. A 1999 national survey of 400 parents found that two-thirds say their children define their self-worth by their belongings.[3] Parents, worried that their children won't fit in, give in to the pressure from today's kids and feed their "buying habit"—even if it means they have to work longer hours to do so.

The "buy, buy" attitude comes not only with a huge economic price tag; our hectic work-and-spend way of life also has huge social costs. In 1998, over 1.4 million families declared personal bankruptcy, credit card debt reached new heights, and the personal savings rate fell to the lowest level since the Great Depression. Millions of Americans report feeling exhausted, pressured, and hungry for more balanced lives. They are seeking greater purpose and more free time to spend with family and friends.[4]

In addition to a culture of consumerism, drug use and a high crime rate also have a profound effect on today's children. Everyday exposure to violence has increased dramatically and has traumatic effects, especially on those children who witness violence at home. The horrific events of the September 11, 2001 attacks on America leave us with a unique set of terrors, and as a nation we are under siege from threats of hijackings, bombings, and bioterrorism. The familiar question, "Did the mail arrive yet?" now arouses fearful images. Colleagues and clients alike report common complaints of insomnia and nightmares, panic, anxiety, depression, and wide-scale acute stress symptoms. While we are all clinging to one another and looking for reasons to be hopeful, the unthinkable has happened and we are left with a sense of vulnerability and powerlessness.

Increasing numbers of children and adolescents are at risk for developing posttraumatic stress disorder, risk-taking behaviors, and psychopathology. Children who witness violence at home are also affected emotionally. While violence is found in every sector of our populace, those who live in poverty may have increased exposure. Currently, 40 percent of persons living in poverty are children. For some, school is also a place of violence. Ricky, who lives in the projects, tells me he worries that he will be assaulted in school and that he needs a weapon for protection. He hides a razor blade in his cheek as he walks to school and keeps it there to escape the bells of the metal detector. Olivia also lives in public housing. She tells me that shootings, stabbings, and gangs are a part of her everyday life.

Research affirms what we already know: Children who live in poverty suffer detrimental effects. Exposure to violence can have an impact on all aspects of development. It can lead to lowered school achievement and internalization and externalization of problems. In addition, exposure to violence can compromise a child's early brain development. More sadly, living with violence colors children's views of themselves, of their world, and of the purpose and meaning of their lives. The 2001 Surgeon General's report on youth violence noted violence of epidemic-like proportion in the years from 1983 to 1993; while there has been a decline in more recent years, the number of adolescents involved in violent acts continues to be alarmingly high. Large numbers of today's kids suffer from maltreatment.[5]

Clearly, kids of today are having a hard time. While large numbers of women and families are homeless, many of today's kids who do have a place to call home often find it empty when they return from school. These "latchkey children" contend with loneliness, isolation, and all too often poor adult supervision. In addition, the divorce rate in this country continues to be very high. Current estimates state that between 50 and 60 percent of first marriages end in divorce. Second-marriage failure rates are about 10 percent higher. More than half of blended families end in divorce. Children of divorce suffer; compared with children in never-divorced families, they have significantly more adjustment and achievement problems.[6]

Today's kids are stressed. Social factors such as poverty, violence, family problems, terrorism, and the drive toward consumerism, "more, more, more," lead to high levels of anxiety. Statistics from the United States National Health Interview Survey found increases in parent-reported chronic and disabling childhood mental health conditions, which are judged to be a major cause of childhood disability. In the years 1992 to 1994 an estimated 1,448,000 U.S. children (2.13%) were identified as having a disabling mental condition. Approximately 80 percent of these children needed special education services and additional health care, significantly impacting the educational and health care systems. The U.S Department of Education reported an increase of 3.8 million children in special education enrollment between the years 1976 and 1993. Psychosocial problems in pediatric populations are also on the rise.[7]

Today's parents are stressed. Along with increased levels of psychosocial problems in children has been a concomitant increase in the prevalence of mental disorders, particularly depression, in adult groups. One in three employed Americans works weekends and there has been a dramatic rise in dual-earner couples. Among this group, "one in four includes at least one spouse who is a shift worker—one in three if they have children." For some women, going to work or maintaining a career is a choice; for others, single motherhood, economic, and social pressures push them to join the workforce. Mothers' multiple roles force them to rush from the workplace only to begin work anew with a night of homework, baths, and housecleaning. The boundaries between work and home have blurred as technology, beepers, cell phones, and faxes have made it impossible to escape work and relax. How do the increasing demands on a parent's time affect family life? Carryover of work stress to home is a problem and troubled marriages are sometimes a consequence.[8] Balancing family life and work is an act that often leaves little time for leisure, social interaction, and family fun.

One of Today's Kids: Eva

Eva is one of today's kids. She's a right-brained,[9] action-oriented 6-year-old who is enamored with television and pleads for every new product she sees advertised. She tells me that she loves video games, chat rooms, and her Sony PlayStation®, and hates homework and school. Both her parents have high-stress careers. My first contact with her and her family was through a despairing phone call from her mother, Yvonne. "My husband, Eric, and I can't stop fighting about how best to handle our daughter Eva's behavior." Yvonne described Eva as irritable, aggressive, and stubborn. In part, Eva was difficult for her parents to manage because she had problems with self-regulation. She seemed to have little capacity for self-soothing and little ability to be soothed. Eva had a heightened physiological response to noise, textures, and bodily sensations, such as hunger. Diagnosed with attention-deficit/hyperactivity disorder, Eva was prescribed a psychostimulant medication, Ritalin, which recently she was refusing to take. She had problems getting along with other children, tended to blame everything on everyone else, and had few friends. Because of the heated disagreements between Yvonne and Eric, and Eva's obstinate ways, the temperature in the house was hot. Yvonne sadly noted that she was constantly critical and negative with Eva. Yvonne, who reported herself as suffering from depression, added that Eva's erratic nature mirrored Eric's.

Despite the fact that she had been in different types of therapy during the last three years, there had been no intervention that seemed to manage Eva's difficult behavior. Yvonne wept as she told me how previous treatments had gone. "We feel as if we tried everything. Eva's first therapist worked only with Eva. They played games together, which Eva loved, but there was no carryover to the real world. I had only a few concrete ideas of how to handle her at home so, for a while, my husband and I met weekly and were trained how to manage Eva's behavior. Her second therapist didn't gratify Eva's wishes to play and Eva flatly refused to go. Now she and I go together and my husband comes sometimes. Nothing seems to stick. She either sits there week after week and gives the therapist all the right answers or is argumentative and jeers and snickers at him. She can be quite charming sometimes and tells him everything she thinks he wants to hear. When we get home, it's another story. Sometimes she doesn't even wait until we get home; she stops listening the moment we step out of the office. Our current therapist is dismissing Eva from treatment and told us that my husband and I have to learn to work together and stop arguing. He says Eva gets stuck in our struggles and her difficulties are a reflection of our troubled marriage.[10] He tells us that Eva's problem will not go away until we work on our relationship. I feel very pessimistic about our situation."

As I listened to Yvonne's story, many questions came to mind about why Eva's treatment was not going well. For example, was Eva's diagnosis clear and linked to treatment? Was Eva a collaborator whose voice was being heard in the treatment? Did her parents use inconsistent management techniques? Was there follow-through in the home? Was Eva getting pulled into her parents' conflict, thereby diverting the marital tensions? Whether for these or other reasons, therapy was not working.

An Inclusive View: A Biopsychosocial Framework

There are many lenses through which to view Eva's struggles. One is through the biological lens that explains the causes of disorders in terms of "the dysfunction of tissues and cells."[11] Proponents of this model would examine biologic causes of Eva's reported disinhibition and poor attention and concentration. They might discuss a dysregulation in the brain's chemical messengers implicated in attention disorders,[12] weaknesses in certain regions in the brain,[13] neuropsychological deficits,[14] or difficulty integrating sensory information.[15] A focus might be on the body's response to stress.[16] Another perspective offers a psychological explanation of the disorder and looks at "patterns of thinking, feeling, perceiving, cognating, and behaving."[17] Eva's anger may be understood as a difficulty in social information processing, the impact of her automatic cognitive style[18] that results in poor coping strategies, and difficulty with anger management. A third explanation for Eva's problems offers a social perspective and focuses on problems in interpersonal interactions.[19] Clearly Eva's social world is tense and she has problems in getting along at home, at school, and with friends. Are her stressed social relationships the cause of her problems, or are they the result?

There is no one "correct" lens through which to view Eva's case. Her behavior has multiple causes. Every child's internal makeup and experience of the environment is shaped by biological, environmental, psychological, and social factors. These biopsychosocial influences include genetic endowment, temperament, and "fit"[20] with the environment. A biopsychosocial model presents a holistic, multidimensional perspective that integrates these views and gives a broad picture of how they all contribute to the presenting problem. There are distinct advantages when this view is practiced:

> Evidence is accumulating that both biological and psychosocial factors are relevant in understanding the causes and mechanisms of major psychiatric disorders. In this modern-day reframing of the nature versus nurture controversy, we have learned that gene expression is inextricably bound to environmental influences and to the meaning those influences have to the individual.[21]

As we will see throughout this book, using a biopsychosocial perspective provides a framework for intervention across several domains. Psychoeducation may help Eva and her parents understand the role of biology that contributes to her fierce inherited temperament, restlessness, high level of motor activity, and intense moods.[22] Genes however do not act in isolation and, as we will see in Chapter 4, are "inextricable partners" with the environment.[23] Nature and nurture both have crucial roles in child and parent behavior; both influence the patterns of interactions that family members develop.

The mind and body are also inextricably linked. As we will discuss in Chapter 7, early experiences, bonding, and attachment shape the developing brain, including affect regulation. Eva's difficulty with affect regulation impacts on her experiences. Her experiences, in turn, shape her developing personality. Psychological interventions might include working with Eva to learn ways to stop and think and manage her behavior.[24] Teaching her ways to relax and cope better will be helpful.[25] Multiple interventions across home and school environments are required. Interactional problems that are a result of the mutually shaping influences of beliefs, expectations, gender, and culture can be addressed in family sessions. Yvonne and Eric's high expressed emotion[26] (which have been found to be indicators of chronic psychiatric and medical illness) should be reduced. Intervention in the school setting, such as instituting a contingency management program, is also essential.[27] Most of all, ways to help each family member use and practice new competencies and skills in the different settings must be found—therapy then will become part and parcel of life outside the treatment room.

Children with Brain-based Disorders

Children like Eva often have difficulties in multiple arenas. They might have social problems, interpersonal difficulties, learning disabilities, or suffer from a spectrum of related psychiatric problems. These problems might include internalizing disorders (those of anxiety or mood) and/or externalizing disorders (those of attention, activity, opposition and defiance, or conduct).

When we imagine what an optimal *educational* setting for children with these disorders might look like, we envision an environment that is rich in opportunities to learn. Because research tells us that children with brain-based disorders do best in settings that offer hands-on and sensory-rich learning, instruction would rely on a multisensory approach.[28] The very nature of their strengths and weaknesses would demand that instruction be provided *differently*. In keeping with this demand, an educational intervention plan would take into consideration the child's strengths and weaknesses and use them to develop strategies to help her succeed in school. Unfortunately, only rarely is such consideration given to a child's neuropsychological profile in the treatment setting where words, that is, talk therapy, is still the norm.

In therapy, not enough consideration is given to how these children take in and understand information, and learn. Statistics indicate that the majority of children show preference for, and perform better, when learning is presented in a tactile-kinesthetic manner.[29] This percentage might be considerably higher in groups of children who struggle in academic and/or social-emotional domains. These children might be restless, have impaired ability to integrate sensory information, suffer from cognitive and social skill weaknesses, and/or have difficulties in initiating, sustaining, and shifting attention. These children may know the right action to take, but innate temperament and biology make it difficult for them to choose it. This often leads to social problems that leave them lonely and unhappy.

Most of the traditional schools of psychotherapy are language-based and rely on explanation, analytic skills, and interpretation. They are geared toward left-brain learning, knowledge, and skills. However, for many of the children and families we see in therapy, some of whom are our treatment failures, words are not enough. For clinicians working with these children, this book presents sensory-rich therapy techniques that maximize involvement. This book advocates inclusion of a "learning by doing" approach, in line with the Chinese saying "I hear and I forget, I see and I remember; I do and I understand."

A MULTIFACETED APPROACH

The therapy described in this book helps the family understand the child's difficulties from multiple perspectives.[30] It weaves a tapestry that leads to fresh understandings of often confusing and misunderstood children, those who suffer with disorders having biological origins. Therapy for the child is family-based, and discussion begins at the neurobiological level. Together, the therapist and the family look at behaviors in the child's individual profile. Family members work as a team, strategizing and collaborating in a child-friendly, systemically informed treatment. Psychoeducation and a descriptive approach help to demystify the child's problem by providing the family with shared knowledge and information.

Treatment also takes into account that families have genetic predispositions and tendencies to certain disorders. The characteristics and behaviors of the referred child are often present in their parents. In some cases the parents may have had experiences with these behaviors in their families of origin or with other family members. History and experience predispose them toward certain ways of believing, understanding, and behaving. The biopsychosocial approach advocated in this book examines how these beliefs and behaviors shape one's relational world and family life and cause families to get stuck in vicious cycles. One of the goals of therapy is to help families end these vicious cycles by changing the home environment and creating a more positive atmosphere. Therapy opens doors to understanding a child's struggles and provides intervention with the family and in the child's world outside the home.

In my clinical practice, I find that more rapid and long-lasting therapeutic gains are made in child-focused family-based therapy that includes action-oriented techniques in addition to talking. These techniques, which engage family members through right-brain learning, include visual imagery, metaphor, and imaginative play. The child is recognized as a person in and of him- or herself, is actively engaged, and becomes a protagonist who learns in the presence of and *along with* the family. Although I am deeply committed to systemic thinking and work within an overall systemic framework, I use a number of different techniques. My work is a combination of family, cognitive, narrative, and behavior therapies. It integrates a "doing" aspect, incorporating skill-building, multisensory activities and games the whole family can do or play together. These techniques help to enhance family relatedness, increase empathy for one another's plight, and provide family members with new ways and a positive language with which to talk about their trouble spots. In addition, these activities help families practice and consolidate new learning, as together they build a more hopeful future.

A basic goal of therapeutic work with families is to bring about change through new information[31] and new ways of seeing, feeling, and understanding. While there are standardized tests, there are no standardized children. Thus, treatment for today's unique minds must reflect the novel, dynamic approach of an interested, involved therapist. Therapy must take into account a multiplicity of factors including the physical environment, cognitive variables, such as language, memory and attention, and learning styles. At the heart of the therapist's work should be a play-full approach that helps keep the child and the family involved.

IT'S EVERYBODY'S PROBLEM:
THE FAMILY IS CENTRAL TO TREATMENT

Few would dispute that the family is a major influence on all aspects of a child's development and adjustment.

> The strong tie between the quality of key family relationships and general functioning numbers among the best established findings in social science. . . . Innumerable studies in developmental psychology demonstrate that patterns of child rearing and family process have vital and lasting impacts on the development of virtually every personality characteristic and form of psychopathology.[32]

The family context has a profound impact on the extent, the severity, and the long-term outcomes of a child's problem.[33] The family is also a resource for healing and must be involved in the therapeutic process.[34] Each member of the family holds a key to helping other family members and the therapist to better understand the child and to cultivate solutions. "When therapists involve families in children's therapy, they help the child access the greatest healing source the child has: the child's family."[35]

When one person in a family has a serious difficulty or problem, that problem often acts as a stressor for the whole family. Seven-year-old Shirley is an example of such a case. Shirley was referred for treatment because she was soiling. As is often the situation, everybody in the family was affected. Her brother, Timmy, wouldn't let her play in his room or sit on his furniture and screamed that Shirley "smelled." He was punished for this behavior, and of course blamed Shirley even more. Joan, her older sister, tried to protect Shirley and cover up whenever Shirley had an "accident" by washing Shirley's underwear. Joan worried about Shirley and had difficulty concentrating in school. Shirley's parents, Brian and Toni, fought all the time about how to deal with this problem and how to decide on the best course of action. Brian thought that Toni babied Shirley. He'd grown up in a family where he always resented the fact that his mom protected and babied his sickly younger brother. The way that Toni handled Shirley's distress was related to the fact that she grew up with a depressed mom who did not attend to her needs. As a child, Toni never really felt cared for and supported. This fueled her determination to be a different kind of mom to her kids. Toni's feelings of lack of support made her turn to everyone in the neighborhood. Everybody got caught up in Shirley's problem; grandparents, Aunt Patsy, and even the next-door neighbors offered suggestions to the family.

That it's everybody's problem is especially true for families of children whose disorders have biological underpinnings. Because there is a heritable or genetic basis to biological disorders, as mentioned before, they aggregate in families.[36] Thus, symptoms are often seen not only in the child who presents for treatment, but also in other family members. Even mild forms of more serious mental problems have the potential to undermine the parent's ability to respond appropriately to the child's needs.[37] Because of this, when clinicians see children whose disorders have biological underpinnings, it is imperative for them to develop family-based interventions to treat the child, and other family members as well.

Without parallel involvement and possibly concurrent treatment of other family members, change is often short-lived or at times impossible. Let's look at an example with attention-deficit/hyperactivity disorder (ADHD). A child diagnosed with ADHD does best in a structured environment.[38] Because ADHD belongs to a spectrum of heritable disorders, it is possible that one of the child's parents may also have ADHD.[39] Genetic makeup may cause that parent to be labile in mood, easily aroused and angered, irritable, and explosive. He or she may have difficulty in planning and carrying out strategies to manage the child. A parent with ADHD may have difficulty prioritizing issues or carrying through consistently with promised rewards or consequences. As a result, parent-child interactions may actually exacerbate the child's difficulties. As in the example of Shirley and her family, despite the fact that each person in the family system may in fact be trying hard, family members can feel exasperated, frustrated, demoralized, and bewildered. The mother feels she is doing a bad job. The child feels misunderstood, disconnected, like "a bad person." The self-esteem of both the mother and the child plummet. Often secondary symptoms such as depression or acting-out develop. Vicious cycles between parent and child add to the parents' sense of guilt and failure, which in turn negatively affect a child's sense of belonging to the family. This may make the child act out even more. Sadly, children may end up feeling "expendable" and choose some desperate measures because they believe the family would be better off without them.[40]

FAMILY THERAPY PREMISES

Family therapy's rich contributions help us understand human behavior.[41] A fundamental premise is that the family is a patterned system of mutually shaping influences.[42] Family therapy "takes as its subject matter interpersonal processes in the intimate psychological context of the person, that is, couple relationships, family of origin or family of creation."[43] Sessions may include different parts of the family constellation—individuals, siblings, and/or couples. The whole is equal to more than a sum of its parts, as a family is more than a collection of its individual members: "It is a system, an organic whole whose parts function in a way that transcends their separate characteristics."[44] The family therapist places a central focus on the system and not on the individual. The tenets of family therapy represent the shift from an intrapsychic view of behavior to a relational perspective of human suffering.

Family therapists are trained as systems thinkers. Instead of searching within the individual for a singular cause or chain of causes resulting in a behavior, they understand behavior as multidetermined and complex. Family therapists look at the multiple influences on a problem. Instead of viewing behavior as a linear process, they perceive it as a circular, repetitive, continually developing, and changing pattern of behaviors and beliefs.[45] According to family therapists, behaviors and beliefs are affected by, and have an impact on, all members of the system.

Family therapy also assumes that problems both shape and are shaped by the context in which they occur. All aspects of the context of a problem are examined, starting with the family and moving outward to include important relationships beyond the home, such as those with teachers and friends. Exploration includes looking at the wider circles of association; larger systems, beliefs, expectations, and the impact of culture and gender are examined. Another current perspective in systems theory involves the process by which meaning is created and maintained by social interaction. This point of view considers how our experiences are colored by our perceptions, which in turn affect the way we think about them.[46]

For discussions in this book, I offer the following often-cited definition of family therapy:

> Family therapy may be defined as any psychotherapeutic endeavor that explicitly focuses on altering the interactions between or among family members and seeks to improve the functioning of the family as a unit, or its subsystems, and/or the functioning of individual members of the family.[47]

A Slice of Life

Working with the child and the whole family provides the therapist with a slice of family life right in the office. It helps the therapist see firsthand what the family contends with daily. It is frequently "messy." There are distractions, whining, spilled drinks, interruptions, nagging, varying attention spans, dirty diapers, more balls to keep up in the air, and often more explosions. But, being there with the family, whether there are two or seven or more members, says to all of them that you are ready and willing to roll up your sleeves and tackle their life's problems with them in the milieu in which these problems take place.

Problems do not occur in a vacuum; assessing and understanding the family context is essential to bringing about change. In order to understand a child, one must learn about the family he lives with. Involving the whole family in sessions has many distinct advantages. Meeting with the important figures in a child's life allows the therapist to obtain multiple perspectives on the referral problem, get a more comprehensive understanding of the interpersonal nature of the problem, observe family structure/dynamics, and see what the child learns from his parents' marriage and their treatment of each other. In essence, the therapist can get a better understanding of how the family shapes the child and how the child shapes the family.

Ten-year-old Kenneth and his single mom, Sally, were referred for family therapy by social services. They live in a small studio apartment. Sally complains that she has no privacy and Kenneth never knows when enough is enough. He doesn't respond to direct commands and when he wants something, he doesn't quit. Sally often screams, pulls his hair, or cries "to shut him up." In our second session Kenneth wanted special paper that he had seen in my office the previous week. I let him know that I would look for it at the end of the session. For the next 30 minutes, Kenneth said the word "paper" over and over and over and over. He did not respond to questions, but instead continued his flat monotone demand for paper about every 10 seconds. This in-vivo vignette of family life provided a bird's-eye view of an interactional pattern that at home often led to out-of-control behavior. In an attempt to describe Kenneth's behavior in a different way, I asked Sally if this was the typical level of *determination* that Kenneth pursues in all his life's desires. I noted that while this behavior generally serves one well as an adult, it made living with Kenneth now very difficult. Sally said that it was hard for her to think of his annoying behaviors in this way, but agreed that she could see that there might be another way to look at his relentlessness. "Do you think that if you look at his behavior this way, you might be a little less angry?" She and I worked together to think of some positive things that this relentless behavior would afford him some day. Sally laughed and commented, "I feel sorry for the customers if he decides to be a door-to-door salesman." By the time the session was over, Kenneth had begun to contribute to the list we were creating.

The experience and stress of this type of daily and protracted interactions with Kenneth had changed Sally over time. Her history with a demanding, unrelenting father made Kenneth's behavior even harder for Sally to tolerate. In turn, Kenneth's functioning and behavior evolved in response to his mom's harsh responses to him. In sessions with both of them, I was able to serve as a coach to Sally to find an alternate response. In the treatment that followed, "paper" served as a topic of discussion and a focus of problem solving.

Please Don't Leave Me Home

It would seem obvious that when a child presents with a problem, a family therapist would include that child (and all the children) in the family treatment, but for a variety of reasons this is not always the case. Popular explanations for leaving children home vary. Some therapy approaches advocate an adult focus and concentrate on the adults' families of origin, or on the parental subsystem.[48] Another explanation involves a practical consideration, for example, worry that the child will be unable to maintain attention, or that the child's presence will distract the parents from the task at hand.[49] Another reason cited for leaving the child home is that children's language and communication skills will impede treatment, thus requiring the therapist to use play as a medium of expression.[50] Many therapists feel vulnerable, unequipped,[51] and don't know what to do with these "squirmy little people with such limited verbal facility."[52] It is a "source of sadness, even embarrassment, that the voice of the child is sometimes overlooked within family therapy."[53] Often, children are excluded because of the therapist's comfort level, and when they are included, they are not involved in the session.[54] Numbers of family therapists lack adequate training and supervision for work with children.[55] The end result is a "for adults only" family treatment,[56] leading some to conclude that exclusion of children is a "case of neglect."[57]

While children's presence may be disquieting at times, their absence is palpable and presents the therapist with an incomplete family picture. A range of books and articles on play and family therapy offer various strategies for engagement and facilitation of children's active involvement in treatment.[58] The inclusion of children in sessions brings smiles, liveliness, freshness, honesty, and delight.

> The family cannot be well understood if some members living under the same roof are known only by hearsay. Moreover, those who include young children in sessions testify that each child brings to the session not only a separate viewpoint, but also uniquely evocative and contributory modes of communicating, often characterized by immediacy, spontaneity, and refreshing candor.[59]

Although children's minds and attention may wander in school, I am always struck at how observant they are about what happens in their families. I find that children are some of the best historians and reporters of the family culture. When cousin Hal's name was brought up in a session, the parents signaled to me that they didn't want to discuss him in front of the kids. Four-year-old Daniel, who looked half asleep, jumped off his brother's lap, came up to me and whispered, "He lives in jail."

A CHILD-FRIENDLY THERAPY

One of the best compliments I ever received came from 7-year-old Joey, a former client. His mom Sonia called me because Joey was having some problems adjusting to his new teacher in school and she was concerned that some old social problems were once again "rearing their ugly heads." It seemed that Joey was refusing to do his class work. No amount of controlling or convincing helped to get him on a good track. When Joey's teacher told him that she was going to have to involve his mother, Joey replied angrily, "If you do that, my mother will get you." The teacher answered, "That won't happen, Joey, your mother and I are a team. We work together." "Then I'll get my father to get you," Joey answered. The teacher disengaged herself from this struggle with Joey and immediately called his mother. When Joey came home from school his mother and father told him that his behavior was unacceptable and he would not be able to have any playdates for two weeks. After her call for an appointment, Sonia told Joey that they were going to come to see me the next day to talk this over. Joey looked up at her in confusion and said, "I thought you said that I wasn't going to have any playdates for two weeks."

The fact that play has an important role in a child's life has been well documented. Piaget believes play is essential in shaping the mind.[60] Similarly, Alfred Adler states that play is a child's work.[61] Incorporating play in family work conveys interest in children. It sets the stage for creative ways to approach family concerns.[62] Playful methods are a great way to solve life's problems. These methods include play-filled interactions, silliness, fun, and humor.[63]

> Like the twin masks of comedy and tragedy, play reflects both the mirth and pathos of the human experience. When children and adults meet, play provides a common language to express the breadth and depth of thoughts, emotions, and experience—in this we share a lingua franca.[64]

There is an extensive literature base on the importance of play in therapy.[65] Play helps parents understand the problem from the child's perspective. When working with children, especially young ones, play must be encouraged and valued. The vital role of play to children formed the basis of play therapy, which was introduced in 1919 by Hug-Hellmuth.[66] Psychoanalytic play therapy emphasizes the use of interpretation and views child's play as symbolic of internal concerns.[67] Virginia Axline applies the concepts of client-centered therapy to children in her classic work on a nondirective play therapy framework.[68] Gil describes play therapy's anchors in psychoanalytic, humanistic, behavioral, and Jungian approaches:

Play therapy offers children an opportunity to release pent-up emotions; express themselves verbally, nonverbally, and through their use of symbols; compensate for problems in reality; find solutions to problems; and through pretend play rehearse the myriad situations children might encounter. The goal of play therapy is to help children to identify and express their feelings in healthier, non-symptomatic ways, as well as to encourage working through the difficult emotions while finding and using alternative non-problematic behaviors.[69]

Play in the context of family therapy is an effective process. Through play, family members learn forgiveness and how to support one another, and develop a capacity for understanding. It also provides an opportunity for family members to experience each other in different ways.[70] As we will see in the chapters that follow, the "play" that I use is often goal-oriented and structured. The child is not the *sole* director in the therapy room. This work is often action-oriented; it has a "doing" component. The therapist takes an active role, with the high level of engagement that is often found in family therapy.[71] The learning of new skills is facilitated through play and play-filled interactions and transactions in the sessions. This facilitation is particularly important with the child who has difficulty in sustaining attention, or the child who has cognitive weaknesses. The play is not used as a particular strategy to explore dynamic issues, although these do arise. Interpretation and analysis of play for unconscious meaning is not the goal.

Learning Through Concrete Activities

In a classroom setting, children, especially young ones, learn best through concrete activities. According to Piaget, the "intrinsic activity" of the child is a key source of learning. "The child must act on things to understand them." Sidestepping this process and using only verbal means of communicating information results in superficial learning.[72] The therapy room, in a sense, is a classroom for life. Interactions and transactions that occur there represent a microcosm of the child's life in other settings. I find that providing an array of activities in therapy helps maintain interest and encourages involvement. The tools and techniques I use to foster this "we're learning while having fun" approach include involving the senses, metaphor, gadgets, computer-made games, a digital camera, expressive arts activities, story telling and creating, puppets, music, movement, and more. The activities stimulate communication and give the family a new metaphor, tool, or family problem-solving activity to take home and use outside the consulting room.

In the context of psychotherapy, action methods have been defined elsewhere as: "those processes that have clients engage in purposeful physical activity at the direction of the therapist."[73] There are a multitude of action methods that are employed in family therapy, such as role-playing, enactment,[74] ceremony,[75] ritual,[76] sculpting,[77] and letter writing.[78]

Involvement: "You've Got to Be in It to Win It"

The first step is involvement, getting your foot in the door. Children are often dragged to therapy and present themselves as unwilling partners, but a therapy that is imbued with imagination, creativity, fun, and novelty is hard to resist. Certain children we see in treatment are prone to externalizing the reasons for problematic behaviors rather than accepting responsibility. Due to the biological underpinnings of their disorders, numerous youngsters lack the requisite competencies for observation or evaluation of their impact on others. Thus they think it is *the other* people who have the problem and who need the therapy. It is essential to find a way to get these youngsters involved and to enhance their motivation. Collaboration and involvement are key ingredients. Using children's expertise about themselves, and actively involving them in problem solving, are motivation enhancers.

Make It a Sensory Experience

Albert Einstein once said, "Learning is experience. Everything else is just information." Getting the information through the senses facilitates learning and remembering—just what we want to do in therapy. Try this experiment and see for yourself. First, picture yourself attending a lecture on handwriting difficulties in school-age children. The lecturer presents a cogent discussion of development of the small muscle groups and the importance of the coordination of the senses, such as the eyes and hand. The lecturer goes on to explain in detail about the struggles children with handwriting difficulties have in school when they are asked to write in their notebooks. When they do expository writing, their final products are shorter than those of classmates. This is not because they don't have thoughts to convey, but rather because they just get too tired writing.

Next, take out a piece of paper. Pick up your pen with the hand that you usually write or draw with. Now put your pen in your other hand and write a paragraph that tells about how you spent last weekend. Remember, don't switch your pen back to the hand that you usually write with. Give yourself a five-minute time limit. Then ask yourself: How did I feel? Were my thoughts moving faster than my hand? Did I get frustrated? Feel like giving up? Did I give up? How did my handwriting look? What about letter size and shape? Did I start off neatly and lose control as I was writing? What if your boss told you that in order to get paid next week, you would have to write all your reports with your nondominant hand? Would you feel like going to work?

Which of these two methods facilitated your understanding of the struggles of individuals with fine motor weaknesses? Our sensory systems are the means by which we come to understand the world. Babies less than a week old are thought to be able to recognize their mothers through the gustatory and olfactory systems. Piaget, in discussing the sensorimotor stage of development, highlights its importance to later cognitive development. He views this as the first stage of cognitive development that begins at birth and extends to about two years of age.[79] Infants make sense of the world as they take in information through the senses. It is through the visual, auditory, kinesthetic, olfactory, and gustatory systems that information is sent to the brain.

Learning first comes in through our senses. As we explore and experience our material world, initial sensory patterns are laid down on elaborate nerve networks. These initial sensory patterns become the core of our free-form information system that is updated then becomes more elegant with each new, novel experience. These initial sensory patterns become our reference points and give us the context for all learning, thought, and creativity. From this sensory base we will add emotions and movement in our life-long learning dance.[80]

If therapy is presented only in a single mode, such as verbal, using only explanation and analysis, the child may find it too challenging, or even impossible, to understand and generate alternative solutions. There needs to be consideration of a child's learning style and the way he learns and understands the world around him. If a child is "not getting it," it doesn't necessarily indicate his denial or resistance. "Not getting it" might result from our failure to provide information in a manner that is in harmony with the learner's preferences.[81] Cognitive variations have an impact on the therapy process. Utilizing more than one sensory modality helps facilitate the child's ability to make use of therapy.

Multisensory refers to "any learning activity that includes the use of two or more sensory modalities simultaneously to take in or express information."[82] Multisensory instruction has been widely employed in educational settings. Involving all senses to encode new learning helps send therapy home and promotes generalization and maintenance. This is especially important with individuals who have learning difficulties and impaired channels of knowing and understanding, such as those represented in Figure 1.1.

Think Right-Brain

Paul Watzlawick, expert on human communication, suggests that the therapist employ the language of the brain's right hemisphere to bring about real change. In discussing the two hemispheres he posits the idea that each

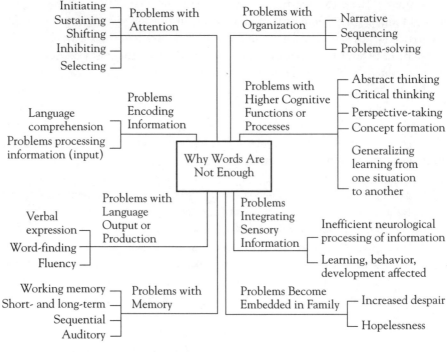

Figure 1.1. Why Words Are Not Enough

employs a different language. The language of the left hemisphere is the
language of most schools of psychotherapy. It is the language of definition—
objective, logical, analytic: "It is the language of reason, of science, explanation, and interpretation."[83] The language of the right hemisphere,
Watzlawick suggests, resonates on different levels of our experience. It is
the language of imagery, of metaphor. The uniqueness of the right hemisphere lies in its ability to synthesize complex patterns, configurations, and
relationships from the perception of a small part into a whole. "The ability
of the right hemisphere seems to be based on the *pars-pro-toto* principle,
that is, the immediate recognition of a totality on the basis of *one* essential
detail."[84] An example might be our quick recall of the entire Happy
Birthday tune from listening to the first few notes. From a part, we grasp the
whole.

The use of metaphor as a learning tool has also been extensively discussed
and widely employed with both children and adults. Metaphor can be used in
language and action to help people move toward behavior change. Using
metaphor "circumvents intellectual defenses that are activated through verbal
representation."[85] Metaphor can be employed when joining with a family and

as means through which interventions are presented.[86] Some therapists employ metaphor to enliven the sensory system.[87] Many forms, such as fables, stories, anecdotes, fairy tales, tasks, drawings, paintings, and sculpture can carry meaning metaphorically[88] and can be used as therapeutic tools.

Carla loved the Greek myths and was studying them in school. We talked about our favorite myths and when she mentioned that she had just studied the story of Icarus, I seized upon the opportunity. We dramatized the story of Icarus who was held prisoner. In order to help Icarus escape, his father, Daedalus, made his son wings from wax. He warned his son to stay away from the sun's heat, but Icarus did not heed his father's counsel. He flew too close to the sun, his wings melted, and he perished in the sea. Carla's mom, Nancy, commented that similar things happened in their home, that is, that "people often don't listen." In a discussion of this issue, Nancy complained that she had to tell Carla the same things repeatedly. Carla agreed and commented, "It just feels like nagging to me." Carla hated the way her mom reminded her to do things. Nancy hated to remind. They were stuck. We assessed each person's view of the problem and decided that maybe Icarus could help. Instead of Nancy's telling Carla to do something, we decided Nancy would simply say, "Remember Icarus." These two words served as an acceptable reminder for Carla without Nancy telling her what to do and what not to do. Icarus served as a metaphor for listening and responding at home.

Color Outside the Lines: Therapy Is Creative

Working with difficult populations has impelled me to come up with new ideas to engage them in treatment. It has forced me to develop techniques that involve "coloring outside the lines and thinking out of the 9-dot frame." Therapy that targets areas of difficulty in creative ways enhances the motivation of participants and increases their sense of ownership of the treatment. Children and families can use the expressive arts to create material for their own healing. Therapy is often hands-on, their own. It gives families a new way to talk about old problems, a new language that they develop together. The final product, book, game, activity sheet, video, "invention" goes home with them. Leona made a "worry zapper" and hung it over her bed. Before she went to sleep she breathed deeply and imagined her worries, one by one, getting zapped and disappearing. Jed invented a game called "the right place at the right time." We developed a point system with his mother whereby Jed earns points in the morning when he is at the breakfast table prepared to eat or when he is at the front door, jacket on, books in hand, when it is time to leave for school.

This work stimulates fantasy, what dreams are made of, the inner world of the child. Using fantasy in work with children provides a connection to their inner lives.[89] Fantasy is where the limited reality of objects disappears: a tissue box might become a train station or a schoolhouse, a pen is a magic wand. The possibilities are limitless and one is hampered only by forgetting to use imagination. Having the children present enlivens my imagination and often turns up a light on a road that only a few minutes earlier had seemed dimly lit. It often starts a synergy of shared thoughts and ideas that spark the child's creative juices. This opens up new options, which in turn lead to hope, which is not a bad place to end up!

T.E.A.M! Together Everybody Accomplishes More!

Collaborating and cocreating solutions also helps to enhance the child's sense of ownership of the treatment. Children and families have expert knowledge about themselves. Valuing this knowledge and using it in sessions helps to develop collaboration. "I don't have all the answers; I need and appreciate your involvement and participation" is an important message. When children, families, or couples ask me, "How long do we have to come here?" I take the position, "A lot depends on how hard you are all willing to work." When children complain, "I don't want to be here," I tell them that I understand that. I ask them how quickly they can "fire" me. I ask what they think they have to change at home or at school so that their mom and dad will know they can work on these issues and concerns without my involvement. I add, "I can't wait to get fired. Some people hate it, but it makes me feel great. In fact, my family always asks me how many people fired me this week? How fast do you think you can fire me? What do you think you need to do?" I then eagerly reach for my pencil, because children often come up with the entire treatment plan.

Make It Relevant

In my practice I find that the most useful, relevant, and practical interventions, the ones that help families stay involved, are those that are developed not for, but in collaboration with, the child and family. It is essential to develop focused interventions that will translate ideas into real life changes. Parents, teachers, and children provide descriptions of problems that beg for intervention. It is most helpful to work on specific, targeted problems, while dealing with broader-based and long-term issues and concerns. It is also important that the treatment be relevant to the child and family's connections to the world outside the therapy room. Getting off the chair and into the life of the child in school is imperative.

Nine-year-old Harris was referred for therapy by the family physician. Those who knew Harris well described him as a sensitive boy whose feelings were easily hurt. "He's like a summer peach that bruises easily," commented his teacher in a phone interview. "He is always crying on the playground and other kids tease him about it." Harris lives with his biological parents and 15-year-old sister, Donna. In a family interview it became apparent that Harris bore the brunt of criticism from his dad, Myron, who pointed out that Harris "just needs to get tougher." "Big boys don't cry" was the lesson Myron learned growing up with four brothers who tormented and teased him. His wife, Lila, disapproved of any "get tough attitude." She noted that there was constant fighting and tension in the home and this was one of many areas that they disagreed about.

While there were several long-term family issues, including differences in parenting styles, marital stresses, and general tension in the home, Harris needed some targeted intervention to deal with feelings he had and conclusions that he drew concerning what other children did and said. We did an experiment. I sprayed water on a cloth and Harris watched it seep in. I then showed him a cloth I had already treated with Scotchguard™ (in preparation for this experiment). I asked Harris to make a prediction about what would happen when we sprayed water on this second cloth. He was surprised that the water beaded up and rolled off, rather than soak into the cloth. I used the two cloths as examples of two different kinds of temperament. Picking up the soaking-wet cloth I said, "Some people are like this. Everything just sinks in and affects how they feel. This is not a bad thing, because often these are people with a lot of sensitivity toward others. But, when too much sinks in, it can leave them feeling upset. Some of our work together will be to learn how to make other people's comments roll off your back."

Harris made the connection right away and commented that this was just like his ski jacket, "it never gets wet!" The cloth became a metaphor for other family members' abilities to have the harsh talking or criticism that was directed at them "bead up" and "roll off." Lila revealed that many things Myron said would sink in and upset her. Lila and Myron decided that was one of the reasons he had married her; she was sensitive to his feelings—something he missed in his own house. Donna, generally quiet during these discussions, agreed that she looked like a person who is tough, but on the inside, the fighting in the house was "sinking in" and making her worry.

"Keep Up with the Joneses"

I find that learning and keeping current with today's kid culture helps me find a language to connect with children and develop interventions with them. What kids are interested in, interests me. I became Pokemon-fluent and learned about the powers and evolution of the characters. Pikachu and Charizard[90] provide consultation and direction. Harry Potter[91] has become one of the best cotherapists I ever had! When children talk of a movie that has influenced them extensively, I find out about it and often make it my business to see it.

Tim loved video games. His mom, Florence, felt they "consumed him, just like his anger." "He's addicted to them and gets nasty when we try to take his game away. It is so bad," she continued, "that when Tim enters a room he never makes eye contact." Tim did not want to part with his hand-held video game during the session. Even if it wasn't on, he clutched it in his hand, interrupted, and asked about when he could put it on. I noticed a spark in his eyes when I asked him if he thought we could invent a video game about anger. We decided that like his video game, anger also has levels (Figure 1.2). You start at the coolest level, Level 1 (three Cs, calm, cool, and collected), and move up to the hottest. He reminded me that sometimes you skip all the levels in between! At the bottom levels, you still have a chance to stay in control. When you get to Level 3, red alert, we decided you might still have a chance. Once behavior gets dangerous and the fire department and the police are summoned, it's often too late. At Level 6, your "guy" is losing life; surely anger will be the winner. Tim told me he hated when anyone else was the winner. I asked him what he could do to be the winner instead. Family members joined in and talked about their anger levels. Tim's dad commented that he often starts out at Level 5.[92] The family assigned points for "winning" at the anger game. Starting and staying at a lower level earned bonus points. Criteria were set up and the family took home an intervention tool that "spoke Tim's language." Questions such as who was winning, how, and who stayed at what level, became a way to talk about a troubling family problem. It opened the door to new conversations about a tough family problem.

INGREDIENTS FOR CHANGE

Gregory Bateson, the well-known anthropologist and major contributor to family systems thinking, advanced the idea that change comes from new information.[93] In family therapy we talk about this as "news of a difference." This thinking advances the idea that people change in reaction to information, which, it is believed, comes in the appearance of difference. The therapy experience outlined on these pages seeks to help children and families change in response to new information provided in a multiplicity of ways. Even a small difference can be a springboard for change, for new ways of developing "the 3Bs" that are so important to family life: being, believing, and belonging. Stir these with a huge dose of "the 4Rs," respect, regard, responsibility, and reciprocity of kind acts in the family, and we have the beginning of an ingredient list for a recipe for hope and change.

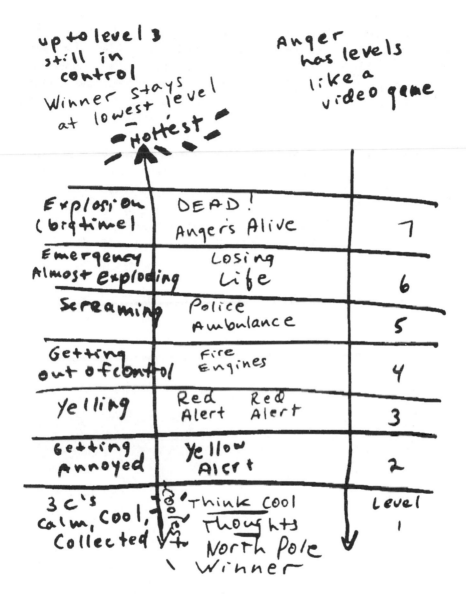

Figure 1.2. Tim's Video Game About Anger

Problems can quickly become embedded in family life. They increase despair and hopelessness. Using the active and sensory-rich techniques that I will present throughout this book creates optimism, enhances involvement, and promotes change. Adopting a biopsychosocial framework provides a lens that shows multiple avenues for understanding and treating a child and his problems. It is helpful for the therapist to embrace a playful philosophy and cultivate such valuable abilities as connecting to the child within, silliness and the love of fun, balance between the left and right brain (with a willingness to develop the right brain), intuitiveness, readiness to experiment, and "coloring outside the lines." And, of course, there is no substitute for acceptance, caring, warmth, empathy, genuineness, respect, and regard.[94] These create meaningful connections and facilitate attunement in sessions.

Interventions have an underlying theme that embodies an "I can do it" attitude. Families feel and often comment, "We're getting something done here." This treatment seeks to find ways to send therapy home with clients. It highlights resources and strengths that may have taken a back seat to individual and family problems. Children and parents start to recognize, appreciate, and value their talents and assets while they learn to overcome their struggles.

CHAPTER 2

Principles and Practices

General Anchors and Guides

This chapter presents principles to guide therapeutic work with children and families. Many of the anchors and guides are part of time-honored practices that enhance connection, empathy, and understanding of, and with, clients. Innovative strategies, activities, and exercises outline ways to help therapy move from the analogue setting into a child's life outside the consultation room. In child-focused work, this includes building relationships with teachers and schools.

THERAPY IS EMPOWERING, COLLABORATIVE, AND RESOURCE-ORIENTED

Clients are often engaged in courageous struggles to reclaim their lives from oppressive problems. Whether the pain that leads them to a therapist's office is short-term or chronic, it has often diminished their coping resources. The therapy process helps individuals and family members find and celebrate strengths and knowledge. Inquiry into problems is collaborative. Each family member is viewed as an expert and an important contributor. The therapist is not there to take over, but rather to encourage family members to assume an advocacy role.[1] Taking inventory of family strengths helps families remember that they are resource-full. Completing a Family Strengths Inventory (see "Tools for Gathering Information" in the Appendix) highlights resources family members have that can be utilized for creative problem-solving.

THERAPY IS ABOUT REPAIR

Therapy concerns itself with building, enhancing, and repairing fragile connections between parent and child. For the therapist, one difficulty in working with families lies in the need to be vigilant, to carefully maintain a balance between being attuned to the parents' affect and the child's, balancing between the child and parent.

Gloria became tearful as she told me about her shattered fantasies since 6-year-old Sam's birth. "From the day I took him home from the hospital, I couldn't please him." Sam was planned, longed for, and talked about for years before his conception. Gloria and her husband, Jim, were thrilled and eager to be home with their new son, but right from the start life as a family was not as they had imagined. Sam's cries pierced the stillness in an otherwise quiet home. He was difficult to calm and soothe, and he seemed distressed through much of the day and night. As he nursed at Gloria's breast he was distracted and never seemed to get enough nourishment. This left him hungry and restless, and sleep eluded them all. Tension in the house heightened and anxiety mounted. To make matters worse, well-meaning child-rearing "experts" in the extended family jumped in and tried to take over. In a family session, Gloria sadly recalls the beginning of misunderstandings and ruptures in attunement that still persist, and, through a sea of tears, Sam yells that no one likes him. While tracking Sam's meltdowns, the family becomes keenly aware that his explosive behavior often occurs at times of misattunement, particularly with his mom. Therapy helps the child and parents learn how to have mutually enjoyable experiences and rebuild family connections.

THERAPY IS NURTURING
AND REDUCES SHAME AND BLAME

It is imperative to connect with caregivers (often the mothers) and help them feel nurtured and cared for in the therapy. Remember the old Hindu saying, "Water the root and enjoy the fruit." Many of the parents themselves had poor experiences of attachment in their families of origin, so it is essential to get the parents' descriptions and understandings of their own histories and memories. Therapy offers the possibility of healing past wounds and ruptures in bonding. The process is deeply concerned with the therapist's attunement or misattunement to the parent and with helping caregivers feel valued and appreciated.[2] One of the jobs of the therapist is to provide a safe, protective setting, a *holding environment*.[3]

In family therapy, the therapist's task is to provide a helpful environment in which the whole family can participate and which it can shape according to its unique expressions of need, thought, and feeling. The environment derives from the design of the office, from the way arrangements for consultation and therapy are handled, and from the ability to listen thoughtfully, to engage, to be affected, to tolerate anxiety, to reflect upon experience, and to communicate understanding intent. This ability has been called the therapist's *contextual holding capacity*.[4]

If a rupture between the therapist and a parent occurs, it can be used as an opportunity to build and enhance understanding. The therapist will do best in acknowledging his or her part in any rupture while exploring the client's part; the therapist takes a "let's look at this" attitude. It is most helpful to connect the event to the client's own history, which in a profound sense may be a recapitulation, a reiteration of a trauma or shame of the past. Jen felt that I sided with her daughter, Kristin, on an issue. She became angry with me and called after the session to let me know her feelings. Jen could become quite volatile in the sessions and it was difficult for Kristin to present her point of view. When I supported Kristin, Jen felt marginalized, just as she had felt in her family while growing up. She could not tolerate this happening in therapy. We had several individual sessions to help her find ways to be less reactive, both in sessions and at home. This opened the door to the new closeness with her daughter that Jen longed for.

Parents learn how to tune into their children's inner feelings. When there is a shaming experience, they learn how to repair the misattunement. Reducing shaming experiences helps the family diminish blow-ups. The therapy room must be a "no blame" zone. Developing ways to talk about everyone's struggles without finger-pointing is no easy task.

Barbara's mother started talking about her as she pulled my office door shut. "Here she goes with her list of everything I do wrong," Barbara shouted as she covered her mother's mouth. "Well I have a list too." Often shame is an enormous issue in sessions. The therapist needs to find ways to talk about difficult situations. The therapist is responsible for setting a safe and useful context in which to discuss difficult material. Using a structured tool or technique is a helpful way to slow things down and creates a calmer atmosphere in which to discuss events or incidents. **Rewinds** (see "Tools to Get and Stay on Track" in the Appendix for a blank worksheet) are a helpful way to accomplish that goal. They are also a great way to take a look back and see the steps one took to make something work well.

▫▫

Rewinds

Just about every child is an expert at operating the VCR. Using the idea of the VCR remote control provides a technique for "rewinding" the tape of an event and then reviewing the tape. "Rewinds" presents a nonshaming, nonblaming way to help children and adults take a look at a previous behavior or incident, review events, and think about new ways to act and react. To do a Rewind, anyone involved in an incident is asked to fill out a Rewind Sheet. The sheets are then reviewed and a new plan of action is developed. (There is a tendency to spend the most time reviewing and talking about events that didn't go well. Since there is as much to be learned from good situations as from bad ones, it is important to also use Rewinds to take a look at things that did go well. How can you repeat the sequence that resulted in a positive outcome? Write down the steps.)

1. "Rewind the tape" and take another look at what happened.
2. Write or draw the steps.
3. Review what happened.
4. Think about how you could do it differently if you did it again.
5. Come up with a new plan.
6. Write or draw your new plan.

I rewind the tape and look back at what happened.

1.

2.

3.

4.

I think about what happened. If I could do it again, I would do it differently. Here is my new plan.

_____

_____

_____

Signed: _____

□□□

THERAPY IS CONTAINING

Explosiveness might be a frequent "visitor" to sessions. When working with explosive children, therapy must not become a punishing, contentious, and thereby unproductive experience. Therapy must provide a safe container for anger and a safe place in which to develop alternative responses. While enactments of family events might produce intense feelings, the therapist is responsible for safety[5] and for "keeping the lid on everybody's id."

During a session, Andrew started to whine and complain that he wanted a snack. He pulled out his package of chips and started to open it. His mom, Dorothy, said, "No. When we bought them I told you they were for after our time with Marcia." His father, Jonathan, said, "You'd better listen to your mother and put them away now!" Louis, Andrew's brother, grabbed his pistachio nuts and announced, "If he eats his chips I'm eating my pistachios." Both parents had fury written all over their faces and they hurled threats of loss of privileges at the boys. Voices were raised. Neither child noticed.

This little vignette of family life typified what happens at home, presenting an in vivo enactment of the trouble spots and conflicts the family deals with on a daily basis. Finding ways to slow down the action is essential. I called "pause" to get everybody to freeze. I then asked Andrew to look at his mom and dad's faces. I asked him to "read" them for me. We had previously discussed face reading and other nonverbal cues that tell that someone is upset or angry. We had played feelings charades and acted out home-life scenarios. Andrew and Louis were beginning to learn important life skills. The boys looked at their parents' scowling faces and Andrew told me that he saw they were very mad. I reminded him that he told us he hated when they yell and scream at him. He reconsidered, whined a bit more about his chips, but put them away. Louis followed. Through experiences like this one, Dorothy and Jonathan were learning that threats, screaming, and punishment were not effective agents of change. The cues they now use to prompt the boys are visual ones, such as pointing to a stop sign or using their hands to show how their patience is shrinking, and verbal ones, such as saying the two-word statement "eye contact."

THERAPY HELPS BUILD EMPATHY

A popular cartoon strip caught my eye one day, as it was about empathy. It was Nipper and his pal Wellington.[6] Nipper was stuck on a homework problem and showed the problem to Wellington who couldn't figure it out either. Wellington asked if he could put on Nipper's shoes because his mom had told him that if he were in Nipper's shoes he could understand Nipper's problems better. Therapy helps family members learn about, understand, and empathize with each other's plight.

Carrie and Tanya are twins. Carrie is agile and athletic. Tanya is poorly coordinated and awkward. In session, Carrie bemoans the fact that she has such a klutz for a sister. "Why do I have to get stuck with the worst player on my team? Tanya can't even catch or run fast. She doesn't even try." Carrie leaves early for practice without Tanya and makes her feelings known to her teammates. This exasperates their parents who discipline Carrie harshly for her behavior. Carrie blames Tanya for getting her into trouble with their parents and pays Tanya back whenever the chance arises. They are stuck in a vicious cycle with no solution in sight. Their mother comments that she is very concerned that Carrie doesn't show empathy for her sister. "How can we help her understand?" I asked. We came up with a plan that had the family play volleyball together. Everybody except for Tanya wore rubber boots instead of sneakers. Carrie wore her father's gloves as well. During the game, Carrie dropped the ball, tripped over her feet, and even tumbled to the ground a few times. This firsthand experience helped them all to see what Tanya is up against. The new way of seeing Tanya's problem helped Carrie develop a more compassionate understanding of her sister's difficulties.

Laurie, diagnosed with attention-deficit/hyperactivity disorder, is always in trouble with the adults around her. In a family session, her parents claim that she doesn't try to do better. The finger pointing is nonstop and so is the screaming. I ask Laurie's parents to talk about one of the worst mistakes they made or about an incident that made them feel ashamed. After they fill in the details and describe what happened and how they felt, I ask Laurie if she ever felt that ashamed. She lowers her eyes and says, "Every day." Family members need compassion and understanding for each other.

THERAPY LOOKS AT "FIT"

Common sense and a great deal of research clearly indicate that the temperament and nature of the child have an impact on interactions between the parent and the child. "Fit," in this context, concerns itself with understanding the match between the temperament of the child and his or her environment. A mismatch between the two can have serious consequences. The idea of "goodness of fit" (consonance with one's environment) as proposed by Chess and Thomas is an important one to understand.[7] *Consonance* with one's environment provides an opportunity for optimal learning where positive growth is possible and children can blossom. In contrast, *dissonance*, poorness of fit, may provide the fodder for behavioral difficulties.

As a psychologist and family therapist, I often hear anecdotes from family members about temperament characteristics that were present from the infant's first days. "Danny was a stubborn infant. He knew just how he wanted to be held and never settled down, until I got it just right." Georgia told me, "When I was pregnant the baby was so active, we came to call him 'our little jumping bean' and the name still holds true today!" Burton's parents commented that while Burton had many strengths, adaptability was clearly not on the list. As long as he was on "the Burton channel" and did what he liked, family life was pleasant. However, it seemed as if Burton was born with a broken channel-changer, and transitions were torture for the whole family. In these cases the problematic behaviors were not part of a symptom cluster reflecting pervasive difficulties with sensory integration, attention, or hyperactivity. Instead they were part and parcel of the individual temperament characteristics of these children and resulted in problems in self-regulation that impacted on the child's interpersonal world. The impact on family life was palpable and was a source of vicious cycles that fueled arguments in the home.

Vivian, age 7, lives with her mother, Mona, a single parent. Both were described by the referring agency as highly reactive. Recently, a neighbor called social services with a report of abuse. Vivian was evaluated and found to have ADHD. She responded well to a trial of psychostimulant medication and her behavior at school improved dramatically. The fact that her classroom teacher had a calm nature made it easier for Vivian to deal with her frustrations and inner tensions. At home, however, her mother's physiological unease and impulsive response style made change elusive. The similar genetic "wiring" of both Vivian and Mona made them a "poor fit" and made Mona's nurturing and caring for her daughter a yeoman's task. Family therapy was targeted at reducing Mona's critical comments and reactivity, while working concomitantly on the heightened levels of arousal and reactivity in both her and her daughter.

The idea of "fit" applies itself to many settings. A poor or inappropriate fit between a child and a teacher often spells disaster in school. There also needs to be a good fit between the child or the family and the therapist. (Some of the questions that help determine how successful the fit is include: Does the family feel comfortable with the therapist? Does the therapist's style work well with the family's style? Do family and therapist feel they can work well together?) Finally, there needs to be a good fit between the family and the proposed interventions. Cognitive and learning styles, temperament, brain organization, and multiple intelligences need to be considered in developing and/or adapting appropriate interventions.

THERAPY EXPLORES EXPECTATIONS AND BELIEFS

Because family expectations and belief systems shape behavior, it is essential to explore them in therapy.[8] Jerry and Joanne brought their 7-year old child, Perry, into treatment because of behavioral difficulties at home and school. While completing a multigenerational genogram, the therapist finds that Joanne's brother, Barnett, had similar problems. Barnett was often aggressive at home and in school. Throughout her life Joanne was ashamed of her brother and his inappropriate behavior. At school she was often called on to bring home notes containing news of incidents or suspensions. At lunch, Joanne was embarrassed when Barnett threw food, acted silly, or bothered her while she was playing with her friends. Barnett's arrival home from school was often the beginning of endless disagreements that lasted way into the night. Their parents argued over management issues and each blamed problems on the other. Joanne blamed them both and was contemptuous of her parents for failing to control Barnett. Secretly she wished that Barnett had never been born and often felt guilty about these wishes. While she loved her brother, she was embarrassed by his behavior and angered by the fights he caused at home, depriving the family of fun. He never sat still, and anyone's prized possession was fair game when he was around. She felt relief when she married and left this all behind her, but when her son began exhibiting some behaviors that were similar to Barnett's, Joanne feared that she had given birth to her worst nightmare. Joanne's experiences in her own family of origin clearly shape her beliefs and expectations, and have a profound affect on her parenting of her own difficult child. Joanne needs to explore and understand how her expectations and beliefs affect her parenting and what she can do to change old patterns.

THERAPY HELPS CLIENTS UNDERSTAND HOW THEY THINK AND LEARN

Therapy helps individuals learn about themselves as well as come to know and understand the world around them. Time is spent on meta-cognitive processes, thinking about how we think and how we learn. Therapy emphasizes that people function in different ways. Uniqueness and differences are viewed as examples of the diversity in the world. Our inner clocks, sleep cycles, and circadian rhythms are all part of the therapeutic conversation: Do interactional problems occur in the morning when you wake-up? Do you seem to have a morning fog and general irritability that takes time to burn off? Are you someone who can delay gratification in the moment to attain a future goal? Do you operate only on I.S.T. (Immediate Standard Time, i.e., NOW!)? What do you know about how your brain works? How do you learn best? In therapy, people learn that grey matter matters. They also learn how to develop their own strategies.

Individual learning profiles (which include strengths and weaknesses) and preferred learning styles[9] and modalities (auditory, visual, tactile-kinesthetic) provide rich terrain for understanding and intervention. For example, how does a child's learning style impact on a problem? Twelve-year-old Ivan is a visual learner, who does best when auditory information is presented along with charts, graphs, and pictures. His teacher, Mr. L, uses a lecture style in class. Ivan has trouble taking notes, gets distracted, daydreams, and doesn't complete assignments in a timely fashion; he is in danger of failing language arts. Ivan says he hates Mr. L and feels he will never pass the class. His mother takes away privileges because she believes Ivan is not putting forth any effort.

In a discussion about learning preferences during our session we uncover how Ivan's preferred learning modality shapes the way he functions in Mr. L's class. Ivan tells us he can't learn the way Mr. L teaches. His mother had not been aware of the different way in which Ivan learns. With this new information, she stops blaming Ivan and advocates for him with Mr. L. Once Ivan feels his mother is listening to him, he becomes less angry and more open to finding solutions. We make a plan for Ivan to get the notes from a friend. Mr. L also allows Ivan to bring a tape recorder to class, and his parents hire a tutor.

New information, explanations, and understandings of old problems can open doors to interventions. Weaknesses that may plague an individual at school and rob him of feelings of self-efficacy do not end at the finish of the school day. Cognitive variations[10] need to be understood and taken into account when developing appropriate therapeutic interventions.

John, age 7, complains bitterly that no one likes him and that he feels left out and without friendships at school and at home. His crying and whining behavior is like a fingernail on a chalkboard for all family members. John's father, Tom, argues with his wife, Toby, that she babies John. His 10-year old brother, Stuart, reports that John never seems to know "when enough is enough." Stuart explodes when John doesn't get the message to leave him alone because he has had a bad day at school. Despite Stuart's growling voice and grizzly looks of disapproval, John dares to cross the threshold to enter Stuart's room. Stuart glares at John in a family therapy session. He throws his hands up in the air and exclaims, "John has never failed a vocabulary test and he understands the English language, but he seems to get lost every time someone asks him to go to the store or to put something away. How convenient."

Children with these behavioral difficulties may suffer from a nonverbal learning disability with right-hemisphere deficits[11] and may lack the "social language of success."[12] These children have difficulty fitting in with their peers and, due to weaknesses in right hemisphere visual perceptual skills, literally don't notice the social cues from others. John isn't aware of the scowls from his brother and doesn't heed the warning not to enter his room without an invitation. Facial clues elude him and directions mystify him even more. He gets lost, anxious, and confused. Yet in some arenas, such as a vocabulary test, John may function adequately. In part, treatment for children with these problems involves targeted interventions aimed at enhancing their social skills and helping them encode new information so that behavioral change is possible.

Sonia, age 9, has a history of oppositional and negativistic behaviors. Temper tantrums have been a way of life since she was small and it became easier for family members just to give in to her rather than suffer listening to her screams. Therapy was viewed by her brother and sister as a further intrusion into their lives; wasn't it Sonia who had the problem? Upon careful examination (through cognitive testing and observation) with the assistance of Sonia's teacher and a learning specialist, it was discovered that Sonia had a moderate expressive language deficit. Weakness in communication impacted on all areas of her functioning. Treatment strategies that are not informed by this knowledge might result in yet another tragic failure to improve Sonia's ability to regulate her affect. Testing and observation provide new information that often helps targeted interventions have a greater chance of success.

A discussion of how we come to know and understand the world should also take into consideration the idea that there are many ways to show intelligence.[13] Therapy can provide another avenue to understanding individual learning styles and to developing interventions.

THERAPY SEEDS NEW IDEAS

The therapist, in a sense, is a farmer, "seeding" the session with new ideas, and a framer, reframing struggles in a light that can help the family look at them through a positive new lens. "He can't keep his hands on his own property," exclaims Raymond about his 10-year-old son Mitchell. "That's for sure," Mitchell's sisters declare. I ask, "Are your curious hands being curious in the wrong place or at the wrong time, Mitchell? More at home or at school?" Mitchell bursts into tears. We take out an octopus puppet, a friend of mine who also has "digital exploration struggles." The family comes up with strategies to help the octopus keep its curious hands near its sides. They begin to discuss who else in the family is curious. Stories emerge about traits that involve a high-energy boy who is very much like his pioneering, inquisitive, successful-entrepreneur dad.

Another way of reframing is to point out that all family members have traits that caused problems for them at one time, but that are now clearly assets for them. The **Time Capsule** activity is a fun way to explore these. Parents are asked to think of a trait or behavior that is a problem today, but might be an asset in the future. For example, a doodler in school now may be a cartoonist like Walt Disney later; an asker of a million questions now can become a police captain, a troubleshooter in business, or an investigative reporter. Therapists can ask: "Think about the child's behaviors that are troubling you now. How can they be positively translated into behaviors that will help your child later in life?"

THERAPY CONSIDERS PERSPECTIVE-TAKING

Mario is a boy who has many ideas. Usually, this is an asset. Certainly an "idea man" often grows up to be an inventor, entrepreneur, producer, writer, designer, or comic to name a few. However, there is a problem when one's ideas do not leave room for others' points of view. Mario seemed to get "married" to his ideas.

Could this be inherited? His mom, Clara, and grandpa Arthur, were noted to have a similar trait, a tendency toward all or nothing—black-or-white thinking. Once they "fell in love" with an idea it was very difficult to "divorce" themselves from their way of thinking. This caused endless tangles between Clara and Mario. It is very difficult to get along with friends and family without the ability to understand someone else's perspective.[14] While Mario could understand that we all have our own ideas and perspectives, in practice this was difficult (as is most often the case). Making a visual representation often helps children look at a problem in a different way. In this case, a **flow chart** helped Mario see a connection between his behavior and his angry feelings.

After we made the flow chart, I used a marker on a piece of plain paper to draw a large **scribble** (a simple unstructured drawing) and made copies of it. I gave one copy each to Mario and Clara, and kept one for myself. I said that each of us should use the scribble to make a drawing. It didn't matter if we used markers or crayons. It didn't matter which way we held the paper, any side we wanted could be the top, but we couldn't look at anybody else's paper. When we compared finished products we saw that each of us had used the same scribble in

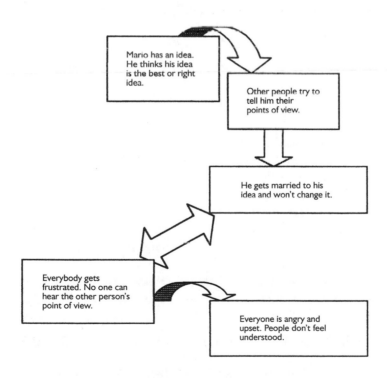

Connecting Feelings to Actions: Mario's Flow Chart

a very different way: Mario had used one part of the scribble and made it into a boat, Clara had used a different part to draw a lady with a hat, I had used the whole scribble to make a garden. When I asked Clara and Mario if they were surprised that we all made different drawings, both replied, "No." Clara commented that she and Mario have different ideas about many things. For example, she and Mario love ice cream, yet each likes a different flavor.

Visual images are a playful and helpful way to invite people to "stretch" their thinking, to generate and entertain new ideas. Since the image presented is only an "as if" situation, this exercise often helps clients get unstuck. I enlarge and use one of the ambiguous figures shown below.[15] Each picture is actually one of two figures, depending on your "point of view," which way you look at the image. For example, looking at the one on the left you might see either a seal or a donkey. If needed, I provide clues to help everybody see both figures. Once everybody sees the two figures, we are ready to argue both sides of a situation.

| Seal or donkey | Rabbit or Indian | Duck or squirrel |

Sixteen-year-old Albert feels that his parents treat him like a younger child. He wants a later curfew. His parents are worried that Albert's lifestyle is dangerous and his school grades are suffering. Albert and his parents are at an impasse. A discussion is initiated. We use the rabbit/Indian figure, labeling Albert's position, a later curfew, the rabbit and his parent's stance, the Indian. I take notes on the two kinds of thinking on the table and give each side my notes. In this phase of discussion, each side is only allowed to present the opposite side's thinking as outlined in the notes and from our discussion. The intriguing game-like quality of this activity helps everybody "play" with new ideas. The new ideas often open the door to new possibilities for solving the problem.

THERAPY GIVES THE FAMILY A SHARED LANGUAGE

Giving families a new nonshaming language helps them use therapy tools and techniques at home, especially in problem situations. This new language is developed with family members and most often comes out of the work we do together in the session. Barbara, Terry, and Peter are siblings. Their teasing and fighting resulted in hair-pulling one week. Their mother, Marjorie, brought them in because things in the house were out of control. After tracking the sequence of behaviors that led up to the physical aggression, we came up with the antecedents of *teasing* and *touching*, and made a new rule, **The 2T Rule**, shorthand for "no teasing, no touching." Infractions brought a hefty penalty to all parties. The statement "remember the 2T rule" replaced accusations and threats, which had been Marjorie's previously ineffective intervention. Similarly, **Caught Ya Points** are a way for children and parents to know they have been caught doing the right thing. Shortcuts and shorthand, as well as visual signs such as a traffic light or symbols, help the family use the techniques at home.

Eddie complains that his brother calls him fat. "You are," shouts Harry. "Keep it up, you two, and no ice cream after the session," yells their mom. These zaps are like lightning in the house because they always precipitate a storm. I introduce an activity, **The Shrinking and Expanding Feelings Game**, by asking the question, "Did you ever hear the saying 'sticks and stones can break my bones, but words can break my heart'?" We discuss this. I place my hands approximately twelve inches apart, palms facing each other and say, "Everybody, hold your hands up with the palms facing one another like this. Let's think of the space between your palms as your good feelings. I'm going to tell you some encouraging words like 'Good job!' or 'Nice going!' How does that make you feel? Does it make your good feelings get bigger or smaller?" Move your hands further apart when you hear encouraging words to show that your good feelings expand or grow. "Now I'm going to tell you some discouraging words like 'That was a dumb idea.' Does that make your good feelings get bigger or smaller? Move your hands together when you hear discouraging words to show that your good feelings shrink or get smaller."

Have family members use their entire bodies for shrinking and expanding. This gets everybody moving and helps provide a visceral way to understand the experience. Ask one of the children in the family to model the game. Have him stand slouched over a bit. Tell the child encouraging words, such as: "Way to go!" "You can do it," or "Keep trying." With each word of encouragement, the child should "grow" a few inches, getting taller and taller, until he stands upright, beaming with pride! Then reverse the positive comments and say discouraging words, such as: "You can't do it," "You're dumb," or "Give up," so that the child's good feelings shrink. With each comment, the child should shrink lower and lower until he reaches the floor. Then mix up the comments, some encouraging and some discouraging. The child should shrink and grow accordingly. After one or two practice demonstrations, divide the family into pairs. Invite each pair to practice shrinking and expanding each other's good feelings. Remind everyone that they are just using words that discourage, they are not "attacking" the other person with their words. (You may prefer to have the family do this activity as a whole. Ask everyone to stand up. When you tell them words that encourage, everyone should stand taller. Conversely, when you say words that discourage, each person should move closer to the floor.)

I often use my hands to demonstrate quantity. This is especially helpful with young children and children who have expressive language weaknesses. I start by asking children to use their hands to show me how much is a little, medium-sized, and a lot. This provides an interactive way for everyone to participate. Family members guess what the other ones will say or show with their hands. It's a way to keep all on their toes and to heighten participation.

In Myrna's family, words fell on deaf ears. Her incessant repetition of commands taught her children that they didn't have to listen the first time they were asked. Not surprisingly, when her patience shrank, she blew up. Myrna would start out using a nice tone and positive affect, but once the children did not listen, she would lose her patience. In therapy, she learned to use visual prompts instead of words. She would signal, "Look what's happening to my patience," by moving her hands close together. This became a nonconfrontational cue for her children to follow directions.

Three additional examples of development of a new, shared language are **The Dancing Finger**, **Invitations**, and **The No Game**.

The Dancing Finger

Arnold gets into trouble because he can't stop touching his sister Monique's CD player. He says, "If she didn't leave it out, I wouldn't touch it." Instead of accepting responsibility for his actions, he points his finger at his sister.

Cynthia forgets her books at school and can't complete her homework. She points her finger at her last-period teacher: "It's his fault, he rushed us out of the class."

Kendra wakes up late for school. While she's dressing, she screams at her mother, "It's your fault. If you would wake me up earlier, I could get there on time."

Finger pointing is done all the time, especially in what I call the "shame-blame game." When somebody points a blaming finger at another person, the person being pointed at often feels ashamed and tries to get rid of the bad feeling. One way to get rid of the feeling is to blame somebody else. The shame-blame game is like holding a hot potato in your hand and getting rid of it by passing it on. The problem is that fingers most often point out toward others, rather than in toward ourselves. I ask Kendra, "Can a finger that 'dances out' turn around and 'dance in'?" She replies that others don't admit they are wrong, so why should she? I agree that others need to take or admit responsibility, and ask her if she can dance her finger around and tell me how she is also responsible. To give an example I say, "I am planning a wonderful afternoon at the movies. Because there is a lot of traffic I arrive at the theatre about ten minutes after the movie has started. I am annoyed and blame all the other drivers on the road." Then I slowly dance my finger toward myself and ask Kendra, "What could I have done? How could I have been responsible for getting to the movies on time?" Kendra tells me I could have gotten myself ready to leave my house earlier!

Once the concept of the dancing finger is introduced, everybody in the family is assigned a special job. I tell them, "This is one of the most important jobs in the world (and maybe one of the hardest, too!) The job is to be a monitor of yourself and only of yourself."

When the dancing finger is brought out in session, if I see it moving in only one direction, I may lightheartedly say, "Uh oh, I think we might have the dancing finger at work here. The trouble is, it seems to be pointing in only one direction. What do you think? Do you think I'm right? Does anybody else notice the dancing finger?" I gently ask the person who is pointing to others as culprits to "see if you can dance your finger back around to yourself and talk about your part in the problem or situation." All participants in turn get to dance their fingers back to themselves to think and talk about their roles.

Invitations

Helping children see their responsibilities in their transgressions is crucial. The idea that they might do something to cause a negative consequence is a foreign concept to some children. Dean, for example, thought that blame was a one-way arrow that points directly at the other person. Using "invitations" helps children learn the important idea that their reactions and behaviors often "invite" others to respond opposite to what the child wants. I start by telling about Irwin, who *invites* trouble for himself in school. I tell them that this is what Irwin said:

> I don't listen.
>
> I don't do what other people tell me to do.
>
> I argue with them.
>
> I am not polite to them.

I then asked Dean if he thought that teachers like Irwin's behavior. Did Dean think that if Irwin did any or all of these things he might have a bad day and get in trouble in school? Did he think that Irwin might lose a privilege? Dean agreed that these behaviors had in fact caused a problem for a boy like Irwin the previous week. "Who is in charge of his behavior? Who decides if he will listen or not listen?" I queried. "The boy," he answered. "Then something that this boy did caused the teacher to take away a privilege," I continued. "Even if he didn't mean to do it, but got angry or was upset because someone else bothered him, still, it was his decision about whether or not to listen and be polite. His behavior *invited* the teacher to take away a privilege." I told Dean that I thought Irwin had begged the teacher to take away a privilege because he had had several chances and still made a bad choice.

Dean was able to see that sometimes we do things that *invite* other people to also do things, such as take away a privilege. The principal had recently placed Dean on a conduct card because he talked back to the teacher. Dean made a connection between his behavior and the principal's actions. (This was no easy task as he insisted that the teacher had talked rudely to him first! I agreed with him that the teacher had not made a good choice, but reiterated that he had had a choice too.) I asked Dean what he could do to have the principal take away his daily conduct report. He commented that he could start following the rules. We compiled the following list of behaviors he could do to invite other people to do *nice* things for him.

1. Do what the person says to do.

2. Listen.

3. Don't argue.

4. Even if you want to say something bad just say it in your head, not out loud.

5. Be polite.

6. Try to behave the best you can.

Dean agreed that he could *invite* either fun, like a reward for himself, or trouble.

This concept was also useful for 10-year-old Maureen. She and I spent a lot of time talking about "invitations." She had been observing her behavior and noticed when she behaved a certain way; very often she didn't get what she wanted. We decided to make a list of behaviors that invited a "no" response. On the computer she wrote:

This is a list of things that I do that invite other people to say "NO" to me.

Screaming or crying

Yelling back

Saying "no" to them

If they say, "not now," just keep asking over and over

Ignoring them

Fighting with somebody

Saying, "one minute," and you don't come

Have a little amount of patience

There are things that we do that invite other people to help us or give us what we want. There are things that I can do to invite other people to be nice with me. When I do these things, people want to say yes to me more times.

We took the list and then made it into a chart, which Maureen used to record her behavior.

If I do these things my life is happier and I feel happy and good.

MAUREEN'S "INVITATIONS"	MON	TUES	WED	THURS	FRI	SAT	SUN
Be a good helper.							
Make a good choice.							
Use nice words.							
Have patience (don't expect to get what you want the first mimute).							
When they call you, come right away.							
Say yes! Say okay!							
If they say "not now," stop asking and wait.							
Treat other people in the family nice (no screaming at them).							
Listen the first time they ask you to do something.							

The No Game: Going from No to Yes

This game is an intervention that the family (Mom and Dad in particular) can use with the child who seems to be having difficulties in conforming. The "No Game" teaches children about how their behavior *invites* reactions and other responses from family members and how their actions create cycles of reacting that have become intractable to change.

The essential first step in this intervention is to sit down with the entire family to explain the game. This family meeting should include all the children in the house, not just the child whose behavior is being targeted. I say to the child, "I'm going to teach you two words that could change your life." I try to pique interest by asking the child to guess what the two words are. The usual reply is "please and thank you," or something similar. I encourage several guesses, and then say, "The two words are 'yes' and 'no'."

"Now, I'm going to take a piece of paper and divide it into two columns, one headed 'yes' and the other headed 'no.'" I ask the child, "What do you notice happens in your house when you say yes? Are there usually more smiles? Are people more cooperative? Are things generally better? Do you often get more privileges, like staying up later? In the "Yes" column, I list all the things that happen when everybody is saying yes. Then I ask the child, "What do you notice when you say no? Is there more screaming?" Generally, children say there is. "Do you get sent to your room?" Frequently, this is true. "Do you usually have time out? Does saying no invite people to have friendly relationships? Does it sometimes rob family members of the chance to have fun together as a family? Does it sometimes leave people feeling hurt and unhappy?" I write down all the things that happen when anybody is saying no. Here's an example:

YES	NO
good times	bad times
nice talking	yelling
fun	sent to room
prizes	no prizes
smiles	mean faces
hugs	hit
feel happy	feel sad
happy house	mad house

Let's see how The No Game works. Mom asks Aaron something like, "Please get the milk for me." When Mom makes this request, Aaron has a moment to choose, to decide, if he will say yes or no. If Aaron says "no" Mom waits for a few seconds and then Mom is to say, "Are you inviting me to play The No Game?" This question is a discriminative stimulus, a cue or reminder for the child that his behavior is inviting a reaction or a behavior from the mother. Aaron knows that this means that in response to any requests Aaron makes subsequently, Mom will be using this phrase, "I'm sorry, I can't say yes because you invited me to play the No Game." She won't say "No." Rather, she will point out how his behavior invited her to play The No Game, which lets Aaron know that her answer is no without her saying the word.

This is the important part! There is an enormous difference here between the mother saying, "No, I'm not going to do this because you didn't get the milk when I asked you to," and her referring to the idea of The No Game. When she refers to The No Game, she constantly restates *calmly* and in a *matter-of-fact manner*, that the child's behavior indicates his choice, and his choice has consequences. (A caveat: While I often use the No Game with different types of children, as you might suspect, it does not work well with those who are very oppositional.) An idea here that must be underscored is that we need to get away from language such as, "I'm not saying yes to you because you never say yes to me." That becomes a signal, the throwing down of the gauntlet to begin the escalation to war.

SEND THERAPY HOME

Shared language, along with activities, games, stories, and metaphors, supports the transfer of learning from the analogue situation, the therapy room, to the everyday world of the child and the family. The goals are generalization[16] and maintenance.[17] The interventions that are presented are offered within the context of other work with clients. They are not stand-alone interventions; they lead to discussions, new ideas, and unique solutions for each family. Each chapter of this book highlights ways that therapists can help families take therapy home.

As therapists, we have a responsibility to offer the best practices available to alleviate human suffering. Managed care gives us little time to help solve difficult problems. There is a plethora of articles using controlled outcome studies that helps guide the practitioner toward proven therapeutic interventions.[18] This literature base is informed by developmental psychology and psychopathology, examines how therapeutic change occurs, and offers empirically supported practices.[19] Incorporating these practices into ongoing work with children and families is vital. Keeping up with current practices includes ongoing study and reading to keep informed.[20]

THERAPY IS TARGETED
AND HELPS TO BUILD COMPETENCIES

Sometimes therapy targets particular skill weaknesses in order to help children learn new skills to manage their behavior. By developing new competencies, behavioral repertoires are increased, allowing interactional patterns to be changed.

Lenny has difficulties with planning and prioritizing. Socially, he has difficulty inhibiting inappropriate responses. In school, his impulsivity gets him into trouble daily. He loves racing and we often talk about it in sessions. He told me he moves "lightning fast." Using Lenny's interests when developing interventions makes it easy to segue into discussion with him. We set up a start line and started a race. We practiced what I call "the **3 Gs**": (1) Get on your mark, (2) Get set, (3) Go. We talked about why each step was important and what could happen if the runners were to "go," before "get on your mark" and "get set." Along with Lenny's mom, we identified that it was Lenny's difficulty with steps one and two that often caused him trouble at school. We talked about how important it was to practice the 3 Gs and decided that we invite or cause trouble for ourselves when we don't practice them. We concluded that if everybody practiced "get on your mark" and "get set," life would be better everywhere. Lenny decided to start practicing this. Mom decided that she and Dad needed to work on this too. They made a plan to help each other practice at home. One of the ways they would practice was by using the expression "3Gs," which was an instant reminder of our important conversation. They decided that each time they practiced they would make a happy face on the calendar. When they had fifteen happy faces they would rent a movie and eat pizza, Lenny's favorite activities.

Jesse needed to learn flexibility. We wrote this story together and talked about how his difficulty with this important skill affected relationships at home. He monitored himself at home using the recording form that follows his story.

Flex-ability

"Flex" means, stretch, move, grow, relax, having thinking that could bend and change.

A plant has flex-ability. Flex-ability means it can move. People can have flex-ability.

I like when Mom has flex-ability. I like when other people have flex-ability.

When you don't have flex-ability you get like one idea and you don't want to change it. Sometimes, I don't have flex-ability. Sometimes things like a pen don't have flex-ability and they could break if you try to make them flexible (move or bend). Once it breaks it is garbage.

A brick wall doesn't have flex-ability. People who have flex-ability are easier to get along with. You can get along with people who don't have flex-ability, but it's harder. In my house when I don't have flex-ability I am usually mad. I get stuck in my thinking and later I realize that I'm wrong. That happens to me a lot. When we don't have flex-ability we can't think if something is right or wrong. You just say it.

Later, when I think about what happened it doesn't make sense that I got so mad. Later, I feel like I'm dumb. In school that happens and I say something and later I figure out that I made a mistake. I used to stay mad for a long time, now I figure it out quicker.

We followed up at home with a chart to monitor progress. Each day Jesse rated himself (1) yucky, (2) fair, (3) good.

	Monday	Tuesday	Wednesday	Thursday	Friday	Saturday	Sunday
Did I have flex-ability today?							

THERAPY'S PARTNERS IN SCHOOL

Therapy places importance on the involvement of other systems and participants in the life of the client. These significant others—parents, extended family, teachers, coaches, and friends—become part of a team of helpers to move therapy along. The school is an essential partner.

When a child's struggles are school-related, we must make treatment "portable" so it can be carried to the educational setting. Bonny, age 10, was having a tough year in school. She loved to clown around and laugh. The problem was that she did it at the wrong time and certainly in the wrong place. For example, Bonny called out all the time or threw her books off the desk and announced that she was testing gravity. She attended a structured religious school where appropriate comportment was emphasized. Bonny complained that she couldn't understand why she got into trouble. "The teacher is mean to me and never talks nice. She talks nice to other kids," she grumbled. I asked her to do some detective work with me and to observe what it was that pleased the teacher. What behaviors did other students do that got praise, a smile, a positive comment, or nice talking from the teacher? The next week we made a diagram from her observations (see next page).

We then went through the diagram in a step-by-step fashion and saw what Bonny did and didn't do in class. We rated each of the behaviors on a scale of (1) yucky, (2) fair, (3) good. We sent a note to the teacher and asked her to review Bonny's chart and to rate her on these areas using our 1-2-3 rating scale. I thanked her for her comments and her willingness to help Bonny develop some new skills for life. Bonny and I reviewed the chart and guessed what the teacher would say. This helped Bonny make a more honest assessment of her trouble spots. She decided to work on one of the behaviors she needed to improve, and as a starting point chose "do what the teacher says the first time she asks." A daily progress sheet with different opportunities to practice the target behavior traveled between home and school. In session, we developed a reinforcement menu with a list of privileges that Bonny could earn for improvement on specified target behaviors.[21]

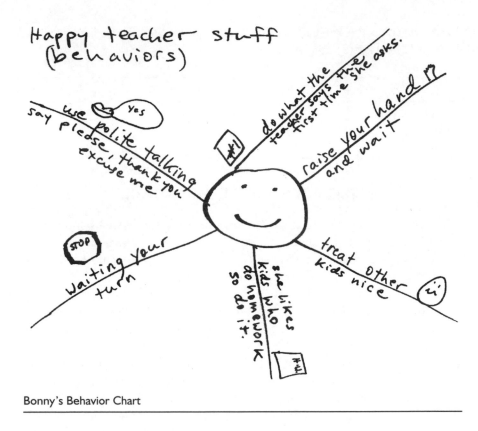

Bonny's Behavior Chart

ARE WE THERE YET?
CHART THE COURSE AND MAP PROGRESS

Charting progress toward specified outcomes is an important part of treatment. How will you know when you've arrived, if you don't know where you're going? Goal-attainment scaling is a useful way to set practice-based, realistic, individualized goals for clients.[22] It has been used widely in the fields of rehabilitation[23] and geriatrics,[24] and as a method of evaluation with learning disabled individuals,[25] and in family[26] and play therapy.[27] Those who work with goal-attainment scaling find it quick and simple to use.[28] I find that it helps clients monitor progress toward goals. I like to use the example of monitoring the size of the spot in the treatment of enuresis. The size of the spot may be larger than a dinner plate when we begin treatment. After a time the spot is not gone, but it may now be down to the size of a saucer. We look for progress, not perfection. Mapping progress helps children and family members combat feelings of defeat and a "nothing's working" notion.

THERAPY UNDERSCORES WHAT'S WORKING

Solution-focused therapists encourage clients to be goal-directed and collaborate with the therapist to create solutions. They ask, "Suppose that one night, while you were asleep, there was a miracle and this problem was solved. How would you know? What would be different?"[29] They ask if the problem is happening now and about times when the problem or referral complaint did not exist, or was not in evidence. (These latter times are "exceptions" and can be deliberate or spontaneous.[30]) "Miracles" happen all the time. Clients inadvertently stumble upon useful solutions, frequently attributing the locus of control for success to something outside of themselves: Jay's lucky penny that *helped* him pass his math test. When I hear the client talk of "a good day," a success, or an accomplishment, my ears perk up. By exploring successes and figuring out how they happened (miracle, accident, plan), clients learn how to use these solutions to solve new problems and attack new situations. Any time someone comes up with ideas, solutions, or strategies that bring about a desired result, it is important to *punctuate* the success. We write down the solutions. Each time, I am awed by the unique and creative means people employ to succeed. We figure about how they can "Xerox" a success, to use it again. After a solution is written down we work together to figure out how we will be able to (1) select, (2) highlight or bold, (3) copy, (4) cut, and (5) paste the solution for future use. It becomes a living document of a person's keys to success. I often use the computer to show children how this works and to reinforce the metaphorical life skills inherent in every step.

Cora struggles with anger. We have been collecting a list of ideas that help her feel more in control. She especially liked our discussion of anger and danger and decided to put that on her list. When people are very angry, she decided, dangerous things can happen, like something could break or somebody could get hurt—even if you didn't mean it to happen. She writes her 10 secrets for having a good day and tells me that when she does these things she gets along better with people and has a better day:

My Secrets of Success

1. When you make a good choice you feel good.
2. When you make a lot of good choices you could earn something special (sometimes).
3. Choose wisely and it invites other people to do nice things with you.
4. Ignore people when they are annoying you.
5. Don't get very angry. Keep your anger small by doing what you are supposed to be doing.

6. If you want to do something and somebody wants you to do something else, you should listen to the other person and not get angry.

7. The only difference between anger and danger is a "d." Anger can be dangerous. It's okay to be angry, but you have to be the one in control of the anger. There might be danger if you are not in control.

8. When you get angry use good words and not your hands. Say why you are upset.

9. Go to school every day!

10. Sometimes you could get angry if you miss something in school, but you should ask somebody what you did. Get help if you need it.

When I follow my secrets of success I have a good day.

All of us may have our own secrets for success that we employ in our work with children and their families. Chapter 3 offers tactics to help the therapist get and stay on track, which is one of my secrets of success.

CHAPTER 3

Principles and Practices

Strategically Organized Sessions

While working with children has its delights, it sometimes presents your worst therapy nightmares. In a recent course I taught, one therapist/participant related being handcuffed to a chair by a 7-year-old who gleefully ran to the waiting room to tell of his feat. The look of horror on the other attendees' faces told the story of recognition.

There are many ways to get "handcuffed" in a session. For example, a child's provocative and aggressive behaviors can threaten to dominate a session. The same challenging behaviors that are exhibited at home also "visit" the consulting room. What can you do?

Michelle sent me a handwritten note via her mom: "I want 18 minutes of play and then I'll talk." I should have guessed her mood the minute I saw her in the waiting room. Her coat was still on, her collar was pulled up, and her baseball cap was pulled down low so as to avoid eye contact with me. Her mom, Rosa, watched intently to see how I would react. She knew that giving in to Michelle came with a price, and if we reinforced her behavior we could be assured that this would become a weekly event.

Rosa and I strategized. Our plan was to de-escalate the situation. In order to negotiate a settlement, the next 15 minutes were spent passing notes back and forth between Rosa and me in the office and Michelle in the waiting room. In one of the early notes we acknowledged Michelle's right to choose to stay in the waiting room and remarked that she could be proud of herself for using words today to let us know what she wanted to do. This was important to Michelle, who often complained that no one ever listened to her requests.

We told her that using words was something that grown-ups did and was a sign that Michelle was growing up. She could also be proud of herself for staying in control of her anger.

Michelle looked surprised, possibly because this was a departure from the way Rosa usually handled Michelle's noncompliance, that is, with threats, and menacing behavior. There was a visible change in Michelle as she moved from the role of combatant to the role of co-negotiator. Her face softened, and her tone became quieter. Rosa also seemed pleased and her worried look began to dissipate.

Rosa and I then proposed a solution. We said that we were going to start the session, and when Michelle was prepared she could join us. We created an open door policy that allowed Michelle to make a choice and enter the room when she was ready. As Michelle "overheard" Rosa and me talking about what we might do during the session, she edged her way toward the door. When we decided to take out the video camera and moved the puppet theater, Michelle asked to videotape a play that she directed and wanted to take home the tape.

Near the end of the session I told Michelle that what had happened reminded me of a story. A lady went to a restaurant for lunch and ordered a hamburger. The waitress brought her lunch, but instead of the hamburger, there was a roast beef sandwich. The lady immediately got up from the table, stomped out, and went into the beauty shop next door where she began to complain to the owner that she had gotten the wrong lunch. The beauty shop owner said, "Lady, I can't do anything about that. I do hair. You need to speak to somebody who can do something. When you have a problem, take it to somebody who can help you." We had a discussion about the similarity of what had happened in the story to what had happened today with Michelle. She had started threatening Rosa in the car about not participating in the session. If she had a complaint about the sessions, we needed to find a way for her to discuss it with me, the person who could do something about it.

In a phone call later that night Rosa told me that she had learned a valuable lesson herself, about not taking up the challenge, using words, and thinking calmly.

In our work it is important to consider brain-behavior connections. Chapter 4 will discuss the importance of keeping the brain in mind during therapy and ways to discuss the brain with clients. I always think about the impact of physiology and prepare myself to handle "uninvited guests," the problem behaviors that haunt families every day. Larry can't sit still; he fidgets constantly and no one wants to sit near him in the session. Orin is easily distracted and can't sustain his attention; he is the first to let me know that someone pulled into the driveway or that it just started to rain. Maurice has difficulty organizing and planning. Without help in the session, he can't organize his thoughts. This makes him so frustrated he often explodes. His mom's biology makes her tense and her mood mercurial, adding fuel to Maurice's fire. Allison blurts out answers and can't wait her turn; family members become exasperated with her behavior at home and in the session. I have to batten down the hatches when George has an appointment, as everything is fair game for his curious hands. Both he and his younger brother have difficulty with self-control. If a song could describe Derek it might well be "I can't get no satisfaction." His insatiability interferes with his tolerance for boredom. Laura's song might be "Little things mean a lot." She often makes a mountain out of a molehill.

This how-to chapter provides suggestions for promoting success in working with today's unique minds in therapy. It presents practical guidelines for enhancing client listening, participation, self-monitoring, and on-track behavior and for organizing sessions strategically to solve various therapy dilemmas. The chapter offers ways to develop tools to talk with children, activities to help them connect with their feelings, and techniques to facilitate sessions, help the therapist deal with the impact of physiology, and keep from getting "handcuffed." I find that it is especially disconcerting and demoralizing when serious disruptions and outbursts occur in a place that the family feels is a site of help and healing. If looks could talk, the expression on a parent's despairing face may say, "Not even you can help us with this uncontrollable child. It's hopeless."

GETTING ON TRACK

"Getting on track" begins with my first contact with a family member, usually on the phone. After listening to a brief description of the problem, I gather basic information such as the names of those who live in the home and contact numbers for parents and the referral source. Frequently callers are anxious and worried, and I spend a few minutes connecting with them. I also explain that when I work with children, family involvement is essential. I emphasize that while I may have sessions with the child alone or with different combinations of family members at different times, I find that children do best when parents are included. I add, "Your involvement is key. We need to make sure we send therapy ideas home to use outside my office. If therapy is conducted only with the child behind closed doors, how can we make that happen?"

Some parents are relieved when I tell them this and welcome the chance to be involved. Others, however, are concerned about how to make change happen. They worry that they will be blamed for the problem. They want the problem (often the child) to be fixed. I tell them that I wish it were as simple as changing a battery or the distributor cap in a car, but it is not. Problem

formation is complex and we need to examine and explore the issues together. *I* cannot *fix* something, but *together* we can find solutions that will work in
their family. My asking how others get involved and are affected by the problem helps the caller understand the need for the presence of others. I explain
that our work is a joint effort and the family is an essential part of the solution. We arrange a time for the consultation and decide who will attend.

The Physical Environment of the Therapy Room

One size doesn't fit all, and the therapy room must reflect this. In a sense,
the room becomes symbolic of what therapy will be like. When you open my
closet, you find surprises: novel, interesting, and imaginative toys, puppets,
and games. There are different mediums for creative craft projects. The
inventory includes: dolls, small figures, animal families, human families;
chips, tokens, counters; stickers; picture books; pick up sticks; easily manip-
ulated puppets of all sizes, including finger puppets; signs (e.g., "How Am I
Doing?" and "The Floor"); colored paper, construction paper, crayons,
markers, round-tipped scissors, glue, stapler, pipe cleaners, paper plates; a
stopwatch; game-making supplies; bubbles; small cars; play telephones,
walkie-talkies; dry marker board, blackboard; basketball hoop, sponge balls,
and rubber balls.[1]

The physical environment is cozy, with comfortable pillows, and there is
seating at the child's eye level, including a small table and chairs for young
children. A pop-up tent[2] provides a quiet spot where a child can go to re-group
yet still be part of the session. Portable active games[3] that can be folded up and
put in a closet are also useful.

Another valuable piece of equipment is a laminating machine for making
thematic placemats, games, game boards, and story covers. I also make use of
technology and have a computer, a video camera, and a digital camera on
hand. Children may bring in their toys, stuffed animals, and trinkets whose
images can be captured on a computer disk and then inserted into a story using
a word processing or publishing program.[4]

Listening Enhancers

It is essential to set the tone that the therapy room is a place where we listen to
one another. This is especially important in families that don't have this skill as
part of their behavioral repertoire. I may focus *attention on attention* by using the
questions "Why do you think we have two ears and one mouth?" and "What other
important word can we make from the same letters as listen (silent)?" I sometimes
forget about using a tool only to be reminded by a child asking, "Where is 'the

floor'? I think we are going to need it!" "The floor" and the "talking rock" are examples of token objects we pass to whomever we designate to be the speaker.

Monitor of Myself

Helping individual family members self-monitor often moves the session along. Victor had little tolerance or patience for family sessions. He repeatedly exploded and refused to participate. Since he enjoyed games, I introduced a match game where he rated his behavior in the session by using the "How Am I Doing?" sheet.[5] He received one point when his self-monitored rating matched the rating given by his parents. He earned a bonus point for describing why he rated himself the way he did. Others gave themselves ratings as well.

Asking, "How are we doing?" puts responsibility on all family members to make judgments about their own behavior. It moves them from the role of passive participators to the role of active listeners, observers, and evaluators. When someone is rated a 1 (doing yucky), we ask, "What can we do to make it a 2? How can we help you?" Harry told me that he had rated himself a 1; he wasn't paying attention because he was bored. "Can we play a game?" he asked. We made a contract with Harry for 10 more minutes of conversation and chose one of the many games in the closet that employ a more active approach.

During a difficult discussion with the K family I asked, "How do you think you are doing staying on track and talking about this?" Each one commented they were doing great. With Mom acting as the recorder, we brainstormed what was helping them focus and participate. They decided their success was because: (1) no one interrupted when another person was talking, (2) there was no teasing, (3) everyone looked at one another, and (4) there was no shouting. We typed the list into the computer, printed it, and they took it home as a guide so they could practice during the week at dinner. They also took home "How Am I Doing?" sheets for rating themselves (see "Tools to Get and Stay on Track" in the Appendix).

Tush In Seat: T.I.S.

Norman's family was like popcorn popping. Maintaining a focus was difficult because no one stayed seated for more than five minutes. Every time Norman jumped up, his father would drag him back to his seat or yell at him in an angry tone and Norman would retaliate in kind. We decided to use T.I.S. (tush in seat) points when in-seat behavior was required. The family found them a helpful motivator. One of the children even pointed out that T.I.S. spelled backwards is sit! For T.I.S. we used a stopwatch and counted how many points the child could accrue by staying seated during a given time period. I usually find that prizes are not necessary, but for the few occasions when they are needed I have used hard-to-get stickers (such as special dinosaur or hologram stickers) or ones that I make myself with a computer program.[6]

Do What Comes Naturally

For many children, sitting without doing something just doesn't work. Encouraging movement that does not disrupt the session channels activity into acceptable avenues. I sometimes encourage doodling, cartooning, and playing with paper clips or pipe cleaners while the child is waiting or listening. Actually changing seats to get a new perspective sometimes helps. Having an active child work as my assistant, drawing pictures or taking notes like a court reporter, is also useful. Taking turns with Simple Simon is a tried and true way to get a bossy, oppositional child involved. A television remote control device that we use to pause, start, and stop the discussion can be employed. Velcro darts, hopscotch, and golf are also popular activities. In order to make these games useful therapeutic tools, there is a caveat: The child must answer questions in order to collect points. A stress ball, bubbles, and relaxation exercises, such as "Robot–Rag Doll,"[7] are helpful and can also be used at home.

Encourage Active Participating

To keep everybody involved, I often use a "thumbs up or down" approach; when there is a discussion or a question, I might ask, "Thumbs up or down?" Everybody gets a chance to respond and stay involved. Or sometimes I use this don't agree/agree meter that we make together from a paper plate.

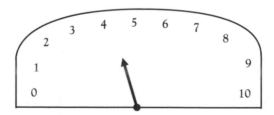

With young children, I ask, "How much?" After deciding what represents "a little," "medium," or "a lot," I suggest that they demonstrate with their hands, holding them close together or far apart to show how much or how little something is a problem. Or I draw pictures of cups filled to varying degrees and place numbers under them: (1) a little, (2) half or medium, and (3) a lot. You might add (4) full. One child even reminded me, "Marcia you need one 'over the top'!" To be sure that the children understand, I first ask them simple questions, "How much do you like pizza? Video games? Television?" These techniques, "Thumbs Up or Down," "Don't Agree/Agree," and "How Much," are all useful in both ongoing and assessment sessions (see "Tools to Get and Stay on Track" in the Appendix).

I sometimes use a counter, purchased at a local office supply store, to keep track of "smooth cooperator points" or give out actual tickets similar to those used at a carnival or raffle. These help to motivate participation and reinforce listening and attending behaviors. In a particularly difficult discussion, I might give out double cooperator points. Austin's outbursts threatened to disrupt the sessions. He liked nothing better than to argue with his parents, his sister, or me. He deemed these arguments the reason for coming to therapy. For Austin, a good fight relieved boredom and got his "juices" flowing. But he also loved getting points! We made up agreements about listening and reviewed them together each week. He gave each agreement a point value, from (1) easy to do (sitting) to (5) difficult (no screaming and fighting). He kept track of his points during the session. He loved a challenge and enjoyed earning bonus points for accomplishing the difficult behaviors. His dad, Ryan, had an equally fierce fighting spirit and was easily sucked in by Austin's "industrial strength vacuum." Ryan needed to work on his side of the equation in order for any work to progress. He also agreed to a point system and monitored his own arousal level. Everybody received extra points for using words instead of a jab or a piercing comment.

STAYING ON TRACK

To help everyone focus I may start by asking, "What can we do to stay on track?" The R family developed the following list to help them stay on track: Look at the person talking; listen to the person speaking; do not argue or interrupt; keep your hands to yourself. They decided to make different family members responsible for monitoring how they were doing.

Another way to keep everyone on track is to hand out index cards with jobs for the session. Some of these jobs might be "summarizer," "recorder," and "best listener." One person can be the "echo," and repeat a comment if necessary. I occasionally ask, "Who knows what we are talking about now? Who can tell me?"

Andre starts a session talking about what he considers an unfair punishment he received for his failing grade on a social studies report about the rain forest. Within a few minutes he is shouting about a family trip to Florida. "How did we get here?" I ask. Andre thinks and then tells me that talking about the rain forest reminded him of the restaurant that was just like a rain forest in the mall in Florida, which reminded him of a disappointment about a toy he didn't get in the mall, and that made him angry all over again.

Kayla's family also makes "side trips"; when they go off the topic, it takes the family "off purpose." Kayla loves to serve as a monitor and keep us focused. It helps her brain stay awake and involved. The G family also tends to switch tracks and introduce one topic after another. When someone switches the track, Hannah brings us back. "Do you know what's happening here?" I ask. Marie, Hannah's mom, correctly observes, "Yes, no one lets anyone finish and the first thing that got started never got finished."

Interrupting often keeps a session off track. Thomas blew up every time his brother William interrupted him. He would give William a jab in the ribs, start yelling, or storm out of the room. Patience and "waiting behavior" did not come easily to William either. As the younger of the two boys, he often struggled to have his voice heard. I suggested that instead of interrupting, William could hold onto his finger when he had something to say. I assured him that he would have a turn. This gave William a way to "hold on to" his ideas and a means for others to see he had something to say. It was also a helpful way to cue William about an upcoming difficult conversation where extra waiting and control might be needed. In addition, I keep paper handy so children can write words or draw quick pictures about what they are planning to talk about when it is their turn.

Think on Your Feet

Sometimes a family session begins in the waiting room. I opened the door to my office to hear piercing screams ordering Ira to stop playing with his paper airplane. Strong-willed Ira refused to stop. The youngest of three boys, he rarely had a chance to be an expert and was eager to demonstrate his skill. He entered the office proudly carrying the paper airplane. His determination to fly it around the office was matched only by his father's determination to stop him. I saw that we were on a collision course and asked Dad if he minded if Ira instructed us on how to make an airplane. Ira's five minutes in the limelight calmed him down. When I asked everyone how we might use the airplane in the session, the boys came up with the idea that we could go out into the waiting room and fly each other messages. The last five minutes of our time together was spent sailing thoughts through the air.

Gather Ideas: Here, There, and Everywhere

Each of us has an inventive spirit. One certain way to jump-start your innovative spirit is to trust your hunches and intuition and develop your right brain.[8] A child's world is filled with fantasy; sharing it helps me cultivate my creativity. There are four qualities of a person's creative C.O.R.E.: curiosity, openness, risk, and energy.[9] It is important as a clinician to ask yourself, "Do I tap into my C.O.R.E.?" Do you think you are imaginative, or do you consider yourself "creatively challenged?" Do novel ideas "spark" your thinking? Do you say to yourself, "I can try that," or do you make a list of reasons why you can't do that? Write down your thoughts about the questions and examine them.

Ideas to use in treatment come from here, there, and everywhere. An article about movies, "This Year's Hits and Pits," in the local newspaper sparked a useful discussion with an adolescent. When we talked about some of his struggles I said, "It sounds like this week was the pits. Was any part of it a hit?" Since then we often touch on the topic of "the week's hits and pits." Another idea came from a saying printed on a calendar: "It's not the first angry word that starts the fight, it's the second." On a different day, when I was stuck in a traffic jam, I looked over and saw this message on a bumper sticker: "It's never too late to have a good childhood." I filed both away with another of my favorite quotes, "Whether you think you can or think you can't—you are right."[10] I find many opportunities to incorporate these expressions.

One of my favorite interventions involves a maze and **blocked alleys.** I showed Myles a simple maze and told him to imagine with me that if I solved this maze and got to the end without going into any blocked alleys, we would win a million dollars. I told him he couldn't help me but he could watch. As he stood by my side I took my pencil and slowly went down the first road. I carefully negotiated the first blocked alley but got stuck in the second. Myles, who was prone to quick arousal, looked quite annoyed and began to get upset. I told him to calm down, that we had a second chance. I again put my pencil on the maze and, following the same road, working slowly, went into the same blocked alley. At this point, Myles was looking quite annoyed. I wondered out loud if he was thinking, "Boy, Marcia, you must not be too smart. How could you get stuck in the same blocked alley two times?" I told him not to worry, that we had one more chance. I picked up my pencil and put it back on the maze. I very slowly negotiated past the same blocked alley that I had gone into, but then I went back and went right into it.

Now, Myles looked exasperated. He asked me, "What happened? Why did you go into the same blocked alley each time? Didn't you see that you weren't going to get out that way?" At that point, his dad piped up and said, "Isn't that what you do in the house all the time? We tell you something once, we tell you something twice, we tell you something three times and you still go and do the same thing over and over." We talked about a tough incident that had happened that week, incorporating the metaphor of blocked alleys. "Blocked alleys" became a term that they took home with them, an idea that the family could use during the week. When Myles kept pursuing something that was going to get him in trouble or relentlessly went after something despite the fact that his mom or dad had said no, his mother or father would look at him and say, "Myles, this is a blocked alley."

Time and again, children enter a session bearing a gift of a story, a specific situation, or an event from the week that I can incorporate into the treatment. This gift could even be a pet, which might serve as an "unlicensed co-therapist."[11] Six-year-old Robert was described as fearful by his parents and teacher. Whenever he encountered a new situation, signs of anxiety appeared. His eyes would blink uncontrollably, his respiration rate would increase, and as he struggled to get words out, his tongue would dart in and out of his mouth as if he were a lizard or frog searching for insects. Robert's mother was particularly distressed because this behavior had begun to interfere with Robert's friendships and his school functioning.

In one session Robert animatedly told me about his new puppy, Fluffy. When he was outside with Fluffy she was always running up to meet new people. I said, "I think Fluffy knows just how to make friends. What to you think?" Robert and his mother agreed. I asked Robert if he would watch Fluffy that week and see just what she did to make a new friend. The following week Robert came in and dictated this list:

Fluffy's Rules For Making Friends

1. When you go somewhere be happy.

2. When someone comes to the house be excited.

3. Greet the person.

4. Talk to the person.

5. When you see someone go over and say "hi."

I asked Robert if any of Fluffy's rules might help him make a new friend. Robert thought that he would try rule number 5. We role-played some common situations, with Robert practicing saying, "Hi." We generated a list of other words that he might say when greeting someone. Robert and his mom and dad agreed to practice, and we made a simple checklist to see how many times Robert used this new skill.

Fluffy was a great cotherapist, and so was Libby. Nicky and his parents, Rosalie and Phil, had continuous disagreements about the tone Nicky used when he talked to them. They found it disrespectful, but Nicky would say, "What was so bad about what I said?" Many times, Rosalie and Phil said that they wanted to listen to what Nicky had to say, but could not accept that he talked to them "like they were two jerks." We did role-plays in a session, with the parents imitating Nicky's tone. He, however, insisted that only the words count, nobody hears the tone. He claimed he was not being rude or fresh since he only used nice words. It seemed that we were at an impasse. I decided to make a video to demonstrate the effects tone has on whoever hears it. One weekend I gathered a video camera, some pigs' ears—a special dog treat, and my friend's dog, Libby.

The experiment had three parts. In the first part, I showed how smart Libby was. Instead of saying the word, I spelled out the letters of her favorite treat. I asked her, "Where are the "p-i-g-s-e-a-r-s?" She quickly ran to the cabinet where they keep them and barked until I opened the bag and gave her a treat.

For the second part of the experiment, I used mean words and a nice tone. I looked down at Libby. With a big smile on my face, and in the high-pitched type of voice usually used with babies, I said, "You're a filthy slob. Who's a jerk? You're disgusting." Libby stood up on her hind legs, wagged her tail, and barked with delight.

In part three, I used nice words and a mean tone. I told Libby in a very harsh voice, "I love you. You're the best. Who's a great dog?" Again Libby looked at me, but this time her head went down, her ears went back, and her tail went between her legs. She hunkered close to the floor and moved away.

The whole family roared at the video. Nicky, still laughing, looked chastened as he said, "I guess it's true. It's not only what you say, it's how you say it."

Sandi was studying volcanoes in science. She was animated in session as she talked about them. She showed me a picture of an erupting volcano that was in her science book. I asked her if she thought anger erupts in people. I could see the proverbial light bulb go on as she made the connection. The volcano metaphor became a way for the whole family to discuss anger. Sandi wrote this story:

Imagine your feelings are volcanoes. When your feelings get hurt they erupt. When they erupt you get sad or angry. Everybody has a volcano in them. Some people's volcanoes erupt a lot. Other people's volcanoes hardly erupt. When my volcano erupts it makes me want to scream and I get very angry. Bad words come flying out like birds. Hot lava goes everywhere. The hot lava burns people's feelings. The hot lava ruins people's thinking and all they could choose are bad things. You never know when your volcano will erupt. It is a good thing to memorize how your volcano works. If you know what makes the hot lava get hot you can go on the yes road and make it colder. What happens in my house is that when my volcano erupts usually everybody else's erupt too.

I will see if I can keep my volcano from erupting. I am much happier when I do.

Develop Tools to Talk

Activities and games have many purposes. They are tools that prime the pump, facilitate conversation and talking, increase motivation to discuss difficult topics, help problem-solve, and provide active role-modeling. They make sessions interactive and fun and lend themselves to group play as they engage the family in structured activity. When I find we are headed toward an impasse in a session, I often turn discussion into a game. "More and more therapists are realizing that by 'making a game out of it'—whether it be learning how to make friends or learning how to be a better problem solver—you can teach children more effectively."[12]

Neil hid his face behind a pillow from the couch, literally refusing to face a painful conversation about his suspension from school because he hit another child. I took out a Velcro dartboard that he had enjoyed playing with in the past. Neil put down the pillow, threw the dart, and scored 10 points. In order to collect his points, he needed to answer a probe such as, "Tell what you might have done instead of using your hands when you got upset." For an extra turn (or double points) we made a plan that he could follow the next time he got upset. Even the most resistant children join in when the session is game-like. I have seen a child sit in a family session, cover his ears, and sing while someone was trying to give him feedback about an incident or problem. But when the feedback is part of a game, out-of-control behavior is generally not the rule.

A number of companies specialize in games and books that address the social/emotional needs of children and adolescents.[13] Numerous games are available for purchase, among them The Ungame,[14] and Imagine![15] Richard Gardner describes his Talking, Feeling, Doing Game as a "therapeutic instrument" and asserts that the child's response should serve as a point of departure for therapeutic exchanges. The idea is to get "as much mileage out of it as possible."[16]

You can also make your own board games. A simple, adaptable, and customizable game board that I made on the computer is included in "Tools To Talk and Send Therapy Home" in the Appendix.[17] I often use the same game board but I have several different series of question cards focusing on different themes (home, school, peers, how is it going, self-control, etc.) Before a session, I personalize the game with the child's name and print a set of question cards. (See "The ABCs of Game Making" in "Tools to Talk and Send Therapy Home" in the Appendix for additional information about game pieces, rules, and actual construction.) I have preprinted rules, but we often make up the rules together (e.g., what happens when you land on the star shape, talk bubble). One of the most important rules is that there are no right or wrong answers. Some of the questions carry a bonus for responding to several parts, or for answering a tough question (e.g., tell about a time you lost your temper this week).

Individualized board games help increase the child's motivation to talk about and work on concerns. Custom-made games easily translate into activities that can be taken home so the family can practice new skills. Additionally, the projective nature of the questions (A girl is crying in school. Why?) provides information about the child not readily available through direct conversation. The games provide a rich starting place from which parents and clinicians can gain a better understanding of not only the presenting problem but also other issues.[18]

Louise's Game Board: Making a Friend

This personalized game board was developed with 6-year-old Louise, who has difficulty with making friends. She titled her game "Making a Friend"; here are the rules:

Making a Friend–Louise's Rules to the Game

1. Up to 5 people can play.

2. No cheating. Let's say someone goes to the bathroom, don't spin for them.

3. Start where it says start.

4. Spin the spinner and move your piece to the correct spot.

5. Some of the places tell you what to do, like "say something nice and move ahead one." Do what it says.

6. Here's what to do on the other places.

   Heart: Say something that you say when you love somebody; who is it?

   Grey: Tell about something that made you sad with a friend

   Miss Piggy: Act like a "Miss Piggy." She likes to tell other people she is great and so beautiful. Do you think she has a lot of friends?

   Spaces with words: Do what it says to do.

   Horseshoe: Go down to the black and white talking guy.

   White: Skip a turn.

   Star: Tell us a wish.

   Schoolbus: Tell a time when you made a friend at school.

   House: Say a time when you were a good friend at someone's house.

   Happy face: Tell about a happy time with a friend.

   Kermit: Does he have a lot of friends? How does he act? What does he say to make a friend?

   Talking guy: Say something to someone who is playing with you.

   Radio: Sing a little song together.

   Pencil: Make a picture of a friend.

   Listening guy: Tell a time that you listened to a friend.

   Good idea: Say your best idea to get along with a friend.

   Dance: Make up a dance together.

HAVE FUN

It is important to note that this game was not created in isolation. It was one of the many multilayered activities used to accomplish treatment goals within the biopsychosocial framework. Part III of this book presents a detailed description of how interventions are developed within the overall context of a comprehensive treatment plan.

Another activity I used with Louise involved a magnet metaphor. We started with an actual magnet and objects that it attracted or repelled. I asked Louise if she thought that maybe there was a magnet inside each of us. We did some role-playing to help her see that words or actions could pull people toward her or send them away. We used puppets and videotaping. With permission from some other clients, I showed her their tapes. This is the story that we wrote together on the computer.

A people magnet is someone that attracts people & friends. It works like a magnet. If you put 2 magnets together, they pull to get to one another. Sometimes there's a bad magnet that wants to kick people away. We all have a magnet inside us. One that attracts people or one that makes people go away and not be friendly. You can turn your magnet on either way.

Instructions: How to pull people toward you.

- ★ Be friendly and nice.
- ★ Invite people over to your house.
- ★ Make a play date.
- ★ Look like you're having fun.
- ★ Ask people to play with you.
- ★ Use nice talking.
- ★ Share your toys.
- ★ Be a leader and walk tall.
- ★ Take turns and do what other people want to do.
- ★ Don't tell people everything they do wrong. If you have to say something, say it in a nice way.

Instructions: How to push people away from you. This is the secret for you if you don't want any friends.

- ★ Be mean.
- ★ Leave them out of the game.
- ★ Make fun of people.
- ★ Use bad talking.
- ★ Be sure to use bossy talking.
- ★ Always tattle.
- ★ Be a nagger.

If you want people to like you, you should choose the good list.

If you don't want people to like you, you should choose the bad list. It's up to you.

Connect with Feelings: Activities with a Purpose

There are several activities that help participants learn how to recognize their own feelings and the feelings of others. A version of Charades, where the objective is to "read" people's faces and bodies and guess how they are feeling, is invaluable. I collect magazines so we can cut out pictures to use in role-plays, to make collages, and to match faces to feeling words. Thumbprint faces are an entertaining way to make faces that show the different feelings we have.[19] With younger children I may use a book such as *Today I Feel Silly,*[20] *How Are You Peeling?*[21] *Play with Your Food,*[22] or *The Lonely Seahorse.*[23] With an older child I might use questions such as these, prompting for examples:

- Are feelings inside you or outside you?
- Is knowing the same as feeling?

(For example, you *know* that your baby sister needs attention from your mom, but you still might *feel* sad and mad that your mom doesn't have time to play with you. You *know* that the teacher can't call on you every time, but you still *feel* angry when she calls on other people more often.)

- Do you think that feelings affect your body? How?
- Do you think how you feel affects how you act or behave?

(For example, if you think a teacher doesn't like you, do you think you might be upset in school? Would this affect how you do in school?)

- Do we all feel the same about things?

(For example, does everybody feel happy about going to school?)

- Can you have more than one feeling at a time?
- Are there some feelings you welcome and are happy to have?
- Are there some feelings you don't like and wish wouldn't bother you?
- Is it better to show your feelings or hide them?
- Can a person know how you are feeling even if you don't use words to tell them?

(For example, Can someone tell how you are feeling just by looking at your face?)

- Are your feelings good or bad? [The answer is neither. Remember, they are just your feelings!]
- Do you imagine that you might feel one way on one day (or part of a day) and feel differently the next day? Is that good? Bad?
- Are thoughts the same as feelings?

Children love to draw faces or I use computer clip art Screen Beans[24] figures, which are also fun to use when learning, writing, and talking about feelings.

We might construct a feeling die.[25] Together we make a list of feeling words and write these words or draw pictures on the die. We roll the die and each person makes up a story, draws a picture, or talks about a time he or she had that feeling. Faces can be drawn as well. Here are Trudy's.

I have developed situation cards that cover a wide range of topics. I start with blank index, business, or postcards[26] and write a hypothetical situation on each (you got the best birthday present, you were picked first to play on the team, you were picked last, you lost your homework, etc.). Players pick cards and describe or draw a picture of a feeling they might have in that situation. Everyone gets to play.

Another aspect of this work incorporates cognitive behavior therapy (CBT), which has proven to be useful with a variety of problems.[27] I use this representation to discuss how thoughts affect how we feel, what we do, and how we act/react.

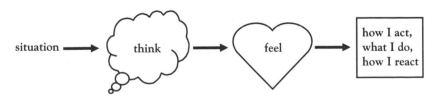

To help children understand the idea that thoughts affect feelings and that feelings affect behavior, I use examples. Here are two.

Situation One. What if your mom is late coming home and you imagine that she has been in an accident and is in the hospital? What are your thoughts? If you were thinking those thoughts, how would you feel? How would you behave and/or what would you do?

situation			act, do, react
Your mom is late coming home and you think she got into an accident & is in the hospital	Marie: "My mother could die."	scared and very, very sad	cry and cry and be scared
	Lester: "Maybe she broke her arm or something."	scared, worried, sad	get my neighbor, call my grandma

Situation Two. What if your mom is late coming home and you imagine that she stopped on the way to get the new toy she promised you? What are your thoughts? If you were thinking those thoughts, how would you feel?

situation			act, do, react
Your mom is late coming home and you imagine that she stopped on the way home to get you a new toy.	Marie: "I can't wait to show it to my friends, I'm lucky, I have a great mommy."	happy, very excited	keep looking out the window because I am so excited
	Lester: I can't wait to play with it."	smiling, happy	be jumping around the house

I also create cards relevant to situations children encounter in their daily lives. "You're in the schoolyard at lunchtime; a group of children are playing a game and you want to join them but they won't let you." In her response to the situation on the card, Joanie says she would think, "They're being mean to me. That's not right; I let them play with my friends." She says that would make her feel upset, angry, and sad. She would probably go over to the teacher and tell him that the other kids wouldn't play with her. On the other hand, Tammy says she would think, "It's okay for them not to play with anyone they don't want to play with." She wouldn't feel mad. She would just be by herself or find someone else to play with her.

Connect with Your Own Feelings

Jay enters the office with an inquiry. "Did you make? It smells in here. Did you, did you, did you?" His mother and father tell him to stop, which only raises the ante. Jay doesn't allow us to move off his topic and his voice gets louder and more insistent. He is literally in my face now, announcing, "If you don't answer me, why should I answer you? Did you make? Did you, did you?" I model a calm and appropriate response, yet it is not without a certain amount of inner consternation. I know that I had better fasten my seatbelt, put on my thinking cap, and remain calm. This might be a bumpy hour ahead! I tell Jay softly, "That isn't the kind of question you ask someone. That's personal. That's why there are doors on the bathroom, it's a private time." I continue, "What do you think would happen if I stood by the bathroom door and asked each person, 'Are you making? Are you, are you?' I don't think anyone would come back to my office." Each time Jay brings up the topic, I look at him and whisper the refrain, "Questions like that are personal; that's not the kind of thing we ask someone else."

We can't help but react to children's behavior. Their plight often pulls at our heartstrings, and their provocations may remind us of feelings we thought were buried with the dinosaurs. They may impel us to feel protective, confused, flooded, frustrated, furious, or anxious. This is especially true when unexpected aggression occurs. It is important during these times to connect with your evoked feelings and notice your reactions.[28] Children and/or adults may push the envelope in sessions. Some are masters of provocation. Careful monitoring is required as a situation can ignite quickly. It is vital to examine and stay in control of the kaleidoscope of feelings.

This is no small task. As Weber and Levine have described, the family therapist needs to be emotionally attuned to the family and is responsible for holding, labeling, and integrating the emotions and the split-off parts of family members, and must do this without "defensively retaliating, withdrawing, rejecting, criticizing, or colluding with family scapegoating."[29] They recommend tuning inward and asking oneself, "Why this feeling, why now?" They conclude: "Being able to listen to and hold one's experience can be helpful in understanding a family member's experience and provide a window for viewing family group process."[30]

Problem-solving

Effective problem solving is crucial. Families habitually get stuck in a more-of-the-same approach[31] and need to determine new possibilities and create new solutions. Jonathan, age 15, is diagnosed with bipolar disorder. He lives with his parents, Helen and Jim, his brother, Scott, and his sister, Eleanor. They are very close with his aunt and two cousins who live in the apartment below theirs. The family is following current treatment recommendations for children and adolescents diagnosed with bipolar disorder, a combination of medication[32] and psychosocial interventions[33] aimed at reducing stress, providing psychoeducation, enhancing problem-solving skills, and improving family functioning.[34] Given that adolescents with bipolar disorder are at greater risk for suicide than their peers,[35] a vital goal is relapse prevention.[36] Ongoing treatment is essential, as are compliance with medication[37] and psychoeducation for patient and family so they may recognize emergent symptoms such as increased irritability, grandiosity, sleep disturbances, and substance abuse.[38]

Taking these important factors into consideration, I met with the extended family to set up a safety/relapse-prevention plan for Jonathan. We brainstormed ways the family might offer support. This is the list of relapse prevention ideas:

> predictable good routines
>
> enough sleep
>
> a calm house (avoiding chaos)
>
> structure to the day
>
> using an alarm watch as a reminder to take medication
>
> keeping up with schoolwork
>
> not getting "too" anything (tired, hungry, angry, hurried, lonely)

To set up the safety/relapse-prevention plan, we began with the metaphor of throwing either gasoline or water on a fire. Family members agreed that adding gasoline makes a fire bigger. They also agreed that it is easier to put out a match than to put out a big fire. Putting out a match requires only blowing it out or throwing a bit of water on it, but putting out a blazing bonfire requires hoses and a fire truck. I noted that sometimes in a family, people throw gasoline instead of water onto a fire. I asked them to think of instances when they threw gasoline instead of water.

The family noted that many things served as fuel; anger and sarcastic remarks, for example, seemed to start big trouble. (This was especially true as symptoms such as grandiosity, manic behaviors, or pressured speech recurred.)

We looked at circumstances that caused disagreement and increased stress levels in the house. Jonathan acknowledged that when he got angry, he generally became spiteful and made poor choices, like not taking his medicine. Some behaviors, for instance, Helen's constant reminders for him to brush his teeth, acted like gasoline, ignited the situation, and made him angry. (Jonathan reminded his mother that he was 15 years old and didn't want his breath to smell bad when he talked to girls so he always remembered on his own to brush his teeth.) Preventing fires before they started, and putting them out immediately if they did start, was critical.

Once Jonathan was experiencing acute symptoms, it was almost impossible to get things under control. The family looked over the list and put check marks next to the suggestions each person thought might prevent a fire. They agreed that when someone noticed cause for concern, that person would notify others that there was gasoline around and they had better be on the alert. Jonathan identified things that would be helpful to him, such as exercising with his brother, dad, and a trainer. They decided these activities were like throwing water on the fire. Staying up late was definitely in the gasoline category. It was negotiated that the computer, another item in the gasoline category, would be removed from his room. Over a period of several sessions, the family developed a management plan they could live with and work on together.

Eight-year-old Jeremy and his dad, Allen, talked about their nightly fights over homework. Allen's own parents had never had the time or the patience to help him when he was in school. While he reasoned that they were busy working, he often felt alone and angry. With his son, he wanted to be the parent he hadn't had. He wanted Jeremy to succeed and not end up as he had, in a "dead-end job." Allen tried to assist his young son with his homework, but Jeremy resisted. He argued, threw objects, books and pencils, and the week before, he had scratched the dining room table. "Dad calls me stupid and screams at me and won't let me watch television," yelled Jeremy. Allen admitted that he often lost control in response to Jeremy's refusal to begin his homework by himself. "Just talking about it makes me all fired up," commented Allen. I observed, "The main fire I see in this room is the one that you make together."

I asked Jeremy if he knew how to keep a fire going. He said, "In scout camp we make a fire with wood. When you throw the wood in the fire, it gets bigger." "The more wood, the bigger the fire," I agreed. We discussed that mean talking is like adding wood to the fire. "What might put the fire out?" Jeremy replied, "Throw water on it." "Is saying 'no' like putting water or wood on the fire?" I asked Jeremy if he thought throwing pencils and books would make the fire between him and his dad go out. "He screams at me," was Jeremy's

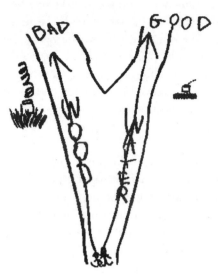

response. I asked Allen if he thought name-calling would make the fire between him and his son go out. I asked both, "Who is responsible for throwing wood or water?" Allen said that he and Jeremy were both responsible. Jeremy blamed his dad. Allen was able to say that he knew he shouldn't call Jeremy names. I asked them which way they liked it better, when there was a big fire between them or when they got along. Jeremy became teary and silent. I asked Allen if he realized that Jeremy was so sad about what happened when they fought. He responded, "I guess I'm like him. I get upset and then I say and do things to make the fire grow." Allen reached across the couch and moved toward his son. Jeremy cried quietly as he collapsed onto his dad's chest. Toward the end of the session, Jeremy made a drawing of a fork in the road. One path, wood, builds up the fire; the other path, water, puts out the fire. We began a quiet discussion that became a focus of therapy, the ways they both make the fire grow and what they might do to make things different.

Use What's Out There

There is a wide range of books that can be used in sessions or taken home to reinforce ideas.[39] I used one such book with Charles, a sixth-grade student who had trouble controlling his impulses and taking responsibility for his actions.

Charles and I read *The True Story of the 3 Little Pigs*, by A. Wolf, which tells the classic story from the wolf's point of view.[40] After discussing the story, Charles used the computer to write this letter to A. Wolf, who was serving time in prison for his crimes against the three pigs.

Dear Alexander T. Wolf,

We think that you over-exaggerated your side of the story. You told us that it wasn't your fault that you ate little animals. That may be true but people should learn to control themselves. Just like I get angry or carried away by being silly and then I try to blame it on someone else or say that's just the way I am. That's not a good enough excuse. You should be responsible for controlling your urges. We all have them but lying about them doesn't help. It just makes people angry at you.

Don't you think that one little pig is enough? Did you need to pig-out on another pig? Don't you know when enough is enough? When I don't know when enough is enough I usually get in trouble. For example, if I don't stop talking I get sent to the principal's office. When I eat too much, I usually have a stomachache.

In the end you are in jail and you act like you did nothing to deserve it. You act like you were the innocent one. I know about this. Sometimes I just give people the innocent face and I almost start believing it myself that I didn't do what I was accused of doing.

P.S. Don't worry, you will be working off the weight behind bars. This is what I learned from thinking about your story:

1. control your urges
2. don't blame things on others and last but not least
3. don't lie because other people won't believe you and when you are telling the truth, no one will believe you.

P.P.S. Don't cry wolf! I think you should read this story from the prison library: The Boy Who Cried Wolf

Charles was able to identify himself as occasionally behaving just like the wolf and putting forth a less than reasonable point of view.

Sending books home with the family is one way to extend the session. Another way is to tape sessions and activities for at-home viewing. Kids love to use technology, and it has been applied widely to a variety of problems.[41] Since children also love to receive e-mail, sending messages, quotes, riddles, and stories are great session extenders. Designing logos and sayings to transfer onto T-shirts, mouse pads, post-its, or magnets is fun, and provides another opportunity to send therapy home with clients.[42]

Activities presented in this chapter have highlighted ways to get and stay on track. Games, purposeful activities, handling "uninvited guests," developing tools to talk, and learning how to problem-solve, all develop out of what the client brings in. Topics and interventions spring from the child's and family's needs and are developed together with them. Another important way to get and stay on track is through understanding the role of the brain, which will be discussed in Chapter 4.

PART II

Assessment

CHAPTER 4

Keeping the Brain in Mind

A Brain Primer

aridad's father, Roberto, looked tense and angry as he discussed what he termed "the latest fiasco." He had taken Caridad and her friend to see *Snow White* at the local children's theater. Caridad watched with rapt attention and shuddered along with the other children at the very sight of the witch. When the witch offered the unsuspecting Snow White a poisoned apple, the crowd jeered and screamed out, "Don't eat it, don't eat it." Caridad jumped up, stood high above the crowd on her chair and shouted, "Eat it, eat it, eat it." Roberto was aghast. "It seemed as if every face in the theater turned to look. Caridad didn't even notice. During intermission the other children and parents looked disapprovingly at me and pointed at Caridad and said, 'That's the girl who told Snow White to eat the apple.'" He concluded his story commenting, "I just don't understand why she does these things."

In a recent session with another family, another parent declared, "I don't understand how his brain works. Every day I tell him the same thing, I tell him to stop doing something and one minute later he's doing it again." Other parents comment similarly. "He doesn't seem to profit from instruction and guidance. He doesn't learn from his mistakes." "Our house operates on crisis mode, everybody makes a mountain out of a molehill." "Tamika begs for a toy, torments me, and then five minutes after she has it, she's bored with it." "We are a family of hand-wringers; worry is our middle name."

Many children are like Jordi. Jordi always notices everything. He's the first to tell you that you might have gained some weight or ask why you have a canker sore on your lip. He may notice that the girl next to him in class has hair on her arms and tell her that it looks ugly. Most of us may think these things and comment quietly to ourselves or to others. Not Jordi. If it's on his mind, it's out his mouth. When he has a thought, he "publishes it immediately." It's as if his "print screen" button works overtime.

77

These behaviors interfere with interpersonal relationships and communication. They become fodder for spats and tangles between family members. If not understood, they may lead to false conclusions or interpretations about a child. Some think troubling behaviors are rooted in the brain's biology, that the individual's brain is hardwired that way.[1] However, hardwiring doesn't tell the whole tale. As we shall see, the brain develops through its interactions with the environment, including experiences with caregivers. The brain and the environment are in constant interaction; the brain is constantly being shaped throughout life.

Frequently, when families enter treatment, they are puzzled and confused. Helping families find new ways to understand their children often begins with encouraging awareness and appreciation of the influences of neurobiology. This new understanding leads them to find new avenues for intervention and additional ways to bring therapy home. This chapter will present simple, easily digestible "brain basics" and provide helpful ways to use this information in treatment. Clinical material will offer suggestions of how to talk to children and families about the way the brain works.

In therapy, it is essential to keep the brain in mind. Scientists discuss how the association and linking of neurons constructs neural circuits and patterns[2] that involve our emotions, memory, ability to self-regulate, and ability to connect with others. Helping clients understand the neuroanatomy of fear and fear conditioning, for example, not only helps them understand themselves better, it also helps therapists to intervene.

Scientific investigation has pointed us in new directions that will surely have an impact on therapeutic practice. Cutting-edge information from neuroscience suggests that we need to change the way we think about families and couples in conflict, about attachment,[3] and about how Mom's affect and biology effect the developing neonate. The investigation is a work in progress; discoveries made within the last decade were inconceivable only a short time ago.

There is good news:

- You *can* teach an old dog new tricks. Experience is a brain shaper throughout life.[4]

- Brain function and structure are in a constant state of change and are changed by sensory input. Synapses, the connections in the brain that make it dense, are developed through interaction. The brain's unique characteristic of plasticity allows it to change in response to experience.[5]

- Brain cells regenerate throughout life; the central nervous system, once believed to be fixed, can change.[6]

- Effective psychotherapy changes the brain.[7]

DECADE OF THE BRAIN

In the last decade, there has been an explosion of articles and books about the brain. We only have to go to the local newsstand to find cover stories such as "Your Child's Brain,"[8] "Mysteries of the Mind: New and Updated Explorations of How We Think, How We Behave, and How We Feel,"[9] "Behavior—Why We Do What We Do."[10] All of these works propose to unveil the dark secrets of this mysterious three-pint, three-pound organ. The last decade of the millennium was declared the "Decade of the Brain" and the research generated by investigators gave us a plethora of new information.

The advances during this period have come from many sources, such as the Human Genome Project.[11] One of the goals of the project, the construction of a genetic map for humans, will be realized in the first decade of the twenty-first century. This map will give us information about the location and lineup of each of approximately 100,000 genes on our 23 pairs of chromosomes.[12] Mapping the human genome will shed light on mind-body connections, on the relationship between genes and behavior, and on exactly how, when, and where genes function. The focus of the project for the past decade has been on isolating genes involved with disease; this research has led to discoveries about Huntington's disease, spinal muscular atrophy, and Wilson's disease.[13] These discoveries will arm us with information to better fight disease and to develop drugs for this purpose.[14]

New noninvasive technologies for modern brain imaging, such as magnetic resonance imaging (MRI), positron emission tomography (PET), and functional magnetic resonance imaging (fMRI) uncover structural changes or abnormalities in the brain. They offer visual representations of the brain in action and how the brain changes after learning or in response to provocative stimuli.[15] They also provide the opportunity to directly examine activity at receptor sites. Recent advances in molecular biology regarding DNA and RNA structure, and protein structure and synthesis, have also widely advanced our knowledge about this intricate organ.

AN ORGANIZED BRAIN

Dr. Paul MacLean, a neuroanatomist, discusses how the brain is thought to have evolved over time. Triune brain theory, MacLean's evolutionary perspective on the development of three distinct parts of the whole brain, is presented here because it provides a simple model for understanding the brain.[16]

In MacLean's paradigm, the oldest part of our brain, the reptilian brain, is concerned with basic survival, with keeping us alive. It oversees such bodily functions as heartbeat, respiration, sleep, elimination, and reflexes such as swallowing. The reptilian brain is not involved in regulating a human's emotional life. One writer concluded, "A body animated by the reptilian brain is no more human than a severed toe."[17]

The next part of our brain to evolve was the "paleomammalian" or limbic brain, the emotional center. The limbic brain contains several important interconnected structures, including the hypothalamus, the thalamus, the amygdala, and the hippocampus.[18] These parts work together and are important regulators of our emotions, attention, and long-term memory. While each plays a vital role, when discussing the brain with patients I often emphasize the importance of the amygdala. I describe it as a key player regarding emotions. "When the amygdala gets activated, it's as if we pulled the fire alarm—the response from the limbic system is instantaneous." Twelve-year-old Jason tells me he doesn't think it's fair that something the size of two almonds causes him so much trouble when he gets angry. Paralyzed by fear, 7-year-old Jennifer makes a plan to have her beanie baby "Panther" guard the amygdala and stop it from letting out all those "scary" feelings. When she starts to get worried, she visualizes Panther standing guard.

According to MacLean's model, the last part of our brain to develop is the neomammalian brain, also commonly called the cerebrum or neocortex. This part of the brain is involved in cognition, abstraction, language comprehension, and production. It is comprised of the right and left cerebral hemispheres. As communication links between old and newer cortical centers evolved, the neocortex came to facilitate, modulate, interpret, and regulate emotional life.[19]

The limbic brain is sandwiched between the primitive reptilian brain and the neomammalian brain. Thus situated, the limbic brain is the intermediary between instinct and reasoning. It comprises a crucial part of the circuits and pathways that send messages to the cortex. It also plays a key role in the attention system. The limbic brain is "the bridge between two worlds [that] stands at the convergence of two information streams. [Its job is to] monitor the external world and the internal bodily environment, and to orchestrate their congruence."[20]

One might be tempted to think that the neocortex, the "reasoner," dominates lower brain structures but this is not so. When the individual is faced with a dangerous situation, the limbic system can and does seize the brain in such a way that emotions call the shots. The fact that our brains are hardwired to react this way in a dangerous situation helps us to survive. It is important that the limbic system be a "default directory" so to speak because when we are at danger's door we have to act in a flash. When we awaken in the middle of the night to a room filled with smoke, there is no time to use reflective thinking and evaluate the level of danger. We need information to take the rapid, reflexive pathway that will move us to instant action.

The scientist Joseph LeDoux traced pathways in the brain to explain about fear conditioning. He identified what he calls the "low road," a path that initiates an instantaneous response to "threatening" events.[21] Importantly, the body does not wait to find out if the threat is real. An "alarm" goes off and the reptilian brain, along with the limbic brain, literally closes down the thinking system as we prepare to fight or flee; no thought is involved. For example, Giovanni's body may react the same way if the teacher calls on him to read aloud or if somebody mugs him on the steps of school. It is important to realize that individuals who are described as "hot-headed," having a "short fuse" or a "hair-trigger" may be people whose "good thinking" gets hijacked because of chronic heightened limbic arousal.

When the client understands the complex interaction of multiple brain areas, it provides the therapist and client with new avenues to talk about and intervene in the family system when fear, anxiety, and anger disrupt family life. Eleven-year-old Carolyn is a worrier. (That all her family members are also worriers is not surprising, as anxiety often runs in families.[22]) In family sessions, one of the ways we work together involves conversations about the brain. After looking at a model of the brain,[23] she draws this picture.

In talk bubbles she writes what her feeling brain tells her, and how her thinking brain fights back. A dialogue is created between the feeling brain and the thinking brain.

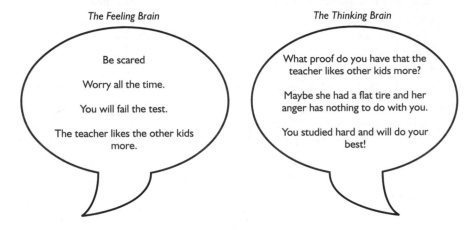

One week, we made a mind map of how the thinking brain helps. Using the computer to make a diagram helped to focus Carolyn's attention and thinking.

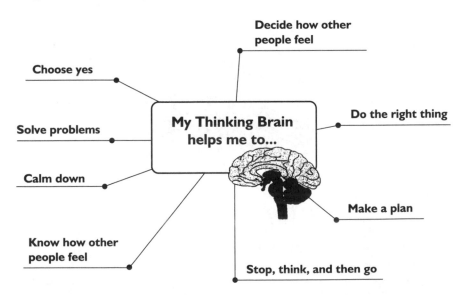

Knowledge of the neocortex, limbic brain, and reptilian brain is useful in discussing behavior with children and their families. It is especially helpful to talk about the new brain, the "thinking cap," and the limbic system, the "feeling brain," where our emotions and our primitive responses such as rage, aggression, joy, and pleasure reside. Clients should be aware that the three brains are not separate entities, but are woven tightly together and are in constant communication with one another.

Diagrams, charts, and pictures help children understand the structure of the brain. A favorite activity is traveling through the brain using the computer. The "Digital Anatomist" for example, examines the brain and spinal cord.[24] I use a model of the brain and explain to 8-year-old Grace and her family that when she gets upset, a special place in her brain wakes up and gets her ready to fight or run away from danger. This place is deep inside the brain and helps us if we need to fight to protect ourselves. Grace tells me that this happens a lot and then she usually gets into trouble. She sadly adds that no one wants to play with her because she always uses her hands instead of her words. Her mom notes that Grace is not invited to parties and is a lonely and unhappy child.

When using the new language, Grace reports that her "feeling brain" wakes up fast, like her dad's brain, and her "thinking brain" doesn't have a chance to get control of her feelings. We draw pictures and act out how the "mean feeling brain" keeps the "thinking cap" prisoner. A new beginning is possible when Grace, not unlike Houdini, learns to escape from the shackles that bind her "good thinking" when she is upset. Dad and Grace agree to work on this together. The family plans how to help support their efforts.

Mark uses his favorite heroes and the computer to draw and tell his story of bravery. Darth Vader threatens to capture his thinking brain and tells Mark, "I will take over your brain and not let you choose with Yoda and Luke. I am going to win." Mark's helpers, Yoda and Luke, are there to help him get back his good thinking. Yoda says, "Mark, you must use your thinking brain. Choose wisely. There is no try, only do or do not." "I do," says Mark. Luke, another ally in the fight to recapture the thinking brain, says, "Sometimes Darth Vader comes and takes over the feeling part of your brain. Use your thinking brain if you need help."

Mark comments that he needs to calm down. His mom and dad help him make the following plan, in the form of an acrostic, using the letters c-a-l-m d-o-w-n.

Calm yourself by exercising.

Ask the thinking part of your brain to tell the feeling part to calm down.

Lighten up and laugh when you're upset.

Monitor the feeling part of your brain because sometimes it can get out of control.

Do let your thinking part advise you.

Open your mouth and take 3 deep breaths.

Wipe out angry thoughts by thinking positive ones.

Now is the time to calm down.

THE LEFT BRAIN/RIGHT BRAIN THEORY:
BRAIN DOMINANCE

Researchers at the California Institute of Technology made groundbreaking discoveries about specialization of the brain. They worked with patients whose corpus callosum, a rich network of fibers linking the two sides of the brain, had been surgically split as a treatment for uncontrollable seizures. They found that the corpus callosum carries messages from one side of the brain to the other.[25] Although the two sides have a similar appearance, they show different types of mental activity and deal with information differently.[26]

All human beings are dominant in either right-hemisphere or left-hemisphere functioning. The brain is thought to be *contralateral,* each side controlling the *opposite* side of the body: If you are right-handed the left hemisphere is dominant, and if you are left-handed the right hemisphere is dominant. Authorities point out there is no precise split and conclude both hemispheres contribute, although unequally.[27]

Research on brain dominance adds to our understanding of human behavior and suggests the need to appreciate individual differences in order to develop therapy interventions. Some research suggests that brain dominance affects behavior. "Brain dominance is expressed in terms of how we prefer to learn, understand, and express something." These cognitive preferences are *preferred modes of knowing,* the ones that individuals turn to for *problem-solving.*[28]

Just what does this mean for therapy? A left-brain dominant person is likely to process information in the "language" of the left brain. His approach to solving problems would be step-by step, rational, concrete, linear, logical, and sequential. He would use verbal means, lists, numbers, and facts. The brain waves of the left-brain thinker demonstrate an alert waking state (beta). This individual is a convergent thinker who makes decisions based on logic. For him a problem always has a correct answer.

The right-brain strategist, on the other hand, thinks and solves problems in a very different manner. His thought process involves understanding of the whole from one detail. A right-brain dominant person may know a symphony from hearing a few bars of hummed music, or see an incomplete line drawing and know the whole from the part. His decisions are made more on emotional preferences, and he "thinks" in a nonverbal mode; intuition, images, pictures, color, rhythm, and music are the "language" of the right-brain thinker. The brain waves of this hemisphere suggest a state that is relaxed (alpha). This individual is a divergent thinker and often solves problems in a creative manner (i.e., outside of a nine-dot frame). There is a general consensus of how the right and left hemispheres of the brain process information. Table 4.1 provides an overview.

Table 4.1. A Comparison of Left-Brain and Right-Brain Information Processing

Left-Brain	Right-Brain
Step-by-step	Holistic
Sequential	Visual (using images)
Linear	Spatial
Logical	Creative
Mathematical (employing numbers	Musical (employing rhythm)
and their relationships)	Artistic
Verbal (using language)	Relational
Rational	Emotional
Concrete (emphasizing literal meaning)	Imaginative
	Intuitive

When faced with a new learning task, a left-brain person may "hit the books" and become immersed in information, proceeding in a fact-based manner of investigation. The right-brain person, on the other hand, is more likely to use the hands-on, doing approach and might in fact become overwhelmed by too much data. For example, Sue and Manny purchase new computer software. Sue needs to read and digest the entire manual before she loads the software in her computer. Manny, on the other hand, rushes home, opens the package immediately, loads the software, and intuitively figures out just what to do. His approach might horrify Sue, who believes her step-by-step approach is the only way to operate. Manny would have little patience for Sue's way and couldn't imagine wasting his time reading the entire manual before beginning.

Each individual appears to have a preferred mode of knowing, a preference that is influenced by dominance in brain function. However, most of the time the left and right brains work together in a cooperative fashion. An example would be singing. Creating the musical aspect of the song, its melody and rhythm, takes place in the right hemisphere, while the left side supplies the words. Both sides of the brain must work together in order for a person to sing. In another example, your school assignment is to photograph a beautiful piece of landscape in your neighborhood and then write a report. As you walk around your community evaluating exactly what to photograph, it is your right brain that is most active as you look. The left brain has the subsequent job of putting the information together to write the report that will accompany the photos.

A FRONT SEAT: THE CEO

Each hemisphere of the brain, right and left, is divided into four lobes: temporal, occipital, parietal, and frontal. The temporal lobes are concerned with speech and hearing; the occipital, with vision; and the parietal, with touch and motor skills. The frontal lobes, however, are concerned with higher-order abilities such as reasoning, problem-solving, and critical thinking.[29] The circuitry in the frontal lobes helps manage the influences of the emotions from the lower brain areas on the higher centers and is commanded by the "executive system," located in the *prefrontal cortex* just behind the forehead.

Executive functions have been "considered by many scientists to be one of the crowning achievements of human development."[30] The executive system is responsible for regulating the self, paying attention, planning, utilizing foresight, and developing a problem-solving set, and acts as a key player in our social adaptation. Patients with damage (lesions, trauma) to the area of the frontal lobes, have deficits in these abilities.

Executive functions have been used to describe many aspects of the emotional, behavioral and social domains of human behavior.[31] Most investigators agree that the duties of the executive system include set-shifting and set maintenance, interference and attentional control, inhibition, integration across space and time, planning, and use of working memory. When all elements are working well, the executive system acts as estimator, censor, and resistor of urges; it helps us evaluate the results of our actions as we play them in our minds—hopefully *before* we act on them.

Scientist and educator Russell Barkley discusses four executive functions that are involved in self-regulation. The first of these is nonverbal working memory, "counter space," where you keep information or a pictorial representation you can use to guide your behavior. The second of these mental activities is the privatization or internalization of speech. Private speech is talk directed at the self that helps you guide your behavior. For example, when you resist eating a cookie that may spoil your diet, you may use inner talk to move you away from the temptation. The third mental activity involves calming yourself, motivating yourself or taking charge of your emotional state. This includes the ability to say "Whoa," and delay gratification of an immediate desire in favor of a long-term gain. The last mental activity is reconstitution. This process involves taking a look at your behavior, being able to see its parts, and then recombining the parts into new actions. When there is a problem with these four mental activities, an individual's behavior is less internally guided, less directed by and oriented to present and future time, and less goal-directed. Barkley, a leader in research on attention-deficit/hyperactivity disorder, believes that problems with these executive functions are implicated in ADHD, a disorder that involves impaired behavioral inhibition.[32]

There are also social aspects of executive functions. These involve such processes as social self-regulation, social self-awareness, social sensitivity, and social salience. Impairment in any of these areas can create a host of difficulties in the social realm; these are often the presenting problems in therapy. They include trouble inhibiting responses in social contexts, insensitivity to others, problems in developing empathy, or problems with perspective-taking.[33]

While there is no universal definition of executive functions, there is a general agreement that impairment in executive function can "have a particularly insidious effect on child, adolescent, and even adult development and may underlie difficulties in poor learners and workers as well as in poorly adjusted parents and citizens."[34] During a discussion, one dad declared, "When there are problems with executive functions, it's like having a Fortune 500 company without a chief executive officer!" Indeed it is, as these problems have an impact on so many aspects of functioning.

I often talk to clients about this area of the brain because of its involvement in attention disorders. I explain it to children in descriptive terms, discussing, for example, the important "jobs" it does. I may ask children if they ever plan birthday parties or other celebrations. They describe the tasks that are involved when planning a party, such as picking out invitations, choosing party bags, and deciding what games they should play. When we talk about the part of the brain that helps them do all these jobs, I explain that it has a front seat, and I point to my forehead. Then we look at a picture or a model of the brain to see where this part is located.

Another helpful way to discuss executive functions is by describing them as the teacher or leader of the brain. I ask the children to imagine how a class might behave and work for a day without a teacher. They commonly relate "horror stories" about what occurs when the teacher leaves the room just to go down the hall. We generally decide that even the best of classrooms would deteriorate without a proper leader to organize the lessons, monitor behavior, inhibit inappropriate responses, start and stop the class, and keep the little details in mind while looking at the bigger picture. After such a discussion, Eddie declared, "The part behind your forehead is like the president of your brain!"

Executive functions are involved in the control of implementation-activation sequences of behavior, the start-stop sequences.[35] The following interchange also illustrates how children can be helped to understand such a role.

MStern: But you see, Donald's brain is a pretty quick brain. And sometimes he steps on the gas when he's thinking or doing something instead of Donald stepping on the - what's the opposite of the gas in the car?

Donald: The brake?

MS: Exactly, exactly. On the brakes. So do you think, like, when Mommy is telling you to get dressed for bed, does she want you to step on the brakes and do nothing, or does she want you to step on the gas and do it quickly? What do you think?

D: Step on the gas.

MS: Exactly, very good. What about your homework, when Mom says . . .

D: Step on the gas!

MS: Step on the—look, he got it right away!

AN INTRICATE ORGAN

Our brains are comprised of neurons (nerve cells) and glial cells, the "mind glue,"[36] which support, nourish, and bind nerve cells together.[37] At birth, an infant's brain contains about 100 billion neurons, "a quantity that rivals the number of stars in our galaxy."[38] The neurons differ from other cells in the body because they communicate with one another and with the central nervous system. Neurons are activated by electrical impulses and form a highly complex switchboard to relay incoming and outgoing chemical messages. When the neuron's threshold is reached, a message leaves the neuron. Outgoing messages leave the nerve cell via an electric pulse along the axon, a single long fiber. Incoming messages are received by very fine branch-like fibers called dendrites. The job of the dendrites is to accept messages across a synapse from other neurons and send them along their way to the cell body. Proteins, the building blocks of the cell, have the important job of carrying messages across the synapse to the next neuron. Sending and receiving messages is a complicated affair.

There are several useful ways to visualize the neuron and this process. I often use one as an adjunct to verbal explanation with clients. The client holds out a hand with fingers extended and imagines that the palm is the cell body of the neuron and the extended fingers are the dendrites. I then ask the person to imagine the information traveling from the fingers (dendrites) to the palm (cell body), and then through the arm (axon or "output system").[39] Furthering this schema, I ask clients to extend fingers on both hands and lay them down flat on their laps so that the fingers are almost touching. Each hand represents a neuron and the space between the fingers represents the synapse.

Information travels through the axon to terminal regions, where it is converted from electrical signals into chemical messages. Chemical messengers (neurotransmitters, some of which are small proteins) float across the tiny gap, the synapse, to the next neuron in line. Just as Olympic runners pass the baton in a relay race, information travels with inconceivable speed from neuron to neuron. The potency and effectiveness of the connections at the synapse directly impact on the rapidity and vigor with which brains function. Experience helps to form, strengthen, and maintain synapses.

Although a newborn's brain has more neurons than an adult's brain, it has few synapses. Starting at birth, the synapses develop like a "firestorm" over time. As the infant interacts with the world, the minute-by-minute discovery process stimulates neuronal connections. "Each experience, whether it is a sight, a sound, or a touch, causes activity in the neuronal pathway."[40] The theory of neuronal group selection suggests that the brain develops through a process of natural selection.[41] Brain pathways that produce useful behavior are reinforced. As a result, there is an increase in the number of connections. Thus, it is more likely that successful patterns of behaviors will be repeated and unsuccessful ones lessened. In this way, the important process of synaptic connection and loss, or pruning, is affected by experience. The baby's brain is a dynamic organ, shaped by experience. It is "a work in progress."[42]

WINDOWS OF OPPORTUNITY: EXPERIENCE-SENSITIVE PERIODS

An environment rich in experiences stimulates growth. Clearly learning enhances brain functioning. Researchers found changes in cortical representations of the brains of string players; Braille readers have similar changes in evidence.[43] Findings extrapolated from this and animal studies underscore the importance of learning and enrichment on the developing brain. Rats raised in an environment where they had access to toys for exploration and social experience with other animals were found to have actual changes in the brain. That is, they had more dense synaptic connections between brain cells and also became better learners than those rats raised in less stimulating environments.[44] Additional research found actual structural change in the individual neurons of the brains of rats raised in a more stimulating environment.

The enriched brains weighed more and had a thicker cortex.[45] *Plasticity*, the ability of the brain to adapt, "to rewire itself in response to environmental stimuli and any kind of learning,"[46] is an essential characteristic that allows the brain to change as we learn. Rich environments are not enough, however. In Chapter 7 we will see how the involvement and attention of an attuned caregiver is vital to the developing brain. As Siegel reminds us, "human connections create neuronal connections."[47] He states:

For the infant and young child, attachment relationships are the major environmental factors that shape the development of the brain during its period of maximal growth. Therefore, caregivers are the architects of the way in which experience influences the unfolding of genetically prepro-grammed but experience-dependent brain development. Genetic potential is expressed within the setting of social experiences, which directly influ-ence how neurons connect to one another.[48]

While stimulation encourages development, deprivation has deleterious effects. Research has highlighted the critical importance of experience on the developing brains of animals.[49] Kittens reared in the dark or with one eye cov-ered were denied the experience necessary to stimulate neuronal pathways in the brain. Marked changes in the visual system of the brain were evidenced. If access to visual stimulation and input was withheld for several weeks, the kit-tens never regained appropriate vision in the covered eye. (It is important to note, however, that lack of visual input later in life did not affect the already developed brains of adult animals.)

Deprivation has many faces. As I discussed in Chapter 1, many of today's children go hungry and are without homes. Many of them are born to teenage mothers, incapable of caring for themselves let alone able to respond to the over-whelming needs of an infant. Many live in drug-infested communities or in homes where violence is a way to solve disputes. Sadly, many children are abused, neglected, or rejected. A tragic, albeit extreme, example that comes to mind was the subject of a book[50] and a television special, "The Secret of the Wild Child."[51] Genie was reported to be one of the most extreme and devastating cases of isola-tion and abuse. She was being raised by a troubled father who dominated his almost blind wife. Genie lived without any sensory stimulation. When discovered in California on November 4, 1970, she was strapped to a potty chair and locked in a room. She had spent her 13 years in solitude and had almost no language, just the babbling of an infant. Even after being reintroduced to the world and given a great deal of rehabilitation and stimulation, she was not able to fully use language. A critical window of opportunity had been lost to her forever.[52]

WRITTEN IN THE GENES—
REWRITTEN BY EXPERIENCE

"As goes the father, so goes the child." Why is this? One reason for familial sim-ilarity is the genetic transcription that lies deep within the cell. The nucleus of the neuron holds the genetic coding, the blueprint for the developing organ-ism. It also supplies "the recipe for how its architecture can get rearranged through life."[53] Although the genetic transcription provides the plan, the influences from the environment have a strong effect on the manner in which they are expressed.[54]

Genes do not act in isolation and "in the dance of life," are "absolutely inextricable partners" with environment.[55] Neither can exist without the other. It's like trying to determine which part contributes most to the sound of a bell ringing, the clapper or the housing. This interactive process continues throughout one's life. The input from the environment actually shapes the brain's architecture and intricate processes within the brain. One's inherited genetic endowment is only partly expressed at birth.[56]

While human interaction is the most critical factor in the development of the infant's brain,[57] any discussion of "heredity and environment" must include discussion of the wider environment, the world beyond the family.[58] Elliot, 11, the oldest of four children, is brought for treatment by his maternal grandmother. He and his siblings live with their mother, 29-year-old Sharon, and their grandmother Beatrice in a deteriorated neighborhood, polluted with toxins, violence, and racism. Sharon works full time at a difficult, low-paying job. She is struggling with issues regarding Elliot and his father, who is a drug user, now in prison for armed robbery. Elliot has many of the characteristics found in his father and in his father's family; in particular he is impulsive and prone to rages. Sharon recognizes these behaviors and is afraid of them. Beatrice does not understand his behaviors and refuses to tolerate them. Elliot seems to be finding his "match" with a street gang. Both mother and grandmother are afraid that Elliot will turn out "just like his father."

Elliot's heredity, his biology, make him prone to a great deal of inner turmoil and make the "fit" within the family system difficult. Stress has been created for everyone. His environment, both the physical community in which he lives and the tone in the home (that is, his mother and grandmother's constant disapproval), exacerbates his tendency toward impulsivity, overreactivity, and rage. His society, an angry, restless street gang, serves to exaggerate rather than modify the effects of both.

A BRAIN SHAPER—STRESS

That which causes tension, is upsetting, or is frightening, is a "stressor." As experience shapes the brain, stress plays an important role. Stressors vary from person to person and change throughout our development from infancy to old age. An individual's explanation and understanding of a stressor depends on his or her cognitive level. Children's definitions of stress however, have a common thread: there is something from the outside that makes them feel something on the inside. Jenny, age 7, says, "When you have to do something hard you get like a stomachache and you feel that you can't do anything." Matt, age 9, states, "I feel upset when I have a lot of homework and tests." He adds, "Stress means popping your brain 'cause there is too much pressure and everything feels like it's overflowing." Sammy, age 7, declares, "When I see somebody I know and my mother says 'say hello Sammy,' I get nervous, I start to shake a little, I have trouble talking, and I like to stay home." Peggy tells me that she gets all upset when she plays video games with her brother. "He always wins and that's not fair."

But stress goes beyond tension, pressure, or worry. Of special concern are recent indications that children are being exposed to severe and chronic violence at younger ages. This exposure has a negative impact on their mood, behavior, school performance, friendships, and physical and mental health.[59] Children who are victims of violence or witnesses to it, either in the home[60] or in the community, are likely to exhibit one or more troubling behaviors. Witnessing or experiencing violence is associated with self-reported use of violence and carrying a weapon.[61]

Stress affects each individual differently.[62] For example, investigators find that exposure to violence, particularly family violence, places the anxious, vulnerable child at risk for developing posttraumatic stress disorder.[63] It has been well documented that genetic, biochemical, and environmental factors interact in a recursive process and affect each of us in unique ways. The stress-diathesis model discusses this interaction in the etiology of disorders. In this model, psychosocial stressors expose and impact on a biological vulnerability. Environmental risks, such as abuse, neglect, conflict, parental psychopathology, and heightened emotions in the family, interact with biological factors and result in clinical symptoms.[64] Intra-individual, as well as external stressors can either exacerbate or serve to mitigate the vulnerabilities.[65] In discussing the mind-body connections in the development of symptomatology, researchers conclude:

> As a cybernetic creature, a human being actively reorganizes his or her behavior in response to an environmental perturbation. Primary mind-body symptoms produce a behavioral deformation in the family, hence, they cannot exist for long as isolated events in the life of the patient and family before further secondary patterns of behavior are triggered. In addition, individuals or families can sometimes initially present with secondary patterns of symptom behavior when the presence of a primary mind-body symptom is only hypothetical or suspected; the perturbing symptom then is a cognitive and internal event.[66]

Exposure to violence does not need to be direct for it to take its toll. In a family session, Rusty's father complains that all the children sleep in his bed. He is tired of it and wants to reclaim his bedroom and assert his right to privacy. All the children comply except for Rusty, age 5, who reports in the next session that he can't sleep alone because he is "scared." It is not the dark that haunts little Rusty at night, it is the voices of "news people" that he hears every evening while his mom prepares dinner. Rusty trembles as he vividly describes news of killings, robberies, bombs, terrorist attacks, natural disasters, plane crashes, and kidnappings. His solace comes from the warmth of the parental bed. It is too frightening to be alone.

Physiologically, stress is the body's adaptive response to events that are emotionally disturbing, alarming, or threatening. When such events are perceived, the body prepares for fight or flight (the limbic brain in action). Adrenaline and other emergency stress hormones are released, causing an increase in heart rate, blood pressure, and respiration rate.[67] When there is persistent arousal of emergency hormones, brain changes occur that can impair the brain's ability to get information into long-term memory. Stress impacts on the brain, particularly on the hippocampus, a crucial structure for learning and the consolidation of new memories. Too much stress, especially of a chronic nature, can also impact on the immune system and result in serious damage to health.[68] Children often convert stress into somatic and/or behavioral symptoms such as worries and fears, nausea, lightheadedness, somatic complaints, sleep and eating disturbances, heightened activity levels, hair twirling, problems getting along with others, irritability, anger, aggression, sadness, and depression. (Many of these become the basis of referral for psychological help.)

As a psychologist and family therapist, I have been keeping a list of stresses that children report. As one might conjecture, daily hassles of school life are high on the list, with homework and tests often at the top. For many children, I've also found that difficulty making friends and concerns about social issues are prominent. As we will see in Chapter 8, a child's learning disability or attention disorder often heads the list of individual and family stressors[69] because they are chronic and unrelenting, sapping the psychological and physical resources of the whole family. Shame and worry about reports, homework, school progress, and the future haunt children and result in diminished feelings of self-worth and self-efficacy.

Many children and families report feeling pressured by their overbooked schedules, with little free time during the week. In the children's book *The Berenstain Bears and Too Much Pressure*,[70] Gran concludes that *doing* is one thing, but overdoing is something else. With the poverty of time we all face, it's no surprise that many more children show signs of behavioral problems these days. But, we must also remember to include what we might think of as "unlikely suspects" on the list of stressors; picture day at school, the car pool, recess, and board games can be significant sources of anxiety. Eight-year-old Mark wrote and illustrated the following story.

This is a story about a boy who gets all stressed out.

When he gets stressed out he loses control. He gets angry. He gets stressed a lot. These are the things that he says get him stressed.

1. "When I don't get my way.
2. When I have to wait for something.
3. When I am under stress, it is easy for my anger to get big quickly.
4. I get mad about tiny things.
5. When someone doesn't let me do what I want, I get stressed.
6. When I can't do something as good as other people, I get very stressed.
7. When I have nothing to do I get very stressed."

Then one day he felt tired of getting so stressed so he went to sit down by a tree. He was feeling sad because he didn't know what to do. Just then somebody spoke. It was the wise owl. Owls are smart. The owl said "Come into my tree, I don't know if you know it: I'm a stress shrinker. A stress shrinker is someone who knows about ways to shrink stress. So come into my tree and I will show you how to shrink your stress." So the boy went into the tree.

The owl showed the boy his stress-shrinker machine. The machine really just made the boy think it was the machine that could shrink stress, but it was really the boy that thought up the ideas not the machine.

Every person has to think of his own ways to make stress smaller. These are the ways the owl helped the boy to shrink his stress.

1. Instead of hitting someone I hit my pillow.
2. I call my anger bad words.
3. I take 3 breaths then I count to 10. By then I should be calm.
4. In my brain, I picture myself doing the thing I'm scared of, like being somewhere without my parents.

5. I made up this song that says "I think I can, I think I can, I know I can, I know I can."

6. I made a decision in my head and I asked myself "should I get in trouble, or should I do it?"

7. I used the thinking part of my brain to calm down the feeling part of my brain.

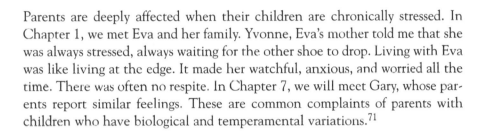

The owl learned a lot from the boy's good ideas.

Parents are deeply affected when their children are chronically stressed. In Chapter 1, we met Eva and her family. Yvonne, Eva's mother told me that she was always stressed, always waiting for the other shoe to drop. Living with Eva was like living at the edge. It made her watchful, anxious, and worried all the time. There was often no respite. In Chapter 7, we will meet Gary, whose parents report similar feelings. These are common complaints of parents with children who have biological and temperamental variations.[71]

INTERCONNECTED CIRCLES

Barry Commoner, a well-known conservationist, proposes that there are four basic laws that govern a functional ecosystem. One is that everything is related to everything else; every effect is also a cause. (An animal's waste, for example, provides nourishment for soil bacteria; the bacterial excretion feeds the plants; animals eat the plants.)[72] Similarly, the bionetwork of the brain provides an example of the idea that all systems are interconnected. Brain structures are wrapped around one another and contain delicate, intertwined circuitry that is engaged in lively interaction. Each part shapes each other part. It is the interaction of the mutually dependent systems of biology and environment that shape psychological and cognitive processes and relational and social systems. Like a mosaic that forms a picture, each tile is an element of the whole.

In this chapter, we saw how environment and genes interact to shape the circle of life for an individual. Each family has its own circle of life. The circle can be conceptualized as multiple interconnected circles of biological, psychological, and social experiences, each of which has bidirectional influences. In order for the therapist to understand their impacts on one another and to engage in collaborative treatment planning, it is vital for him or her to do a thorough assessment. The next two chapters provide guides, tools, and tactics for family and child evaluation.

CHAPTER 5

Zoom Out

Focusing on the Family and School

This ambiguous figure is called "Mother, father, daughter."[1] Can you find all three figures? Identifying them requires eye movement from one area of the picture to another to another. As you look at the picture, your brain is constantly reanalyzing information and drawing conclusions. While it may be difficult initially to find all three figures, once they are perceived, it is easy to move between them. Assessment of clients, particularly when working within a family-based treatment model, requires a similar process. Assessment is a multifaceted task in which the therapist's brain must constantly take in information, reanalyze it, and then make sense of it with the family.

Although family therapists are adept at viewing a problem through a "family lens," they often do not sufficiently consider the role of intra-individual variables. I advocate a type of assessment in which the therapist moves the lens between three different domains; I call these domains *within-the-family*, *within-the-child/individual*, and *larger systems*. The next two chapters offer guidelines and charts to help the clinician's eye move within each domain and from one domain to another. These chapters outline general principles to guide the clinician's work and include examples of how these principles can be effectively applied. The information that is collected becomes a scaffold for intervention. This chapter begins with a general discussion of effective assessment and the biopsychosocial perspective and guides the reader through the evaluation of the family and the school.

EFFECTIVE ASSESSMENT

Effective assessment *is* an intervention, a powerful tool that offers the child, family, and teacher increased means for understanding and collaborative intervention across biological, psychological, and environmental domains. It helps the family to engage in an exploratory *process*. It is not a scatter-shot approach to gathering information, but rather a thoughtful, guided, collaborative inquiry. The goal is a *sharing* meeting in which the therapist and the family bring together information and develop a road map for treatment.

Assessment *is* an intervention because it provides a new lens through which family members can view the problem and each other. Perhaps a child needs information repeated many times. The family's nonunderstanding of this need can lead to interactional problems if they mistakenly view the child as resistant and oppositional. Through ongoing assessment, the family can become aware that this child's current struggles may be related to cognitive weaknesses in attention, language and/or memory, which impede his or her ability to follow directives.

In order for assessment to be effective it needs to be multidimensional and incorporate various techniques to gather information about the interplay of the biopsychosocial systems that the individual inhabits. As mentioned in Chapter 1, the biopsychosocial model is *inclusive*. It integrates biological (hereditary and biochemical influences) and environmental forces (community, housing, toxins), psychological factors (including thoughts and perceptions of experience[2]), social experiences, and sociocultural variables. As Eisenberg notes, "Development is at one and the same time a social and a psychological and a biological process."[3] The method of assessment, therefore, must be flexible enough to allow room for the expression of all of these variables.

The biopsychosocial model does not attempt to answer the question of etiology. It recognizes that each factor has a role. While in some cases, biology might have a "starring role," in other cases, psychosocial variables (past and/or present) predominate. The biopsychosocial perspective incorporates the role of each piece of the puzzle and offers a presentation of how the multiplicity of factors contributes and interacts on all levels. Although the list of variables in Table 5.1 is not inclusive, it is intended to give a sense of the wide range of factors that the biopsychosocial approach takes into consideration.

Combrinck-Graham conceptualized the "biopsychosocial influence of a child as represented by a series of concentric spheres creating a continuum of

Table 5.1. A Summary of Biopsychosocial Variables

Psychological	beliefs, perceptions of the problem, ego functioning, coping history, insight, judgment, resources, cognitive functioning, social and emotional functioning, premorbid levels of functioning
Biological	temperament, genetic influences (role in transmission of predisposition and vulnerability), health and health practices, nutrition, hormones, medical and psychiatric history, trauma
Sociocultural	spiritual, culture and cultural practices, social support (extended family, friends, community), values, family stability
Environmental	school and community, housing, neighborhood, toxins, access to health care and community resources, quality of life

three-dimensional domains encompassing or being encompassed by others." She names the spheres (starting from the center) biological, psychological, nuclear family, extended family, social context, socio-cultural-political.[4]

Developmental outcomes are mediated by a host of psychological, biological, sociocultural, and environmental factors. It is important to recognize that a disruption to one level of influence is likely to reverberate throughout *all other* levels of each system.[5] Assessment in the biopsychosocial model acknowledges that Connor's tummy aches get worse when his parents argue, and that significant stressors from Lorraine's past haunt her and cause her depressive episodes to worsen.[6]

The idea that constitutional and environmental forces are partners and impact on problem formation has led to increased understanding and strategies for intervention in a multitude of problems.[7] A child's innate biology and "hardwired" genetic tendencies actively shape his or her environment in a myriad of ways. Irene's aggressive outbursts cause the family to tiptoe around her; Juan's shyness keeps him close to his mom's side and results in her overprotective stance with him. Irene's genetic tendencies impel her toward acting-out behavior, and Juan's genetic endowment makes him prone to anxiety and introversion. In discussing these issues with families, a key point to consider is the recursive relationship between these areas: how the environment affects the child, how the child's problem influences the home and family milieu, and how the child's difficulties have an impact on peer relationships and school life. Cultural and extrafamilial influences (cohorts, television, gang culture, school, and religion) have an impact. Stress, as we saw in Chapter 4, also plays a *very* significant role in symptom development and onset of a variety of disorders.[8] Table 5.2 outlines the key aspects of a biopsychosocial frame.

Table 5.2. Key Aspects of a Biopsychosocial Perspective

Is multidimensional, multifaceted
Is holistic
Considers interplay between factors and views influences as interactive, reciprocal
Emphasizes health
Is interdisciplinary
Looks at complex interactions in development and maintenance of behaviors
  and problems
Considers stimuli and environmental conditions
Considers effects of conditioning and learning

WITHIN-THE-FAMILY DOMAIN

The Family Context

Problems do not occur in a vacuum. Although assessing family context is essential, often therapists do not devote sufficient time to family evaluation.[9] There is a wealth of information to be collected and, at times, the task may seem daunting. Sometimes, the diverse agendas from school and home make this evaluation difficult to do initially. This is especially true when school suspension or safety issues (e.g., abuse, harm to oneself or others) start the referral process and there is a demand for immediate intervention. In these cases, crisis management is needed. This includes assessment of risk, a safety plan, and involvement of other professionals, such as a child psychiatrist.

Getting to know and understand the whole family means involving everybody, including young children.[10] The present, the past, worries and dreams for the future, and the "sense of total family identity"[11] cannot be fully understood without knowing all members of the family. Zilbach notes: "The tasks of the whole family, at each stage of the family life cycle, are different, and build upon each other." Youngest and oldest participate in family life and influence it during all stages of family development. Therefore, the presence of the whole family in diagnostic sessions is crucial because it helps the therapist understand how everybody gets into the action. (Sometimes the interactions involving the family pet give the therapist clues about how the family functions.)

Dominick, age 10, and his brother Anthony, age 7, were playing in the yard. Anthony hit Dominick because Dominick was teasing him and wouldn't give him back his ball. Their 12-year-old sister Mary ran over to protect Anthony from their "bully brother." Dominick pushed Mary and yelled at her to stop interfering. She started to cry. Lucky, the family dog, started to bark and growl. Then he grabbed the ball and ran away with it, making Anthony cry even louder. As she prepared lunch in the kitchen, Mom heard the screams. She sent Dad out to quiet things down. Dad, annoyed that he was interrupted while reading his newspaper, grunted at Mom as he passed her in the kitchen. He refused to listen to the kids' explanations and sent all of them to their rooms. Even Lucky got yelled at after he refused to give the ball back to Dad. Mom, who had just about finished preparing a special family lunch, was angry with Dad's rough handling of the situation. Lunch was spoiled. "This happens all the time," stated Dominick sadly.

As mentioned in Chapter 1, the family context impacts on the extent, the severity, and the long-term outcomes of a problem. The family can also be an important resource for healing. When one person in a family has a serious difficulty or problem, that problem often acts as a stressor for the whole family. Without the involvement of all family members in the session, the therapist develops an incomplete picture of the child and his world.

There are occasions, however, when it may be necessary to meet with only certain members of the family, such as when there is marital stress and discord. When the presenting problem involves a child, I often meet with his or her parents first. This is a practice I have adopted over the years. I have found that many parents are in agony about their children. They are upset about the child and about failed attempts to solve the family's problems. They need a place to be heard and understood. Parents sometimes tell stories of how the child makes family life unbearable, and identify the child as the source of their failure. I consider these conversations X-Rated for "violence-talk" ("Our daughter Joyce ruins the family, she destroys family life, we don't have a life because of her") and find that they are best reserved for private consultations that are in addition to family sessions.

Some Guidelines for Family Interviews

Interviewing the whole family is an essential but challenging task. Chasin has proposed some helpful guidelines for family interviewing.[12] He starts sessions by examining the family's strengths, as this sets a positive tone right from the outset. He outlines a useful four-step procedure for an evaluation process that takes between one and three sessions. Step one covers the introductions (including "What name would you like me to call you?") and the purpose of the family meeting. In step two, the therapist sets up a contract for the meeting and provides the family with rules about safety, answering questions (a noncoercion rule, i.e., children will not be coerced to answer), discipline (parents are in charge of their children), and about the room and equipment (the therapist is in charge of the physical space).[13] The purpose of step three is to join with the family and the "therapist-family system." In family therapy, Chasin explains, the therapist temporarily *joins* the family and becomes part of the new system, the therapist-family system. In step four the family's goals and problems are explored. Hopes and fears about the future are also discussed. (Later the fifth step serves as a time for the therapist to share impressions and offer recommendations.)

I conduct interviews using Chasin's steps as a general map. What follows in this chapter are more specific guidelines, questions, and solutions that can aid clinicians in developing their own assessment processes.

Establishing a Relationship with the Family

Defining the purpose of therapy for children. When beginning a family assessment, I build upon Chasin's multistep process, starting with introductions, the purpose of the meeting and some ground rules. A noncoercion rule is in force, with some caveats, especially for the young (or not so young) and restless. I don't ask children "Do you know why you are here today?" as they may not have been told or may have forgotten. Not knowing may make them feel ashamed. Very often, however, they also respond with, "I don't care." I use a number of different methods to explain to children why they have come and to establish a rapport with them. Eight-year-old Larry was referred to me because of his oppositional behavior. On the phone, his dad had noted sadly that he dreads coming home to the chaos his son has created. In the first session with this family, I opened by saying: "Your dad called me and told me that your family doesn't have much fun together because there is a lot of yelling at home. He and your mom heard that I was someone who helps families figure out how to have more fun. Dad mentioned to me that he yells too much and he wants to change that. Do you think that you would like to have more fun in your family?"

The language I use varies and depends on the age and interests of the child. To a younger child, I may say, "This is a magic room where we talk together and figure out how you can have more fun as a family. I say 'magic' because here we work together and turn frowns upside down. Have you ever done that?" If a child enters with a Transformer® and shows me how it changes, I may talk about problems that some people have with "morphing." I may also use my famous magic wand and ask, "What would you like to change for yourself and your family?"

Setting the tone about attention and communication. In the session I "pay attention to attention" and encourage conversation about keeping focused. I may ask riddles such as, "What can you pay here that won't cost you any money?" "How is attention like the lottery? You've got to be in it to win it!" These types of statements serve to set a tone and expectation that everybody is going to participate. I provide positive, fun-filled ways to facilitate the process. These methods are especially necessary for children with developmentally inappropriate levels of attention and concentration.

Right from the start, I set a tone about the importance of communication. I emphasize that each person's words are precious pieces of information and must be heard. It is especially crucial to make this clear in chaotic families where individuals may not be accustomed to listening to one another. The therapy session may be the only time the family comes together to talk. Family members may not have any idea of how to make communication happen. From the outset, it is essential to set the expectation that each person's voice is important and to find ways to facilitate communication.

Getting children to participate. Sometimes, in previous treatment, at home, or at school, children have been inadvertently "trained" not to participate. They know that if they act up they will get sent out of the room and are adept at finding ways to make this come about. For example, a child might bring his hand-held computer game to the consulting room with the expectation that he will be asked to leave and will have an opportunity to play it in the waiting room. I am gentle yet very firm about needing "eye and ear" contact and involvement with/from everyone.

I say, "When we talk, you will not be forced to answer and sometimes you can just say 'not now' and we know to pass." However, I also let them know that I allow only a certain number of complete passes in a session. If children say "I don't know," which is often the case, as they really *don't* know, I press for a "guesstimate." "If you could guess, what might it be? Let's guess. What do you think your mom is going to say? Dad?" I never use overt coercion, but at times will use a game like "hit the penny" or "hot potato." If you wind up with the hot potato, we need an answer! I also sometimes use a point system—in order to get points you need to answer a question. I tell everybody, "There are no right or wrong answers in this room, just what each person thinks. That's part of what makes the room magic. This is not like school: you don't have to raise your hand, but we need you to wait your turn sometimes. What happens at home? Do people wait their turn to talk?" I may use a small stuffed animal that we pass to the person talking. I may use "the floor,"[14] the small piece of carpet that is passed from one family member to another. Only the person who has "the floor" can speak.

Simple activities like these help participants go from passive to active involvement. They can act to wake up a sleepy cortex, or can be used to slow things down. I watch for signs of motor restlessness and head it off at the pass, taking a break for "jumping jacks" or "simple simon." These are playful activities that give the message that we can work and have fun at the same time. With these types of interventions, people begin to listen. I watch my cadence and pacing, and check back throughout the session to see if I am being understood. I notice the pace of the family, and if they're doing a waltz, I don't do a polka. Any of these methods may make a small crack in a family's otherwise impenetrable shell.

Examining the Presenting Problem

With the whole family present, the therapist has the opportunity to inquire about and explore unique viewpoints and examine each family member's account of the presenting problem. The following questions, while not inclusive, serve as a guide to understanding the extent of a problem. They also help the clinician consider whether the problem is situational or pervasive.

Defining the Problem
- Who defines the problem?
- Is the problem in the eye of the beholder?
- What is this family's understanding of the problem?
- What are the *unique* viewpoints of different family members?
- What has having the problem meant for the different members?[15]

Coping with the Problem
- How has the family's day-to-day life been affected?
- Who is most/least affected?[16]
- What choices have the family members made in regard to living with the presenting problem?
- What are the values, beliefs, myths that led to those choices?[17]
- How has this family been successful in living with the problem?
- How do they imagine they will continue the success in the future?[18]
- What within-the-family capacities (resources, strengths, coping strategies, resilience, supports across generations[19]) have promoted this success?
- How has the family adapted to and managed other adversities and challenges?

Making Changes
- In what ways has the family actively chosen to make or not make changes in response to living with the problem?
- What has led to these choices?
- How can we use the experience of individual family members to encourage family functioning?
- What assets, strategies and resources do they have that can help them to change?
- How could family resources be supported and enhanced?
- What is already working?

Inquiry and observation around the presenting complaint need to be comprehensive. Also see "Tools for Gathering Information" in the Appendix. Table 5.3 provides one guideline for examining the presenting problem.

Table 5.3. Examining the Presenting Problem

Beliefs	about the problem, about its cause, about solutions, family myths
Narratives	stories about the problem and its origin
Interactional Patterns	around the problem behavior(s), explore vicious cycles, track sequences, examine enactments
Assess	potential harm to self or others, abuse (child, sexual, domestic)
Inquire and Explore	different viewpoints, accounts, and descriptions, mom, dad, siblings, others—everyone's unique account, others have same problem? the problem across generations, solutions tried by family successful? unsuccessful? why? recent or ongoing? onset (precipitants), why a referral NOW? problem in different contexts, are there others not present who are involved with the problem? who is most/least concerned? next most/least worried?
Additional Points to Consider	Why is this a problem in THIS family? Are there projections from families of origin? How does the problem intersect with the dynamics in THIS family? How does the problem organize the family? How is the problem seen across the generations?

Tara and her family enter treatment with the complaint that Tara, a 9-year-old fourth grade student, is unable to complete her school assignments. Because both parents work, after school Tara stays at home with her 13-year-old sister, Robin, until their mother, Lorraine, arrives at about six o'clock. Lorraine's expectation is that at the very least, both children will have begun their homework assignments by the time she gets home. Instead, between 3:30 and 5:30 daily, Tara and Robin call her office about Tara's inability to settle down and do her work. As Lorraine drives home, she has that all too familiar feeling in the pit of her stomach. She knows that each night will involve another argument about homework. When the children hear her key in the lock, they run to the door to be the first to tell her "my side" of what transpired in her absence. Lorraine can barely collect her thoughts or begin to prepare dinner because of the fighting. She realizes this will be yet another long evening and, as her husband, Tim, enters the scene, she notices the familiar grimace and look of disapproval on his face. Tim's booming voice silences the rest of the family as he turns to Lorraine and shouts, "Why can't you learn how to run this house?" Lorraine screams back at Tim, throws the pot down, and leaves the room. Robin glares at Tara and shouts, "This is all your fault." Tara bursts into tears and locks herself in the bathroom.

Although the presenting problem is Tara's seeming inability to complete her homework, there are multiple arenas that need to be examined before intervening to end this vicious cycle. One of the most pressing questions to ask is: Does Tara have the necessary skills to complete homework independently? Some of the following lines of inquiry might be considered in trying to answer this question.

- Does she have a skill deficit in the area of attention, concentration, organization, or visual-motor functioning?
- Is she obsessive and perfectionist in her approach to tasks and thus unable to begin her work?
- Are anxiety or low tolerance for frustration factors here?
- Does she have the correct assignment in her homework book?
- Is there an appropriate place to do homework?

It is also crucial to look at the influences of family relationships on the problem.

- What happens when an adult is home to supervise the work?
- How has the family handled non-school-related problems?
- Who is most/least affected by the problem or is most/least concerned about it?

Examining Family Structure

Assessing the family variables that impact the presenting problem also involves an evaluation of the family structure. Are the boundaries clear, or blurred? Is this a family that is "enmeshed" or "disengaged?"[20] Hoffman[21] states:

> According to [Minuchin], an appropriately organized family will have clearly marked boundaries. The marital subsystem will have closed boundaries to protect the privacy of the spouses. The parental subsystem will have clear boundaries between it and the children, but not so impenetrable as to limit the access necessary for good parenting. The sibling subsystem will have its own boundaries and will be organized hierarchically. . . . Finally, the boundary around the nuclear family will also be respected. . . . Therapy, from a structural point of view, consists of redesigning family organization so that it will approximate this normative model more closely.

Each category in Table 5.4 provides a rich avenue of exploration. The information gained by pursuing these lines of inquiry will help the therapist understand the systemic context of a child's problem. It is important to keep in mind the biopsychosocial model that presupposes that problems/symptoms originate and are sustained in the context of interdependent, mutually shaping systems.

Table 5.4. Within-the-Family Domain: Important Considerations

Family Structure	boundaries, coalitions, cut-offs, triangles, power, conflicts, hierarchy, patterns in relationships across generations
Risk Factors	health problems, poverty, finances, time, loss, trauma, anniversary reactions, expected and untimely life cycle changes, recent events, alcohol, drug use, housing problems, abuse, violence, neglect, psychiatric hospitalization
Family Coping	strengths, resources, resilience, stress level, stressors, ability to adapt, anxiety level, social supports, flexibility, cooperative/resistant
Participation	voluntary/coerced
Family Reactivity	level of emotional arousal, ability to tolerate frustration and control impulses, ability to set appropriate limits,
Stage of Family Life Cycle[22]	early, middle, late
Social Learning Pattern	observational learning: how do family members treat each other (violence?), how do family members treat others outside the family unit
"Fit"	match of person(s) and environment(s), consonance (good), dissonance (poor), attachment histories: each parent/referred child
Family Relationships	within the family, with extended family, marital stability, parenting skills, family unit: intact, single parent, etc.
Siblings	quality of relationships, level and quality of interaction
Family Problem-solving Skills	competent/poor
Gender Issues[23]	level of equality, power dynamics
Culture	beliefs, background, immigration experience, acculturation
Relationships to Larger Systems	school, social services, courts, other

Observing Family Patterns

The family interview gives the clinician an opportunity to observe family dynamics and process. In observing the family in the therapy room, the interviewer takes note of reactions, particularly those evoked by the symptomatic child. The clinician might observe family interaction patterns by giving the family an exercise.[24] Answers to the following questions can help to identify what are sometimes deeply entrenched family patterns. Make mental notes on the following as you conduct your assessment.

Seating, talking, reacting
- What are the seating arrangements?
- Who talks for whom?
- Who directs that process?
- Whose lap is a harbor from distress? Is there one available? (For example, Connie climbed into her sister Tina's lap and snuggled into the curve of her body. No one missed a beat. Is Tina a parentified child?)
- How do others react to the frustrated (stressed, impatient, whiney, angry) child?
- How do family members react to each other's verbal and nonverbal behavior?

Parenting behaviors
- Does the parents' conflict spill over to the child?
- Are the parents using emotions to parent? (For example, one parent said: "Stop it! You're making me sick. I'm going to get an asthma attack, right here in the doctor's office." This comment helped me understand sequences of behavior and how problematic or inappropriate behaviors were reinforced.)
- Do the parents micromanage a difficult child, or do they use a laissez-faire approach and ignore dangerous behaviors? Do they fail to intervene when needed?
- What about "expressed emotion" (EE), emotional overinvolvement and/or hostility as expressed by frequent critical comments, and intrusiveness?[25]
- Are the parents responding to the child in the moment in such a way that problematic behaviors, negative affect states, or negative cognitions are reinforced?
- Is the child overwhelmed by parental emotion?

Family climate and family dynamics
- What is the "family temperament"?[26]
- What is the family temperature? Is this an easily aroused, hot-reactive, high-conflict group?
- Do the child's behaviors serve to distract the family from conflict in the marriage?
- Do family patterns serve an adaptive or maladaptive function vis-à-vis the referral problem?

- Do the observable dynamics suggest that the child's symptoms are serving an adaptive, coping function? Do the dynamics suggest, on the other hand, that the family employs a maladaptive function (e.g., scapegoating) in order to displace the responsibility for serious family problems?
- What is the current stage of the family life cycle?

Triangles

- Do two family members pull in a third (often the child) to side against the other (triangulation)?[27] Is there an overt or hidden partnership between two family members against a third family member (coalition)? Are there cooperative alliances? Is there is an alignment between one parent and the child that causes a split between the parents or other family members (splitting)?
- Is the child torn between conflicting relationships?

A Multigenerational Inquiry: Using the Genogram

Genograms, graphic representations of family patterns over the generations, are widely used by family therapists. The genogram is my favorite way to record the family history as it unfolds in the sessions. In using genograms in therapy, I often find truth in the adage "one picture is worth a thousand words." Monica McGoldrick and her colleagues are leaders in the development of clinical use of the genogram. They note that the genogram inquiry should be a fundamental part of any complete clinical evaluation as it assists the clinician in generating provisional hypotheses. Genograms help the therapist scan for patterns across generations; they are tangible and comprehensive living documents that offer information that can be revised as new discoveries unfold.[28]

Children generally enjoy working on the genogram with the family. They often listen with rapt attention as family stories and histories unfold. There are active approaches to get children involved.[29]

The genogram inquiry provides a way to join with the family. McGoldrick outlines its function and utility as follows: (1) creates a systemic perspective of the problem; (2) provides a means for the interviewer to reframe, detoxify, and normalize emotionally charged issues; (3) allows for a view of the problem that is both current and historical; (4) helps the therapist to examine structural, relational, and practical information in the current family context and vertically across multiple generations; (5) allows documentation of pertinent events, concerns, and issues; (6) provides a means to map out multiple perspectives; (7) helps to track shifts in family relationships.

When family members are questioned about the present situation in relation to the themes, myths, rules, and emotionally charged issues of previous generations, repetitive patterns become clear. Genograms "let the
calendar speak" by suggesting the possible connections between family
events over time.[30]

In addition to gathering the usual information, when looking back at several
generations it is helpful to ask about school and learning histories of family
members, risk factors, losses, trauma, treatment of children in the extended family, significant stressors in the caregiver's and extended environments, history of
psychiatric hospitalizations, alcohol and drug use.

Minnie, age 14, reported that she was feeling hopeless about her life and
often had ruminative thoughts about ending the misery. Minnie had been
hospitalized recently for attempting to jump off her apartment building roof.
A neighbor, planting flowers on the roof garden, had seen Minnie and was
able to talk to her and get help. Family information revealed a history of
depression not only in her parents, but also in a maternal uncle and aunt, and
her paternal grandparents. Several relatives in the extended family had committed suicide.

I asked Minnie what her thoughts had been as she went to the edge of the
roof. We drew a talk bubble and she filled in the words "I want to end my life."
I used her words throughout the rest of the interview to frame our discussion
about suicide and "end my life thoughts." I asked about the frequency and
intensity of these thoughts, and who else in the family had them. Family information and secrets were revealed, including stories of courage in the face of
the thoughts. These stories provided a rich forum for an open discussion.

The neurobiological aspect of the genogram inquiry should include questions about genetic tendencies and endowments, "shadow syndromes,"[31] suspected learning disabilities (school problems), attention disorders, behavioral
difficulties, problems with the law, depression, bipolar disorder or manic depression, obsessive-compulsive disorder, anxiety, panic attacks, eating disorders,
separation difficulties, schizophrenia, autism, pervasive developmental delays,
and mental retardation.

Assessing Family Relationships

The Couple. In child-focused referrals it is essential to assess the quality of the
couple's relationship.[32] At its best, the marital and couple relationship can
offer friendship, stability, a source of mutual support, and a buffer to the stresses and strains of life. Closeness between partners has been linked positively to
the infant's secure attachment and adjustment.[33] Not surprisingly, research
documents the deleterious effects of interparental conflict on infants, toddlers,
and the growing child.[34] Karen tells me that she believes that her parents fight

all the time because of her. She knows she is right; she hears them arguing from the other room. Marvin, her older brother thinks otherwise; he believes their parents argue because they just can't agree on anything. The attributions and appraisal of family arguments affect each child differently.[35] Disagreements are part of all relationships; however, how they get handled and resolved is crucial.

Gottman[36] discusses how marriages function and dysfunction. He identifies seven negative dysfunctional patterns that are useful to keep in mind when observing couple interaction.

(a) greater negative affect reciprocity in unhappy couples, which may be related to the failure of repair; (b) lower ratios of positivity to negativity in unhappy couples and couples headed for divorce (this includes a greater climate of agreement in happily married couples); (c) less positive sentiment override in unhappy couples; (d) the presence of criticism, defensiveness, contempt, and stonewalling in couples headed for divorce; (e) greater evidence of the wife demand-husband withdraw pattern in unhappy couples (though it is probably also there to some extent in happily married couples); (f) negative and lasting attributions about the partner and more negative narratives about the marriage and partner in unhappy couples; and (g) greater physiological arousal in unhappy couples.

For either warring or low-conflict couples, couples counseling can be an essential part of the overall treatment plan.[37]

Siblings. Each sibling has a unique perspective that must be acknowledged. The fact that siblings are so different is not surprising to behavioral geneticists. Siblings raised in the same family have vastly different relationships with their parents and with one another.[38] Each family member has a different experience of divorce, illness, death, family tensions, financial problems, stress, and daily hassles. Individual attributes and perceptions color their experience and make them unique.

What developmentalists once thought was a shared environment turns out not to be shared at all. Although the family may seem to be one environment, it's actually a multiplicity of microenvironments, a collection of niches, consisting of distinct vantage points from which siblings experience the same events in different ways.[39]

The family interview helps the therapist understand a child's experience of family life and evaluate the siblings' relationships with the referred child and with each other. It is important to note whether the sibling relationship is a source of support and comfort or a source of rivalry, tension, and friction. Do siblings have an empathic position toward the child? Do they sometimes act as parental figures and need to be moved out of that position? Do parents see how the problems of one child may keep another child from having his needs met? Do other children feel that the referred child takes up all the family "air space"? How does the temperament of each child have an impact on the function of the whole family?[40]

These last questions are particularly relevant when a sibling has a disability or chronic illness.[41] We know that each child in the family has a unique reaction to a sibling with one of these problems. There is often less parental attention available to the other child, more chores for him/her to do,[42] and an increase in the number of responsibilities. Siblings often experience loneliness because the family is isolated by the problem. Negative emotions lead to fear and guilt responses, ongoing stress,[43] shame, and resentment.[44] Family sessions help to uncover the siblings' distress and find ways to intervene. Some sibling relationships can also be a source of mutual support and comfort, which enriches life and helps each to flourish.[45]

WITHIN-THE-CHILD/INDIVIDUAL DOMAIN

Assessing the family environment also means considering the "within-the-individual" factors that contribute to the family environment. Table 5.5 provides a selected list of these variables.

Table 5.5.   Intra-Individual Variables

General	health & vitality, temperament, genetic endowment, predispositions, tendencies
Cognitive Abilities	learning and/or attention problems, sensory integration difficulties (high or low sensory threshold), speech & language (expressive/receptive)
Social Competence	listening, sharing, negotiating, social skills, empathy
Reactivity	emotional arousal, frustration level, impulse control, responses to limit setting
Coping	strengths, resources, resilience, stress level, adaptability, anxiety level, social supports
Flexibility	cooperative/resistant

Intra-individual variables influence relationship patterns, which influence health and disease in individual family members. The influence is bi-directional. An exemplary model developed by Beatrice Wood, The Biobehavioral Family Model (BBFM), considers the bi-directional influence of family relationship patterns and disease.[46] This model is of import for our discussion here in that it examines biopsychosocial interactions in chronic childhood illness.

Specifically, the BBFM proposes that family proximity, generational hierarchy, parental relationship, triangulation, and interpersonal responsivity are processes that influence one another and interact with individual (family member) psychological and emotional processes in ways that either buffer or exacerbate biological processes related to disease activity in children.[47]

Wood's model employs a developmental biopsychosocial approach, which defines well-being as "a dynamic balance among three levels of functioning—individual physical functioning, individual psychological functioning, and family-social functioning."[48] Imbalances can occur in any (or all) levels of functioning. The goal of treatment is described as "*biopsychosocial balance.*"[49]

Having Family Members Assess Themselves: Taking Inventory

It is helpful for the family to take inventory of themselves. They can be instructed to make a list and draw pictures of what is going "well, fair, or yucky" in such areas as family, school, homework, friends, work, sports, health, and free time. It is always interesting to see what everyone writes or draws. If they choose, the family members can try to guess what is in everyone else's "going well" category. Focusing on the "going well" category gives everyone a chance to highlight what is working. It also gives the therapist a chance to note resources. Sometimes I am told that nothing is going well, only to have one of the younger children jump right in and tell a positive story about a pizza party, a time they played Nintendo together, the huge bag of popcorn they ate in the movies, or how they stayed up late and watched a movie together.

Is the Solution a Problem: Vicious Cycles

The way that family members respond to a difficulty determines whether or not it becomes a problem.[50] Sometimes a family gets stuck when trying to solve a problem, often inadvertently reapplying ineffective solutions instead of taking a step back to examine if a solution is working. When they keep reapplying a solution that does not work, the problem either perseveres or is exacerbated.

Bernardo is having difficulty with his homework and asks his father, Fred, for help. His parents think that Bernardo is lazy and needs to be more independent, so Fred tells Bernardo to try to do the homework by himself and then ask for help if he is still having problems. Instead of starting his work by himself, Bernardo insists that his father needs to help him. Fred refuses to help until Bernardo at least starts on his own. Both Bernardo and Fred begin to get frustrated. Bernardo gets upset and his father gets angry. The more Bernardo refuses to start, the angrier Fred gets. The angrier his father gets, the more Bernardo digs in his heels. They have become embroiled in an interactional problem, a vicious cycle, each one's behavior leading to and following from the behavior of the other. Each blames the other. Fred feels that the problem is Bernardo's because he has not been trying. Bernardo feels his behavior is justified and blames Fred for stubbornly refusing to help and because of his angry talking. At some point this vicious cycle will end with a fight or because either Bernardo or Fred just gives up.

A "more-of-the-same" approach, trying the same ineffective solution over and over again, creates new problems, which are sometimes bigger than the original one. More-of-the-same keeps people stuck and results in vicious cycles or feedback loops. (It is important to query about the solutions a family has employed. Often, those involved make a later, identical attempt to handle the original problem, and the vicious cycle starts anew.) Vicious cycles are part of everyday life. One of the goals of treatment is to identify and interrupt these unhelpful cycles of behavior in the family.

ZOOM OUT TO THE LARGER-SYSTEMS DOMAIN: SCHOOL CONSULTATIONS

In addition to looking at relationships within the family, it is important to widen our assessment/intervention lens to include relationships in the school. Teachers have a central role in and impact significantly on a child's behavior. School problems must be uncovered and understood by the parents, the teacher, and the therapist in order for interventions to be effective. Children who have poor attendance, who are identified as discipline problems, or who are retained, are at risk for exacerbated school problems or dropping out.[51] Although sometimes the relationship between a teacher and a child is a thorny one, when a good alliance is developed, the teacher can be a resource for positive growth.

Teachers often feel confused by a child's behavior and need assistance in understanding the complex picture a child presents in the classroom. The teacher's beliefs about the child's behavior need to be heard and understood. A teacher's attitude toward the child can also color the perceptions that others have of the child. The case of Raymond is especially illustrative.

Raymond was a student in Mrs. S's class. He drove her to distraction. Raymond was always unprepared and never ready to work. Although chronically late, Raymond always arrived at school by 10 a.m. If it was 10:03 and Raymond had not shown up, Mrs. S knew it was going to be a good day. She would find herself breathing what she thought was a *private* sigh of relief: Raymond was absent. Then, one day at 10:10, the door flew open and there was Raymond. "Oh no, Raymond's here," groaned the class. It was as if they reflected Mrs. S's thoughts and feelings. When she heard the reaction of the other students, Mrs. S realized that she had made it apparent that she did not like Raymond. By unwittingly betraying her feelings to the other students, she had caused them to isolate and reject him. From that day, Mrs. S began to be more welcoming to Raymond. She made him a class monitor, which gave him a new status among his peers. His behavior improved somewhat, as did his attendance. This example shows that teachers *do* make a difference! Supporting them on behalf of a child is vital.

A child's behavior is the product of the reciprocal influences of multiple interacting variables, such as temperament, learning history, social setting, and physical environment.[52] Teachers need to understand biopsychosocial contributions to a child's behavior. These variables should be discussed when meeting with teachers. Armed with correct information, they are in a better position to empathize and provide the appropriate assistance to the child. I find a visit to the school is invaluable. Not only do I get to see the child's life as it unfolds, I can also recruit the teacher and guidance personnel as team members and allies. I view my visit as a crucial, albeit indirect, service to the child. At the very least, a telephone interview is a must.

A child's struggles in the academic realm also need to be understood. Children are often angry at a system they feel has failed to understand them. Lucas's drawing (Figure 5.1) depicts his feelings of frustration and anger. Children with behavioral difficulties and heightened emotional arousal must work to keep their aggressive impulses in check. As a result, they may have few resources left over for learning. Learning problems leave them feeling confused, and they harbor worries that they are stupid and can't learn.

Misinterpretation of such a student can cause far more damage than the learning difficulty itself causes. "A child with school problems has a need and a right to be understood."[53]

Interview the Teacher

The teacher is a firsthand observer of the child in the variety of circumstances that involve both social and learning arenas, and so the teacher is often the first to notice that a child is struggling with academic, social, or behavioral problems. A review of the child's cumulative record card offers a longitudinal view of performance, attendance, and behavior and provides a record of the child's academic history, which includes previous assessments and test scores,

Figure 5.1. "I hate my research report!"

as well as past and current levels of achievement and social adjustment. The following is a sample of some useful questions. For a sample teacher interview see "Tools for Gathering Information" in the Appendix.

- What are the child's strengths? What does she *like* to do?
- What concerns the teacher most?
- How does the child function across the day?
- What are the child's weaknesses in school?
- Are the demands of the child's workload appropriate to her developmental level?
- Is there a discrepancy between the child's perceived ability and performance?
- What about peer relationships? The quality of friendships?
- Is he an accepted, sought after youngster or isolated, neglected, rejected?
- Does the teacher make allowances for the child's special needs?

Interview the Child

Chapter 6 will discuss the in-depth examination of the child. "Tools for Gathering Information" in the Appendix provides a guide for interviewing children about learning and attention. To get additional information about the child's perception of school and learning, I often ask the child to help me give the teacher a report card.

- Is the teacher a good listener?
- Does she give the child interesting work to do?
- Is the work too easy/too difficult? (I query about each subject.)
- Does the teacher talk in a quiet manner, or raise his voice often?
- What happens if someone breaks a rule in the class?
- How do kids get in trouble in his class?
- Does the child feel that the teacher likes him?

Giving the teacher a report card can segue into a discussion of other issues. If children have behavioral problems, the clinician can inquire as to why they think they behave the way they do in school.

- What makes it easier to make good choices?
- What makes it difficult?
- What can the child or others do to help?

Assess the Fit

Just as the fit between the parent and the child is important, the fit between the teacher and the child can have positive or negative consequences. Gabriel, a second grader in the school where I was the school psychologist, was in Mrs. T's class. Right from the outset, it was a disastrous match. Gabriel was endowed with a high level of motor activity and a wild curiosity about anything that was in his reach. He suffered from what one might call a "digital exploration" problem. You could identify his desk immediately by the papers strewn around it. His coat made it to the closet, but was often on someone else's hook. Mrs. T was the kind of person who couldn't help but notice every movement in the room. A neat desk was a requirement and organized notebooks and book-bags were essential to success in her class. Quiet, steady students did best in her room. During that year, every time I met Mrs. T, she had a laundry list of complaints about Gabriel and his behavior. While we tried to intervene, Gabriel's behavior never quite met her standards.

The next year, Gabriel was placed with a teacher who didn't particularly notice messy desks or restless children. His mom reported the teacher had hardly a grievance. Mrs. T certainly hadn't been wrong, but the fit between that teacher and that child had been a poor one. The experience was unfortunate for both. There is no substitute for a positive relationship with a teacher. Children work harder when they feel that the teacher understands and appreciates their unique needs. It is a key to enhancing their motivation.

School Consultation: Best Practices

When consulting with a child's school, it is helpful to embrace a systems perspective, which encourages exploration of multiple influences on a problem. "Students' problems usually result from a complex and reciprocal interaction between the child's behavior and the environmental and/or instructional conditions that regularly exist in a particular classroom."[54] Maintaining a systems view means orienting oneself to the organization of the school and the classroom, as well as other variables that might affect the implementation of suggestions for change. Is this a system that welcomes consultation from the outside? Does this system provide the opportunity for teachers to develop necessary skills to resolve specific problems? Where is it best for me to begin? What resources are available within the system?

Forming a collaborative relationship with the teacher and the school is a vital first step. Active listening and effective questioning, delivered in a caring, empathic, and understanding manner, are other essentials. A strong working knowledge of intervention principles, tactics, and techniques for change is also crucial.[55] Leaders in the field of school-based consultation suggest the following steps that constitute good practices: (1) define the problem; (2) identify antecedent determinants of the problem; (3) identify consequences that may maintain the behavior; (4) assess other relevant environmental variables; and (5) identify all available resources.[56]

In guiding myself through the school consultation, I find it helpful to cultivate the following abilities: respect-ability, response-ability, reach-ability.

Respect-ability involves
- Respect and consideration for all viewpoints, including the child's. Frequently, important decisions regarding a child's future are made without the child's involvement. Solutions are then developed without consideration of the child's unique ability to formulate a solution.
- Building relationships with all parts of the system. I find it especially helpful to have a key individual as a contact. When I consult with a

child's school, I keep in mind that as an outsider, I am the guest. While I stay closely involved, I try not to wear out my welcome.

- Reinforcement of efforts and positive attempts to help the child.
- Remembering that a school and teachers are resource-full. Blame and shame have no place in consultation. Getting everybody on the same side is important.[57] I think of myself as a "head hunter" looking to form a team. Most important, I try to remember to be a team player!

Response-ability involves

- Being available and reliable, and making regular contact.
- Gathering information and helping others recognize the biopsychosocial factors at play.
- Reframing the child's difficulties within this framework.
- Recognizing strengths and limitations of the educational setting. (I ask myself, "Can *this* setting respond to *this* child? Do they have the resources? Is a change of educational setting needed?")
- Being responsive and providing information to help the system be more responsive to the child's needs. Is the reason they are not responding to the child that they need new or different skills? See yourself as a resource to others who brings in information that may shed light on a problem.
- Re-evaluating your own resources and competencies. I ask myself, "Do I have the resources to respond appropriately? Do I need to call in help? Do I have the requisite skills to help this youngster and his family?"

Reach-ability involves

- Having reachable goals in each of the domains of the biopsychosocial perspective.
- Having realistic expectations that are developmentally appropriate. The aim is progress not perfection. Start small.
- Reducing stresses and the anxiety of others when possible. Work toward eliminating resistance to change.
- Re-evaluating progress. This may mean meeting with the team players, going back to the drawing board with new resolve, or rethinking the problem.
- Maintaining flex-ability. Using a T.E.A.[58] (try, evaluate, adjust) approach helps.

CULTURAL PRACTICES AND BELIEFS

Family therapy is often the "treatment of choice for culturally diverse clients."[59] It is essential to understand the referral problem within the context of a family's culture and cultural practices, background, and beliefs.[60] In working with culturally diverse groups, it is an imperative to use culturally competent assessment and intervention. Celano and Kaslow[61] remind us that the therapist must include a "culturally informed view of the definition of family health and dysfunction."

> Family interventions are efficacious and culturally competent only when the therapists: (1) recognize the effects of their own cultures on the therapy; (2) acknowledge that family therapy theories and techniques reflect the culture within which they have been developed; (3) attend to the dynamic interplay of the cultural influences that affect the individual's and family's functioning; and (4) devise and implement problem-resolution strategies that are culturally acceptable.

Ashraf's school behavior provides a poignant anecdote about the need to look at culture when examining a child's behavior. Ashraf, a wide-eyed 6-year-old, shook nervously whenever the teacher gave the class a copying task. Although he could recognize all the letters of the alphabet, his handwriting was illegible. When the teacher checked his book each day, she noticed that Ashraf had a thin cord tied around his right wrist. When she queried him about the cord, Ashraf became mute and ashen.

The teacher met with the school psychologist who observed Ashraf in class and completed a brief, informal cognitive screening. It became clear to the psychologist that Ashraf was a left-hand dominant child who was writing with his right hand! When the psychologist asked Ashraf why he wrote with his right hand, tears filled the child's eyes and he twisted his fingers nervously. All he could say was that he had to do what his parents said.

The psychologist and teacher met with Ashraf's parents, who explained that for cultural reasons Ashraf must write with his right hand. The cord tied around his wrist was an important reminder that he must do so. The psychologist carefully explained to Ashraf's parents about brain function and how it related to hand dominance. She detailed the negative impact writing with his right hand was having on Ashraf, whose anxiety mounted each day as it became increasingly difficult for him to complete any work in school. His parents remained adamant in their demand. Eventually, a spiritual leader in their Arabic community was contacted and was helpful in intervening with the family. By the end of the year, Ashraf was writing with his dominant hand and had become a high-functioning member of the class.

Ashraf's story highlights the need to explore all avenues when evaluating the nature of a problem. Exploring all avenues of a problem means learning about the child and understanding the within-the-child variables that make the child who he or she is. Chapter 6 zooms in to focus on the individual child.

CHAPTER 6

Zoom In

Focusing on the Child

In this chapter, while continuing to focus on assessment, we change the lens to examine the "within-the-individual" factors in the referred child that play influential roles in the development and maintenance of problems.

Individual differences in inherited and acquired traits have an impact on many aspects of life. Let's look at the case of Howard, a 10-year-old boy in a class for learning disabled children. Howard became sad when the teacher told the class that they were going to participate with the regular education children in the fifth grade assembly, and that they were going to play reindeer in the holiday play. The rest of the class seemed elated at the news because, in previous years, they had not been included in performances given by children in mainstream classes. Although the teacher, Mrs. K, was somewhat surprised at Howard's reaction, she initially dismissed his sadness. She had often found Howard to be a moody youngster, and thought he was simply having a bad day. As the day progressed and Howard's distress became unusually pronounced, however, Mrs. K thought it was time for a private conversation. She now suspected that his mood was related to a concern about his situation at home. She had met with his mother, Molly, the previous week and learned that she suffered from depression and was not always able to help Howard. Molly had also noted that lately Howard's asthma attacks had been worse,[1] causing the family fright and worry. When Mrs. K and Howard met in private, his eyes filled with tears as they discussed the fifth grade play. Sobbing, Howard finally blurted out the reason for his sadness. When he had heard that the children in his class were going to be reindeer, he became worried that the children in the mainstream classes were going to "ride" him. The idea of having to carry other children on his back was extremely frightening to Howard.

Howard's difficulty with comprehension of language has an impact on his understanding of the world around him.[2] He often struggles to find the words to express his ideas. This makes him tense and frustrated. During a family interview, his father commented, "He leans toward the half-empty-glass view of life, not unlike his mom and me. He's a worrier like me, everything seems to stress him out.[3] He's the oldest of four children and we need his help with the other kids. We don't have a lot of patience for him. Especially since I lost my job." This comment showed me that in order to understand Howard, we needed to look at the reciprocal, mutually shaping influences of biology (heightened arousal, inborn traits), psychology (how he makes meaning out of his experiences), individual differences (strengths and weaknesses in his individual learning profile), family (including culture and belief systems), and environmental stressors (his father losing his job).

GETTING TO KNOW THE CHILD: SEEING THE CHILD ALONE

While it is crucial to understand family dynamics and the impact of family transactions, it is equally important to obtain a comprehensive picture of the child. A perspective that integrates individual and family therapy approaches is often indicated.[4] Getting to know the child fully in family-based therapy often requires meeting with the child alone.

There are many compelling reasons to incorporate individual sessions as part of the assessment/intervention plan. Individual sessions afford the therapist an opportunity to understand the child's perspective, inner feelings, and experience. They offer opportunities to (1) explore the child's unconscious concerns, (2) improve assessment by obtaining a complete picture of the child's understanding of the problem, (3) assess the impact of the child's symptoms and current struggles on his life outside of the family, (4) help the child feel listened to and understood, (5) enhance the therapeutic alliance with the parents, (6) set the stage for collaborative work, and (7) help others understand the child's world view by finding ways to bring her position to the family sessions. This final step is important in helping the child begin to advocate for herself.[5]

Although the number of individual assessment sessions may vary, I find the work can often be accomplished in two to three visits. I use the child's words to explain to him that we are going to meet in order to play, talk, and think together about ways to help "make his worries smaller," help him "have an easier time at home," and figure out why his mad (sad) feelings stop him from having fun. Children are usually very receptive to the idea.

Ellen Wachtel[6] suggests that while the child's symptoms are constantly influenced by the family system, they are also partially separate from it.

By including in our work more focus on the symptomatic child's internal experience and the mechanisms he or she has developed for coping with anxiety and other disturbing thoughts and feelings, we can help children develop a sense of themselves as emotionally intelligent and able to tackle the stresses, strains, and challenges that will surely come their way. . . . By making a concerted effort to include in our assessment an analysis of the symptomatic child's coping and defense mechanisms, we will be able to coach the parents on how to help the child develop more adaptive ways of handling problems.

Wachtel advocates an integrative approach using systemic, psychodynamic, and behavioral orientations. Maintaining different perspectives allows the therapist to accommodate the unique needs of each referral and effectively guide treatment planning.[7]

When using a collaborative child and family therapy approach, there are some instances in which it may be necessary to see other family members individually as well. Seeing other family members alone gives them the message that their opinions are considered and respected; it also sets the stage for cooperation with others. These meetings are sometimes helpful in relieving parental anxiety and the feeling that they are to blame for the child's problem.[8]

GATHER DEVELOPMENTAL HISTORY

There is no substitute for starting with a good developmental history from the parents.[9] While gathering information, it is important to always keep in mind "normal" developmental processes. Maintaining an appreciation of the process by which children mature and develop intellectually may mean reviewing the work of influential theorists, such as Erik Erikson, Jean Piaget, Anna Freud, Albert Bandura, and attachment theorists, such as John Bowlby.[10] (While normative processes provide a guide for comparison, it is essential to keep in mind the recursive relationship between nature and nurture.)

Following is a list of important aspects of the child's development that are crucial to effective assessment.

1. *Conception, birth, and attachment history* (and if applicable, adoption history). Consider these questions in assessing the child as an individual:
   - What were the circumstances around conception and birth?

- What were the details regarding maternal support, stresses, and expectations? Who was involved? How?
- What was happening at the time of the child's birth? (Include extended family events, illnesses, and separations)
- What was mom's response to mothering? What was her level of attachment? Was it easy or difficult for her to care for her infant?

2. *Early development.* Explore early development. Include eating and sleeping patterns, developmental milestones, and temperament in your assessment.
   - How did the parent(s) accommodate the change in the family's life cycle that accompanied the birth of their child?
   - How did each parent's personality and endowments intersect with the child's nature?
   - What were some problems, successes, significant events, or stressors during this phase of the child's life?
   - What kind of toddler and little boy was he?
   - How did he regulate affect, self-soothe, learn to accept "no," handle prohibitions, and play with others?
   - How did the child develop physically?
   - What were his preferred activities?
   - What was his relationship with mom and dad like?

3. *Social development.* Assess the quality of relationships with peers and siblings.
   - Does the child have age-appropriate social development?
   - What are the child's strengths in social relationships?

4. *School history.* A good school history (see Chapter 5 and "Tools for Gathering Information" in the Appendix) is essential; include a look at old report cards. Review evaluations from outside sources.
   - When did she start school?
   - Did she have problems separating from her parents?
   - Did she have problems adjusting to her new environment?

5. *Adolescence.* Note any changes during adolescence in interpersonal contexts, school functioning. Look for drug and alcohol use.

6. *Maltreatment/trauma.*
   - Is there a history of trauma, neglect, or abuse?
   - If yes, obtain a complete picture.

7. *Daily activity.* To get a sense of the family's daily life, I ask children and parents to describe a typical day.

8. *Looking back.* To get a sense of the *canvas* of family life at a particular time, I ask children and their parents to "paint a picture" for me about what life was like during a particular period.

OBSERVE THE CHILD

Assessing a client's functioning involves developing a keen sense of observation.[11] I observe the way a child walks, negotiates steps, talks, tells a story, describes the sequence of a movie or a television show, pays attention, and waits her turn. I also inquire about vision and hearing acuity. An easy way to get a feel for cognitive strengths and weaknesses is to get a picture of schoolwork. I meet with the child alone and investigate different dimensions of his or her school functioning. I also have a selection of age-appropriate books that I can use for informal assessment. I say, "I am always interested in the kinds of work that children do in different schools. Can you show me (tell me about) the kinds of things that you do in your class?"

REVIEW SCHOOLWORK

School notebooks provide a snapshot into the child's academic functioning. With the child's permission, we review the notebook together. I always ask the child to read what he or she has written. When the child reads, I look at how she approaches the task. Can she identify the letter? Does she know what sound the letter makes? Can she blend sounds together? If she can't figure out a word, does she use picture clues or context clues to help her? When faced with difficulty, does she persist? Does the child struggle with the mechanics of reading, or is it poor understanding of the meaning of the word that gives her trouble? I often ask a comprehension question or two about the passage. I have found that all too often a child valiantly copies a passage even though he is unable to read it.

I look for specific comments from the teacher, such as "incomplete," "sloppy," or "good job." Does the child start an assignment neatly and "lose steam" as she works? If I see that there are many assignments that are incomplete, I gently inquire about the reasons. I may say, "Some children tell me that the teacher doesn't give them enough time to finish copying from the board. Does that ever happen to you, too?" "Yes," Barbara told me, "my hand hurts so I can't write too much." We talk about how attention, talking to neighbors, getting to school late, and other factors interfere with schoolwork.

Table 6.1 is a checklist of clinical observations. After seeing a child, it is helpful to review each aspect and jot down your observations.

Table 6.1. A Clinical Observation Checklist

Appearance	physical, neurological, hygiene and grooming (appropriateness of dress for age, sex, weather), general health and vitality
Affect	range, appropriateness, modulation (flat?), congruence between mood and affect, quality of relatedness (eye contact)
Thought Processes and Content	logical, reality oriented, preoccupations, obsessions
Motor Coordination	fine, gross, eye-hand, coordinated or awkward
Motor Activity	level (low/high), impulse control, response to limit setting and/or direction
Mannerisms	tics, atypical, nervous, gestures or abnormal posturing
Reactivity	emotional arousal (anxious? easily angered?), sensory (response to lights, smell, heat, etc.), tolerates frustration, deals with tension, response to praise, to different topics, concerns
Cognitive Functioning	attention span (distractible; focused; sustains attention), concentration, frustration level, memory, judgment, level of abstraction (concrete?), fund of general information
Attachment to Caretakers	interactions with parent(s), reactions before and after separation
Temperament and Adaptability	easy, slow to warm up, difficult
Speech and Language	speech (e.g., speed and fluency, quantity, voice quality, articulation), automatic, receptive (understands questions, directions), expressive (spontaneous language, on demand when questioned, vocabulary, word-fillers—e.g., huh, uh, you know), narrative organization
Flexibility	cooperative, resistant, change: easy to difficult
Social	listening, sharing, negotiating, empathic responding, interpersonal functioning, problem solving, social reasoning

MAINTAIN A DEVELOPMENTAL PERSPECTIVE

As mentioned earlier, in interviewing a child, one must maintain a developmental perspective. "Developmentally sensitive interviewing"[12] considers (1) a child's receptive and expressive language and communication skills, (2) a child's ability to conceptualize and reason, (3) developmental stages of cognition and social understanding, and (4) a child's readiness and capability to share thoughts and feelings. It also considers both transient events and a child's unique coping strategies.

If necessary, a therapist should consult developmental psychology reference texts for assistance. It is imperative that the clinician be aware of normative research, incidence, and the course of normal development. Let's take the case of children's unique fears, for example. Fears and anxieties are quite common among children of all ages. It is important to keep in mind that children's fears vary by gender and other variables at different age levels. "Normal" children have a large number of fears that change as they age and move up the developmental ladder.[13] The question here is not about the "normalcy" of fears per se, but about whether the child's fears are outside the developmental norm in terms of type, severity, or duration. It is also important to keep in mind that many disorders co-occur; they are comorbid.[14]

Understanding emotions is a complicated business.[15] Understanding one's own emotions and making judgments about them occurs within a developmental context; the extent to which children can apply these skills varies by age and gender.[16] As anyone who has done more than one or two child interviews knows, interviewing children about feelings, symptom presentation, and events is very different from interviewing adults. Diagnostic interviews and self-reports for children under eight years of age lack reliability and validity.[17] Children are often found to be inaccurate reporters; they have difficulty noting important factors such as frequency, onset, and duration of symptoms.[18] With preschool children, the picture gets even more complicated because they may confuse fantasy and reality.[19]

Common mistakes adults make when communicating with young children include (1) assuming too much control, (2) asking too many questions, (3) employing "forced-choice" and "close-ended" questions, which often bring forth one-word responses, and (4) providing insufficient structure. In interviewing children, therapists should engage in supportive practices, such as

- creating an atmosphere of mutual exploration
- using a combination of open-ended and direct questions
- encouraging elaboration
- having some awareness of the event or experience child refers to
- employing pictures and manipulatives as aids
- asking more "what" questions than "how" or "why" questions.[20]

Hughes and Baker say that questioning the young child is a "subtle art requiring a combination of open-ended questions ('What will the mother doll do now?'), specific questions that avoid leading ('What do you like about school?'), and a generous sprinkling of 'extenders' ('Oh' and 'umm' and 'I understand')."[21]

CONSIDER COGNITIVE FUNCTIONING:
LANGUAGE, MEMORY, AND ATTENTION

Children naturally focus on outer experience. They often link a feeling to an event: my mom didn't buy me a special toy, the teacher punished the class, my brother hit me. Turning the focus inward is not something they are used to doing. The child's position in the developmental trajectory affects his understanding of emotions and in part determines whether or not he can find the words to describe his inner experience. The child may be aware of a problem, but have difficulty understanding and labeling feelings because of developmental as well as cognitive variables. As a result, information about children is often obtained through parent/teacher observation and checklists.

Therapy has been called a talking cure.[22] While being sensitive to the cognitive level of the client, it is essential for the clinician to develop an ear for listening to the client's communication style, vocabulary, fluency, expressive language, and receptive language. It is important for the clinician to match his or her style accordingly. If the child's thinking is concrete, the therapist must adjust her language to accommodate this style. The therapist must continually observe interactions, cognitive function, attention, language, and memory: he or she should tailor interventions accordingly.

Developmentally inappropriate levels of attention and concentration can impact significantly on communication skills and affect the interview. Peter knew about attention. "Where are your eyes supposed to be when someone is talking?" questioned his mom, Denise. He looked at her and replied, "on the person's face." However, although there was eye contact, there was no "ear contact"!

MStern: Does that happen a lot, that people talk and it's hard for you to understand things?

(Peter nods his head.)

MS: Is it because your mind takes a vacation—or is it because the words I use are too big? What do you think?

Mom: (To Peter) Sometimes you don't understand the words?

MS: Hmmm. Leon, what do you think?

Dad: I think, like, that his mind is somewhere else.

MS: Do you think that if his mind was on it he could understand more of it? Well, you know, maybe that's a good experiment to do for both of you in the house. Eye contact first and then check out ear contact and then see if Peter understands what you have to say.

Quizzical looks, latency in response time, nonresponse, use of nonspecific language (e.g., "the thing"), word fillers, and the parent's continual translation of the child's response are all indicators of possible language difficulties. So, *when in doubt, check it out.* Ask the child or parent, "Did you understand my question?" "Did you understand what I said (meant)?" "If you didn't understand, I'm not doing my job well." "I need to try again." "I'll try to do a better job this time." "Will you tell me?"

DeShaun mentioned that he had seen a movie five times. When I asked him to tell me about it, he could only give me short descriptions and names. He said he "never remembers movies." I always consider memory and listen for ways to evaluate it. An important point to keep in mind is that problems in language and memory often co-occur: A problem in one area will affect the other. Weak attention and concentration will impact as well. When I observe that a child has a lapse in attention or memory, I inquire as to the cause, generally asking in a playful way, "Was your mind taking a vacation? Did it go somewhere else? What do you think?" At times, I may ask someone to serve as an "echo" and repeat in her own words what we are talking about. Children I see who have weaknesses in auditory attention need multiple pathways to get the information in. I aim for novelty and try to link ideas.

If, during the assessment, I find that language comprehension or auditory processing is a problem, I set up a signal (for example, a raised finger or the time out signal used in football or basketball) that indicates a need to stop the action. Prompting or cueing is also sometimes helpful: "Some kids tell me that sitting still and paying attention is a hard thing for them. What about for you?" Some of the successful techniques that have been used with the mildly retarded (for example, using either/or rather than yes/no questions), work well with children who have communication weaknesses.[23] Employing visual aids helps. For example, sometimes I point instead of talk, or use a picture book about school to stimulate conversation. It is also helpful to ask open-ended questions, "Can you tell me a time that it is difficult for you to sit and pay attention? Can you tell me a time that it is easy for you to sit and pay attention?" or to use arrays, "Some children find it hard to understand because their mind is somewhere else when the question is asked. Some children find it hard to understand because people are using big words that they don't understand. Are you like either of them? Which one?" I find the following helpful to keep in mind: speak in small bytes, don't give a lot of instructions, check back, restate, and reword.

CONSIDER TEMPERAMENT

Temperament refers to the manner in which individuals approach and respond to their environments. It includes their reactions to people, places, and situations.[24] Each person has a unique set of temperament characteristics that are evident at an early age. Just as the tide shapes the coast, these characteristics have an impact from the first moments of life.

Consider the G family. They glow as they talk about the ease of learning to care for their infant daughter, Jessica. Her rhythms are predictable; she is friendly, flexible, and a delight to care for. Her mom comments that she feels like a parenting expert, as she is always able to anticipate her daughter's needs. In contrast, the B family told of difficulties with Rick from the first day. Both parents felt overwhelmed by an irritable, colicky, sleepless, difficult baby. Rick was a challenging toddler, and now at 6 is still described by these same adjectives. Children with difficult temperaments present challenges to those who live or work with them. By understanding children's unique styles, we can intervene to make dramatic changes.

Temperament was initially discussed as individual differences and tendencies, which had their impact on behavior.[25] The nine characteristics (dimensions) developed and researched by Thomas, Chess, and colleagues[26] are: activity, rhythmicity (one's rhythms related to eating, sleeping, elimination, etc.), approach/withdrawal (to new people, places, or things), adaptability, intensity, mood (pleasant and friendly or unpleasant and unfriendly), persistence/attention span, distractibility, and sensory threshold. I like to look at each of these dimensions when evaluating or thinking about a child. I ask myself the following questions:

- Which dimensions are areas of strength?
- Which aspects are weaknesses?
- Does this child's functioning in a particular dimension impact (positively or negatively) on daily functioning? Does it affect relationships? If yes, how? To what degree?
- If a child's functioning is impacting negatively (such as when a child is misbehaving), is it because of the poor match between the child and the environment? (It is important to underscore this last point, as the consequences of a problematic match between the child and the environment can seriously affect the child's overall adjustment and development. Predictably, a "good fit" between the child's temperament and the environment (this includes the beliefs, values, and expectations of caregivers, teachers, camp counselors, tutors, etc.) helps a child blossom.
- How do the caretakers' or teachers' profiles intersect with the referred child's profile? Do they "mix"? Is it a question of oil and water? I use a look and listen approach to observe the caretakers' temperamental characteristics and see (or ask) where each caretaker (teacher) fits on each dimension.

CONSIDER SENSORY INTEGRATION

"The label on my shirt bites me," notes Tammy. "The line on my socks is annoying and I feel it when I walk," Todd claims. "I hate the smell of this restaurant," yells Anna as she runs outside to catch her breath. Cara always needs to be on the go; Robbie can't seem to get himself moving. Kyle trips over his shoelaces and no one in the family will lend him anything because he is so careless and breaks everything.

How often do clients present themselves at our offices with complaints such as these? Ben's fight with a teacher over his refusal to remove his baseball cap may not be an oppositional battle over clothing. Instead, Ben's insistence on the cap may arise from his attempt to block out the annoying flicker of the classroom lights that keep him from paying attention. It is important to ask children or adults in treatment about their reactions to textures of clothing, changes in temperature, and unusually high or low activity levels. When I ask such questions, I am often reminded of the timeless fairy tale about the princess who felt a pea through the many mattresses piled high, one on top of the other. In our offices, we see many children with heightened sensitivities. These phenomena, which have biological origins, are often overlooked, yet they may explain a dysfunction in the processing and integration of sensory information.[27] Understanding their origins helps everyone to better understand a child's behavior.

CONSIDER A CHILD'S INNER WORLD

Employment of developmentally sensitive interviewing is one step in gathering information. How else can the individual learn about aspects of the child's inner world that can shed light on the unconscious concerns and conflicts that interfere with his functioning? There are many ways to glean information about family, friendships, conflicts, resolutions, defenses, and coping styles. Both verbal and nonverbal behaviors (e.g., body language) are clues. Mood, appropriateness of affect, eye contact, defensiveness, avoidance, reality orientation, thought processes, and fantasy life also provide essential information. A qualitative look at the child's behavior in the waiting and consulting rooms often gives a sense of the child's underlying concerns. Shannon clings to her mother during the session and looks imploringly at her whenever I ask a question; maybe she has difficulty with verbal expression, is anxious, or fears reprisal from her mom if she reveals any "secrets." Pablo demonstrates a bravado in session; maybe it masks underlying feelings of sadness and depression about his new role in the family since his father left the home.

Observing a child's play or themes in play[28] also provides clues to the child's inner world and offers the therapist a window into the child's cognitive development. Chethik notes that play is the "emotional language of the child." "Play emerges from a child's internal life and typically explicates major conflicts or defenses."[29] He suggests, "the child's capacity to play has diagnostic implications." Useful questions he poses are: "How well and freely does the child patient play? Is she inhibited—is the play frozen, repetitive, or stereotyped? Is the play too impulsive, wild, and out of control?"[30]

Another way to get information about a child's inner world is through the use of projective assessment tools. "Projective testing is based on the notion that, when presented with a vague, unstructured, or ambiguous stimulus or task, the production of the individual will reflect aspects of the personality that might be otherwise unavailable to consciousness or for assessment."[31] There are several projective games and activities that may be utilized. Make a Picture Story (MAPS)[32] (for use with adolescents and adults) and The Storytelling Card Game[33] (for use with children 4 to 11 years of age), are helpful. Both games employ stimulus (picture) cards and cutout figures that the client uses to create a story. MAPS provides both prearranged and indefinite situations (cards) on which the figures are placed and about which a story is created. The Storytelling Card Game provides pictures of ordinary settings on which the various figures are placed and about which a story is created. Sentence completion can also be employed.[34]

I often create my own cards that pertain to the child's life and presenting concerns. I have children bring in stuffed animals. We use a digital camera to photograph them and then make our own story cards to use as part of the storytelling. Children (and families) also enjoy T.A.G. (Take a Guess Game). I customize story starters for the referral problem and write them on index cards. A girl and her brother fight, take a guess why? A mother is crying, take a guess why? A teacher is angry, take a guess why? Another of my favorite projective tools are picture books, such as *How are You Peeling?*[35] The natural curves in the fruit and vegetable pictures in this book can represent a variety of emotions, and are wonderful stimuli for projective questions. Children look at a picture and tell me if the particular vegetable is feeling bad, sad, or mad. Prompts such as "What's happening?" "What happened?" or "What can he do about it?" provide insights.

The Roberts Apperception Test for Children (RATC) is a normed test for children ages 6–11 that has an objective scoring system.[36] Children relate stories to pictures about interpersonal situations. The Family Apperception Test[37] is a projective test that elicits information about family process, problem identification, depression, problem pervasiveness, abuse, limit setting, and relationships with family or peers.

Children's art and drawings also provide windows into their worlds.[38] In the Kinetic Family Drawing, a child draws a picture of his family doing something. Distance between individuals and extent of interaction is examined.[39] Some children want to write stories about their pictures or ask that I take down their dictation. The Kinetic Drawing System for Family and School[40] can also be used to explore interaction in both the home and school settings. It employs a guided inquiry process.[41]

Small animals, puppets, and family figures are helpful in storytelling to uncover and understand defenses and conflicts. Specific assessment techniques, as well as sandplay therapy, are outlined by various play therapists.[42]

REFERRAL TO OTHER PROFESSIONALS

The child's needs dictate the level of assessment that is required. If informal assessment, reports of current status from multiple sources, problem behaviors, child complaints, or problems in adaptation consistently point to a need for further attention, referral to other assessment professionals may be necessary.

Projective measures, as discussed above, although widely employed, have weak psychometric properties. Given the comorbid nature of behavioral and learning problems,[43] a more thorough evaluation of a child's strengths and weaknesses is often a prerequisite for understanding the complete picture. Specialized assessments in ophthalmology, audiology, physical and occupational therapy, or psychiatry may also be indicated.

Psychological testing provides standard and objective information regarding a child's cognitive functioning, emotional functioning, and memory. It also provides information about how someone learns and thinks.[44] (See "Tools and Resources" in the Appendix for a list of well-normed, reliable, and valid instruments that are used in evaluating academic and intellectual abilities in children and adolescents.)

Referral for Testing

If testing is indicated, it is important to develop a list of questions for the evaluator and to provide important observations about the child and all concerned. I explain to children that testing is a way to help us find out what is easy and what is hard for them. I tell children that we will use the information in making a plan to help them. I meet with the child and the family and we complete a simple task I call **A Piece of the Pie.** (See "Tools for Gathering Information" in the Appendix for a blank worksheet.) The instructions to the family follow.

□□

A Piece of the Pie

1. Make a list of any area(s) of difficulty for the child or any reasons that you might observe (e.g., slow copying from the board, can't follow directions, is distractible) that could be keeping the child from getting to her/his goal.

2. Look over your list.

- What do you think causes the most trouble for her/him? Place a number 1 next to that item.
- What is the item on the list that causes the next largest amount of trouble? Place a number 2 next to that item, etc.

3. Make a pie chart. Divide the circle into "slices" that show what "piece of the pie" you believe each problem area on the list represents.

The completed pie chart has many uses—it is a jumping-off point for discussing areas of relative strengths and weaknesses, it gives the examiner an idea of the child's and family's subjective views of the problem, and it becomes a tool to refer back to when testing is completed. The process of making the list engages the child in "detective work" about what is keeping the child from his/her goals.

Communicating with the evaluator (psychologist, occupational therapist, etc.) is a vital step. What important questions need to be answered? How can the evaluation be most useful to the child and the family? What have you and others observed? Sending the pie chart along with a list of additional concerns and questions helps to make the assessment more relevant. I look for threads of similarity that are woven through my assessment, and take note of trouble spots, especially the ones that appear repeatedly. The repetition acts as a "blinking yellow light"; it tells me that I may need to slow down here or that I may need to come back to this spot. I go along carefully, pull the information together, and check it out with the child and the family. I make sure that I write down concrete examples from our work together to provide the examiner with detailed information.

Understanding Testing Results

The data obtained from testing must not be examined in isolation, as scores are only a part of the picture. Because testing is conducted in an artificial, laboratory setting, relying heavily on test data can, in fact, be detrimental and prejudicial. "The mystical powers that are assigned to tests proclaim their misuse and lack of understanding about their supplementary role in the total assessment of the child."[45] Testing needs to be considered along with checklists, observations, parent and teacher reports, interviews, good judgment, and clinical analysis. Obtaining a "multiperson perspective" is essential.[46]

When I receive results of the testing, I read the report carefully and make a list of the reported strengths and weaknesses. Eloise is a 9-year-old fourth grader referred for testing by her school counselor at the request of her paternal grandmother. She has family, medical, learning, and social difficulties. The results of a full battery of tests are reported in Table 6.2. This worksheet is a helpful guide to organizing the information and can be completed as a second step. It helps me make the most of

Table 6.2.   Recording Testing Results: Eloise

Skills, Competencies, and Abilities	– – Very Below	– Below Average	+ – Average	+ Above Average	+ + Excellent
intelligence				verbal; performance	overall
reading				comprehension; oral reading	word attack
math			applied problems	calculation	
writing			grammar; informal sample		
spelling				spelling	
speech			articulation		
language (receptive, expressive)				receptive; expressive	
perceptual discrimination				auditory; visual	
attention and concentration	attention; concentration				
memory		short-term		long-term	
motor skills			fine		gross
acuity			visual; auditory		
personality assessment	depressed	coping skills; social skills			persistence

the testing intervention and provides a pictorial representation of the results. (See "Tools for Gathering Information" in the Appendix for a blank worksheet.)

CONSIDER MEDICATION: SHOULD IT BE PART OF THE TEAM?

In working with children whose problems are at least in part genetically based, medication may be part of the overall treatment team. Psychotropic medications are "agents that affect the central nervous system, resulting in changes in thinking, behavior, or emotion."[47] Psychotropic medication is widely used with adult populations, and the last 15 years have witnessed a significant increase in its use in treating emotional and behavioral disorders in children.[48] Using medication to ameliorate children's suffering, however, still remains a controversial issue,[49] and there are many unanswered questions about its toxicity and effectiveness.

Understandably, putting a child on medication is often accompanied by parental ambivalence and child/parent conflicts. While many recommend trying psychotherapy and behavior management as first-line interventions, others point out that medication has been a viable means of reducing children's symptoms and re-establishing adequate functioning. The social and academic cost to the individual of *not* taking medicine must be weighed against its risks.[50] Each decision depends upon the unique needs of the child.

Stanley had few friends. He was a chronic instant reactor and was unable to put himself on pause. Social relationships were significantly impaired because his impulsivity made any play date a disaster. Aggression became Stanley's way of solving interpersonal problems at home, at school, and on the playground. He even seemed unable to make use of therapy.[51] Once he began medication, the family noticed that it afforded him a small window of opportunity to make better choices and to make better use of therapy. He started to use his words, not his hands. Peers began to notice his considerable athletic abilities and he went from *persona non grata* to a more valued member of his group.

Terri counted the cracks in the sidewalk. She was rarely on time for school because ritualistic morning behaviors consumed her time. Intrusive thoughts competed with her studies for attention, affecting school performance. Rigid, black-and-white thinking interfered with social relationships and, for the most part, she led a lonely life. Terri was diagnosed with obsessive-compulsive disorder and began psychotherapy that used a cognitive behavioral approach.[52] While there was some observable improvement, her suffering continued. Eventually medication was introduced; it served as a helpful adjunct to her treatment, and accelerated her progress to near full functioning.

"Pharmacotherapy should be part of a treatment plan in which all aspects of the child's or adolescent's life are considered. It should not be used instead of other interventions or after other interventions have failed."[53]

Practitioners need to:

- collect data from multiple sources during a careful diagnostic assessment.
- formulate a multiaxial diagnosis based on *DSM-IV* that takes into account all factors contributing to the child's clinical presentation.
- include medical, neurological, and psychosocial variables.
- refer the child for a neuropsychological examination to rule out cognitive deficits.
- remediate specific weaknesses when needed.
- use knowledge of pharmacotherapy to maintain reasonable expectations of what medications can and cannot do.
- intervene before chronic incapacitation occurs and social functioning declines.
- start treatment at the lowest possible dose and titrate slowly upward to achieve maximum therapeutic response while minimizing uncomfortable and/or risky side effects.
- monitor carefully, using objective data (e.g., blood pressure, heart rate, EKG, blood levels, etc.) and maintain close contact with client and family for subjective data in evaluating side effects.
- re-evaluate the need for medication after a 6 to 12 month period of stable functioning, depending on the diagnosis and clinical course of the client.[54]

Medication and Beliefs

Parental consideration of psychiatric medication as a treatment option is often accompanied by worry or fear. The child may also have strong feelings about taking medication. Aurora ran out of a session yelling, "I'm not taking any pills, I'm not crazy!" The use of medication is a personal decision, which often takes a period of time and information gathering[55] before parents are comfortable that it is the correct course of action. In most cases a medication trial is not recommended as a first-line intervention. (There are some cases when medication may have to begin immediately, for example, when hospitalization is required because a child poses a danger to himself or another.) Inviting discussion about the child and the family's concerns, fantasies, beliefs, and expectations regarding medication is essential.[56] These discussions must be followed by clear psychoeducation concerning how medications work and what to expect—or not expect—from its use.

Each parent has a unique perspective about medication. Danny's dad, Henry, had very negative feelings about medication. After all, he reasoned, he had had similar problems growing up and he turned out just fine! Calvin's mom, Beryl, on the other hand, had personal experience with medication. She suffered from depression and had been taking medication for some time. Knowing that depression often runs in families[57] heightened her awareness of its symptoms in her child; she was concerned about Calvin's insomnia, lack of appetite, and loss of interest in his usual childhood activities since his grandpa died. When her husband later blamed Calvin's problems on Beryl's "bad genes," we all discussed this idea in therapy. New understandings were needed before Calvin's father could support medication use for Calvin.

When educating families about medication, it is important to consider the influence that media presentation and reporting about medication usage have on their opinions. It is impossible to turn on the television or to read a magazine or newspaper these days without hearing about the overuse of medication, especially Ritalin.[58] There has been a dramatic increase in prescriptions for preschoolers.[59] Some say the drug companies are "mythmakers" and are responsible for this increase.[60] Many try to make sense of Ritalin and question why millions take the drug.[61] Others tell frightening stories and warn of addiction.[62] One author presents a scathing account of misuse of medical diagnoses and warns of long-term damage to the brain.[63] Use of antipsychotics cause even greater concerns.[64] Invite the family to tell you what they heard, think, and fantasize about medication. Talk about what feelings this decision elicits. This type of discussion will help parents understand their responses to the problem; it will also give them the perspective necessary to develop a well-rounded, sound, evidence-based[65] picture of the positives and negatives, the risks and benefits. When they are armed with correct information, they can make an informed decision.

Getting Everyone "On Board"

Family involvement is essential in helping to heal a child's problem. Lewis, a bright underachiever diagnosed with attention-deficit/hyperactivity disorder, was in constant trouble at school. His raison d'etre was to get a laugh from his peers. Lewis failed to finish work, constantly lost his books, and disrupted other students near him. Initially, both of his parents refused to start Lewis on a trial of psychostimulant medication. His father took a decidedly strong stand against it. His mother, however, finally tired of the daily calls from school and fights over homework. She decided to go against her husband and start Lewis on the trial of Ritalin without informing his father. Lewis knew his dad had strong feelings, and he felt very conflicted about taking the prescribed dose. He loved his mom and didn't want to go against her, but he could not defy his father either. The psychostimulant trial was sabotaged from day one. Therapists and families must understand that in order for medication to work as a viable option, everybody must be "on board."

Positive teacher involvement and understanding are indispensable. Flora did well on her medication regime. Her behavior and accomplishments showed a dramatic difference. Her teacher, Mrs. J, reported that she could tell when Flora was on the appropriate dose. Then one day, when Flora was "off task," Mrs. J shouted in a moment of desperation "What's wrong with you Flora, did you forget to take your medicine today?" From then on, Flora was the subject of ridicule by her peers and became extremely resistant to taking her medication. Any attempt to get her to take her medication involved a fight.

Schools often pressure parents to put a "difficult" child on medication. Clara's private school continually threatened expulsion. The school's rigid position was that they could not provide the structure and management that Clara's behavior dictated. They viewed her parents' refusal to medicate as resistance and unwillingness to cooperate in her education. After a battery of psychoeducational exams and an assessment of the fit between Clara and the school, the family decided that a change of educational setting was in order. While her parents did note an improvement at her new school, the continued reports of inattention and underachievement they received ultimately led them to make an appointment for a medication consult from a child psychiatrist.

Become Partners

It is important to appreciate that medication can actually be a family intervention, since its use has an effect on all members of the family. When a family decides to begin a child on a medication trial, I work closely with all concerned. In order to achieve the best possible results, I collaborate with the child psychiatrist/psychopharmacologist, the parents, and the teacher to inform and educate the family. Parents need to have an understanding of multiple issues. Questions to be explored include: [66]

- What is the reason medication is recommended?
- What symptoms will the medication help?
- What is the risk-benefit ratio?
- How does the medication work?
- What are the possible side effects?
- What is the difference between "side effects" and "toxicity"?
- What are the signs or symptoms, if any, of toxicity?
- How should the family/child react to evidence of side effects? (e.g., given a few days to a few weeks of time, the body/brain often develops tolerance to initial side effects)? to toxicity?

- Have there been studies on the medication? What are the outcomes?
- What tests should be done before medication is started?
- When can we expect to see improvement?
- How will the progress be monitored and by whom?
- How long will the child have to take the medication?
- What will happen if the child forgets to take the medication? What if the child refuses?
- What is the best way to explain to the child the need for medication?

Examine Your Own Beliefs

It is essential for the clinician to examine her own biases and beliefs about medication. The therapist's beliefs do not remain hidden; they will be transmitted to the family and can stand in the way of a child's receiving the most appropriate care. Educate yourself about pharmacotherapy. In the case of ADHD, Tourette's syndrome, tic disorders, obsessive-compulsive disorder, some other anxiety disorders, bipolar disorder, psychosis of any etiology, and severe depression, psychiatric medication is a favored and proven treatment choice.[67] Partner with a child psychiatrist who makes room for collaboration. Don't hesitate to ask questions.

I hold fast to the position that giving children medication without psychotherapy is not good medical practice. With clients who lack definable cognitive and/or social skills, it is necessary to examine whether a problem represents a skill/performance deficit. In cases where this deficit is present, targeted intervention works best. If symptoms don't improve or if they worsen, explore other treatment options. Perhaps the client needs "skills *and* pills." Psychotherapy in conjunction with medication has proven results and can sometimes reduce the need for the medication. Although it was not always the case, I keep an open mind concerning medication because I have witnessed firsthand how appropriately prescribed medication has dramatically opened doors to change and increased options for many individuals. These experiences have all helped me to assist others in making informed decisions.

Educate the Child

Parents and therapists are not the only ones who need education. Children also need to understand how medicine works in their brains. Jerome kept a list of the changes he observed and made a picture of how his medicine helps him (see next page). I also helped Jerome to compile a list of any changes that he made in his behavior, such as writing down his homework assignment each day, bringing home his books, and completing his homework each night. His pictures and charts helped him see that the changes and progress he made were through his effort and hard work, not merely luck or a magic pill.

Jerome's Picture of How His Medicine Helps Him

Consider Diagnosis

Many clinicians think that diagnosis is antithetical to family therapy. Current practice in family therapy encourages movement away from diagnosis because it is considered a way of pathologizing or marginalizing a person by labeling him.[68]

Family therapists need not buy into a biotechnical, reductionistic reframing of illness as disease. Rather, it is more appropriate to conceptualize and work with illness as a narrative placed in a biopsychosocial context. Such a narrative includes how shared responsibility for coping and for finding solutions can take place, without becoming involved in disputes about causal models.[69]

There are many who suggest, or perhaps insist, that when the therapist engages in "problem talk" (discussion of problem behaviors, descriptions, and understandings about problem origins and maintenance), it reifies the problem.[70] Some assert that labeling (categorizing a child as having a learning problem, attentional weakness, mood disorder, or conduct problem) stig-matizes and intensifies an individual family member's view that she or he is in fact causing a problem. They believe that diagnosis keeps the family steeped in describing "problem-saturated" situations.[71]

Other therapists and researchers challenge these assumptions for chil-dren and families with problems with biological origins.[72] They declare that shunning an individual diagnosis in these cases is not helpful. Avoiding a diagnosis may leave a family feeling misunderstood, angry, and alienated. It can also prevent a family from securing appropriate care for their child.[73]

Researchers document that biology plays a key role in the development of many disorders.[74] "All of these biological deficits and/or deviations can have an enormous impact on family interactions and on individual family members' and the child's intrapsychic and other reactions."[75] Miscalculating the key role of biological factors and embracing the "unidi-mensional view" that dysfunction resides only in interactions and relation-ships within the family can result in inappropriate therapeutic goals. The issues and concerns related to problems arising from the biological deficits are left unaddressed.

In my opinion, it is essential to avoid an either/or position; clinicians must take an inclusive stance. As previously discussed in this book, the therapist must shift perspectives between multiple viewpoints when assess-ing a child with a biological deficit. These perspectives can be used to cre-ate a collaborative resource model; through the use of this model, families develop new nonblaming explanations of old problems that have tightly woven themselves into the fiber of their daily family lives. They can be mobilized to find assistance in community groups, parent support groups, and self-help groups. Most importantly, diagnoses can help them find a loose thread which, when tugged, may unravel an embedded problem. Using therapy to aid them in reconfiguring relationships, family members can then be free to try different ways of interacting.

Remember Eloise, the 9-year-old fourth grade student referred by her coun-selor for testing? Information about her came from extensive interviews with her teacher and with the referring school counselor, from a medical report, from the psychological evaluation done at the school, and from a discussion with her grandmother. Table 6.3 illustrates a simple way to summarize and organize the large amounts of information gathered from many sources. This table helps to graphically systematize the information, to identify major biopsychosocial variables and treatment targets, and to plan interventions. (See "Tools for Gathering Information" in the Appendix for a blank worksheet.)

Negotiate a Treatment Plan

What do we learn from the data we collect? I always start my thinking simply, as the following spoof suggests. Holmes and Dr. Watson went on a camping trip. After a good meal and a bottle of wine, they lay down in their tent for the night and went to sleep. Some hours later, Holmes awoke and nudged his faithful friend. "Watson, look up at the sky and tell me what you see." Watson replied, "I see millions and millions of stars." "What does that tell you?" Holmes questioned. Watson pondered for a minute. "Astronomically, it tells me that there are millions of galaxies and potentially billions of planets. Astrologically, I observe that Saturn is in Leo. Horologically, I deduce that the time is approximately a quarter past three. Theologically, I can see that God is all-powerful and that we are small and insignificant. Meteorologically, I suspect that we will have a beautiful day tomorrow. What does it tell you, Holmes?" Holmes was silent for a minute, and then spoke. "Watson, you jerk, someone has stolen our tent."[76]

The information gathered in an assessment comes from a multitude of sources and perspectives. It needs to be analyzed and integrated into a digestible explanation of the problem. Just as gathering information is a team effort, so is deciding how to proceed. Many clinicians choose to hold a feedback-informing session with the parents. I find it most helpful to conceptualize this meeting as a *sharing* conference. Children need to be included, as they are often as bewildered about a problem as their parents are and need help in understanding what is happening. I make a list of the family's concerns and we review them together. Issues that involve dangerous behaviors and safety to self or others are given highest priority. I try to use the family's language and hypotheses about the problems to confirm their observations and hunches about their child. They are, after all, the experts on their child. The sharing conference should help the therapist and the family generate ideas and open the door to possibilities for intervention.

Feedback in a sharing meeting should start with a discussion of strengths. A thorough investigation should have uncovered a variety of positives that can start the conference off on an encouraging note. It is vital to discuss how these strengths can be developed. It is important to remember that a child who is brought to your attention might have a long history of failure and, thus, a fragile sense of self. Many children have been evaluated, poked, and probed by questions. They may have come to view the whole process as

Table 6.3 Biopsychosocial Variables and Treatment Targets: Eloise

	Individual	Family	School/Peers/Community	Resources/Strengths	Treatment Targets and Planning
Biological and/or health, physical	seizures ②; wears glasses; poor appetite ① (−)	mother depressed ②; father drug user (− −)	distractible; problem concentrating ②; anxious in social situations ③ (−)	doesn't give up; agile and athletic; in general good health (+ +)	seizures—continued medical follow-up; neurological psychoeducation regarding seizures; refer mother for a re-evaluation of medication; ↓ stress
Psychological	feelings of worthlessness, hopelessness ① (− −)	mother angry, critical (− −)	low self-esteem—says "I have no brain" "I can't learn"; name calling by peers (−)	above average intelligence (+ +)	↓ dysphoria; ↑ self-esteem; ↓ mother's critical comments; cognitive-behavior therapy; family therapy
Social spiritual, cultural	parents divorced (−); religious, attends church regularly (+ +)	mother unemployed ③; housing problems (− −)	teacher reports social relationships strained①; loner ②; poor coping skills when stressed (−)	warm, involved extended family, participates in church activities (+ +)	↑ social skills; ↑ socialization opportunities; focus on strengths, resources of social support in the extended family; family therapy; peer coaching; social skills group; children of divorce group; Brownies; sports team

Overall functioning: + + (excellent), + (above average), + − (average), − (below average), − − (very below)
Symptoms: ① transient, ② acute, ③ chronic
Treatment targets: ↑ increase, ↓ decrease

a punishment. In order for them to make any changes in their lives, they first need to understand the nature of their strengths and weaknesses. They need to find words that capture their experience.[77]

The following is a simple activity to help a family examine where they are today, where they want to be, and what steps are needed to get them to their goal. First, give each person in the family a piece of paper with instructions to draw a picture of anything that tells about how life in the family is now. I have young children draw a picture of the family. I ask them to tell me about it, and I write down their explanation for them. Next, I give out a second paper and ask them to draw a picture that tells about how they would like things to be in the family. Third, I put a picture of a bridge between their two pictures. Together we begin filling in the lines with ideas of what the family needs to do to go from picture one, "now," to picture two, "future." We number the steps and negotiate a viable treatment plan, one that takes into account the assessment pieces that have been gathered.

In sum, if a child has a disorder with biological underpinnings, the clinician has a responsibility to (1) research pertinent information about the disorder, (2) keep abreast of current findings related to diagnosis and empirically-based interventions, (3) gather information systematically from all involved with the child, (4) consider behaviors across different contexts, (5) collaborate with other professionals to find out what works best for this child, (6) identify strengths and resources within the child and the family, (7) find ways to impart the information to parents and child so they fully understand the impact of the child's challenges, and (8) link the diagnosis to intervention.

A REVIEW: ASSESSMENT

The purpose of assessment is to identify mutually influencing biopsychosocial, individual, family, social, cultural, environmental risk, and protective factors. The following outline summarizes the steps in the assessment process discussed in Chapters 5 and 6. It is presented here as a guide and review.

I.   Preparation phase
     A. Gather information from:
        - phone call
        - referral source
        - review of records (as applicable—school, medical, hospital)
        - testing reports
     B. Begin to fill in charts:

- biopsychosocial variables and treatment targets
- testing results

C. Possibly begin to construct a genogram

II. Joining
A. Organize the session:
- facilitate listening
- discuss the purpose of the meeting and ground rules
- create tone of importance around communication
- observe, observe, observe
  Each session offers an in-vivo opportunity for ongoing observation and collaborative intervention.
  View family patterns
  Move the assessment lens between domains: *within-the-family, within-the-child/individual,* and *larger-systems*

III. Construct a multigenerational genogram and conduct a neurobiological inquiry by gathering information about:
- school and learning histories of family members, suspected learning disabilities (school problems), attention disorders, behavioral difficulties
- risk factors, losses, trauma, problems with the law,
- treatment of children in the extended family,
- significant stressors in the caregiver's and extended environments,
- history of psychiatric hospitalizations, alcohol and drug use,
- genetic tendencies and endowments, temperament,
- depression, bipolar disorder or manic depression, obsessive-compulsive disorder, anxiety, panic attacks, eating disorders, separation difficulties, schizophrenia, autism, pervasive developmental delays, mental retardation.

IV. Have a sharing meeting
V. Negotiate a treatment plan

PART III

Treatment in Action

Sending Therapy Home

CHAPTER 7

Child and Family Work

Attachment, Affect Regulation, and the Family

"I'm afraid of him. He controls us. He's never satisfied." As she asked for help with her 8-year-old son, the woman who had left the message on my answering machine sounded desperate. The message described her son, Gary, as cunning, manipulative, intentionally destructive of property, and never satisfied. "Please, Dr. Stern, we're at the end of our rope and don't know what else to do."

Although I usually work with the whole family in treatment, I conducted the first interview with Gary's parents only. I saw the parents together in order to take a careful history and give them an opportunity to ventilate their disappointment outside of Gary's hearing. The profound sadness they felt was especially evident in Gary's mother, Betty. What follows in the next section is a summary of information I gathered in meeting with Gary's parents, interviewing his teacher on the telephone, reviewing previous testing, consulting with the child psychopharmacologist, and speaking with his former therapist.

OUR WORK BEGINS

Meetings with Paul and Betty

Our work together began with a first appointment with Betty and Paul. Betty described herself as devastated, exhausted, and desperate. She expressed enormous disappointment and profound sadness. She was overwhelmed with hopelessness and questioned her ability to parent Gary. She sobbed as she spoke of the daily struggles. Both Betty and Paul were suffering and needed time to tell their story. It was evident that we needed several appointments to accomplish this goal.

Betty and Paul married late and wanted to start a family immediately. They learned they were infertile and decided to adopt, but the process was not easy. Finally, after several years and many traumatic disappointments, an organization with ties in Rumania informed them of a little boy who was available for adoption, a child they had already decided to call Gary. Little was told to them about his genetic inheritance or the circumstances surrounding the decision to place him for adoption. Nevertheless, they were delighted.

Betty and Paul longed to cradle Gary in their arms, to see his face upon waking in the morning, and to rock him to sleep each night. However, because of legal red tape it wasn't until ten months after beginning the adoption process that they were able to take him home to the United States. They had been permitted one visit during the 10 months that they waited. During that visit, Gary was fretful and didn't sleep well while they were together, but Betty attributed this to her own inexperience as a mother and to the uncomfortable nature of their surroundings. From the first moment of that visit they were deeply saddened at having to separate from Gary. Snapshots and fantasies were the only source of solace and company until they would take him home when he was 15 months old.

Betty cried as she showed me the picture of the "wished for" child they had adopted. She and Paul described daily life with their now 8-year-old son. When told "no," Gary cursed, was intentionally destructive of property, would break furniture, and rip money. His mood changed abruptly and his behavior "turned on a dime." Betty said, "He is never satisfied. He won't let me out of his sight. I'm all used up. He controls us, and we never have a night alone." Betty was devastated and exhausted by this little boy who couldn't accept "no." Paul, while supportive of Betty's position, believed that Betty just didn't know how to handle Gary. Betty felt Paul and Gary got along because Paul always gave Gary whatever Gary wanted. The child they described came across as feral, his mood labile. "It's as if his thermostat is broken," Betty commented. "From the day he came to live with us, life has been in an upheaval. I suspected it wouldn't be easy, but I never expected anything like that. Gary cried all the time and didn't like to be held. Most of the clothes I bought for him had to be given away. It was as if the fabric or texture of the material bothered him. He pulled at the collars, the buttons seemed to annoy him, and even now he complains that the line at the front of his sock bothers him when he walks. Forget labels! I still cut them out because Gary complains that they're 'biting' him. It's been a nightmare," was all I could hear through Betty's sobbing.

While I listened to Betty, I could not help but be aware of the overwhelming pain, disappointment, and sadness she experienced as she struggled to parent Gary. She was concerned that Gary would not cooperate with any therapist, and questioned if it was even possible for things to be better. Gary had already been diagnosed with ADHD, and was taking the psychostimulant medication Ritalin, but still, he was unmanageable. Betty and Paul had previously brought him to see a therapist who quickly discharged Gary and worked only with them. There had been little improvement, and the difficulties were becoming further embedded into family life. As they described the dimension of Gary's symptoms, there was a question in my mind of comorbid disorders such as a mood or oppositional defiant disorder. His outbursts were a concern, and it was unclear whether they were in his control or whether they were the result of an intermittent explosive disorder, a reactive attachment disorder, or possibly a psychotic rage.

Developmental History

Assessment usually begins with a good developmental history, and with information about the circumstances surrounding conception, birth, attachment, early development, and genetic endowment. None of this information was available to Betty and Paul. In fact, in trying to understand Gary we are struck by the absence of information regarding the first 15 months of his life. Through the initial interview with Betty and Paul, I had learned that when they first met him in the orphanage Gary was fretful and did not sleep well. When they brought him home, Gary cried all the time and did not like to be held. He also showed heightened tactile sensitivity and had no ability to self-soothe. Developmental milestones appeared to be within normal limits, except for speech, which was delayed.

From the beginning, Gary could not accept prohibition. As a toddler and little boy, he was always on the go, ignored "no," and wouldn't let Betty out of his sight. Betty tried involving Gary in a playgroup, but his unmanageable behavior caused her to give up this attempt at socialization. Now, at 8, Gary continued to be difficult to manage. Although he was on medication for ADHD, he was subject to abrupt mood changes, was manipulative, cunning, intentionally destructive of property, and never satisfied.

Gary's temperament could best be described as "difficult," in the category of the highly sensitive child.[1] He had a heightened physiological response to noise, textures, and bodily sensations, such as hunger. He was often irritable, prone to temper tantrums, and had both feeding and sleeping difficulties. He continued to have little capacity for self-soothing and needed an enormous amount of attention from parents who were exhausted by his demands. When he entered kindergarten, his peer relationships were troubled and his teacher reported that managing Gary was problematic.

Teacher Telephone Conference

Although Gary had never been formally evaluated, a review of his cumulative school record found inconsistencies in his learning. In my telephone conversation with the teacher, I learned that Gary had been unable to stay in nursery school and had had a hard time adjusting each year, from kindergarten through second grade. Now he was in third grade and the teacher reported frequent outbursts and opposition that made it difficult to cope with him in class. He demanded constant attention from her or from any other adult who would come into the room. Gary seemed eager to participate in class, and had a hard time when the teacher would pay attention to another child or call on someone else. His teacher also noted that Gary worked harder when he liked the teacher. She described him as a child with a short attention span and difficulty focusing. Extremely restless and impulsive, he had problems waiting in general and waiting his turn in particular. His temper and outbursts were unpredictable. He didn't get along with the other children, and sometimes resorted to pushing them or destroying their property. Despite the fact that he wanted friends, he had none because other children shunned him. The teacher added that on good days it was obvious that Gary was a bright, quick, and eager learner. At these times, he could be a very positive addition to the class.

A Despairing Pair

Our work together in the first sessions with Betty and Paul began with lowering the volume on the voices of defeat and despair. In an effort to introduce hope into this dispirited system, I elicited stories of victories in other areas. In hearing their story about Gary's adoption, I was struck by Betty and Paul's persistence and optimism during the long months of waiting to bring their son home. I asked them to describe the details. What was it that helped them keep their goal in view in the face of the overwhelming odds that it might not work out? What kept them going when their hopes dimmed? I asked Betty to recall other times when she had felt hopeless. These questions elicited narratives with the theme of perseverance. Betty demonstrated that she was and is a resourceful person. She came to life as she talked about the almost daily calls she had made to the adoption agency in an effort to move along the bureaucratic red tape. She had called her congressman, her state senator, and the embassy. She animatedly reported that she had been on a first name basis with important government officials, and proudly declared that they had told her that she was the most persistent adoptive parent they had encountered. Her mother, her friends, and her coworkers all cheered her on. Paul was an extraordinary resource for Betty through that period. As he shared his thoughts about that difficult time, he commented that *then* it had seemed easier for him to maintain a hopeful attitude. In doing this, he had used some of the coping skills he had developed at the time of his brother's death, when Paul was 14. These included such things as picturing his brother's face, talking to him, writing him notes, and staying close to others who shared his pain. While he and Betty waited for Gary, he made a rocking chair and involved Betty in decorating Gary's room. He hung photos of Gary around the house. He organized the trip for the two of them to see Gary for the first time. He made a tape of lullabies that he sent to Gary along with a tape player, thinking the music would be a bridge between Gary's two worlds. Activity seemed to help them.

We talked about how the difficulties with Gary disrupted family life to such a degree that they now had few positive experiences together. The problems seemed to engulf them. However, by discussing small victories in other areas, more positive stories began to emerge. At the end of the session, Betty and Paul held hands as they spoke tenderly of happier times.[2] We talked about Gary's perplexing behaviors and began what would be a series of conversations about how biology had "dealt" Gary a "tough hand" of cards to play. We planned for Gary's first session. Paul and Betty raised concerns about getting Gary to come to yet another therapist. They mentioned that Gary would not tolerate sitting for a long time. I explained that I try to have a child-friendly approach that integrates a "doing" aspect. "Not playing games," commented Paul. "I don't want to pay for another therapy where Gary sits and plays games." I explained that we would be playing, and playful, while working on skill-building, multisensory activities, and games the whole family could do or play together. We would work together to find ways for them to take the new ideas home.

Infants and Good Beginnings

In attempting to understand Gary and his family, we must turn our attention to the importance of good beginnings. Each infant needs the loving care of an attuned caregiver. Infants need to be touched and held, they need to be cooed at, talked with, and responded to. In the absence of this, they may fail to thrive and develop.[3] As we saw in Chapter 4, the brain is not a static organ but one that grows and changes over time. The brain is experience-dependent and feeds on stimulation from the environment. Infants interact with their environment from the moment they are born, with the primary caregiver playing an essential role of mediator and modulator of input from that environment.[4] "Mother's presence is like a fixed light that gives the child the security to move out safely to explore the world and then return safely to harbor. She makes the world of time and space sensible and intelligible."[5] A parent's face is a source of emotional support, an affect regulator, an emotional mirror, an arousal regulator, and a reinforcing stimulus.[6] The development of the mother-child bonding and attachment is undeniably critical.[7]

John Bowlby, the British psychiatrist, psychoanalyst, and leader in the development of attachment theory, states that the infant's proclivity to seek proximity to the mother has a biological and instinctual basis.[8] The attachment process is necessary for the infant's exploration of the world around him. The caregiver's closeness helps to maintain and support security as well as provide a "home base" for the infant.[9] The child's sense of self grows from the connection and the predictable care provided by his mother. From this care and connection, the child develops an internal working model of how relationships work.

> Through sucking, clinging, following, smiling, crying, and, when older, by going to mother when in physical or emotional distress or simply when he wants attention, the child explores his relationships and builds a model of how they work. The internal working model, like the wasp's internal map, reflects the child's relationship history, codifying the behaviors that belong to an intimate relationship, and defining how he will feel about himself when he is closely involved with another person.[10]

What does this mean for the infant? From the start, the infant is building a "data base" of how relationships operate. The "interpersonal world of the infant" is developed through a highly interactive process.[11] A parent's availability, responsiveness, and ability to tune in to her infant are fundamental to all aspects of that infant's psychological development. Through her love and caring, she helps the infant experience the world in "small doses."[12]

Early-established patterns of interactions with the mother are thought to have implications for the child's ability to adjust in the future. Infants with mothers who responded predictably and consistently to their needs developed "secure" attachments.[13] Throughout our lives, most of us seek connections and develop bonds. We look to those close to us for "protection, comfort, and support."[14] It is often the solace and comfort from family members, friends, and others in our support systems that help to sustain us during bleak times. Learning how to build these connections starts with a sense of belonging that develops early on.

Mutual Gaze Experiences and Brain Development

The building of bonds and creation of templates for connection are not the only results of the interaction between the caregiver and the infant. Critical structures in the brain, particularly the right orbital prefrontal cortex, which is responsible for development of affect regulation, evolve through the process of reciprocal exchange. The socioemotional environment shapes this part of the brain; for the infant, "the mother essentially *is* the environment."[15] Early interactive experiences shape brain development, which in turn molds experience. Regulatory functions help to shape the social self.

Events that occur during infancy, especially transactions with the social environment, are indelibly imprinted into the structures that are maturing in the first years of life. The child's first relationship, the one with the mother, acts as a template, as it permanently molds the individual's capacities to enter into all later emotional relationships. These early experiences shape the development of a unique personality, its adaptive capacities as well as its vulnerabilities to and resistances against particular forms of future pathologies. Indeed, they profoundly influence the emergent organization of an integrated system that is both stable and adaptable, and thereby the formation of the self.[16]

How does this begin? It is the gaze at the primary caregiver's face and the subsequent stimulation of the visual pathways, which cause changes in the infant's immature brain. Visual encounters through mutual gaze between the infant and the caregiver allow for affect to be transmitted between the pair.

> The sunshine of thine eyes,
>   (O still celestial beam!)
> Whatever it touches it fills
>   With the life of its lambent gleam.[17]

The "sunshine," the gleam of the mother's eyes, is a powerful stimulus that attracts the baby.[18] At the same time, the infant plays an active part in its interaction with caregivers. How do we know this is happening? Observation and microanalyses of films of mother-infant dyads reveal a system of communication between the pair. A process occurs in which the mother attends to the infant's cues for connection and response, and then ends the connection when the infant averts its gaze.[19] Just as ballroom dancers move in a harmonious manner, the responses of the attuned caregiver and the infant are in harmony.

The enjoyment of these harmonious interactions is clearly evidenced by the delight on the infant's face and is also thought to have an effect on the infant's inner state. In fact, the effect is bidirectional; the infant is stimulated by the mother but also stimulates positive affect in the mother. Through the matching of affective patterns, they generate similar inner psychophysiological states.[20] It is this matching and reciprocity that is attunement at its best: a baby bathed in the warmth of the caregiver's delight, caring, and comfort.

Now let us consider Gary. What assumptions can we make when we think about his year in the orphanage? If his fussing and complaining were ignored, he learned the lesson that his cries did not bring help. He did not learn how to discharge tension from the presses of his needs and drives. It is during this time, perhaps, that the seeds of his feelings of unworthiness and shame were sown. There was no constant face to gaze upon Gary and no individual with whom he could engage in mutually connected and mutually enjoyed experiences. Absent was the gaze between parent and infant that results in bursts of neurotransmitters that impact on the brain's emotional architecture. Most probably Gary wasn't touched and held as much as babies need to be held, massaged, and spoken to.[21]

Betty's current reports that Gary reacts negatively to noise, sensory stimuli, and textures of clothing, suggest that he has sensory integration difficulties.[22] Because of these difficulties, Gary's heightened physiological state, and the absence of an attuned caregiver, we can conclude that sufficient amounts of physical comfort were probably unavailable to him. He never learned how to soothe himself or be soothed.

By the time that Betty and Paul brought him home, Gary was toddling around. He would climb up the stairs, pull over small tables and objects, rip up important papers, and eat anything from the floor that was in his path. Betty reported that she was very anxious and worried that she couldn't provide adequate safety for her baby. Screams of "no" pervaded her otherwise quiet home. The face that Gary gazed at did not have a smile, but rather a look of disgust or annoyance that was often accompanied by tears of exasperation. A "smack on his bottom" was appropriate under the circumstances, Betty reasoned. Gary's accomplishment of walking around did not bring delight to his mother's face. Instead, Betty's face showed looks of horror when she saw a broken vase or a mess that Gary left in his wake.

Continued experiences of shame without reattunement by a loving caregiver can have a profound effect on a child's affective and self-regulatory development. Of course, the caregiver cannot be expected to always be in sync with the infant; there are times of dyssynchrony in every parent-child relationship. However, the process of repair itself is crucial to healthy growth; it is through the process of repair that we move from feelings of despair to positive emotions. Dyssynchrony and its *successful* resolution contribute to the best possible outcomes. Infrequent or absent opportunities for repair have deleterious results.[23] For Gary, the seeds of shame had already been sown with early neglect and now, continual shame experiences[24] further shaped his sense of self.

FAMILY MATTERS

The Family Context

Betty was oversensitive to anger in others. Despite a successful career and obvious abilities and accomplishments, she constantly doubted herself and her competence. Anxious and a worrier by nature, she was plagued with feelings of pessimism and failure in regard to Gary and she reported that she was both critical and impatient with him. Paul commented that Betty's nature made it difficult for her to look away when Gary was doing something that she didn't like or approve of. She tended to micromanage him, correcting him at every opportunity. Paul, on the other hand, was "laid back." He coped by avoiding, and adopted a "peace at any price" attitude. He did not take a stand alongside Betty in regard to Gary's behavior and, essentially, he undermined her attempts to control him. Paul described how, like his father, he used his job to escape family tensions. He portrayed himself as a workaholic who didn't know how to enjoy himself. Betty noted that Paul had recent stomach problems that the doctor thought might be the beginning of an ulcer. Although both Betty and Paul had thought that a child would enhance their relationship, this had not been the case. Instead, they found their relationship suffering as they attempted to deal with an angry, manipulative, out-of-control 8-year-old. Betty's accusations that Gary came between them and her resentment when Paul seemed to take Gary's side added to an already tense and stressed home. Betty reported the unpredictability of Gary's reactions was most troubling to her. She felt like she had to walk on eggshells and reported some symptoms of traumatic stress disorder. When there was an incident with Gary, she often had flashbacks. These troubling behaviors, as we shall see, had roots in her own childhood.

Families of Origin

Why is this difficult child more difficult in this family? It is important to remember that Gary's endowment and behavior elicit old feelings from Betty and Paul; their feelings toward their son stem from their own temperaments and from their places (real and psychological) in their own families of origin. (On the following page is a multigenerational genogram of Gary's family.) Gary's difficulties must be viewed within the dynamics of this particular family. We will see that Betty and Paul's personal histories make it especially difficult for them to deal with Gary's anger. Their own transferences, expectations, beliefs, and anger get projected onto Gary, making it impossible for them to respond in helpful ways. In addition, Betty and Gary's similar temperaments exacerbate the situation.

Betty's Family History

Betty was the youngest of three children in a working class, suburban family. She described her father, Carmine, as a "depressed, crazy, angry, suspicious,

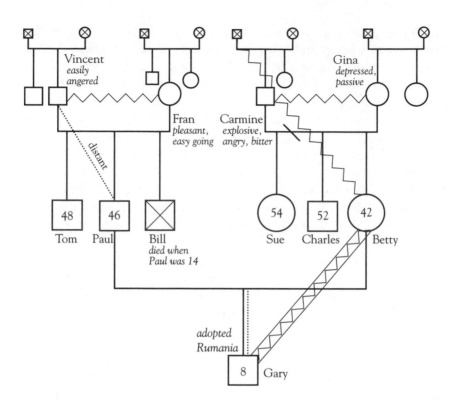

and frightening man" who displayed a false and charming nature to those outside the home. Betty, her brother, Charles, and her sister, Sue, never knew what was waiting for them at the end of the day. Charles and Sue were 10 and 12 years older than Betty and often didn't come home until late in the evening, so Betty often became the focus of their father's fierce rage. In my office, she cried as she described cowering behind the sofa and covering her ears to block out his biting, critical comments. Her father had a suspicious nature and repeatedly got stuck on an idea. He ruminated over decisions and often accused Betty, Sue, and Charles of wrongdoing. Betty knew her mother, Gina, worked long hours and was herself depressed and worn out by the years of living with Carmine. Dread often overcame Betty as she left her school building and watched the other children run happily toward their homes.

When I asked Betty whom Gary was most like, she immediately made a connection. "He's my father, the worst and best of my father." Betty noted many similarities between the two. Gary was a particularly engaging child with a sharp wit, a quick mind, and an inviting smile. At times he could be extremely charming. When Gary was having a good day, there was no one

Betty would rather have been with. Yet like her father, Gary had an angry, controlling, and at times rather chilling presentation. When confronted with Gary's unpredictable explosions, Betty felt as if she was once again cowering in front of her father, without any resources for fighting back. As she talked, she began to understand her desperation to "fix" Gary. During incidents with Gary, the past merged with the present, and Betty became flooded with rage and anger that gnawed at her insides. She felt powerless in the face of this all too familiar vulnerability and these terrifying feelings. Just as in her childhood when there wasn't anyone to protect Betty from her "crazy" father, Betty felt she was alone in handling Gary. She needed help from Paul, but his own history made it difficult for him to respond in helpful ways.

Paul's Family History

Paul, the middle of three boys, was raised in a middle class, suburban family. He portrayed his early upbringing as positive and connected, especially in regard to his mother and brothers. However, in stories about his father, Paul described an angry, irritable man. His father, Vincent, worked nights and didn't spend much time at home. Paul noted that that was probably a good thing; when his father was home, there was tension and fighting. Paul had many interests outside the home and learned that he was happier if he tuned out and "minded his own business."

Growing up, Paul had developed the habit of distancing himself from the explosions and anger that were common in his house. Logic told him that the best way to avoid confrontation was to remove himself from it. Paul had watched his brother Tom fight every day with their father. Paul saw there was no winning, so he either withdrew or practiced a policy of appeasement. He developed calluses to his father's temper; Vincent's raised tones may have pierced the air in the house, but they didn't hurt Paul anymore. Paul commented sadly that, after a time, the calluses "covered his heart"; he found consolation and success in academic pursuits.

When Paul turned 14, tragedy struck the family when the youngest brother died in an accident. His mother, a quiet woman, spent most of her days alone grieving the loss of her favorite son. Although the family stayed together, "it was never the same."

It was this history that led Paul to distance himself when Gary and Betty fought. He diminished the importance of follow-through and urged Betty to stop fighting. He didn't protect Betty from Gary's explosions and intentional destruction of Betty's property; instead, Paul used a strategy similar to the one that had worked for him his whole life: "distance yourself and avoid the confrontation."

GARY

Gary's First Appointment

The day of Gary's first appointment arrived; Paul had to work overtime and could not come and Betty and Gary were late. Betty called my office from a pay phone to inform me that Gary was refusing to come; he had broken the windshield wiper on the car and was screaming loudly. I urged Betty to get Gary to the office, telling her, "It's your job to get him here, my job to keep him here." They arrived ten minutes later and Betty looked beleaguered. This was a perfect opportunity for me to view firsthand exactly what Betty was up against when Gary had one of his explosive outbursts. As they entered the office, I coached Betty on how to handle the situation. Gary screamed angrily at me and was furious that his mother was listening to my coaching. We gave Gary several choices. He could lie down on the couch while his mother talked to me, he could sit on the floor, or he could sit in the waiting room with us. Betty stood her ground and informed Gary that he was not leaving. They were going to stay until the session time was over.

By the time Gary calmed down, there were only about five minutes left of our time together. He appeared curious about some of the interesting materials he saw in my office, such as the puppets hanging on the wall, and the abundance of art materials and toys in the closet. He asked me about working with them. I quietly informed him that he could pick something and we would work on it together the next time he came. Betty mentioned that this vignette in the office was typical of the way Gary reacted. It seemed clear that he used his anger to control Betty.

The Next Few Sessions

Gary came to the next session with both Betty and Paul. He was a willing partner. He chatted with me about his school day and took the lead in a discussion about anger in the house. After listening to everybody talk about how quickly anger grows, I commented that it sounded as if anger came quickly, like this, demonstrating with a snap of my fingers. The following activity helped us talk about anger and reactivity.

Note: A word about the symbols that will appear throughout the text:
🏠 indicates tools or activities that are sent home with the family. These are not homework assignments, but rather ways to reinforce, punctuate, and practice what was discovered or learned in the session.

🗨 Another way that families take therapy home with them is through a new language with which to talk about their struggles. "🗨" indicates a new idea, concept, phrasing, or metaphor that can be utilized at home.

Fuses and Boom

I asked Gary if he had ever seen a firecracker. "Firecrackers go 'pop,'" I told him. "No," he said, "They go 'boom.'" We discussed how that happens, and his father explained that first you light the string on the firecracker. The string burns, and when the flame reaches the end of the string, it sets off the firecracker. "And then the 'boom,'" Gary finished. "Yes, that's exactly how it happens," Paul told him. I asked Gary if there was a "boom" when he, Mommy, or Daddy got angry. He said, a "big boom." We talked about who gets to "boom" the quickest in their home. Gary said he and his mother did. We drew pictures of firecrackers and their strings, and talked about how long it takes for the string to burn and for the "boom" to happen. Betty acknowledged that she had a short string. Gary agreed and said, "You go boom too fast." Betty became defensive and looked upset. She told Gary, "So do you." I remarked that this often happens in families and wondered aloud, "Gary, do you think this is why you and mom have trouble sometimes, because you both go boom fast?" Gary thought this was a good possibility. I asked, "What would happen if you learned how to make the strings longer?" Everyone decided that it would be a good thing. They also decided that dad has a medium string, but because of the recent fighting it had been getting shorter and shorter.

🗨 "Strings," "boom"

○○

What kind of string (fuse) do you have?

1. List all family members.
2. Write, draw, or circle how short or long each person's fuse (string) is. Do they have short fuses (strings) and react quickly, medium fuses, or long fuses?

   Example: Mom has a short string (a quick boom)

   Dad has a medium string

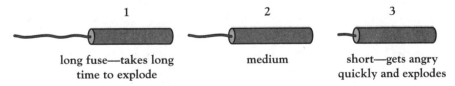

1	2	3
long fuse—takes long time to explode	medium	short—gets angry quickly and explodes

3. Check It Out: How did I do? Give yourself a "1" if you take a long time to go "boom," a "2" if it is in the middle, or medium, and a "3" if you go "boom" fast. How can I stay calm and make my string longer?
4. The family works together to think of how they could make their "strings" longer.

○○

In the next session Gary and Paul told the story of how they used strings and boom at home. Gary told Paul that Paul yelled and wanted Gary to get ready too fast in the morning. Paul said, "I'm trying to keep my string long and not go boom. I will try not to get angry." "How did it end," I asked. I could tell from their smiles that the incident had a happy ending, that they had managed to keep their strings long.

In the session they made a morning plan. They drew pictures of all the things that they needed to do for the morning, for example, have books ready to go and clothes picked out and on the chair by the bed. They put these on a chart for Gary and Paul to see and consult with. Gary decided that to save time he wanted to sleep in the clothes that he was going to wear the next day. While neither Betty nor Paul really approved of Gary's "original" idea, they agreed to try it.

    ⌇ "My string is getting shorter." Say out loud, "I need to stay calm and keep my string long."

The following is a description of a conversation during one session with Betty, Paul, and Gary. I had suggested that both Betty and Paul use a combination visual-verbal representation to show Gary how long their strings were. They were to hold their hands up and say to Gary, "My string is getting a little short and I don't want to go 'boom'." This was a reminder for all of them. It helped Betty and Paul remember that they had to be the grown-ups and stay in control of their anger, it slowed things down, and it also helped Gary see what was happening.

At first, it seemed to make Gary feel quite powerful that he could "make them go 'boom.'" "This is better than the best present I could buy him," Betty commented. "It feels as if he loves to see me that way." We talked about the process: what happens and how it ends. Generally there was a punishment, crying, and sometimes an "I'm sorry." No one liked that ending.

They decided that if they could change the beginning, then maybe there would be a different ending. Gary's poor frustration tolerance and diminished impulse control made it hard for him to do this. When he wanted something, there was no waiting, only "now." "It feels as if it is life or death to him," Paul commented. "To Gary it is! It doesn't matter if he wants an ice cream cone or your undivided attention; delaying gratification of his desires is hard for Gary," I said. "He gets fixed on his idea and has a hard time changing to a different channel. It's almost like an automatic tape in his head starts and tells him to think, 'I have to have it, I have to have it, I have to have it.' It's like his brain gets locked tight on that idea and won't let him have relief and think about another one."

I asked Gary if he thought it was hard for him to stop wanting something when he wants it. "Very hard," he replied. "Does that cause trouble for you sometimes?" I asked. "Yes, a lot." "Is it hard to hear 'no'?" I queried. "Very, very hard," Gary answered. Hearing this conversation helped his parents understand a little more about the way that Gary's brain makes it harder for him to stop thinking something and to change his mind. Paul said he was worried. "He has to learn this, because he can't always hear a yes. Life isn't about that." "Are you worried that Gary won't learn this important lesson about accepting no?" His eyes filled with tears as Paul talked. "Certainly I am." Betty took Paul's hand and squeezed it. Gary moved closer too. We acknowledged that this was something that would take time and work. Paul and Betty agreed to find ways to keep their strings longer and work toward better control over their reactivity. They knew that when they stayed calm, it was easier for Gary to remain calm. Their reaction and subsequent reactions affected the outcome.

🏠 Betty and Paul used their hands as visual representation for Gary to see when his parents' patience was shrinking, when their "strings" were getting short.

Individual Sessions with Gary

Gary and I met alone for two sessions. His behavior varied in each. He is a very appealing child with a broad smile that lights up his face. In the first session he separated with hesitation and seemed subdued and sad. It was

clear that this was an anxiety-provoking situation for him. (Betty reported Gary had had difficulty separating since he was small). His drawings and stories reflected themes of loneliness. Gary described this drawing: "This is a boy crying. He got hit by a boy. He was sad." It appeared that Gary's outer tough guy bravado masked feelings of sadness. In this session Gary's play with toys was unfocused.

The next time we were to meet, Gary ran into the office and pushed open my office door without knocking. To his surprise, I was sitting with someone else. His face went from excitement to shame. Betty pulled at his arm and told him sharply, "I said to knock." Gary's elation deflated instantaneously; it was like the air going out of a balloon. I told Gary that I would be a few more minutes and then we could start. I could hear raised voices through the closed door. Not uncommonly, Gary's level of motor activity revved up and I had to coax him to enter the room. He was angry, grabbed something off the shelf, and threw it to the floor. Gary invoked a no-talking stance about what had happened. I had hurt him and he was angry. (I always appreciate when these incidents happen in the office. They provide a window into interactions at home and they open the door to a discussion of what happens there.)

   Gary's presentation in the second individual session was decidedly different from his presentation in the first. It took him considerable time to recover from the incident of barging into my office and he was much more intent and focused on his play. He demonstrated difficulty with tolerance for frustration and adherence to limit-setting (he pulled things down off the shelves, ran through one door of my office and out the other.) At the same time, he could be redirected when he was interested in a new toy or puppet he wanted to play with, and he persevered and demonstrated keen interest in working with his hands. He particularly enjoyed building a house for small animals. His play with animals was fierce; each one was attacked and died.

MAKING SENSE OF INFORMATION GATHERED

As I gathered material from my notes of the first telephone contact with Betty, the interview with Gary's teacher, my early sessions with Betty and Paul, and Gary's sessions, I began to fill in the following biopsychosocial chart. (Note: the chart is not completely filled in after one or two sessions with the family, but is a tool that can be/is constantly revised and amended. Gary's chart, Table 7.1, was developed over a period of time.)

Treatment Planning

Collection of this information helped us begin to understand Gary's difficulties from multiple perspectives. Gary's family and I identified several major areas that would become the focus of treatment.

   1. *Building family connections*. The goals of therapy here were (1) to have positive experiences together,[25] (2) to repair ruptures that were the result of insufficient bonding,[26] and (3) to deal with issues of attunement and misattunement. It is important to note that Gary's difficulties were *not only* a result of his early history. There were many influencing elements, such as an inherited temperament that made him prone to limbic arousal, sensory integration difficulties, and developmentally inappropriate levels of concentration and attention. A major task for this family would be to build connections that had been lost to them because of the neglect Gary experienced in the orphanage.

   2. *Improving family functioning*. Here the goal was to improve family functioning through a change in family dynamics. Betty needed to see Gary as separate from her father, Carmine. Also, the anxiety that Paul and Betty felt about Gary's anger had to be diffused. Betty needed to change her view of Gary; instead of seeing him as a "crazy" child, she needed to embrace the idea of Gary as a child with many strengths, who could manage his anger. Betty and Paul also needed help in becoming a firm and assertive team (although it was preferable to sacrifice firmness on behalf of connection). Betty needed to see that she could be a

Table 7.1 Identifying and Recording Biopsychosocial Variables: Gary and His Family

	Individual	Family	School/Peers/Community	Resources/Strengths	Treatment Targets & Planning
Biological and/or health, physical	restless, sleeping and eating difficulties, ADHD, tactile sensitivity, heightened physiological responses, irritable ③	mother overly sensitive to anger in others; father, "peace at any price"	hard to stay in his seat, oppositional behavior, demands teacher attention ① to ②	determination, persistence, tenacity, engaging, appealing, sense cf humor (+ +)	medication consult, sensory integration, slowing down/stopping ↓ stress ↑ coping skills
Psychological	temper tantrums, abrupt mood changes, angry, controlling, inability to self-soothe, curses, manipulative, uncooperative, never satisfied; destroys property, chronic shame, demands constant attention (– –) ③	defeat, despair; mother anxious and worried, rage and anger, feelings of disappointment, pessimism, and sadness; father avoids conflict and confrontation, tends to withdraw	feeling of not belonging in regard to classmates	above average intelligence, quick mind, sharp wit, engaging; mother persistent, resourceful; father optimistic, persistent, (+ +)	↑ attachment (repair) ↑ rebuild connections psychoeducation ↑ family functioning ↑ anger management ↑ empathy ↓ family reactivity ↓ feelings of defeat and despair
Social spiritual, cultural	only child, intact adoptive family	support system of family and friends (+ –)	poor peer relations, managing him in school problematic ③	can be a positive addition to the class, is interested in making friends (+)	↑ calm, cool environment ↑ friendships ↑ social skills ↑ expressed emotion ↑ parental warmth and positive involvement

Overall functioning: + + (excellent), + (above average), + – (average), – (below average), – – (very below)
Symptoms: ① transient, ② acute, ③ chronic
Treatment Targets: ↑ increase, ↓ decrease

competent, in-control, effective mother. Paul had to be drawn into the process and become more involved when Gary raged. Betty, Paul, and Gary needed help to find ways to reduce the chronically high stress levels in the house.

3. *Changing reactivity*. The goals were for Betty to be able to say "no" and to stand up to Gary's rages without being afraid of his anger, and for Paul to be more responsive when a problem occurred. At the same time, Gary needed to develop mechanisms for self-control and self-regulation. He needed techniques to manage his behavioral disinhibition, his anger, and his level of stress. Together, Gary, Betty, Paul, and I would become behavioral engineers; we would work to reduce expressed emotion and create a calm home where *everyone* was in charge of his or her anger. Keeping in mind Gary's biological make-up, temperament, brain development, and developmental delays, we would begin building "executive functions" by working on areas of weakness. Through psychoeducation, family members would gain new understandings of Gary's difficult behaviors, such as his intense reactions and need for control.

WORKING TOGETHER

New Understandings: Psychoeducation

Everybody needed to understand Gary's troubling behaviors. Betty and Paul thought these were due to an overdose of "won't." Some learning and thinking together was in order. Psychoeducation approaches are helpful. The therapeutic goals of this approach are as follows:

> The first is to impart information concerning the illness itself—its etiology, symptoms, expected course, the environmental determinants of exacerbations, and the conditions conducive to optimal quality of life. Information helps patients and families anticipate disruptions and changes in life style required by the illness, thereby increasing their capacity to cope constructively with these transitions. A second and perhaps more important effect of patient and family education is that it reframes the definition of and responsibility for the illness.[27]

Betty, Paul, and Gary worked with me to first understand the reasons for Gary's rages. We discussed his sensory integration difficulties, his executive function deficits, the poor habit training that resulted from problems of contingency management, and his feelings of not belonging. On one occasion, Gary wanted to get a new game that a classmate had. When Betty told him no, Gary fell apart, throwing things and screaming, "I hate you, you're a mean mommy, you never buy me what I want." Betty was unable to stay in control and Paul intervened. The scene ended as usual, with crying and later making up.

I suggested that it sounded like things got stormy very quickly. "Yes, a lot of thundering and lightening," commented Paul, picking up on the metaphor. I suggested that we all become "storm trackers." In session we "tracked the storm" of Gary's outburst regarding the game. We discovered that Gary felt that several boys were going to Roger's house because Roger had new games. Gary felt left out of the fun and reasoned that if he had this game, he could be like the popular kids. His reaction to Betty's telling him no had little to do with the game per se; it was more about Gary's feelings of belonging/not belonging.

Watch Out for Attacks

We discussed different kinds of "attacks" that make it difficult to be in Gary's skin. Gary laughed as I described the attack of the labels. We acted it out and he used his hand to demonstrate how they "bit" his neck.

He loved the idea of a "snack-attack." I wondered if the sense of urgency around food might have roots in his sugar levels. We tracked some explosions and they seemed to occur more frequently when, as Paul put it, "Gary's tank was on empty." This seemed worse at the end of the school day. We made a plan to have food available before anyone talked to him. This helped him stay calmer.

Betty's voice was irritating to Gary and felt like a "blame attack." Gary commented that he hated when his mother talked to him in her "list voice" (Gary do this, Gary do that . . .). Betty and I worked together to stop the "shower of commands,"[28] which made him furious at her.

We discussed the idea of "shame-attacks,"[29] which by far had the most serious consequences. Betty's history left her vulnerable to feeling overwhelmed by shame as well. Helping Betty and Paul to understand Gary in new ways changed the way they saw him and understood the meaning of his behavior. Instead of selfish, demanding, insatiable, they began to understand that some of Gary's behaviors had their roots in his biology.

Meltdowns

Gary was prone to "meltdowns"[30] that were not simply willful acts, but were responses that took place at times of misattunement, disconnection, or missed connection. Meltdowns may happen when the child experiences a "no," a shaming experience, or what seems to the parent like a well-deserved punishment. In Gary's situation, it appeared that he had become sensitized[31] to what he experienced as slights from others. It is important to note that his appraisal[32] of any feeling of having been slighted resulted in an instantaneous response. One of the techniques to counteract meltdowns is soothing, but just how does a parent encourage soothing, especially self-soothing? Gary had never seemed to enjoy calming activities such as lap-time, story reading, or parallel play activities. As a result, he and Betty had a paucity of these experiences in the "mother-son bank."

We needed to increase the level of empathy between them and help Betty understand Gary's experience. It was crucial for Betty to see Gary in a more positive fashion to convey a more positive attitude to her child. Often, these restless children aren't even "there" enough to absorb the soft gaze or the moment-to-moment offerings by the mother. Let's not forget what these moments mean, not only in the bonding sense, but also in the development of the architecture of the brain.[33] In therapy, over time Betty and Gary were able to increase the level of empathy for one another by broadening their joint tasks. Making lanyards together, cooking, learning the keyboard, and making a spice garden were all activities that promoted new feelings of connectedness. Gary was the leader. Betty and Paul found different activities to enjoy with Gary. They began with very small doses and increased the time gradually.[34]

Family Meetings

The family agreed to meet at home once a week. Snacks, a game, and a shared activity would follow the meeting. The rules were developed and agreed upon by all. The family decided how they would tally and use the points they would earn during the meetings. We typed up the following document:

Earn Points	Cost Points
"T.I.S." Stay in your seat	Yelling
Listen when someone talks	Using your hands instead of words
Wait your turn to talk	Leaving the room
Keep your hands and feet to yourself	
Use Stop & Think	
Use nice talking	
Participate	
Stay in the room	
Follow directions	

Teaming up: The Problem's the Problem

One pervasive problem for this family was that anger often took up residence in their home. When anger was there, family members succumbed to its powers and acted in ways that caused them to feel badly about themselves and their behavior. The problem was the problem.[35] The family decided that when Mr. Mean and Mr. Anger were around, good judgment went out the window. We tracked times when these heinous guys weren't around and what the family could do to resist their powers when they were around. The family joined together to make a team to stop Mr. Mean from taking over.[36] We made a video together of Gary yelling at Mr. Anger. Betty and Paul shouted too. Gary smiled as Betty scolded Mr. Anger, "Stop bothering my boy. We don't like you. Leave us alone!" This was a paradigm shift for the family. Gary wasn't the problem.

    ◯ Mr. Mean and Mr. Anger

TOOLS AND ACTIVITIES

The 4 Cs: Calm, Cool, Collected, and Connected

Children like Gary who have difficulties with self-control do best in environments that are "calm and cool," where everyone is "collected" and in charge of his or her emotions. Because family reactivity was high, one of the first goals of therapy was to help this family create a calmer home environment. Working on this became a whole family experience. Self-control, if present in the child, is usually modeled by the parent. The interactive nature of some problems mandates that treatment be focused on all parties involved. Thus, it was essential that the child and his parents be treated concurrently.

The first 3 Cs, staying calm, cool, and collected, are not enough without the fourth C, staying connected. Connection was such a crucial step with this family that we focused on this aspect. Gary's early experience had been profoundly lacking. His early experiences, deeply etched onto the template for future relationships, were easily evoked. (For many children like Gary, these early experiences are perceived as enormously shameful ones. When they are evoked, the child responds to them violently.)

A child with heightened states of physiological arousal, who is hypersensitive to stimuli and easily frustrated, does best in a home environment with low expressed emotion (i.e., low levels of hostility and criticism expressed by the caretaker, generally the mother or the father).[37] Because Betty had not found an appropriate way to get Gary to comply with parental requests, events had spiraled out of control. Gary was aggressive with his parents; out of desperation, Betty reacted in kind. Instead of downshifting whenever Gary got excited, the family went into overdrive. This, in turn, caused Gary's anxiety to mount and his behavioral difficulties to become exacerbated. We searched for ways to turn down the volume on the screaming, yelling, hitting, anxiety, and tension. When Gary got angry it was as if his brain got locked. He dug in his heels and it seemed as if his choice was written in stone. Often, when overwhelmed by environmental stimuli, he had rages and tantrums.[38]

Children like Gary also have tantrums because it's exciting; it activates other family members. They also report then feeling calmed down because something is released in the brain during the tantrum. Using the word "no" with these children is like waving a red flag in front of a bull. "Charge" is written all over it! We work together on finding positive ways to say "no." One simple approach to help parents encode this is to teach them to use "when-then" command sentences: "*When* you finish your homework, *then* you can put on the television."[39]

Here is Betty and Paul's list.

Write all the ways you can say "yes."

1. Yes you can watch TV, as soon as you finish your homework.

2. When you put this game away, then we can go to the park.

3. Sure we can go to the park; let's pick up all the toys and we'll go.

4. First you brush your teeth, and then we'll read a story.

♡ Track the storm, when-then sentences, brain locking, the 4 Cs

Other approaches that Betty and Paul used to help calm the storms in the house came from didactic instruction in therapy that will be described in many of the following activities. An important aspect of our work together involved learning and using contingency management principles.[40] They learned how to pinpoint problem behaviors, reinforce appropriate behaviors, eliminate or extinguish inappropriate behaviors, use punishment appropriately, and set limits. We discovered that they inadvertently taught Gary to misbehave by using "the 50-50 rule" (about 50 percent of the time they didn't follow through and allowed Gary to refuse to comply with requests). We called this "oops" because it inadvertently trained Gary to misbehave.

♡ "Oops"

Stop/Stop & Think

When we started our work together, Gary did not know how to slow down or how to stop. Some of the first activities that we did together focused on finding words and actions that would facilitate Gary's slowing and stopping. First, we learned and practiced "snail-time." After hopping all over the office like rabbits, Gary and I practiced moving slowly like snails. Then we reminded ourselves about how we need to learn how to put on the brakes on a bicycle and how to stop when we're wearing roller blades. Gary used his expert knowledge to demonstrate these stops. For help with *when* to stop, we looked at a traffic light I have in my office and we reviewed what the different colors mean.

I told Gary, "We want to start something. Which light would tell us to do that?" "Go," he said, "that's a green light." Stopping something, we decided, was a red light; the yellow light means slow down, like when the teacher tells you to stop running in the halls. Betty, Paul, and I took turns asking Gary about different activities and Gary used the traffic light to answer. As we asked about common things he does each day, Gary would put his hand on the right color light. "Gary, it's time to start your homework, brush your teeth, come to the table, put on your pajamas (green lights)"; "no yelling, shut the television, time to stop playing" (red lights).

I gave Betty and Paul large colored circles to take home as prompts. I suggested that they play a game by naming an action and asking Gary whether he should be starting, stopping, or slowing down. Gary would respond either by guessing what color circle he thought they were hiding behind their backs, or would put his hand on the appropriate colored circle displayed in front of him.

Snail-time, green light, red light, stop, stop and think

Another activity that facilitated learning to stop was **Red Light, Green Light, 1, 2, 3,** which Paul and Betty both remembered playing as children. In this game, whoever was "it," played the "stoplight." The rest of the players tried to sneak up and tap "it." Everyone lined up about 15 feet away from whoever was the stoplight. That person would turn facing away from the players and say "green light." Everybody would keep moving toward the stoplight. Suddenly the stoplight would say "red light!" and quickly turn around. Anybody caught moving after "red light" had been called, was out. Play resumed when the stoplight turned back around and said "green light." The stoplight won if all the kids were out before anyone was able to touch him or her. Otherwise, the first player to touch the stoplight won the game and earned the right to be the stoplight for the next game.

They played Red Light, Green Light, 1, 2, 3 at home. **Freeze** was another game we used to work on stopping. Using a portable tape player that I keep in the office, we played music and then froze when the music stopped.

Gary rated us on how we did. These playful games were helpful in getting Gary to respond to "stop."

🏠 I laminated a stop sign and gave it to Paul and Betty to take home. Everybody worked together on stopping.

💬 Freeze

Learning to stop and think is essential in interactions in the family. Gary seemed better able to control himself with his friends than with his parents. He decided this was because he didn't want to embarrass himself in school. However, when someone slighted him, he often had retaliatory fantasies. Betty and Paul talked to Gary about the difference between thinking and doing. "We all get angry, but you can't hurt anyone," they said. Gary told a

 story about a girl, Carol, who didn't let him play with her group during lunch. Gary felt like punching Carol, but he used "stop and think" and then, instead of doing what he wanted to do, he *drew a picture* of what he wanted to do and named it "Slap." "It's okay to think it, but you can't do it. Hands are not for hitting," we decided. "They are for pointing, writing, hugging, picking up French fries, making bead necklaces, but not for hitting."

The next step was to practice **Stop and Think.** I provided these representations and Gary drew his own.

🏠 Stop and Think signs.

💬 Stop and think

Tug-of-War

Betty and Paul reported that they often got into major tangles with Gary. "Some days we are at war." Gary agreed. I took out a jump rope that I save for these occasions. I gave Betty and Paul one end, and Gary the other. "Pull," I suggested, "and let's see what happens." Betty and Paul took turns tugging at their end of the rope, with Gary, at the other, saying that he wanted to win. At one point, Gary pulled so hard that he caught Betty by surprise and Betty almost fell down. "Someone could get hurt when both you and Mommy pull at the rope," I commented. "Does that ever happen at home, that you and Mommy or Daddy want different things and you fight to see who wins?" "All the time!" was everyone's quick reply. I asked: "What could happen if Gary comes to you and asks you to have a tug-of-war and you don't pick up the rope?" Paul said, "I probably would be more in control of my anger." Betty agreed. I asked Betty and Paul to list all the things that might help them to stay away from the rope.

Betty's List

1. Breathe.
2. Keep the angry words in my mouth.
3. Talk to myself to calm down.
4. Tell Gary I don't want to fight with him, I would rather play with him.
5. Ask Paul for help.
6. Use my words to tell Gary that I am getting upset and need to calm down.
7. Put on my yoga tape and ask Gary if he wants to do it with me.

Paul's List

1. Say over and over to myself, "I will not pick up the rope."
2. Keep breathing.
3. Stay calm.

Afterward, Gary rehearsed with Betty and Paul, trying to give them the rope. Each time I asked him to rate how they did in not picking it up.

Another important aspect of the work with Betty and Paul involved discussing behavioral principles. I predicted that it was very likely that, as they tried to extinguish their old response of picking up the rope, Gary would *increase* his "in-your-face behavior." "Stick-to-it really counts," I told them. Giving in and picking up the rope would reinforce Gary's unacceptable behavior. He would learn that there was a payoff for persistence. Getting them involved and upset was a huge reinforcement for him. Detaching coolly, without sarcasm or annoyed body language, was an essential skill for Betty and Paul to learn.

🏠 Betty and Paul took home their lists of ways not to pick up the rope, and re-read them each day. They rated themselves on their progress. This was ongoing work.

💬 Tug of war, "I won't pick up the rope"

Ready, Aim, Fire

In one session, I brought in a ring toss game. Gary was eager to play and we all talked about how ring toss works. I asked him, "If I closed my eyes and threw the ring, would I get it on the stick?" Gary told me that closing my eyes wasn't a good idea and that I had better look before throwing. I then asked him, "If I threw the ring in back of me would that work?" He told me that I needed to throw the ring to where the stick was. I thanked him and asked Betty and Paul if they knew what word described what I needed to do. They said I had to "aim" the ring at the stick so that when I threw the ring, I could send it to where the stick was waiting. We decided the first step in ring toss was "get ready," then "aim," then "throw." We wrote down these steps. I told Gary there was a game called "ready, aim, fire" that had these same steps. Paul remembered that when he was small he had played cowboys and had a toy gun. When pointing it, some kids would say "ready, aim, fire."

I have a plant in my office and we decided to use the water sprayer to "spritz" the plant. Gary demonstrated how the sprayer worked and we all practiced. First we got ready by stopping any other activity, then we aimed, and then we fired. We talked about what could happen if the person doing the spraying didn't get ready first. Gary told me that water could get all over the place. We talked about what happens when the person spraying doesn't aim before firing. "We make a mess and the plant still won't have the water," Gary responded. I told him that I was thinking that this was a lot like Stop and Think before we do something. He already knew how to play Freeze and Red Light, Green Light and was practicing how to stop. I told him that this is a new way to practice. I asked Paul and Betty if they were practicing Stop and Think. Betty said it was hard for her, but that she was trying. I asked them whether they usually "get ready and aim" before they "fire," that is do or say something. Betty said she often "fires" and skips "get ready and aim"! "What happens then," I asked? "Boom," said Gary and everybody laughed. Betty, Paul, and Gary drew pictures of what it looks like when they use the steps and what it looks like when they don't use them. They all voted for the way they like it better. Betty said that she would try to "get ready" *before* she says something with a mean tone. Paul told us that he would try to use nice talking also. Gary said that he would try to "get ready" *before* he screams. He would try to use his words and nice talking. Each night at dinner they would talk about **Ready, Aim, Fire.**

🏠 Ready, Aim, Fire star sheet. The family filled in a star every time they used the steps in Ready, Aim, Fire. When the sheet was filled, they decided they would celebrate by bringing in Chinese food and renting a video.

💬 Ready, aim, *before* I fire.

The Thinking Cap: Learning Self-Control

We also worked on ways to help Gary develop his *thinking cap*. I used a model of the brain[41] and showed him where the "thinking cap" is. We then looked at where the feeling part of the brain is and saw how the thinking brain covers it. We talked about how all the parts of the brain have "telephone wires" that help them "talk" to the other parts. Sometimes, the feeling part talks louder and tries to be the "boss." This can be a good thing or not such a good thing. This is the list we made together.

Good Thing	Not a Good Thing
Tells you when you feel bad	You get too mad
Lets you be happy	You get too happy and can't do your homework
Tells you if there is something scary	Get too excited
I like my feelings	Can't listen to your thinking cap
Feelings are fun	No part should shout

From our discussion we decided that if the feeling brain was shouting, "Be mad, be mad, be mad," over and over, then we couldn't listen to what the thinking cap was telling us. The thinking cap tells us stuff like "Calm down," "Make a good choice," and "Use your words." If we listen to these messages from the thinking cap, we usually don't get into trouble. The problem is that when your feeling brain is screaming, it's hard to hear the advice from your thinking cap. Gary concluded that this would not be a good thing! The family decided that it is good that the feeling part talks to us, but we have to be careful when it shouts, "Be mad." "What could happen," I wondered, "if we listened. We could get even angrier; what happens then?" "Boom," Gary replied. Everybody agreed. We discussed what they could do to listen to their thinking caps. Betty said she would "Stop, think, and breathe." Paul said, "Don't do anything, just listen." And Gary would try to "Use stop and think."

They all drew pictures of doing what they said they were going to do. They took the pictures home to display in a special place as a reminder of this conversation.

We had many other conversations about the thinking cap. One week, we made a model of it, another week we wrote a play about the thinking cap and the feeling brain talking to one another. Gary had a fertile imagination and eagerly helped to develop activities for all of us. We played "How to Win a Million Dollars" by answering questions about the thinking cap and the feeling brain. Gary, of course, was the moderator.

 Thinking cap

As part of the session one week we made talk bubbles and wrote down some of the ideas that everybody had about how to use the thinking cap.

They took the sheet of talk bubbles home. We folded a piece of paper into sixteen boxes. Each time Gary read or used his talk bubbles, he drew a happy face on the folded sheet. When he filled in the whole page they ordered a pizza and he got to watch television for an extra half hour.

Going from Hot to Cool

In this exercise, Gary drew pictures of "cool thoughts," and Betty and Paul cut out pictures of "cool thoughts" from magazines. Gary commented that Betty picked out a lot of pictures about shopping. "That's right" Betty said, "Shopping relaxes me." Gary's pictures are shown below.

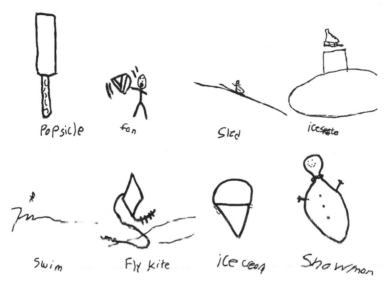

PoPsicle   fan   Sled   iCeskate

Swim   Fly kite   iCe cean   Showman

"I can think cool things and calm down!!!"

We discussed how talk "heats" you up. When you get "hot" it's very hard to use your thinking cap. Here is a story that Gary dictated and I typed.

Hot talk is the kind of talk someone does that gets a person angry or upset instead of calm. My father says it's like having flames around a pot and you make them bigger. The more angry you get the bigger the flames get.

These are examples of hot talk: "Why should I clean up, the other kids were playing," "It's his fault," "She just likes to get me in trouble," "That's not fair," "I'm sick of this," "Other kids do things and they don't get in trouble." "How come they never believe me?"

I'm working on using cool talk.

💬 Hot talk, cool talk

Ping-Pong and the "Tell–Don't Yell Rule"

As a systems thinker, I always consider the interactive nature of the struggles that families bring to each session. Working on Gary's part of the problem without the rest of the family would be a lopsided treatment. Gary could not change without change taking place in the family system. In one session, I asked Gary to explain how ping-pong is played. He told me that one player hits the ball over the net, and then the other hits it back. I asked him to tell what happens when one player hits the ball a little harder. Does the other player hit it back a little harder? What about a slam? If one player slams the ball does the other slam it back? We decided that the way one player hits the ball affects the way the other player hits it. "Just like us at home," Betty said. "When I yell, Gary yells back." "When I yell, Mommy yells. It's like ping-pong," Gary retorted. "Is it fun?" I asked? "No way! I hate it," said Gary. Paul and Betty agreed. From our discussion we concluded that the way one person behaves could affect another person's behavior. They decided that if one person "picks up the rope" the other person would pull at the other end. If one person yells, the other person will yell. I asked everybody to figure out what would help him or her not yell. Gary said that if his mom and dad *tell* instead of *yell,* it would help. The "tell-don't yell rule" was born.

🏠 When someone yells, the other person pointedly says, "I want to listen, please tell—don't yell."

💬 Tell—don't yell

Chaining Trouble Result Cycles:
Learning about "More of the Same"

In one session, Paul came in talking about a persistent struggle that he and Gary got stuck in at homework time. I listened and then suggested that we "chain" the struggle. *Chaining* an event is a helpful way to break it down into small steps. Chaining offers a hands-on approach and a visual way to examine the sequence of an incident. It provides a way of looking back to figure out what happened. Paul described the struggle, and I wrote down the sequence of events, each step on a separate strip of paper. When the first step in the cycle had been identified and written down, we stapled the ends of that strip together to form a circle with the writing facing outward. We wrote the next step on the next strip, placed the end of the second sentence strip through the first circle and stapled the ends together. We repeated this, and each step became a link in the paper chain.

Links in the Chain (as Dictated by Paul)

1. Gary annoys me to do his homework with him the minute I get home.

2. He sits there and doesn't try to do it himself.

3. That makes me angry and I scold him.

4. He yells back at me.

5. The more I scold him, the more he gets angry.

6. The more he gets angry, the more I get angry. (I'm even so angry that it starts in the car when I'm on my way home.)

We constructed the paper chain, a visual representation of the entire incident in which each link represents one of the steps. We held up the chain and examined it to see where Paul and Gary could have made different choices. We read each step aloud. We looked at each step and I asked Paul and Gary if they could have done something differently to change the way the chain of events ended up. I encouraged Paul, Betty, and Gary to brainstorm ideas that could change the chain of events. We concluded that there were certain points in the chain where they could have made different and better choices. We cut the chain to visually demonstrate "breaking off" the rest of the trouble sequence and throwing it away.

I told the family that theirs was a "more-of-the-same approach"[42] that usually got everybody into trouble. In this case, the more Paul used his solution to the problem (scolding) the more it caused trouble between him and Gary. The more Gary used his solution to the problem (nagging) the more he got in trouble for not starting on his own.

I explained that when we can't solve a problem, it's not always because we don't try hard enough. Sometimes, even though we are working hard to solve a problem, we get stuck. We keep trying that same failed solution over and over again. This can create new problems. And sometimes the new problems are bigger than the original problem! This "more-of-the-same approach" approach keeps us stuck. We call it a "vicious cycle."

📖 Strips to make a paper chain

💬 "Let's chain it," "vicious cycle," "more-of-the-same approach"

Examining Negative Reinforcement[43]

Betty and Paul discussed typical family interactions and we examined them together. Through situations like the following, the whole family learned that each influences the others' behavior and that using aversive behavior gets a payoff (a reward). The solution becomes an immediate, but highly ineffective way to end conflict. This cycle of behavior is coercive, and can easily escalate to an act of physical aggression.[44]

Situation One: Betty or Paul asks Gary to bring his plate to the kitchen → Gary engages in "in-your-face screaming" → Betty or Paul repeats the request → Gary engages in more "in-your-face screaming" → Betty or Paul can't stand listening to the screaming and pick up the plate and carries it to the kitchen for Gary.

What happened: Betty or Paul withdrew the request, which stopped the aversive stimulus (Gary's "in-your-face screaming"). In behavioral terms, this is called negative reinforcement. Gary was negatively reinforced for his screaming; he escaped having to carry the dish into the kitchen by using "in-your-face" screaming. The likelihood that he will employ this same tactic the next time he doesn't get his way is *very* high. A negative reinforcement cycle resulted in which (1) Gary, when confronted with an aversive stimulus (e.g., a request, command), (2) engaged in an inappropriate behavior (screaming), (3) parent(s) gave in, stopped asking (aversive stimulus is removed), (4) Gary gets reinforced for screaming, (5) cycle repeats.

Situation Two: Betty or Paul asks Gary to do something → Gary refuses → Betty or Paul repeats request → Gary whines and complains and doesn't comply → Betty or Paul walks over and grabs Gary's arm, pulling Gary up → Gary complies → Betty or Paul gets reinforced for using aggressive behavior to get Gary to comply.

What happened: Gary complied after Betty or Paul used physical force. As a result, the parent's action was negatively reinforced because it served to end the aversive whining, noncompliant behavior. What is the likelihood that they will continue to employ aggression? No doubt, Betty and Paul will be extremely likely to use the same tactic the next time Gary refuses their requests. What became clear from the dissection of family interactions was that Betty and Paul, as well as Gary, were rewarded (reinforced) for their behavior. When Gary commented that since Betty and Paul grabbed his arm or pulled his hair it was okay to grab theirs, Betty and Paul stopped and looked at each other sadly. I commented that while these types of solutions may work in the short-run, they have disastrous effects long-term. [45]

"Good Result" Cycles

In the next session, we looked at cycles of behavior that produce good results or happy endings. If we can figure out what we did right, then we can do that over and over again. It's like practicing the right steps of a dance that we want to learn. I asked them if they agreed. I told them about John to illustrate the point.

1. John wants to talk to his teacher but she is busy.
2. He waits patiently.
3. The teacher notices John's patience and hurries to finish what she is doing so she can speak with him.
4. John uses polite talking. Then he thanks her and goes back to his seat.
5. The next time John wants something from the teacher she looks to help him as quickly as she can.

We decided that *the more* John helps the teacher by waiting patiently, *the more* the teacher looks to help John. We made a list of situations where "more of the same" gets you good results. Then we made chains of several good result cycles.

- Sharing with a friend who comes over to play
- Studying for a test
- Helping at home
- Following instructions the first time you are asked to do something

📖 Gary drew a picture of John's story and took it home as a reminder of a good result cycle.

💭 "This looks like it could have a bad ending" "I think this is a good-result cycle" "How can we make this have a good ending?"

Making Friends

Rejection by his peers was not without consequences.[46] Gary was an isolated, sad, and lonely boy. Betty and Paul believed that Gary lacked the necessary skills for making friends. More correctly, he seemed to have many requisite skills, but appeared unable to use them. I offered a helpful conceptualization from Gresham,[47] a well-known researcher in the area of social skills training who looks at social skill problems along the dimensions of skill deficits, performance deficits, and self-control skill deficits (Table 7.2).[48] Those individuals with "skill deficits," he posits, may not have acquired the necessary cognitive and behavioral skills for social competence. There appears to be another group that includes individuals who seem to have the skills as part of their behavioral repertoire, but they do not perform them (performance deficits). Self-control deficits, he explains, are evidenced in children who lack the sufficient behavioral restraints required to impede aggressive or impulsive and disruptive behaviors.

Table 7.2. Gresham's Classification of Social Skill Problems

Emotional Arousal Response	Acquisition Deficit	Performance Deficit
Absent	Social skill deficit	Social performance deficit
Present	Self-control skill deficit	Self-control performance deficit

Gary had both acquisition and performance deficits. Our beginning work focused on finding targets for social skill intervention. Gary's teacher and Cub Scout leader were helpful in acting as coaches in other settings. Play dates were kept short and supervised, so as to build in successful experiences.

In addition, Gary worked with me in concrete ways to examine his choices. A medication consult proved valuable, as Gary's new medicine helped him to be less impulsive. We decided that he was developing a "pause" button. Gary and I drew a trouble-result cycle. While it had a bad ending for him, he was able to identify times in the sequence when he might have made a better choice. This was progress.

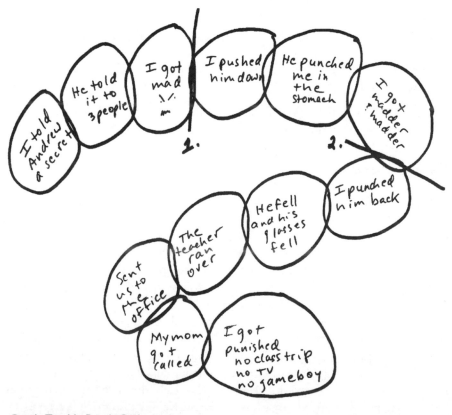

Gary's Trouble Result Cycle

"Larger-Systems" Work: School

Children spend a large amount of their time in school. Sending therapy home with a child also means getting them to transport new skills into other settings and the larger systems they participate in. Gary and I worked together to find the secrets of getting along with the teacher. We listed things that would make a teacher happy and unhappy:

A Happy Teacher	An Unhappy Teacher
Good listening	Talk when you're not supposed to talk
Raise your hand	Call out
Do homework	Sharpen pencils when she talks
Pay attention	Make faces
Do your work	Make fun of her
Sit up tall	Lie on the table

We also worked with Gary's teacher to help her understand how she could help Gary in the classroom. Fortunately, the fit between Gary and Mrs. M was a good one. We talked to Mrs. M about how Gary has "curious" hands and a squirmy body. He needs to move around and take wiggle breaks. His relentlessness was reframed as persistence and tenacity, important qualities for life.

The End: No, the Beginning

My work with Betty, Paul, and Gary took place over two and a half years. Along the way, Gary was diagnosed with a mood disorder. Medication was one of the best helpers on the team. As he learned more self-control, his dosage was reduced. The tools we worked on together acted like the casts around broken bones that help them heal. Increasing bonding, improving attunement, strengthening Gary's abilities to self-soothe and self-regulate, and developing Gary's executive functions, began to create changes in the whole family. Simple activities like collecting "caught ya" points (as they caught each other doing something right) helped to change how they saw each other. Betty started to notice Gary's best behaviors instead of accidentally reinforcing his worst behaviors (remember, "oops"). This made Gary happier and clearly very proud. He often flew into my office to tell me about all his good choices. Paul's response to Betty was very warm as he noticed that she was now on the lookout for positive rather than negative happenings. The house became a place where he wanted to be. He commented that instead of running away as he did in his family when he was young, he now looked forward to coming home. At the end of our work together Gary was no longer internalizing anxiety to the same extent. He didn't feel the need to maintain his position of inflexibility in order to protect himself from the ever-present assaults from the environment and from his chaotic sense of self. Paul became active in handling disruptions at home, and Betty became a more attuned mom. Gary's capacity for relatedness increased. Betty, who had previously seen herself as incompetent, began to gain confidence in her mothering and relax. The 4 Cs, calm, cool, collected, and especially connected, are the "glue" that is helping them become the family she wished for. As she began to separate Gary's rages from events in her own traumatic past, she was able to tune in to Gary's inner moods. As a result of their efforts, the family found themselves on a new path.

A Group Intervention for Children with Learning Disabilities and Their Families

A Biopsychosocial Approach

In this chapter, we move from treatment of individual families to treatment of more than one family at a time. The chapter also offers a biopsychosocial perspective as a guide to understanding variations in learning. The first part of the chapter discusses different definitions of learning disabilities and includes a discussion of how these disabilities affect an individual's development, the lives of those with whom that individual lives, and the world outside the home. The second part of the chapter discusses *The Unique Minds Program*, an innovative multiple family discussion group intervention[1] developed by the Unique Minds Project at the Ackerman Institute in New York City. Included in the discussion of the program are strategies to address biopsychosocial targets. The techniques presented are easily translated for use with individuals and individual families.[2]

I'M JUST STUPID

Mitchell and his family started the session arguing. His father, Kevin, said he was disgusted with his son, who at age 11, "still can't find his way to the store around the corner." "He'll never grow up, the way she [pointing to his wife] babies him. She practically wipes his nose."

"He needs help; can't you see he needs help?" sighed Frances, Mitchell's mother.

Kevin yelled, "I had the same problems in school and I made out okay."

"Help? *He* needs help? What about me?" shouted Dolores, Mitchell's older sister. "Helpless Mitchell needs a personal driver, maid, butler, and homework helper. There's nothing left over for me. It's his fault that we have to come here, too."

As the family drama unfolded, I looked over at Mitchell, whose eyes were downcast. Then he looked up and our eyes made contact. "His are sad eyes," I thought to myself. Mitchell's response to his father's tirade was barely audible: "I'm just stupid. They think I'm lazy and tell me that if only I would try harder I could do better. I try but I can't."

The travails of childhood make it tough for many kids, but it's even tougher when failure casts its dark shadow at home and at school. This is what we found when my colleagues and I interviewed families in which at least one family member was diagnosed with a learning disability. Children struggle to get through the day while others call them "lazy." They may work hard, but have little to show for their efforts. Fights over homework, book reports, and getting out in the morning become daily events. Like a pernicious virus, the fallout that accompanies a learning problem infects family life. Common threads weave a patchwork of sadness, failure, defeat, shame, and blame. Those who are able to talk about it say they feel enormous shame and self-doubt. Parents, many of them learning disabled themselves, are haunted by their own school failure. Those who succeed, talk about a sense of fraudulence. My colleagues and I were deeply touched by their stories and their valiant efforts to get help and find answers.

LEARNING DISABILITIES

A Definition

The definition of a learning disability[3] is, in itself, a subject for extensive review.[4] While approximately 5 percent of the school-age population is diagnosed as learning disabled,[5] investigators in this field have considerable difficulty agreeing on what exactly is meant by the term. They continue to encounter the basic problem of finding a qualified definition.[6] The variety of definitions results in confusion for those who struggle to make sense out of a child's uneven school performance, testing reports, teacher's feedback, the child's complaints, and their own observations. Not having answers leads to increased anxiety, worry, and concern. It also leaves family members feeling helpless.

In the last decade, there has been a growing consensus to employ the definition proposed by the National Joint Committee on Learning Disabilities.[7]

Learning disabilities is a general term that refers to a heterogeneous group of disorders manifested by significant difficulties in the acquisition and use of listening, speaking, reading, writing, reasoning, or mathematical abilities. These disorders are intrinsic to the individual, presumed to be due to central nervous system dysfunction, and may occur across the life span. Problems in self-regulatory behaviors, social perception, and social interaction may exist with learning disabilities but do not by themselves constitute a learning disability. Although learning disabilities may occur concomitantly with other handicapping conditions (for example sensory impairment, mental retardation, serious emotional disturbance) or with extrinsic influences (such as cultural differences, insufficient or inappropriate instruction), they are not the result of those conditions or influences.[8]

Mel Levine[9] offers a most functional understanding of learning disabilities. He uses a developmental view of learning and asserts that, since we all have unique neurodevelopmental profiles, it is understandable that at times in a child's development the fit between the expectations of the environment and the child's profile will be poor. His user-friendly, experience-based framework helps parents to understand their children's learning weaknesses and needs, and to devise strategies to help them. The fundamental premise is that each child learns differently. Each child, family, and teacher should understand the child's particular learning profile, which includes strengths and weaknesses. Levine's model discourages labeling in favor of informed observation and description. He believes that the term "learning difference" is more appropriate than the current nomenclature, "learning disability." Labeling children is often a prophesy of failure. He suggests that when children are struggling with academic work, educators, psychologists, and parents should carefully examine the "phenomena" that impede academic achievement.[10]

Biopsychosocial Impact on Individual Development

Confronting the continual challenges posed by a learning difficulty takes its toll. Stress is one byproduct. Kate tells us her hands start sweating as the reading period approaches. The bathroom frequently becomes her refuge. The day-to-day tension affects her and she often wakes up with "awful butterflies" in her tummy. The fight to get her out of the house in the morning is nothing short of monumental.

Researchers find that a learning disability contributes to the shaping of a child's development. The psychological consequences on children and adolescents are cumulative and traumatic.[11] There are common patterns such as low-level chronic depression, distress, stress,[12] and anxiety. Negative inner representations clearly color the world of the child with a learning disability—who he is and who he will become.[13] Learning difficulties cause negative attributions and negative affect, which impact on achievement and behavior.[14] For some individuals, this impact is lifelong and chronic. "Except for those few with a maturational delay, the learning disabled child will be the learning disabled adolescent and, later, the learning disabled adult."[15]

Many individuals with learning disabilities fail to clear the hurdles that are the demands of our complex society. They are "success deprived."[16] They move along the developmental trajectory, but they often don't seem to fare better in adolescence. In interviewing families, we find that as the children get older there is increased turmoil and anger. The needs of the child with a learning disability pull for closeness and supervision from adults; in direct contrast, the pulls of adolescence are toward autonomous functioning.[17]

While the discussion here focuses on the collective cost of uphill battles, it is important to note that dealing *successfully* with difficulty has a positive impact on individual development. Many people tell us that it fosters an "if at first you don't succeed, try, try, again" attitude. With an understanding of their own strengths and weaknesses and huge doses of assistance and support from educational and home environments, many children succeed and grow. Dealing with their differences and struggles teaches them perseverance and gives them confidence in their ability to overcome obstacles.[18]

Impact on Social World and Relationships

I took the train into Manhattan last week and exited with the crowds during the morning rush hour. People pushed through the sea of humanity that hurried toward a long escalator. In the midst of the hurriers, I noticed a man sauntering along slowly. One commuter pushed past him and grimaced, as if to say, "Don't you know the unspoken rule? If you're not in a hurry, move over to the side and let the others pass." I noticed an unspoken rule also held true for those riding the escalators (and the moving sidewalks at the airport). The "rule" there seemed to be that there were actually two lines, a right and a left on each step. The right line was for those individuals who didn't want to climb the stairs as they were moving upward. The other line must be left open for the climbers. Heaven help anyone who doesn't figure out the rule! An unsuspecting person who does not comply with "escalator etiquette" can expect to be shoved, yelled at, told to "Move over," and probably insulted, "What are you, dumb or something? Can't you see you're in the way?" Kids and grown-ups who learn differently often can't figure out the rules. Take a minute to mull it over. How would you feel if you couldn't figure out the rules? Would you start to feel a little anxious? I know I would.

Many of the stories woven throughout this book tell of the effect that cognitive variations have on our interpersonal worlds. Negotiating the social world and understanding social nuance help us make sense of our experiences. The existence of learning disabilities might be most obvious in schoolwork, but the problems are insidious; they have an impact on other arenas as well. For example, learning disabilities affect relationships: How can you get your needs met, connect with others, understand your feelings, and grasp what is expected of you in relationships if you can't put your feelings into words or make sense of communications from others? Researchers report that there are differences between the social skills and social competencies of children and adolescents who have learning disabilities and those of their peers who do not. The social world of the child with a learning disability is different.[19] "No one likes me, I never get invited to parties,"[20] comments Lily. "People are mean to me, they talk and act angry."[21] Fourteen-year-old Curtis reports, "They act like they want to be my friend and I go over and they act like I'm invisible."[22] "I'm lonely." His 16-year-old sister, Victoria, tells him, "You act like a baby. Your friends act like they're 14, no wonder they don't want to be with you. Grow up.[23] Maybe then you'll have friends." Many children with learning disabilities are youngsters who have deficits in nonverbal social perception and comprehension, whose social problem-solving skills and behavioral adjustment are poor.[24]

In social situations, the effects of learning disabilities can be demoralizing. Zoe was so excited to be going out to lunch with her friends that she looked forward to it all week. It was finally Thursday, the day she would eat at the corner luncheonette with her buddies Susie and Cindy. The waiter brought the menus and Susie and Cindy quickly selected what they wanted to eat. Zoe had planned with her mom to order fish and chips so that she wouldn't need to read a menu. Much to her dismay, the waiter informed her that they served fish and chips only on Fridays. He handed back the menu and told her he would be right back to take her order. Zoe broke into a sweat and her fingers trembled as she opened the menu. The words on the pages were a blur, just as they were in her classroom during reading. She became so anxious she could hardly think. The waiter came back, pointed to the specials on the menu and asked Zoe if she would like to order one of them. Zoe was too embarrassed to tell him or her friends that she just couldn't read what was there. Susie and Cindy looked at her with great surprise as her face reddened and her eyes filled with tears. Zoe jumped up and left the restaurant with hunger pains in her belly and sadness in her heart.

Impact on School Adjustment

"Do you like school?" I ask Claudia. "I like coming, I like going; it's the part in between that I don't like." Ervin drew a picture: "Burn down the school" was his

solution. Manuel said that he wanted to put the principal's head in the toilet and just keep flushing. He wanted to place something on his teacher's seat that would make it sound like he passed gas. All the kids in the class would laugh at the teacher, just like they laugh at Manuel when he doesn't know the answer.

Children with learning disabilities often begin school with less "in the bank." Their accounts in the areas of making friends, attention and concentration, communication, and frustration tolerance may not have enough in them. When these children need to make withdrawals, there just isn't enough there. They start school in deficit spending and sometimes they never catch up.

Moreover, the demands of the academic world may not be in tune with the child's neurodevelopmental functioning. At any time, in any school, there are some children who are just not ready for the standard curriculum. Their differences make teaching a difficult job for today's educators. A mismatch between the child and his learning environment and its expectations can have tragic results.

Clearly, school is the shaping context in which children spend most of their time. The child who has a learning disability is much too frequently a loser at school because the people around him might not understand what's preventing him from performing.[25] Evan's relationship with his fourth grade teacher was not the best. He decided to try extra hard and had worked an entire weekend on a complicated graph. He was very proud of the fact that he had actually completed a project for one of the first times that year. It was Parent Night, and his mother went to his classroom with a smile, knowing that at last Evan had a piece of work that he was proud of. Outside the room, on the bulletin board, Ellen saw many, many graphs, but her son's was not among them. When she asked the teacher about this, remarking that Evan had finally put his heart into a project, Mrs. C replied that Evan's graph was "not colorful enough" and that she "did not choose to reward mediocrity." Evan did not complete another project that school year.

Children like Evan get frustrated and may give up; their self-image suffers and they develop a mind-set of failure that can generalize to other areas of their functioning. The cumulative nature of these experiences leads some students to withdraw and feel deeply ashamed that they don't meet the standards. Like Evan's, their papers are never displayed on bulletin boards and they tell me all the time, "The teacher is mean to me." They turn to alternative ways to get attention, such as assuming the role of class clown. As one student said, "I'm in charge of the laughs. At least they're not laughing *at* me."

Seven-year-old Zach comes from a single-parent home. His mother, Rosie, works full time, and her trip from work to home adds an hour and a half onto her day. For the past year, Zach had been getting into trouble in school. Conduct sheets and behavior reports were covered with marks of P for "poor," then N for "needs improvement," and finally U for "unsatisfactory." His academics were deteriorating. Rosie was called to the school for guidance meetings, and her parenting methods and long work hours came under scrutiny. Zach became more and more sullen and angry. In Zach's case, fortunately, the guidance counselor was aware that behavioral problems are often the result of learning difficulties that are unaddressed. An exhaustive evaluation was done, serious learning problems were diagnosed, and an intervention plan was initiated. All too frequently, however, children with learning disabilities do draw attention to themselves because of their behavioral difficulties. The learning problems masquerade as emotional disturbance and, while behavioral problems are addressed, the underlying learning disability is often neither diagnosed nor adequately treated.[26] A further consequence of this failure to diagnose and treat is that adolescents with learning disabilities commonly do not complete their education.

A learning disability impacts in school beyond academics. Teachers frequently comment to us about how messy the desks of learning disabled students are. Parents comment that their kids make a mess and leave a trail behind them. "She left for school looking neat as a pin but by the time I dropped her brother off half an hour later she looked as if she'd been ravaged." "He wears his clothing inside out; he can't even button his shirt." At the school where I worked as a psychologist we asked one of our colleagues to send up two students to help us collate and staple some parent notices. "Of course," she replied, "I'll send them right up." About ten minutes later, the two breathless students knocked at our door. "Where have you been?" we asked. We received the familiar reply, "We got lost." We sat them down and gave them simple instructions. But when the job was completed, many pages were upside down and backwards, with staples in the wrong corner.

Impact on the Family

It was not unusual when Roger pointed accusingly at his brother and complained bitterly, "There's not enough money to do *anything* because *he* needs tutoring and speech therapy." Time, too, is often unevenly spent, with stress a by-product.[27] Projects become family endeavors and parents often say, "We couldn't go out this weekend because 'we' had a book report due on Monday." While on the one hand, siblings may feel jealous and angry, and bemoan the sacrifices they are asked to make, on the other hand they worry about their siblings or feel responsible for them. In interview after interview, we saw small shoulders carrying big burdens.

Behavioral difficulties are common, but when the functional nature of the child's difficulties is not understood, families often create their own, possibly misconstrued, explanations for a child's behavior. A lack of adequate information can result in distorted explanations; these explanations interfere with the family's ability to empathize with and respond to a child's internal struggles, academic problems, and emotional needs.[28]

Schools and families often think that behavioral difficulties stem from underlying emotional problems. When these difficulties are not understood as related to learning disorders, the family may mistakenly be urged to seek psychological counseling. All too frequently, the psychotherapist, in turn, sees the problem as stemming from emotional issues within the child, low self-esteem or poor self-image, or from conflicts in the family. In addition, psychotherapists may not have the knowledge and experience to address underlying learning problems. The likely failure of their efforts may further demoralize both child and family. Because a family often unwittingly addresses the wrong end of the problem, they experience deep frustration at their failure to provide help for their child. This frustration can serve to exacerbate the child's problem by generating offsetting approaches that result in conflicts among family members. In addition, these interactions can generalize and become a part of the family's pattern of behaving, further undermining the family's capacity to respond appropriately to the needs of other family members.[29]

Impact on Society

In the absence of early and adequate identification and intervention, learning disabilities can contribute to serious problems. These problems include diminished self-esteem, school drop-out,[30] juvenile delinquency,[31] and poor literacy skills.[32] College students diagnosed with learning disabilities when they were young, recall more family stress during childhood and adolescence, and report more drug abuse, more delinquent acts, and more suicidal thoughts than the non–learning disabled.[33] Large numbers of adolescents undergoing treatment for substance abuse have learning disabilities.[34] Learning disabilities and substance abuse are the most common impediments to moving from welfare to work.[35]

The most deleterious outcome for society is that the chronic and consistent failure of these individuals results in their bowing out of the race, or as Levine so aptly puts it, "failure to strive."[36] The humiliation of school failure often results in rage against the school community and violent acts perpetrated against it. I worked as a psychologist on an inpatient ward and I'll never forget the chilling pronouncement of a patient who injured a teacher: "Paybacks are a bitch." Some may choose acceptance in a gang as an avenue to belonging. The end result can be a life of antisocial acts.

UNIQUE MINDS PROGRAM FOR CHILDREN WITH LEARNING DISABILITIES AND THEIR FAMILIES

As we have seen, learning disabilities impact on the individual, the family, and society. Our interviews with families struggling with a learning disability pointed out the extent and degree of their impact and made it obvious that there was a need for intervention. Table 8.1 presents a summary of the biological, psychological, and social dimensions and impacts of learning disabilities, as well as possible targets for interventions.

Over the past few decades, many interventions were developed to deal with children's problems with reading, writing, and math. Education has seen the evolution of special programs, including Orton-Gillingham and "Reading Recovery" for the slow reader, the nonreader, and the "different" reader. There are Chisenbop[37] and *Math Their Way* for remediating math failure, and approaches such as "whole language" and "creative spelling" for remediating problems with writing. While there was recognition of the devastating effects a learning disability has on the individual, there were no programs to help the family as a whole deal with the impact and the toll this disability takes on their emotional and relational world. The Unique Minds Program, a multiple family discussion group (MFDG) in action, was developed as a viable format for intervention with the family.

Psychoeducational multiple family discussion groups have a long history of usefulness. They have been effective with various populations such as those with chronic illness[38] and schizophrenia.[39] Researchers looking at the efficacy of MFDGs in preventing relapse of schizophrenic patients found them to be significantly more effective than a single-family treatment modality.[40] Additionally, with today's managed care restrictions, the MFDG is a cost-effective way of reaching more families. It is also a useful model for working with children with neurobiologically-based disorders. The groups provide psychoeducation and mutual support for the identified children, their siblings, and their parents. They address key areas of difficulty (behavioral, relational, and psychological) as these play out at home and in the educational setting.

Table 8.1 LD: Summary of Biopsychosocial Dimensions and Intervention Targets

	Individual	Family	School/Peers/Community	Resources/Strengths	Treatment Targets & Planning
Biological and/or health, physical	Variations in learning and attention that are biologically and neurobiologically based; health problems such as stomachaches and headaches, tension from chronic stress	Often a genetic component, hence found in other family members as well; others see child as immature, less developed in important areas of functioning	Social problems such as social misperception, impulsivity, anxiety in social situations; academic underachievement	Uncover strengths and hidden talents; how can the strengths be amplified? biological vulnerabilities in one setting can be strength in a different setting	↑ understanding of child's strengths and weaknesses; ↓ impact of biology through psychoeducation and referrals as needed; ↑ enhance learning by involving multiple senses in experiential activities
Psychological	Low self-esteem; depression; cumulative trauma; negative attributions about school, learning, and oneself; anxiety; stress; shame; problem understanding social nuance	Colors individual family members' view of the child; shame and blame	Neglected or rejected by peers	Identify many ways child and family demonstrate intelligence; respect the unique strengths of each family member	↑ normalization and reframing of LD as part of normal variations in learning that we all have; ↑ can-do thinking; ↑ hope & family co-operation; ↑ understanding of the LD child; ↑ problem-solving skills; ↓ can't-do thinking, isolation; ↑ advocacy
Social spiritual, cultural	Drop out; delinquency; substance abuse; failure to realize potential and contribute to society	Sense of aloneness and isolation; strained relationship with school and teacher	Social world affected; siblings affected	Explore helpful beliefs; find ways each family member is resourceful	↑ belonging; ↑ sibling understanding and help as needed; ↑ collaboration; ↑ social & network; ↓ blame

Treatment Targets: ↑ increase, ↓ decrease

The Unique Minds MFDG model is based on the idea that families who share a common problem (in this case a learning disability) are best able to help each other.[41] This program helps families to understand learning differences as part of normal variation. Normalizing of the problem begins to help families "find a place for the problem and put the problem in its place."[42] Instead of the learning disability always being on the front burner, its impact and influence are lessened as family members work together. Our model takes into account individual and family resources and strengths. We believe that families are "resource-full." The groups help to locate and develop strengths and affinities so that success is less elusive. Traditionally, problem solving has been an element of psychoeducational groups[43] and it is an important element of the Unique Minds Program.

The diverse needs of the children with learning differences call for a collaborative team approach that includes the family, the child, school personnel, and outside professionals who are involved with the child. Each member of the team, including the child (who must have an active role) has expert knowledge. Encouraging a child to become an expert on his own learning strengths and weaknesses and to engage with parents and teachers in creative problem solving helps him move from being a passenger on the bus to being in the driver's seat. An important goal is to have the child become an advocate for him- or herself.

The Unique Minds Program brings together five to six children with learning disabilities and their families, including siblings, for eight highly structured, scripted sessions. The aims of the program are to demystify learning disabilities, help families understand the emotional impact of learning disabilities on the child and the family, help families develop problem-solving skills and strategies, and ultimately learn to collaborate with larger systems (such as their children's schools). Other central goals of this intervention are to help families recognize, celebrate, and build on the unique strengths and talents of their children and help to increase each child's self-esteem and motivation for success. The program builds on the strengths and resources of the child, the family, and the school. It works to establish a climate of collaboration in which families and school personnel become partners and resources for each other. It also helps families develop a new language with which to discuss difficulties and to intervene in more helpful ways. Through the intervention, parents learn positive ways to work with their children.

The program tools are interactive, lively, experiential, and multisensory. These fun activities and simulation exercises help the participants see the world through the lens of the learning disabled child. The family context enhances the feeling of "we're in this together," the *esprit de corps* that has been lacking for many. There is wonderful group support, and families become cheerleaders for one another.

Principle Interventions[44]

1. The MFDG provides information about the nature of learning disabilities.
   - All group members participate in simulations that are "hands on." By experiencing what it feels like to have a learning disability, they validate the learning disabled child's subjective experiences of frustration and confusion. In this way, family members develop increased empathy for and understanding of the child's struggle.
   - The group helps families to perceive the learning disability as affecting only a small part of a child's overall potential. Howard Gardner's book, *Frames of Mind: Theory of Multiple Intelligences*, which develops the idea of multiple intelligences, is used as a model for the identification of other intelligences and strengths.[45]
2. The group enables the children with learning disabilities and their families to develop more effective strategies at home.
   - The group attempts to disrupt the negative emotional sequelae of the learning disability by exploring the child and family's beliefs about the learning problem and its impact on family relationships.
   - Children with learning disabilities become more aware of their educational and emotional needs and learn to communicate them, without shame, to other family members. By articulating their needs and gaining family support and acceptance, the children are empowered to become more active participants in their education.
   - Siblings are helped to understand the nature of learning difficulties and strengths. They need to understand that different children have different needs, and that each family member has his or her own contribution to make to the family. Most important, brothers and sisters must have an opportunity to discuss their own conflicts and difficulties with their learning-disabled sibling.
   - All family members, including the child with the learning disability, are helped to develop problem-solving skills that respect the unique needs and strengths of each family member.
3. Families network with other families.
   - Families gain perspective by listening to the experiences of other families.
   - Sharing with others serves to eliminate family isolation and helps families discuss the uniqueness and commonality of their own experiences.
   - Families collaborate to develop strategies that will work for their children.

- Children with learning difficulties and their families are provided with an ongoing support network. In order to provide continuity for families over time, a format exists for reconvening the groups at regular intervals.

4. Families are encouraged to develop strategies that enable them to become advocates for their children within the educational system.

- Families are educated about their legal rights and entitlements.

- Educators join the group for a practice session in which families are helped to acquire skills that will enable them to create collaborative partnerships with school personnel.

Sessions One to Three: Creating a Framework

Session One: Demystification

Session One focuses on demystifying learning disabilities and understanding them within the context of the strengths and weaknesses we all possess. It incorporates the belief that children cannot work on their problems if they do not understand them.[46] Families and children are helped to identify, celebrate, and build on individual differences and strengths in other areas that may generally be overlooked or minimized. No talent is too small to be recognized and appreciated. Group members tell what is unique about each of them. The applause that begins in Session One resonates throughout all the group meetings.

"I'm cute," Seth stated, "and I like that about me."

"I'm a good cook."

"I'm a tic-tac-toe champion. No one in my class can beat me."

"I get to school on time, most of the time."

"I make the best apple cake in America."

"I can cross my eyes and hold my breath at the same time for 30 seconds."

Playful metaphors and novel activities help family members develop new understandings about learning. They begin to appreciate that learning is complicated. When we know how to do something, we take for granted all the smooth operations that are involved. Performing the task becomes automatic; we don't think about it. In order to read, write, or communicate our ideas, the smooth cooperation of certain brain functions (e.g., attention, memory) is required. There are parts of our brains that need to work together smoothly in order for us to complete a task successfully. When these functions do not work together smoothly, children and grown-ups alike may have trouble. Parents are asked, for example, to think about the complexity involved in reading a simple word such as bat. If you don't already know the word, you have to look at it carefully. You have to know that "b" is a "b," not a "d" or a "g." You have to know that it makes a certain sound, then place that sound in working memory, look at the next sound, a vowel, and think, is it a short "a" or long "a," blend that with the "b," and so on. Hard work!

When an individual has difficulty in the input or output of information, it affects how he learns, acts, and interacts. To a degree, these difficulties are common to all of us and are seen as neurobiological variations. I, for example, have a problem with directions and map reading. If you tell me to meet you on the southwest corner of 33rd Street and 2nd Avenue, you might be standing there for very long time while I try to figure out which corner you're referring to. You would do much better if you told me to meet you near that certain record store or restaurant. In my case, these difficulties do not significantly interfere with academic or life functioning. However, this is not the case for many children diagnosed with learning disabilities.

The participants' understanding of learning disabilities is enhanced through the interactive exercises that begin in this session; simulations turn family members into "learning disabled" individuals and give them a chance to "walk in their children's shoes." We ask family members to take a spelling test and write with their nondominant hands. The children smile with delight as they watch their families struggle to write and spell. When asked, "How did you feel?" they answer, "I felt stupid, frustrated, like giving up, ashamed, nervous." "Now hang that on the refrigerator," one child exclaimed, after viewing the final product of his father's efforts.

Session Two: Infusing Hope

Many children with learning disabilities feel so different from other children that they give up. They don't believe they can make it in this complex, competitive, confusing world. In session two, children and families are helped in identifying successful role models (from public life or from their own communities) who have learning disabilities but who have been able to succeed and even excel. By learning about famous and successful people, from various areas of life, who have managed to overcome "tough stuff," children learn what is possible.

Many children with learning disabilities do have the courage and belief in themselves, and the family support to become adults who help enrich our culture: artists, filmmakers, inventors, comedians, writers, athletes, scientists, actors, and leaders in politics and business. The list of famous people with learning disabilities is long and includes Nelson Rockefeller, Albert Einstein, Thomas Edison, Winston Churchill, Benjamin Franklin, Picasso, Leonardo Da Vinci, Walt Disney, Cher, Steven Spielberg, Tom Cruise, Bruce Jenner, Patrick Ewing, Magic Johnson, and Whoopi Goldberg. Growing up wasn't easy for many of these individuals. Einstein was withdrawn, talked late, and had poor scholastic achievement. Franklin, one of our greatest statesmen, had difficulty in math and reading and left school when he was 10 years old. Picasso was a poor student who was scolded for drawing in class. Walt Disney, also a low-achieving student, was surely reported for doodling in his schoolbooks. (A few weeks after the end of one of our groups, we heard from a mother who had just returned from a trip. "When I was in Disneyworld," she said," I was telling everybody that Walt Disney had a learning disability. I was almost proud of him.")

Celebrity Sweepstakes is an activity in which the group matches 18 famous people with short descriptions of their experiences with learning troubles in school. It is a fun way to demonstrate that a learning disability does not preclude achievement. During Celebrity Sweepstakes one group concluded: "If they had learning disabilities and they're successful, there's hope!!" After watching a video clip of a successful businessman who has a learning disability, the parents realized that the diagnosis of a learning disability does not have to mean the child is doomed to failure; they recognized that the child might be "abled" in other ways. The parents said, "Confidence and belief in oneself is important," "Anybody can make it as long as they have the will," "Nobody's perfect."

There is also a focus on what helps people succeed, beginning with "if you think you can, you can; if you think you can't, you can't." With the introduction of "helper" and "robber" thoughts, group members identify patterns of thought that impede or enhance achievement. Helper thoughts help you get the job done. They are like having your own personal trainer inside your head rooting you on. Robber thoughts, on the other hand, cheat you of your good prospects. When you listen to them and say, "I'm dumb, I'll never do it," failure will surely be at your door!

Session Three: Multiple Intelligences

Session three is anchored in the work of Howard Gardner and his theory of multiple intelligences. This work presents a different approach to the assessment of human intelligence.[47] Gardner describes eight kinds of intelligence and makes the point that no one of these is to be viewed as more important than the others.

1. Verbal-linguistic

2. Logical-mathematical

3. Visual-spatial

4. Musical

5. Bodily-kinesthetic

6. Interpersonal

7. Intrapersonal

8. Naturalist

Variations in abilities and biodiversity are part of what makes our culture and heritage so rich. Individual families meet and develop family profiles, highlighting the different ways in which they are smart. Families begin to focus on the talents their children possess that are not often recognized in the traditional school setting. Participants begin to celebrate their differences and start to uncover the many hidden treasures in each of the family members. Through this family profile exercise, they discover new areas for positive connection. As parents work along with their children, they get new and helpful information. With a broad smile on her face, Janie said, "I learned that my daughter likes gardening, she's a real naturalist. I think I'm going to get a seed catalogue and order some bulbs. We can plant them together." Phillip told us, "I learned that Alexis thinks she's smart with people. I'm happy to learn that she feels she can make friends."

Sessions Four and Five: The Emotional Impact of Learning Disabilities

Sessions four and five of the Unique Minds Program explore the emotional impact of learning disabilities on the child and on the family. In these sessions, we meet the character U-Candu. Participants learn about words that encourage and words that discourage and how these affect our good feelings. Negative attention and embarrassment, and the subsequent anger that these children suffer, come to light through descriptions, stories, and energetic puppet plays. Family members join together to shrink the dark clouds of doom and failure and the "can't-do" theme that often prevails when children have learning problems.

Through the technique of "externalizing the problem,"[48] participants playfully objectify and personify "can't-do" problems, from getting up on time in the morning, to learning how to drive, to passing a math test, to organizing the house, to getting along with others. The family unites in the struggle and works together to come up with solutions to escape the "can't-do" influence.

Externalizing the problem helps the person with the problem understand that it is not embedded in his or her being. When the individual sees the problem as an alien invader, an external force to whom he has yielded certain powers of influence over his or his family's life, he can marshal often forgotten or devalued strengths and skills to defeat its hold on his life.

The families also meet two heinous characters, Can'tasaurus and Zapper, who cause trouble for children and grown-ups. The Can'tasaurus, a sneaker-wearing dinosaur, waits for an opportunity, such as when we make a mistake, and springs into action. When we listen to the Can'tasaurus's stream of conversation, we feel that we want to give up. The Can'tasaurus loves to comment on our errors and frailties. It loves to visit people and tell them that they can't do things. The families learn about how the Can'tasaurus behaves and what they can do to prevent it from taking away their "can-do" feelings. Theresa tells us, "The Can'tasaurus robs us of our courage." This is the Can'tasaurus's best talent; it is a great talker and a great convincer. When we believe its words, we end up feeling bad and our performance suffers. The "can't-do" feelings it stirs up may result in lowered self-esteem, depression, and avoidant behaviors.

Since learning disabilities have a genetic basis, more than one family member often has a similar condition. As they develop empathy for their children's plight, parents speak of the times *they* were visited by the Can'tasaurus and reveal the profound sense of shame surrounding their own school difficulties. Children listen with rapt attention as their parents talk about their own, often-agonizing struggles in school. One mother, Eleanor, took the Can'tasaurus puppet and, as the children watched, told her story. "When I was in school it used to attack me really bad and this is what it said, 'Who do you think you are, thinking you can do this. You can't! You're not smart enough. Give it up. Give it up.' I said, 'I'm not giving it up. Yes I will get up and I will do this'." As the kids cheered, she said, "It was a battle, but I won."

Eleanor was joined by Marc's father, who had sat quietly lost in reflection before he added, "You know, all during third grade, I heard this voice in my head telling me that I was the worst reader and I would never be able to get it. I never knew that it was the Can'tasaurus and that I didn't have to listen to it."

Equally universal are the angry, impatient feelings that are externalized in another character, the Zapper. The Zapper's sting causes trouble for the one who is stung and for everyone else! When the Zapper stings teachers, parents, and classmates, it causes them to make unhelpful comments. The Zapper may convince a parent to say, "What's wrong with you? I don't think you'll ever pass that test," or a teacher to say, "Look everyone,

Elizabeth has lost her place again." When the Zapper is around and it stings us, we might respond with words that sting someone else. When the Zapper is in the classroom, it can sting the teachers who then lose their patience. If the Zapper stings the teacher, she might forget that Avery, Juana, or Buddy has to hear directions presented many ways before beginning work. When the student approaches the teacher to ask the same question for the third time that hour, the teacher might comment in an unhelpful way, "How many times do I have to repeat myself?" These words sting and smart for hours.

Parents are quick to pick up on and use the language of the program; this language provides playful ways to discuss many concerns and issues that often hinder us as we try to achieve our goals. This was evident in one mother's response to a question. "I think the Zapper followed me home." "Did it get you before you got in the door?" "Big time!" "Did it help you handle things more calmly?" "No way!"

Families get together and develop strategies about how to tame or defeat the Can'tasaurus. They talk about how tired it makes them when they listen to it, how it makes them feel they don't even want to try, and that they should just give up. Families join together, and with other families, to defeat the Can'tasaurus and diminish its impact on their lives. They begin to recognize the times when they are vulnerable to the Zapper and understand its ability to make them sting. When talking about ways to keep the Zapper from stinging, one mother and father read their list: "Count to 10 before I talk, try to think about something nice that happened that day, think about how the cup is half full, not half empty." Other parents decided on these strategies: "Get more rest, it stings more when I'm tired, and think about how much we love each other."

Through the structured puppet play sequences, children and parents act out what happens when the Can'tasaurus and the Zapper invade family life. A scene is set and parents and children act out bedtime or getting up in the morning with some "help" from the Can'tasaurus and the Zapper. Therapy is sent home with the family as they make colorful door hangers and scorecards to track their progress in defeating these fiends.

The Can'tasaurus and the Zapper are favorite characters that I use in my consulting room. Paula tells me the Can'tasaurus tries to convince her that she can't be an in-control mom. Sylvia says, "It tells me that I'm not a good mother." When she listens to the creature and believes its words, she feels sad. Walter tells me that he can't seem to get ahead at work. After many "can't-do" stories, I tell him about the Can'tasaurus and he readily concludes it must be there at the office. He laughs and begins a conversation about his "can't-do" thoughts. A new door has opened that leads to strategizing and planning. Edward wrote this poem about the Can'tasaurus.

It is the monster it is the beast,

On your good feelings it will feast.

It is trouble it is bad,

If you listen, it will make you feel sad.

If you refuse it, you will confuse it

When you get in trouble you will amuse it double

So as the good inside you gets taller and taller

The Can'tasaurus and its trouble get smaller and smaller!

Six-year old Simon said he would spit on the Can'tasaurus. He drew this picture to remind him of his plan.

Sessions Six and Seven: Problem Solving

Sessions six and seven provide families with a problem-solving model that comes from behavioral psychology and incorporates the concept of vicious cycles from family therapy. Children and parents join the "Problem-solvers Club." They are given concrete tools that enable them to actively identify a problem, sequence it, and find places for intervention. Families meet as individual groups to brainstorm solutions and find interventions that are new or unique to them. As an old adage goes, "Give a man a fish and you feed him for tonight. Teach him how to fish and he feeds himself for life." We teach the model, and then assist the families in developing strategies to experiment with at home. Children and families develop strategies specific to dealing with the learning disability. Families strategize with each

other to develop new ways of handling emotional and behavioral problems stemming from the child's difficulties. This occurs in an atmosphere of mutual support.

Session Eight: Family-School Collaboration

Session eight focuses on collaboration with larger systems such as the child's
school and the medical community. It helps the families work together to ban-
ish blame and discusses how parents can partner with others to advocate for
their learning-disabled children.[49] Bruce drew this picture as a reminder to ask
for help. Collaboration and cooperation help build bridges between the home
and the school.[50] The family is encouraged to engage in a cooperative partnership with outside professionals. They are encouraged to view a referral for
special education, remediation, or medication as a positive step toward helping the child. In a role-play, children and parents join together to discuss ways
to get "your foot in the door" when forging alliances with the school. Different
points of view are represented, and parents offer sage advice to each other.
When a father in one group said that if a teacher has a dispute with his child,
"I give all the credit to the teacher," one of the mothers shared an important
memory. "The teacher said I behaved in a particular way. It wasn't true but my
mother said she agreed with the teacher and said she was ashamed of me. This
was something I carried for years." The group supported her when she voiced
the opinion "I think *we* all know our children."

The final activity of the last session involves passing around a magic wand. The parents make wishes for their children's future, the children make wishes for themselves, and everyone has an opportunity to describe what the program has meant to him or her. As the wand passes through each participant's hands, it becomes a real symbol of expressed hopes for the future. One of the children told the group it helped her to see that grown-ups who had problems did okay. Smiling broadly she said, "It was nice to see that someone very accomplished was someone like me. That really got me a little bit happy, to know that some people might not be totally smart in every way but they can be brilliant." Other children in turn shared their dreams for successful lives and careers, such as becoming a banker, a basketball player, and a writer.

There is a training film that comes with the Unique Minds Program manual. I admit I still get teary whenever I watch this section of the film. It reminds me of how important and useful it is for families to come together to grapple with issues near and dear to their lives. It also speaks to the healing power of relationships within and between families. One mother remarks about how bogged down we get in life when any of us has a difference. Another looks at the children and says, "I learned how unique and wonderful my children are." Yet another becomes choked with emotion as she turns to the children and says, "We want you to know how smart and how special we think you are."

The conclusion of the group marks a new beginning for participants who comment about the new ways of seeing, feeling, and understanding. "It's been an eye-opener." "It's given me an understanding about learning disabilities." "For me it's like getting a better grip on things." "I understand my child better, I know when to back away." Families are empowered through education, information, affiliation and mutual support, development of new skills, and enhanced problem-solving practice. Working together reduces the profound sense of isolation that these children and families often report. Families learn from one another; they band together to defeat the common enemies of learning disabled children. The families take home tools, including new ways to talk about and cope with troubling problems. "Can't-do" talk, the voice of discouragement, is turned down, and the voice of hope and promise is enlivened.

CHAPTER 9

Partings and
Parting Thoughts

The stories woven throughout this book come from experiences I have shared
with children and families as they navigate life's struggles. Witnessing acts of
courage and participating in the healing process are very powerful experiences.
Each child and family resonates in the therapist's life in a unique way. Collective
feelings at the time of termination represent the gamut of human emotion; we
feel relief and sadness, as well as happiness. It is essential for clients and therapists to take time to plan and reflect on the parting.

This chapter briefly discusses the termination process, a phase in child therapy that Lewis and Blotcky tell us is "overlooked and underestimated."

> In the process of effective therapy, battles have been fought, tears often
> shed, painful realities faced, fears encountered and hopefully overcome,
> vulnerabilities exposed, and risks taken. Like a war, these conditions result
> in strong bonds among previous strangers, and the relinquishing of these
> ties is an important dimension of the termination process.[1]

The first part of this chapter will review practices related to terminating therapy with children and families. (Of note is that there is a dearth of family
therapy literature on this subject.) Child-friendly culminating activities as well
as suggestions will be offered. In concluding, as it is now time for *us* to part, I will
also present some of my reflections as we end the child-friendly therapy journey.

TERMINATION

Termination is an active ongoing process that extends over months.[2] The process
itself is thought to have "therapeutic potential;" it assists clients in maintaining
new ways of handling problems. Some writers suggest that termination can be

empowering to both the client and the therapist.[3] They note that a "successful termination" should: (1) consolidate or reinforce the therapeutic changes the client has made; (2) bring closure to the therapeutic relationship; (3) assist clients and therapists in coping with feelings related to the ending of the relationship; (4) help therapists understand how they were helpful to clients; (5) leave clients with improved confidence to manage their struggles independently.[4]

There are various types of termination: client initiated, therapist initiated, forced, and mutual.[5] Whatever the type, it is important to recognize that termination may be experienced as a loss and may prove to be a difficult time for both therapist and client. For example, if the client initiates termination, the therapist may feel insecure about his or her abilities. If the therapist initiates termination, the client may feel abandoned.[6] Barker discusses ending therapy and states:

> Inexpertly managed, it can appear to clients as a rejection, but, just as the death of a loved one can be the occasion to celebrate that person's life and achievements, so can the ending of treatment be an occasion to celebrate what has been achieved. Nevertheless we must always be on the lookout for signs that termination is proving difficult for the children we see.[7]

The last therapy session has been likened to other separations experienced within the life cycle. For therapists as well as clients, it often brings to mind feelings and themes concerning independence and self-sufficiency.[8] In discussing termination in child therapy, Chethik suggests allowing a long enough time during the termination period to deal with the feelings of loss and separation. Setting a specific date is important. He advocates a concrete way to plan is by constructing a calendar together with the child.[9]

Sometimes, practical considerations dictate when therapy ends. This is especially true in the age of managed care or when therapy has to end because of scheduling problems (not so unusual for today's overbooked kids). At times, therapy has to end before the work with a family is complete. Lewis and Blotcky point out that sometimes logistical, dynamic, and practical, as well as other circumstances, proscribe an optimal termination. Within these constrictions, they suggest it is best to look at the course of therapy as part of a "patchwork quilt" completing a "piece of work."[10]

In a discussion of when to conclude family therapy, Nichols and Schwartz offer the following termination checklist.[11]

1. Is the presenting problem resolved or greatly improved?

2. Is the family satisfied that they have gotten what they came for or are they interested in continuing to learn about themselves and improve their relationships?

3. Does the family have an understanding of what they were doing that wasn't working, and how to avoid the recurrence of similar problems in the future?

4. Do minor recurrences of problems reflect lack of resolution of some underlying dynamic or merely that the family has to readjust to function without the therapist?

5. Have family members developed and improved relationships outside the immediate family context as well as within it?

The meaning of therapy is different for each person in the family; hence, each person handles termination in a personal way. (It doesn't surprise me when a child or a family member who seemed unengaged protests vociferously when we talk about ending our work together.) Common therapeutic practices during termination in family therapy include spacing out the sessions, placing the family in an expert role by helping them articulate what they have accomplished, and predicting relapse and temporary setbacks. It is also helpful to mention something about the client(s) that will remain with you, something they have taught you.

A relationship with a family is often ongoing, and although it may end for now, the door is open for future consultations. Follow-up sessions are often viewed as an integral part of the work.[12] Saying good-bye to children often comes at natural times of transition, such as at the end of school. We may take a vacation and then reconvene in September for a booster session to help the child make a smooth transition to the new school year. This is not an uncommon practice in child-focused treatment.

In my clinical work, I find these practices helpful:

- Keeping termination in mind from the first session, since ending actually starts at the beginning.[13] I ask, "How will we know that it is time to end? What needs to happen?"
- Using the biopsychosocial formulation chart to summarize the multifactored nature of problem formation and resolution; using the chart and goal-attainment sheets to monitor progress
- Enhancing understanding of problem formation and resolution as part of family functioning rather than the functioning of one individual[14]
- Pausing during the treatment to look backward and forward to check out where we have been and where we are going
- Imagining a future without therapy; I ask family members, "What will it be like for each of you? What are your thoughts and feelings about ending?

What have you learned? How will you use what you learned at home, at school, and in the community?"

- Tracking family successes and underlining accomplishments
- Highlighting change as it occurs and documenting it
- Collaborating with the family to develop a more realistic view of problems
- Focusing more on process and the steps along the way than on the product (the endpoint of therapy)
- Planning how to handle unresolved issues[15]

SAYING GOOD-BYE

Focus on the Feelings

Even when you make great efforts to ease the transition, parting is not always smooth. Saying good-bye is an important part of life and, as in life, it is sometimes fraught with feelings. Owen and his family left with hardly a word or a reason, but Corinne was angry and experienced our ending as a betrayal and abandonment. Her history of loss and deprivation made it especially difficult for her to say good-bye.[16] She was considerably more attached than Jack, who was happy and relieved when he finally got to "fire me." Each week Jack and I would review the list of what had to happen at home and at school so that he wouldn't have to attend sessions any longer. He pointed out that while he "kind of" liked me, he had many more important things to do on Wednesdays at 6 o'clock. As we monitored progress toward each goal, I would comment that he was getting close to firing me. I pointed out that being fired under these circumstances was a very happy occasion. We planned together about how to celebrate.

In the D family, each person had different feelings about ending therapy. Ten-year-old Bernie was worried. "How will we figure out what to do if we don't talk about it here?" he asked. He didn't feel like the family was okay. Gladys, Bernie's sister, commented that she was fine and didn't need to come anymore. Mrs. D said she felt that she had learned a lot and thought that she handled things better at home. Mr. D noted that he was glad the family had come to therapy and was equally happy that they wouldn't have to come any longer! In a discussion, the Ds decided that they would schedule family meetings for the same time they had come to my office. Each week, they would talk about one thing that was going well and one thing they had to work on.

Marian was sad that we weren't going to see each other every week. We talked about how saying hello and good-bye were parts of life, just as in nature, when the flowers that bloom in the front yard say hello and then "go away." I asked her if she might look at how things had been when we had first said hello.

"Not so happy," she commented. "How are you feeling now?" I queried. A huge smile came to her face. "Pretty good." I asked her to look at what behaviors she had said good-bye to that had previously kept her from getting along with others in her family. We typed "good-bye" and "hello" lists together:

Saying Good-Bye To	Saying Hello To
tantrums	good feelings
big anger	yes road
talking back	good choices
screaming	happier life
fighting with mommy	proud feelings
not listening	getting along with others
people feeling angry with me	
feeling grumpy all the time	

We discussed how she had made the items on her good-bye list "leave" and what she could do to keep them away. "It isn't going to be so easy," she thought aloud, "I still get angry pretty fast." She concluded that she liked the things on her hello list much better than those on her good-bye list: She got along with her mom and life at home was calmer. Marian decided that it was worth it to keep on working and felt ready to do some work on her own.

Use Games

Two minutes into a conversation about treatment progress and outcomes, Logan announced that he was bored. A favorite child-friendly way to have a useful discussion about termination is through playing a structured game. With Logan and his family, I used my special version of Bingo. We followed the traditional rules with some modifications: When a number is called, (e.g., B6, N42, G53) everybody checks to see who has it; before covering the number on the Bingo card, each person who has it must respond to one of these corresponding queries:

B   Tell one thing you can do to help you *behave* at home, at school, or at work.

I   Tell about something "*I*" learned in therapy.

N   *Name* something that you can do when you get stressed.

G   Tell about something that you are *good* at.

O   *Open* your eyes, look at someone, and say something nice to him or her.

Logan participated in the game. He was no longer bored, but enthusiastically involved.

Plan a Celebration Together

Endings are a time to applaud and celebrate the work that the family has done and to review the tools the family plans to use at home. It's a time for giving certificates, recognizing progress, and acknowledging change and triumphs.[17] Melvin tamed his anger; Leta shrunk her worries; Wayne and his family worked on sending "Mr. Mean" out of the house; Juliana told me that she says "no to Mr. No." We planned ways to commemorate these accomplishments, and feats like them, for each family.

Review

In the ending sessions, I review the course of treatment with the child and family. We review progress and talk about our experiences in working together. During our last session, Brendan said that he would remember to use his brain, heart, ears, and eyes to help him solve problems (see next page). He also made a list of the steps that he now uses when he is faced with a problem. His honest appraisal of himself revealed that his first step is still denial and blaming. The steps, as outlined by Brendan, are listed below.

1st step is denial and blaming

2nd step is realization

3rd step is confession

4th step is will

5th step is action

Brendan decided that he still uses his "won't" (I won't do it) power. We talked about the ways that he might increase his "will" power. With his mother and father present, we worked on a family action plan that they took home.

Children most often suggest activities that they would enjoy. Mindy made a book. Vera took home a video that she produced over time, which chronicled her ideas, and included her favorite stuffed animals as "stars." Frank, age 8, loved animal crackers. I brought in a box for each family member and, as we munched, each person talked about something he or she had learned in our work together that the family could take home with them. We recorded the ideas in a document. Frank held up his bear cracker and told us that the bear taught him not

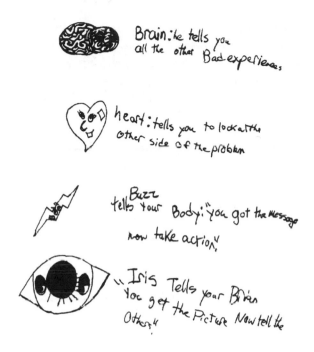

Brain: he tells you all the other Bad experiences

heart: tells you to look at the other side of the problem

Buzz tells Your Body: "you got the message now take action,"

"Iris Tells your Brian You get the Picture Now tell the Others"

Brendan's Drawing of What He Would Use to Solve a Problem

to growl and be mean. It makes people angry with him. Ina, his sister, looked at the elephant and commented, "I learned to keep my nose in my own stuff. My brother and sister already have a mother, no one likes when I stick my nose in too." Before Dad ate his lion he said, "I learned that no one listens when I roar. I promise not to come home from work so angry." Mom said, "I learned that like each animal in this box is different, so are my kids."

PARTING THOUGHTS

As this is the last stop on our child-friendly therapy voyage, it is a time to pause and reflect on our travels. As I reviewed the practices and research of investigators, and reflected on my own, I found universal themes that make *common sense* but are not necessarily part of *common practice*. Some of these are: including children in family therapy, including the family in child referrals, encouraging consistent collaboration between schools and parents, employing evidence-based practices, and understanding and incorporating biology, temperament, and cognitive variations when developing interventions in child referrals.

It has been demonstrated that both nature and nurture are executive producers in a child's development. The metaphor of the newborn infant as clay on the "potter's wheel of life," passively being molded by the hands of others (caregivers, experience, environment, peers, school) has given way to an image that is more complete. In a recursive process and in profound ways, from the very first moments of life, the infant's own innate characteristics mold its environment and affect the behavior of others.

It has also been demonstrated that problems are multidimensional and usually have multiple causes. Therefore, the biopsychosocial perspective is a helpful format for understanding complexity[18] and recognizing the important roles not only of nature and nurture, but also of stress and resilience in the face of adversity.[19]

Another helpful metaphor is that of the bank account. Capital starts accumulating from the very first day of life and interest is compounded. Children who grow up with more capital[20] in the bank—that is, income from friendships, school, and home relationships—have more choices. Families with more capital enjoy a better quality of life. What might we do to help children and families increase their personal and family bank accounts?

Nurture the caregivers and provide needed support. There is the claim that "parenting is probably the most important public health issue facing our society,"[21] yet it is something we are often poorly prepared for. When we purchase a $30 toaster, we leave the store with an owner's manual and a 24-hour toll-free number to call for technical assistance. When new parents begin life with their infant, there is no such book or number. They are told to provide protection and care of physical needs, together with "love, care, and commitment, good enough parenting, consistent limit setting and the facilitation of development."[22] Supporting parents as they work to provide these important ingredients means providing for the needs of the parents as well.[23] Assisting them through support, education, and involvement is critical.

Offer "HOPE" (Have Opportunities for Positive Experiences) by helping families to work together to improve family life. This means helping them reduce criticism and blame, and increase warmth.[24] Increasing the amount of positive experiences means finding ways for family members to talk and listen to one another. The consulting room serves as a laboratory in which families develop new ways of being in and belonging to the family.

Nurture strengths and success. A therapy that acknowledges the struggle yet highlights the strengths and resources of each family member inspires hope. We don't have the answers; there aren't any simple solutions or quick fixes for the complex problems that drive families to the therapist's office. (This is true despite what managed care may insist!) Respect for the family is vital. They may be doing the best they can under the most difficult circumstances.

Send therapy home. One of the therapist's jobs is to help the therapy go home with the family. Parents, children, and other family members, and teachers work alongside the therapist as coresearchers and collaborators. In developing interventions, particularly those for children with biologically-based disorders, consider involving multiple senses and different kinds of intelligences, preferred learning styles, and cognitive variations. Employ right-brain learning by including visual imagery, metaphor, novelty, and imaginative play. Find opportunities for clients to practice skills and competencies by making therapy child-friendly and developing tools to talk.

Listen and learn. My own child-friendly journey never ends. I know that children will always be a part of my life and my work. Each child and family brings unique challenges and inspires me in new ways. I am never bored, but rather awed by their courage, sometimes overcome with sadness for their struggle, and always grateful for the privilege of participating in their triumphs.

Listen! Some of the best advice is often from children:[25]

1. Never trust a dog to watch your food.

2. When your dad is mad and asks you, "Do I look like an idiot?" don't answer him.

3. Stay away from prunes.

4. When your mom is mad at your dad, don't let her brush your hair.

5. You can't hide a piece of broccoli in a glass of milk.

6. Don't wear polka-dot underwear under white shorts.

7. If you want a kitten, start out by asking for a horse.

8. When you get a bad grade in school, show it to your mom when she's on the phone.

9. Never tell your little brother that you're not going to do what your mom told you to do.

10. Don't ever be too full for dessert.

Notes

CHAPTER 1. CHILD-FRIENDLY THERAPY: AN OVERVIEW

1. See Healy (1998) for an excellent review of why children don't think and what we can do about it.

2. Cowley (2000); Epstein, Wing, & Valoski (1985); Fruhbeck (2000); Sokol (2000).

3. Wride (1999).

4. The Center for a New American Dream, www.newdream.org/core/ index.html.

5. Home violence: Hershorn & Rosenbaum (1985). Children witnessing violent and nonviolent marital discord were affected. Also see Groves et al. (1993).

Posttraumatic stress disorder: Glodich (1998); Pynoos (1994).

Poverty increases exposure to violence: National Coalition for the Homeless Fact Sheet #1 (1999, June). In 1997, 14.6 million people (41% of all poor persons) had incomes of less than half the poverty level. This represents an increase of over 500,000 from 1995.

School violence: U.S. Department of Education (1997). In a 1996–1997 survey of a representative sample of 1,734 regular public schools, principals reported the following statistics: approximately 4000 rapes or sexual batteries, 7000 robberies, 11,000 physical attacks or fights with a weapon, and 188,000 physical attacks or fights without weapons. The full report is available at nces.ed.gov/pubsearch/pubsinfo.asp?pubid=98030.

Poverty's detrimental effects: Dubow & Ippolito (1994); Luthar (1999); Pagani et al. (1999). Gonzales et al. (1996) discuss neighborhood influences on academic achievement. Seccombe (2000) offers an excellent review of families of poverty in the 1990s. Also see McLoyd (1998), who found that children experiencing both persistent and transitory poverty do less well than never-poor children. Higher rates of perinatal complications, less access to resources that buffer the negative effects of perinatal complications, increased exposure to lead, and less home-based cognitive stimulation partly account for diminished cognitive functioning in poor children. The study also found poor academic readiness for school and lower teacher expectancies. Other variables that impacted were harsh and inconsistent parenting as well as exposure to acute and chronic stress. *Working with Families of the Poor*, Minuchin, P. et al., (1998) is a valuable resource.

Violence and development: Gorman-Smith & Tolan (1998); Margolin & Gordis (2000); Osofsky (1995).

Lower school achievement: Schwab-Stone et al. (1995).

Internalization and externalization of problems: Margolin & Gordis (2000).

Early brain development: Eisenberg (1999) discusses the role of experience. Also see Nelson & Carver (1998); Perry et al. (1995); Shore (1997); Siegel (1999); Weiss & Wagner (1998).

Children's views: Garbarino et al. (1991).

Youth violence: U.S. Department of Health and Human Services (2001). Earls (1994) reported that juveniles are increasingly the perpetrators of violence with reports of a 165% increase in the rate of murders committed by 14- through 17-year-olds from 1985-1993.

Murder rate by adolescents: Renfrew (1997, p. 172) cites statistics from the 1990 *Uniform Crime Reports*. Adolescent homicide arrests were up 60% as contrasted with a 5% increase for adults.

Maltreatment: Margolin & Gordis (2000) cite statistics from the National Committee for the Prevention of Child Abuse that 15 out of every 1000 children are victims of child maltreatment. Eckenrode et al. (1993) and Laird & Doris (1993) discuss the school performance of abused and neglected children.

6. Homeless—women and families: National Coalition for the Homeless Fact Sheet #2 (1999 February). Cites a range of statistics from almost 5 million to over 9 million were homeless in the latter half of the 1980s. Masten et al. (1997) discuss the educational risks for homeless children and found academic achievement to be lower when compared to that of the general population.

Latchkey children: Lamorey et al. (1998).

Divorce rate: Gottman (1998). Bumpass (1990) notes that approximately 40% of all children will experience parental divorce before the children are adults.

Divorce first marriages: Martin & Bumpass (1989).

Divorce second marriages: Gottman (1998).

Children of divorce: Kelly (2000).

7. Kids' stress: Witkin (1999).

National Health Interview Survey and additional health care statistics cited in Halfon & Newacheck (1999) note that the most common causes of disability were "mental retardation, attention-deficit/hyperactivity disorder, and learning disabilities" (p. 600).

Special education enrollment: U.S. Department of Education (1996).

Pediatric psychosocial problems: Kelleher et al. (1997) found an increase in attentional problems from 1.4% to 9.2%.

8. Adult depression: Weissman et al. (1994).

Works weekends: Presser (1995) cited in Presser (2000). Also see Schor (1991), who reported an increase in the work hours of both men and women from 1969 to 1987 of an extra month per year. See Teachman et al. (2000) for a discussion of the changing demography of America's families.

Dual earner couples: In the 1997 National Study of the Changing Workforce, Bond et al. (1998) report that 78% of workers are married to employed spouses.

Shift worker: Presser (2000, p. 93). "Americans are moving toward a 24-hour, 7-days-a-week economy." She found that nonstandard work schedules impact on marital stability.

Women in workforce: Hayghe (1997). Perry-Jenkins et al. (2000) found that the rate of employment for women in 1997 was 59.5%, and that 63.9% of women with children under age 6, and 78.3% of women with children ages 6 to 17 are employed.

Mother's multiple roles: Light (1997) reports on the strains of working mothers and concludes that "it's not just single mothers or mothers without adequate social support who showed unusual strain: it was any working mom" (p. 360). She cites a pattern of constant vigilance, responsibility to complete chores, and the need to be on call as causing harmful physiological reactions that impact on health and adjustment (such as high blood pressure).

Work and home boundaries blurred: Imber-Black (2000) writes about the "new triangle: couples and technology." Also see Fraenkel (2001).

Carryover work stress: Crouter et al. (1999), for example, found that mothers' and fathers' work pressures and role overload impacted on the adjustment of their adolescent children.

Troubled marriages: Presser (2000) cites shift work schedules as affecting marital stability. Fraenkel & Wilson (2000) discuss the effects of time and rhythms on relationships.

9. Large numbers of today's kids are visual-spatial learners, or right-brained thinkers. Their brains are wired to learn holistically rather than in the step-by-step fashion of left-brained thinkers. Visual input, not words, plays an important role in how these learners process information. Freed & Parsons (1997) discuss the right-brained thinker as a "product of today's short attention span culture, which demands constant stimulation and bombards us with sensory overload and rapid-fire images. From birth his environment literally wires and rewires pathways in the brain" (p. 33). Also see Healy (1990).

10. As Wachtel (1994b) states: "When family therapists see marital problems and troubled children, they tend to assume that the marital difficulties came *first* and in that sense caused the child to have problems. Often insufficient attention is given to the possibility that the marital problems may have partly arisen out of the stress of attempting to deal with a difficult and troubled child" (p. 9).

11. Dilts (2001, p. 11).

12. Castellanos (1999, p. 179). "The thesis advanced is that ADHD is a disorder of deficient and delayed self-regulation, due largely to genetics differences in the rate of development and functional integrity of brain systems modulated by dopamine, norepinephrine, and possibly epinephrine, that encompass at least 5 anatomic components: the prefrontal cortex, basal ganglia, locus coeruleus, cerebellum, and amygdala-septo-hippocampal system."

13. Castellanos (1999, p. 187). The brain regions implicated include the prefrontal cortex, basal ganglia, locus coeruleus, cerebellum, and possibly the amygdala.

14. Pennington & Ozonoff (1996) reviewed the neuropsychology literature and in 15 of the 18 controlled studies found significant executive function deficits. See Chapter 4 in this book for a discussion of executive functions. Also see Barkley (1997b) and Hughes et al. (1998).

15. Kranowitz (1998).

16. Baum & Posluszny (1999) discuss stress and biobehavioral contributions to health and illness. They conclude: "Stress and other emotional responses are components of complex interactions of genetic, physiological, behavioral, and environmental factors that affect the body's ability to remain or become healthy or to resist or overcome disease" (p. 137). According to Negrao et al. (2000), the body's response to stress involves activation of the neuroendocrine system: the hypothalamic-pituitary-adrenal axis (referred to as the HPA axis) and the sympathoadrenal medullar systems. Van Goozen et al. (2000) found that children with disruptive behavior disorders have increased activation of the HPA axis. Also see Chapter 4 of this book.

17. Dilts (2001, p. 12).

18. For a review of the processing of social information and how it impacts on social adjustment, see Crick & Dodge (1994). Webster-Stratton & Lindsay (1999) report that children with conduct disorder overestimate their own social competence and misattribute hostile intent to others' actions. Also see Cadesky et al. (2000); Duke et al. (1996).

19. As Dilts (2001, p. 225) notes: "The *social model of mental illness* proposes that mental illness derives from pathological social interactions."

20. Chess & Thomas (1991, 1999).

21. Gabbard & Goodwin (1996, p. 543). Also, Combrinck-Graham (1989, p. 67) advocates consideration "of the biopsychosocial influences of a child." Engel (1977, 1980) proposed a biopsychosocial model in medicine. He attempted to incorporate biological, psychological, and social causes of illnesses. He thought the biomedical model of disease to be a reductionist view. Campbell (1998, p. 339) cites the research in the field of psychoimmunology (e.g., Ader et al., 1990) as supporting connections between psychosocial and biomedical processes.

22. See Carey & McDevitt (1995); Chess & Thomas (1989); Thomas & Chess (1968, 1977, 1984).

23. Hyman (1999, p. 27). Also see Diamond (1988); Eisenberg (1998, 1999); Kandel (1999); Kotulak (1993); Nash (1997); Steen (1996).

24. See, for example, Kendall & Braswell (1993); Kendall & Panichelli-Mindel (1995).

25. See Forman (1993).

26. Expressed emotion, (criticism, hostility, and emotional overinvolvement) has been the subject of study since first introduced in the 1960s. For example, Brown et al. (1962) looked at the influence of family life on the course of schizophrenic illness, Kanter et al. (1987) reviewed expressed emotion in families. Also see Schreiber et al. (1995); Wamboldt & Wamboldt (2000); Weintraub & Wamboldt (1996). Butxlaff & Hooley (1998) report that expressed emotion in the family is an indicator for a more troubled course of chronic psychiatric and medical illness and therefore should be reduced.

27. Henker & Whalen (1999) discuss the child with attention-deficit/hyperactivity disorder in school and peer settings.

28. Birsh (1999). This edited text is based on multisensory structured language education and presents effective teaching practices for students struggling with academics.

29. Rief (1993).

30. This therapy is an outgrowth of an approach developed by my colleagues and myself on the Unique Minds Team at the Ackerman Institute and NYU Child Study Center. The reader is referred to the introduction for more information. The Unique Minds Team develops and evaluates psychotherapeutic interventions for children and families whose emotional, behavioral, and/or learning problems are related to neurobiologically-based disorders.

31. When we examine two or more things, differences become apparent. We learn new information by examining differences or changes in relationships. See Bateson (1979).

32. Lebow (2000, p. 1084).

33. Whalen & Henker (1999, p. 150). Wamboldt & Wamboldt (2000) note that problematic family interactions can lead to poor outcomes for children.

34. Bailey (2000).

35. Bailey (2000, p. xviii).

36. Rutter et al. (1999) provide an excellent review of genetics and child psychiatry. For discussions of genetic mechanisms in childhood psychiatric disorders, also see Biederman et al. (1990, 1992); Faraone et al. (1994); Kuntsi & Stevenson (2000); Lombroso et al. (1994); Plomin et al. (1997); State et al. (2000). For a discussion of autism, see Bailey et al. (1995); Steffenburg et al. (1989). For a discussion of Tourette's, see Pauls et al. (1999). For a discussion of reading disorders, see Beitchman & Young (1997); dyslexia, Grigorenko (2001).

37. Mild forms of more serious mental problems can affect our lives and our experience; Ratey & Johnson (1997) see these as "shadow syndromes" with origins in the structure and chemistry of the brain.

38. Barkley (1998). ADHD: see DSM-IV (American Psychiatric Association, 1994). Dixon (1995) reviews the impact of ADD and the family; Ratey et al. (1995) discuss the impact on relationships.

39. Biederman et al. (1990, 1992) found evidence for family-genetic risk factors in ADHD. Heritability has been noted in twin studies (Goodman & Stevenson 1989) and adoption studies (Cadoret & Stewart 1991; Morrison & Stewart 1973). Whalen & Henker (1999), in their chapter on the child with ADHD in family contexts, conclude that genetic and other biological contributions (see Castellanos, 1999, p. 150) are "paramount in the etiology of ADHD." Also see references referring to ADHD in note 50.

40. Sabbath (1969) first proposed the concept of the expendable child as one of many factors contributing to adolescent suicidal behavior. It was found that the adolescents' feelings of abandonment and the subsequent compliance with the felt parental wish for them to die were important factors leading to a suicide attempt.

41. Hoffman (1981), a classic book. Nichols & Schwartz (1998) review family therapy concepts and methods. For brief discussions of definition and therapy models, refer to Piercy et al. (1996).

42. Systems theory views the family as an interrelated system in which everyone affects and is affected by everyone else. Bateson's (1972, 1979) biological view of systems brought together many fields; also see Bowen (1978). General systems theory, as outlined by von Bertalanffy (1962, 1968), has its roots in mathematical expressions and models as applied to biology: Bertalanffy (1962) explains system as a complex of interacting components.

43. Szmukler & Dare (1996, p. 198).

44. Nichols & Schwartz (1998, p. 8).

45. Communications between human beings consist of repetitive feedback loops, which mutually reinforce and influence each other. A way to bring about change then is through the disruption of feedback loops, which interrupt problem-generating patterns or sequences of individual behavior/communication or those of a larger system.

46. The social constructionist point of view in family therapy would add the following ideas (quotes are from Piercy et al., 1996, p. 17, who credit Kenneth Gergen with introducing these ideas). "Knowing and knowledge are socially constructed through language and discourse and are context dependent." That includes self-identity, which is thought to be socially and reflexively created (it's a recursive process). Who we are then, our self-identity, changes with the context and the relationships. Adherents believe identity is interactive; hence we might "be" different people in different contexts. This point of view, the narrative approach, studies the construction of stories and narratives and analyzes them at different levels. Language and the meaning we make from it are powerful, and affect the stories and narratives we create. Stories that keep repeating are called "dominant narratives." An unrelenting story about oneself, such as "I'm dumb, I can't do anything," will limit one's options and hamper one's ability to act. See White (1989); White & Epston (1990).

47. Gurman et al. (1986, p. 565). They add (p. 566) that family therapy typically involves "face-to-face" work, with more than one family member, which may be in fluctuating combinations.

48. A conclusion of Chasin & White (1989). Murray Bowen (1978) focuses on the family of origin and works with adult family members in a process for which he coined the term "differentiation." Individuals are engaged in this process throughout their lives—one needs to differentiate in order to define the self within the family emotional system. Also see Kerr & Bowen (1988).

49. Villeneuve (1979).

50. McAdam (1995). Zilbach (1986, p. 20) mentions that exclusion may be a result of "inner reluctance or even a strong aversion to playing with children."

51. Korner (1988); Wachtel (1994b).

52. Rotter & Bush (2000, p. 172).

53. Stratton (1995a, p. 167). Stratton (1995b) devotes an entire issue to hearing the voice of the child in family therapy.

54. Diller (1991); Johnson & Volker (1999). Including a child does not always mean that the child is involved. Ruble (1999, p. 501) raises the issue of inclusion versus involve-

ment and notes: "many family therapists feel that they work with the whole family just by having children in the therapy room (usually coloring in the corner while the therapist talks to the parents)."

55. Korner & Brown (1990); Nickerson (1986); Ruble (1999).

56. Nickerson (1986) suggests the "for adults only orientation" needs to be addressed, that family therapists lack training and experience in working with children and adolescents. Family therapists have been lax in only working with parts of the system. Learning about and incorporating innovative practices is essential.

57. Korner (1988). Ruble (1999) conducted a systematic review of studies concerning the inclusion of children in family therapy and found that they are "routinely" excluded, most often based on "personal preference."

58. Ariel et al. (1985) uses children's make-believe play in family therapy. Barragar-Dunne (1997) suggests the use of narrative, drama, and dramatic play with young children. Freeman et al. (1997) discuss a "child-inclusive family therapy. Harvey (1990) recommends the use of art, drama, dance, videotaping to stimulate and organize changes in the ways the families interact. Rotter & Bush (2000) emphasize the need to involve children in the therapeutic process and suggest play as a vehicle; they assert that good judgment is required as sometimes it is appropriate, reasonable, safe, fair to exclude or include children. Also see Landgarten (1981); Linesch (1999); Schaefer & Carey (1994); Villeneuve & LaRoche (1993); Wachtel (1994a, 1994b). Wiener (1999) discusses the use of movement and expressive techniques in clinical work; Wolfe & Collins-Wolfe (1983) discuss action techniques.

59. Chasin & White (1989, p. 5).

60. Nicolopoulou (1993) presents a summary of Piaget's view on play. Also see Rubin & Pepler (1982), who discuss Piaget's extensive contributions to the study of children's play.

61. Sweeney (1998, p. 71): The play of children was considered by Adler as their work in preparation for the future.

62. Scharff (1999).

63. Gross (1995) recommends playful exchanges, which aid children's participation and brighten the mood of the session.

64. Freeman et al. (1997, p. 4).

65. Gil (1994); Gil & Sobol (2000); Freeman et al. (1997); Anderson & Reynolds (1996); Ariel et al. (1985); Barragar-Dunne (1997); Kaduson et al. (1997); Kaduson & Schaefer (1997); Keith & Whitaker (1981); Rotter & Bush (2000); Schaefer & Carey (1994); Scharff (1999); Smith & Renter (1997); Villeneuve & LaRoche (1993); Wachtel (1994a, 1994b); Webb (1999).

66. Cited in Gil (1994, p. 3).

67. Just as Freud believed that dreams were the "royal road" to the unconscious in adults, Klein (1975, p. 15) maintains, "The more primitive nature of the child's mind makes it necessary to find an analytic technique especially adapted to the child, and this we find in play analysis. By means of play analysis we gain access to the child's most deeply repressed experiences and fixations and are thus able to exert a radical influence on its development."

68. Axline (1947). Tenets of her approach involve the therapist developing a warm, friendly relationship with the child; accepting the child; establishing a "feeling of permissiveness" which facilitates a child's expression of feelings; reflecting back the child's feelings thus allowing the child to gain insight into his or her behavior; maintaining a "deep respect" for the child's ability to solve problems, hence the child is in charge of instituting change; not attempting to lead or hurry the therapy along; imposing limitations that are necessary to "anchor the therapy to the world of reality and to make the child aware of his responsibility in the relationship" (pp. 73–74).

69. Gil (1994, p. 33).

70. Anderson & Reynolds (1996) explore the integration of child-centered play therapy into family therapy.

71. Such as found in the work of Minuchin & Fishman (1981).

72. Ginsburg & Opper (1969, p. 221).

73. Wiener (1999, p. xii).

74. Enactment is a technique widely employed in structural therapy whereby the therapist encourages the family to demonstrate how they deal with a particular problem. (Creating an enactment has been likened to directing a play.) See Minuchin & Fishman (1981); Nichols & Fellenberg (2000).

75. Combs & Freedman (1990).

76. A ritual, as described by the Milan group, Boscolo et al. (1987), is a prescription of action or series of actions designed to change the family's roles. Also see Imber-Black et al. (1988).

77. Duhl et al. (1973); Hernandez (1998); Lesage-Higgins (1999); Papp et al. (1973); Satir (1972); Simon (1972).

78. Penn (1991); Penn & Frankfurt (1994); White & Epston (1990).

79. Ginsburg & Opper (1969).

80. Hannaford (1995, p. 49).

81. Dunn (1984). Rita Dunn researched learning styles for over 30 years. She posits that our unique learning styles determine how we learn. This idea has been applied widely in structuring an educational setting that facilitates learning by understanding the learner's preferences and matching teaching methods to his or her learning style. Environmental preferences, such as light, sound, noise, and temperature, are also considered.

82. Moats & Farrell (1999, p. 1).

83. Watzlawick (1978, p. 14).

84. Watzlawick (1978, p. 22).

85. Duhl (1999, p. 80).

86. Martin (1984). Also see Barker (1996) for suggestions and principles of constructing psychotherapeutic metaphors, and Combs & Freedman (1990).

87. Mills & Crowley (1986). A part of a problem may lie in the "out-of-conscious" sensory system. In creating therapeutic and living metaphors, Mills & Crowley discuss and make sensory assignments (visual, auditory, kinesthetic) to help a child develop an aware-

ness of the blocked sensory system in the area of the problem. They may suggest using a camera for visual senses, carrying weights for kinesthetic, or listening to nature's sounds to become more aware of the auditory sense. Barker (1996) suggests ways to evaluate the preferred sensory channel and communication style of a client.

88. Barker (1996, p. 31). Combs & Freedman (1990) point out that stories appeared to be Gregory Bateson's favorite form of metaphor; he believed "metaphor was inescapable in living systems, as every thought we have is *about* something" (p. 29). Also see Mills & Crowley (1986). Gardner (1993) discusses storytelling in psychotherapy with children.

89. In an article presenting an integrative expressive approach in work with young children in therapy, Harvey (1990) cites a premise of the model, "that creativity is a naturally occurring ability that greatly influences the tenor, style, form, and meaning of interpersonal interaction" (p. 239).

90. Pokemon characters, ©Nintendo.

91. The title character in J. K. Rowling's books, available from Scholastic.

92. From a social learning perspective, the experience of observing aggression teaches children that aggression is acceptable and a norm in the way to behave in relationships. Gerald Patterson's work is exemplary in this area. See Patterson (1975, 1976, 1982).

93. Bateson (1979). When we examine two or more things, differences become apparent. We learn new information by examining differences or changes in relationships.

94. Examples are found in Moustaka (1996) and Rogers (1995).

CHAPTER 2. PRINCIPLES AND PRACTICES: GENERAL ANCHORS AND GUIDES

1. Boyd-Franklin & Bry (2000) discuss this as a key concept in reaching out in family therapy. It remains a vital aspect of all therapeutic work. Narrative therapists, such as White & Epston (1990), focus on strengths. Levine (1994) talks about the importance of developing a profile of a child's strengths and affinities. See Singh et al. (1997) for a discussion on families, children with emotional disturbance, and "empowerment status." Echevarria-Doan (2001) writes about accessing client resources through interviews and dialogue. Also see Rudolph & Epstein (2000) for a discussion of strength-based assessment using the Behavioral and Emotional Rating Scale (BERS), available from PRO-ED, Austin, Texas, 1-800-897-3202. This article can be found online at www.air.org/cecp/interact/expertonline/strength/empower/1.htm.

2. Lewis (2000) cites his previous research that noted the importance of adult relationships with spouses, therapists, and teachers as a source of healing in the sense of "reversing the effects of adverse childhood experiences." What seems to be important in healing relationships is "the establishment of a strong affective bond, the inevitable disruptions of that bond, and the repair of such disruptions. These interactional dynamics, if repetitive, are believed to establish the relationship context in which internalization and subsequent

development may occur. A strong affective bond involves reciprocal gratification. Each participant receives something important from the other. Disruptions are inevitable because it is impossible for one person to be completely attuned to an important other all the time. Empathic failures or misattunements are therefore relatively common. The repair process is concerned with recognizing the signals of misattunement, acknowledging the error, and exploring the topic or feeling that was not initially responded to. Repair is usually a collaborative activity that may be initiated by either participant" (p. 1375).

3. Weber & Levine (1995) describe this task as a core component in engaging families in therapy. A holding environment is described as "a safe, reliable, therapeutic space within which change and growth can occur" (pp. 48–49). Goldman (1993a, 1993b) provides an overview of the work of Donald W. Winnicott, British pediatrician and psychoanalyst. The concepts and ideas that he proposed and developed were presented in over 200 papers and included "good-enough mothering" (the parent is oriented to the infant, hence is ready to meet the infant's needs and dependence), holding environment (the attachment process necessary for the infant's sense of security), and transitional object. Also see Winnicott (1965).

4. Scharff (1999, p. 87). Also see Scharff & Scharff (1987). The Scharffs have written extensively on object relations theory (a combination of systems and psychoanalytic theories). Nichols & Schwartz (1998) comment that object relations is quite complex and describe its essence as follows: "We relate to people in the past partly on the basis of expectations formed by early experience. The residue of these early relationships leaves *internal objects*—mental images of self and other, and self in relation to others, built from experience and expectation. The unconscious remnants of those internalized objects form the core of the person—an open system developing and maintaining its identity through social relatedness past *and* present" (p. 209).

5. Weber & Levine (1995) talk about "emotional containment" and propose that the "message to the family is that in this room, in this space, nothing is too dangerous or too frightening for discussion" (p. 49).

6. King Features Inc. (1975).

7. Thomas & Chess (1968, 1977, 1984); Chess & Thomas (1989, 1991, 1999). Psychiatrists Thomas and Chess are outstanding contributors to the field. In *Temperament and Development* (1977), they identified nine dimensions of temperament and proposed three clusters of these dimensions: the difficult child, the easy child, and the slow-to-warm-up child. More recently, in *Coping with Children's Temperament* (1995), Carey and McDevitt adapted the original nine dimensions into: activity, rhythmicity (one's rhythms related to eating, sleeping, elimination, etc.), approach/withdrawal (to new people, places or things), adaptability, intensity, mood (pleasant and friendly or unpleasant and unfriendly), persistence/attention span, distractibility, and sensory threshold.

8. Nichols & Schwartz (1998) discuss belief systems, perspectives, or world views.

9. Dunn & Dunn (1978).

10. All complex learning tasks require the smooth assembly and coordination of a number of brain functions, including attention, memory, language processing, and language pro-

duction. The execution of such tasks generally requires successful use of complex fine and/or gross motor skills.

11. Rourke (1989, 1995); Rourke & Fuerst (1991). An essential aspect of nonverbal communication is the interpretation of facial expressions of emotion. Children diagnosed with a learning disability have been found to be less accurate than their peers who don't have a learning disability.

12. Duke et al. (1996). Also see Hart & Risley (1999).

13. Gardner (1983). Dr. Howard Gardner and his team of researchers at Harvard University posit that there are multiple intelligences/forms of intelligence. Lazear (1991), author of *Seven Ways of Teaching*, based on Gardner's work, presents ideas for educators that I often apply to therapy interventions. He postulates that we can employ one kind of intelligence to help us learn in what may seem to be unconnected areas. For example, we can use body movement to help us learn vocabulary words, or we can use music to facilitate learning math concepts. Teaching the family that there are many ways to learn helps build acceptance for individual differences. It places a spotlight and turns up the volume on areas of talents and resources.

14. Flavell (1992); Selman (1981). It is important to keep in mind that perspective-taking has a developmental trajectory.

15. Fisher (1968a).

16. Generalization is when a new response or behavior is utilized under conditions different from those surrounding the initial learning. Difficulty with generalization is referred to as a "crucial problem" in optimizing treatment effectiveness (Baer et al., 1987), and maintenance of responding is thought to be "similarly critical" (Gresham, 1981). An important concern in evaluating the success of an intervention relates to the extent that generalization has taken place (Baer et al., 1968).

17. Maintenance relates to the perpetuation of generalization responses over time. Stokes & Baer (1977) point out that active planning for generalization and maintenance of training effects across physical settings, contexts, time, and interpersonal situations is fundamental. We can't presume generalization will occur automatically. A "train and hope" approach doesn't work. Programming methods to ensure generalization into treatment is required.

18. Kazdin (2000a, 2000b). He cites (2000a) a 1500 total of empirical studies as a "conservative" estimate.

19. See Abikoff & Hechtman (1996); Anastopoulos et al. (1996); Borduin (1999); Henggeler et al. (1998); Kendall & Braswell (1993); Kendall & Chambless (1998); March & Mulle (1998); Mash & Barkley (1998); Norman & Gorman (1998); Quay & Hogan (1999).

20. There are many review articles on a variety of topics. Beardslee et al. (1998) discuss children of affectively ill parents; Beitchman & Young (1997), learning and reading disorders; Bernstein et al. (1996), anxiety disorders in children and adolescents; King & Bernstein (2001), school refusal; Ladd (1999), peer relationships; Loeber et al. (2000), oppositional defiant and conduct disorder; National Institutes of Health (2000), ADHD;

Taylor & Biglan (1998) child-rearing-behavioral family interventions; Toppelberg & Shapiro (2000), language disorders; Velting & Albano (2001), social phobia.

21. There are many programs available with guidelines about how to use behavioral shaping principles to change behavior. See Barkley (1998) for details on how to use a daily report card. Alberto & Troutman (1999) provide a wonderful source regarding applied behavior analysis principles for teachers.

22. First described in Kiresuk & Sherman (1968). Also see Kiresuk et al. (1994); MacKay et al. (1996); Ottenbacher & Cusick (1990, 1993).

23. For a discussion of its use in rehabilitation, see Malec (1999); Malec et al. (1991); Joyce et al. (1994).

24. See Stolee et al. (1999).

25. Young & Chesson (1997).

26. Fleuridas et al. (1990); Simeonsson et al. (1991); Woodward et al. (1978).

27. Gil & Sobol (2000, p. 350).

28. See Martin & Thompson (1995).

29. de Shazer (1988, p. 5).

30. de Shazer (1988); Walter & Peller (1992).

CHAPTER 3. PRINCIPLES AND PRACTICES: STRATEGICALLY ORGANIZED SESSIONS

1. See "Tools to Talk and Send Therapy Home" in the Appendix for a list of additional supplies, puppet- and game-making tools.

2. The following site offers a wide variety of tents: www.biznest.com/toy-store/outdoor.

3. Portable games are available from Playhut at www.playhut.com. The Game Center Deluxe has three games, including skeeball, and folds away for storage.

4. A list of useful software is included in "Tools and Resources" and "Tools to Talk and Send Therapy Home" in the Appendix.

5. This is a modification of the match game presented by Kendall & Braswell (1993).

6. Avery Printertainment Software can be ordered over the phone: 1-800-GO-AVERY.

7. In this activity developed by Kendall & Braswell (1993), the child first acts like a robot—stiff and tense, walking without bending limbs, and then like a rag doll—floppy, relaxed, limp. Also see Forman (1993).

8. Harary & Weintraub (1991) discuss holistic thinking, seeing similarities, visualizing, recognizing patterns, and intuition. Also see Buzan (1991).

9. Ayan (1997, p. 28). Curiosity prompts investigation. Ayan suggests that we move out of our "comfort zones." In therapy this might be exploring the use of a new medium with a client. Each time we incorporate something new into our repertoire we increase our "risk tolerance." Energy relates to the "fuel to work and the spark of passion" (p. 33).

10. Henry Ford, quoted in Davis (1996, p. BS5).

11. Freeman et al. (1997, p. 172). The authors point out that "co-therapists in the form of puppets and other toys or even imaginary or mythic entities can be called upon to support the therapist and enliven the conversation."

12. Schaefer & Reid (1986, p. ix).

13. Some of these companies include: Childswork Childsplay, 1-800-962-1141 or www.childwork.com; Western Psychological Services Creative Therapy Store, 1-800-648-8857 or www.wpspublish.com; and A.D.D. Warehouse, 1-800-233-9273 or www.addwarehouse.com.

14. The Ungame® Parents, Kids and Other Animals™ (available through Talicor Inc. in Anaheim, California at www.talicor.com/communication.html).

15. Burks (1978) (available from Western Psychological Services, 1-800-648-8857).

16. Gardner (1986, p. 43).

17. I use Microsoft Publisher or Microsoft Word, but any word processing program has options for including pictures, shapes, scanning, etc.

18. See "The ABCs of Game Making," in "Tools to Talk and Send Therapy Home" in the Appendix.

19. Emberly (1977).

20. Curtis (1998).

21. Freymann & Elffers (1999). These authors, or food artists, use natural curves, wrinkles, and bends in fruits and vegetables to demonstrate a variety of emotions. The wrinkles of a pepper may make it look sad, happy, or mad. The simple text asks questions that direct children to think about emotions. This project is loads of fun.

22. Freymann & Elffers (1997).

23. Freymann & Elffers (2000).

24. For information about or to purchase Screen Beans: www.bitbetter.com.

25. See "Tools to Talk and Send Therapy Home" in the Appendix for a blank template.

26. These are available from Avery Dennison Products, 1-800-GO-AVERY or www.avery.com.

27. For a discussion of cognitive behavior therapy (CBT), see Braswell & Kendall (2001) and Kendall & Panichelli-Mindel (1995). For CBT used in specific disorders, see Bernstein et al. (2000), school refusal; Kazak et al. (1999), cancer; Kendall & Braswell (1993), impulsive children; Lewandowski, Gebing, Anthony, & O'Brien (1997), bulimia; March & Mulle (1998), obsessive compulsive disorder; Mendlowitz et al. (1999), anxiety; Satterfield (1999), bipolar disorder; Sensky et al. (2000), schizophrenia; Thase et al. (1998), depression; Turkington & Kindon (2000), psychoses.

28. Chethik (1989, p. 23) discusses the "counterreactions" to the child patient and notes that because sudden strong eruptions can occur, a therapist might be bewildered and experience "complete disorientation." Reactions can be "dramatically evoked."

29. Weber & Levine (1995, p. 49).

30. Weber & Levine (1995, p. 50).

31. Watzlawick et al. (1988).

32. Antimanic agents (primarily lithium or valproic acid) are the mainstays of pharmacotherapy.

33. See Johnson et al. (2000).

34. Similar to research on schizophrenia, adult studies on bipolar disorders identify family interaction patterns that are predictive of relapse, such as high expressed emotion (criticism, hostility, and emotional overinvolvement). See Geller & Luby (1997); Miklowitz & Goldstein (1997); Miklowitz et al. (1988).

35. Strober et al. (1995).

36. American Academy of Child and Adolescent Psychiatry (1997). Goals of therapy involve the lessening of symptoms and relapse prevention, reduction of long-term morbidity and promotion of normal growth and development. Also see Perry et al. (1999). For a discussion of lifestyle regularity, see Frank et al. (1997). For a discussion of interpersonal and social rhythm therapy, see Frank et al. (1994, 2000).

37. Strober et al. (1990), in a study of adolescents with bipolar disorder, found that 90% of those who were noncompliant with lithium relapsed over an 18-month period.

38. See note 36.

39. Pardeck (1989); Pardeck & Markward (1995); Pardeck & Pardeck (1997). Bibliotherapy, usage of books in therapy, helps children deal with a variety of situations such as divorce, hospitalization, and death. It is utilized as an adjunct in many settings. Pardeck & Pardeck (1997) outline a process for employing books in therapy. Pardeck (1995) points out that research on the efficacy of bibliotherapy has found mixed results. Manning (1987) recommends books as therapy for children of alcoholics. Slade (1987) uses bibliotherapy with siblings of handicapped children. Also see Cohen (1987); Krickeberg (1991); Lenkowsky (1987).

40. Scieszka (1989). Raintree Steck-Vaughn also publishes Point of View Stories, which retell classic stories using the points of view of the main characters, such as Cinderella, the wicked stepmother and her daughters. The reader reads the book and then flips it over and reads the same story told from a different perspective. See "Tools to Talk and Send Therapy Home" in the Appendix for availability.

41. Computers and video use: see DeMaso et al. (2000), medical illness; Bosworth et al. (2000), multimedia violence prevention; King-Storm et al. (1998), using the Internet in therapy; McConatha et al. (1995), institutionalized older adults; Ross (1992), occupational therapy; Schinke et al. (1989), AIDS prevention.

Video use: Arauzo et al. (1994), treatment of childhood sexual trauma survivors; Furman (1990) and Gardano (1994), video therapy with adolescent girls; Getz & Nininger (1999), families; American Academy of Psychiatry & the Law Task Force (1999), forensic psychiatric evaluations, Taylor et al. (1999), video modeling for children with autism; Wark & Scheidegger (1996), engaging children in therapeutic enactments; Webster-Stratton (1996), videotape vignettes to teach and model parenting skill; Zelenko & Benham (2000), as a therapeutic tool in psychodynamic infant-parent therapy.

42. For example, Hanes® T-ShirtMaker® & More. See "Tools to Talk and Send Therapy Home" in the Appendix for information.

CHAPTER 4. KEEPING THE BRAIN IN MIND:
A BRAIN PRIMER

1. Rowe (1994) asserts that there are limits to the influence of the family, that the story is written in the genetic material.

2. Siegel (1999, p. 26), in developing his excellent integration and explanation of the neurobiology of interpersonal experience, cites Hebb's (1949) axiom as "the essence of how the neural net remembers." This axiom is widely cited as "neurons that fire together, wire together."

3. Siegel (1999) offers a wonderful synthesis of attachment and how disruptions in attachment affect self-regulation. Also see Atkinson (1999); Goldberg et al. (1995); Schore (1994, 1997); Walker et al. (1999); Wright (1997).

4. Elbert et al. (1995). This group of investigators, using brain-imaging techniques, studied changes in cortical representations in the brains of string players (violinists, cellists, and guitarists) and compared them to the brains of controls. Changes in the primary somatosensory cortex were found and thought to be correlated with the age at which the person began to play. Sterr et al. (1998) found similar changes in the cortical representation of Braille readers.

5. Kolb & Whishaw (1998) report neural changes, such as modifications in brain size, neuron size, cortical thickness, dendritic density spine density, synapses per neuron, and glial cells (the brain's glue), in response to experience. McEwen (2000, p. 172) states, "the brain is resilient and capable of adaptive plasticity." Gould et al. (2000, p. 715) claim this is true for adults as well as children: "enriching experiences including learning have been shown to enhance the survival of new hippocampal cells." Also see McEwen (1999).

6. McEwen (2000). Lowenstein & Parent (1999, p. 1126) assert, "it is time to lay to rest the dogmatic assumption that the central nervous system (CNS) of adult mammals cannot repair itself. . . . [It] has a much greater potential for repairing damage than previously thought." Eriksson et al. (1998, p. 1313) demonstrated potential of the human brain for cell growth throughout life. They note that although new neurons grow (neurogenesis), it has not been proven that the "newly generated cells are functional."

7. Baxter et al. (1992). In treatment of obsessive-compulsive disorder using cognitive behavior therapy, actual changes in brain metabolism were evidenced. These changes were also noted with medication. Thase et al. (1998) found changes in depressed subjects after cognitive behavior therapy.

8. Begley (1996).

9. *Scientific American* (1996).

10. *Discover* (October, 1997). There has been a concomitant increase in books exploring these questions, including Greenfield (2000), Hamer & Copeland (1998), Kotulak (1996), Pinker (1997).

11. *Science Magazine* devoted an entire issue (February 16, 2001) to human genome contents. Included in the issue is a timeline (with pictures) as well as articles on genomics and

medicine, genomics and behavior, and genomics and society. This issue can be found online at www.sciencemag.org/content/ vol291/issue5507.

12. Steen (1996, p. 3) proposes to sequence the entire complement of deoxyribonucleic acid (DNA), the hereditary material in the genes. Wade (1998) writes that a new field, "computational biology" or "bioinformatics," handles the flow of information entering computer data bases about DNA. Wade (2001) reports on recent articles in *Nature* and *Science*, which indicate that there are probably considerably fewer genes, more likely around 30,000.

13. Scientists have found other genetic links. Wade (2000) reports on the discovery of the type 2 diabetes gene named calpain-10 (2000); on the role of two genes, known as BRCA1 and BRCA2, involved in breast cancer (1997a); on the link between genes and clues to deafness (1997b); and on the discovery of two new human genes linked to epilepsy (1997c).

14. Snyder & Ferris (2000). There has been an increase in the identification of new chemical neurotransmitters (chemical messengers in the brain that mediate the action of all psychoactive medications). They note that late in the 1950s we knew of only two neurotransmitters and now we know of about 50 to 100. The knowledge of these new neurotransmitters provides more opportunity for intervention. Also see Wade (1999) for a discussion of differential response to drugs on a "genome-wide scale" and the emerging field of pharmacogenomics.

15. Rauch et al. (2000) used MRI with veterans suffering from PTSD and found heightened amygdala responses to viewing "masked-fearful" versus "masked-happy faces." Shin et al. (1997) found changes in blood supply when obsessional thoughts were provoked by certain psychological stimuli. McIntosh (1998) discusses how neuroimaging tools provide new ways to study autism. Also see Andreasen (1997).

16. MacLean (1970, 1990). It is important to note that others, such as LeDoux (1996), have challenged some of MacLean's framework as not representing the brain as it is today.

17. Lewis et al. (2000, p. 23).

18. MacLean (1990).

19. Barnet & Barnet (1998).

20. Lewis et al. (2000, pp. 51-52).

21. LeDoux (1996, p. 161).

22. Barrios & O'Dell (1998); March (1995). See Bernstein et al. (1996) for a review of anxiety disorders in children and adolescents.

23. I might use the pop-up brain model in Van der Meer & Dudink (1996).

24. Zephyr Press, at www.zephyrpress.com, has many books and comics. Also see Marguiles (1997). Two favorites are: Digital Anatomist, available online at: www9.biostr.washington.edu/da.html, and A Brain Tour, www.faculty.washington.edu/chudler/introb.html#bb. Also see www.brainpop.com for videos about the brain. See "Tools and Resources" in the Appendix for other resources on the brain.

25. Gazzaniga (1972). Sperry (1974) discusses lateral specialization in the surgically separated hemispheres, which is cited in Bloom & Lazerson (1988, p. 282). "Each hemisphere . . .

has its own . . . private sensations, perceptions, thoughts, and ideas, all of which are cut off from the corresponding experiences in the opposite hemisphere. Each left and right hemisphere has its own private chain of memories and learning experiences that are inaccessible to recall by the other hemisphere. In many respects each disconnected hemisphere appears to have a separate 'mind of its own'." The original reference is in F. O. Schmitt & F. G. Worden (Eds.), *The neurosciences: Third study program*, Cambridge, MA: MIT Press.

26. Healy (1994).

27. Barnet & Barnet (1998); Gazzaniga (1972).

28. Herrmann (1995, p. 17).

29. For developmental consequences of frontal lobe damage, see Eslinger et al. (1992).

30. Eslinger (1996, p. 368).

31. See Lyon & Krasnegor (1996), chapters 14–19 for a summary of various theoretical and empirical approaches to executive functions. Eslinger (1996, p. 380) postulates, "there is no universal definition." See Pennington et al. (1996) for a discussion of executive functions and working memory, and Pennington & Ozonoff (1996) for executive functions and their relationship to developmental psychopathology.

32. Barkley (1996, 1997a, 1997b).

33. Grattan & Eslinger (1992).

34. Eslinger (1996, p. 387).

35. Denckla (1996).

36. Coyle & Schwarcz (2000).

37. Restak (1995). Kandel & Squire (2000, p. 1113) cite Spanish anatomist Santiago Ramon y Cajal, who showed that the brain is made up of distinct cells—neurons—which likely serve as "elementary signaling units." Cajal advanced the fundamental premise that neurons form highly specific connections with one another. In discussing the neuron, Kotulak (1993, p. B6) cites information that links the first brain cell, or neuron's appearance in animals about 500 million years ago: "Able to form flexible connections with other cells to send and receive electrochemical messages, the neuron marked a crucial leap in evolution, second only to that of the DNA molecule, which appeared about 3 billion years earlier."

38. Hyman (1999, p. 12).

39. Healy (1990).

40. Barnet & Barnet (1998, p. 23).

41. Edelman (1987).

42. Begley (1996, p. 55). Eisenberg (1998) claims that nature and nurture have a "reciprocal relationship" in shaping development and discusses this in terms of social experience.

43. Elbert et al. (1995); Sterr et al. (1998). Also see Kandel (1999).

44. Kempermann et al. (1997) found that there were significantly more new neurons in mice reared in settings enriched with wheels, toys, and tunnels. Kempermann & Gage (1999) found experience-induced modification in neural networks in the hippocampus of adult mice reared in enriched environments. Also see Diamond (1988); Greenough et al.

(1987). Kolb & Whishaw (1998) cite Hebb as one of the early investigators (in 1947) who discussed changes in the brain as a result of enriched rearing. Kotulak (1993, p. B6) reported on research that demonstrates how early stimulation "boosts the brain to maximum power."

45. Renner & Rosenzweig (1987).

46. Conlan (1999, p. 176). Kolb & Whishaw (1998) provide a good review of brain plasticity and behavior. Greenfield (2000, p. 13) notes: "As the brain becomes more sophisticated, it appears to exploit instinct less and less and instead uses increasingly the results of individual experience, of learning."

47. Siegel (1999, p. 85).

48. Siegel (1999, p. 85).

49. Hubel & Wiesel (1965), and Wiesel & Hubel (1965). These Nobel Prize winners investigated the impact of early sensory deprivation on newborn kittens. They found that deprivation of visual input resulted in a profound change on the organization of columns 18 and 19; Zeki (1993) provides an overview of the research of Hubel and Wiesel. Hockfield & Lombroso (1998a, 1998b) provide a brief synopsis of development during "critical periods," citing as an example the presence of a congenital cataract in a child. If the cataract remains undiagnosed or is not removed "during the first years of life," the child will be permanently blind in that eye. In adults, once a cataract is removed, vision is restored. Also see Brainard & Knudsen (1998) and Knudsen (1998) for results of studies on the early-altered visual experience of young owls.

50. Rymer (1993).

51. Public Broadcasting System. The tape was first aired as an episode of NOVA on PBS on October 18, 1994. The broadcast transcript is available online as NOVA #2112G: Secret of the Wild Child: www.pbs.org/wgbh/ nova/transcripts/2112gchild.html.

52. Rymer (1993).

53. Hyman (1999, p. 16).

54. Steen (1996). Also see Eisenberg (1998).

55. Hyman (1999, p. 27).

56. Schore (1994).

57. Barnet & Barnet (1998, p. 27). "The most critical factor in the development of an infant's brain, assuming that he or she is neither seriously malformed nor malnourished nor subjected to dangerous levels of heat or cold, sensory isolation, infective agents, toxic chemicals, or radiation, is human interaction." Also see Schore (1994); Siegel (1999); Sroufe (1995).

58. Rutter et al. (1997). The interplay of nature and nurture is discussed with a focus on the person-environment influences, considered along with the wider social contextual features.

59. Cooley-Quille et al. (1995); Garbarino et al. (1991); Glodich (1998); Margolin & Gordis (2000); McCloskey et al. (1995); Miller et al. (1999); Pynoos (1994); Shrier (1997); Straus (1994).

60. McCloskey & Stuewig (2001, p. 94) found that children of battered women are at significant risk and show early indications of social problems.

61. Durant et al. (1995); Gorman-Smith & Tolan (1998).

62. Negrao et al. (2000) review the literature on neuroendocrine responses and differential reactivity to psychological and physical stressors.

63. Silva et al. (2000).

64. Benes (1997, p. 259) explains that, "during the life cycle, genetic and environmental factors probably interact in a dynamic fashion to give rise to what we identify phenotypically as the selective 'vulnerability' for a particular mental illness, such as schizophrenia"; Paris et al. (1999) discuss the stress-diathesis model in the development of borderline pathology; Campbell et al. (1997) report that a schizophrenic family member is thought to have a vulnerable central nervous system; Kendler et al. (1995, 2000) discuss depression.

65. Diamond et al. (1996) cite such factors as an individual's cognitive development and quality of caregiving. Barron & Earls (1984), for example, found a child's inflexibility (a characteristic of the child's temperament), high family stress, and negative child-parent interactions are related to poor behavioral adjustment.

66. Griffith et al. (1989, p. 146).

67. Selye (1975). Selye (1978) discusses the general stress reaction and notes that almost all organs and chemical elements are involved. Stress, according to Selye, is the body's response to any demand made on it. The first stage in stress response is characterized by "alarm," and it is followed by "resistance," at which time the initial symptoms lessen or disappear. If there is extended exposure, a state of "exhaustion" follows. According to Negrao et al. (2000), the body's response to stress involves activation of the neuroendocrine system: hypothalamic-pituitary-adrenal axis (referred to as the HPA axis) and the sympathoadrenal medullar systems.

68. Siegel (1999). Kolb & Whishaw (1998) note that stress impacts on brain structures as well; a particular focus has been placed on the hippocampus, which is involved in long-term memory. McEwen (2000, p. 172) reviews research and concludes, "Stress-induced structural changes in brain regions such as the hippocampus have clinical ramifications for disorders such as depression, posttraumatic stress disorder and individual differences in the aging process." The brain, along with the other systems, such as the immune, metabolic, and cardiovascular systems, is a target of stress. Stress hormones can play a protective or damaging role. Gould et al. (2000) report that negative regulators of adult-generated neurons were deprivation, adrenal steroids, excitatory input, and stress. Nelson & Carver (1998, p. 793) present a review of research on the brain, stress, and memory, and "suggest the developing brain is particularly vulnerable to the harmful physiological effects of stress, which in turn has the potential to lead to impairments in memory." Cohen (2000) reports on the relationship between stress and mental health. Hoes (1997) discusses adverse life events and psychosomatic disease. Sternberg & Gold (1997) write about the mind-body interaction in disease. Also see Chrousos (1998); Gould et al. (1998); McEwen & Sapolsky (1995); Sapolsky (1996).

69. Ackerman Institute, Families and Learning Disabilities Project, NY. See Dyson (1996); Geisthardt & Munsch (1996); Strubbe (1989); Walker & Shimmerlik (1994); Wenz-Gross & Siperstein (1998); Zetlin (1993).

70. Berenstain & Berenstain (1992).

71. Researchers find increased parenting stresses in parents of children with biologic variations. Baker & McCal (1995) found higher parenting stresses due to child character-istics; Mash & Johnston (1983) found that mothers of hyperactive children have signifi-cantly lower levels of self-esteem with regard to parenting, engage in more self-blame, and suffer from more social isolation than mothers of children without ADHD; Dyson (1996) found that parents of learning disabled children reported higher levels of stress when com-pared with mothers of nondisabled children.

72. Commoner (1971). Gregory Bateson (1972, 1979) examined patterns in biological relationships in one system and looked for them in other complex systems in nature. Through his search across systems he found patterns that described larger connections. He underscored the interconnectedness in nature.

CHAPTER 5. ZOOM OUT: FOCUSING ON THE FAMILY AND SCHOOL

1. Fisher (1968b).

2. Thoughts, perceptions, cognitions, and beliefs influence one's experience of events. It is essential to assess the meaning that each client ascribes to the presenting problem and the issues and concerns each brings to therapy. See Bugental & Johnston (2000) for a review article on parental and child cognitions in the context of the family.

3. Eisenberg (1998, p. 213).

4. Combrinck-Graham (1989, pp. 67–68).

5. von Bertalanffy (1962, 1968). General systems theory views a system as a complex of interacting components. One part of the system is not more important than the other parts, and change in any part is likely to cause a ripple effect through other parts of the system. In fact, there are influences between the levels. Wamboldt & Wamboldt (2000), for exam-ple, discuss the reciprocal influence between chronic illness and family process. While they note there is practically no evidence that family processes foretell the onset of illness in youngsters with a genetic risk of developing a specific disorder, childhood illness can change family dynamics.

6. Many disorders have a psychological-physical interface, with psychosocial factors such as stress, anxiety, and depression influencing the presentation of the symptoms and their severity. For discussions of gastrointestinal problems, see Drossman (1998); Wood (1991); Wood et al. (1987). Carlier et al. (2000) write about trauma and depression. They found that there is a high probability that depressed individuals experienced trauma in the past. Epker & Gatchel (2000) discuss coping profiles of patients affected with temporo-mandibular disorder (TMD). Patients assessed to have poor coping scores suffered more

chronic symptoms. Main et al. (2000) found relationships between psychosocial factors and pain in individuals with chronic back pain and psoriasis.

7. See McDaniel et al. (1995) on medical family therapy—a systems approach to psychotherapy with patients and families experiencing a medical illness, trauma, or disability; Moltz (1993), bipolar disorder; Renfrew (1997), aggression; Wood (1993, 1994, 1995), Wood et al. (1987, 2000), and Miller & Wood (1994), chronic childhood illness; Zucker (1994), alcohol.

8. Gabbard & Goodwin (1996, p. 535) conclude that stress plays a role in such disorders as: major depression, bipolar disorder, panic disorder, and PTSD. Baum & Posluszny (1999) map biobehavioral contributions to health and illness. They look at disease processes and how these can be modified by "health-protective" or "health-impairing" behaviors. They highlight research that suggests strong ties between how individuals think, feel, and behave and the impact on outcomes when the individuals are faced with poor health.

9. Nichols & Schwartz (1998). See Stern & Walker (2001) for a brief overview of children's learning and emotional problems within a family context.

10. Zilbach (1986, p. 50–55) outlines different functions of young children in family therapy, which include their being: (1) the "flag bearer," alerting others to the presence of problems in the family; (2) the "tip of the iceberg," whose troubling behavior(s) may alert others to family problems that would otherwise go unnoticed; (3) allies of the therapist and "direct explainers" of family concerns through words or play; (4) "the early detection" of family problems; and (5) the elucidator of entire family interactions.

11. Zilbach (1986, p. 55).

12. Chasin (1999, pp. 58–67).

13. Chasin (1999, p. 58) suggests that since play is the essential mode of communication, collaborative playthings, such as puppets, dolls, and drawing implements, should be available. The therapist needs to allow for spontaneity, but unlike in individual play therapy, should maintain a directive role when necessary. For example, children have access to toys only when the therapist deems it appropriate. Chasin states: "If the therapist is too nondirective, impulsive families will become chaotic, and repressed ones will freeze in the face of so much freedom."

14. Gottman et al. (1976) use "the floor" in couples therapy. Consult Chapter 3 in this book for a variety of listening enhancers.

15. See note 2. Each individual has a different understanding of the problems and concerns based on that individual's beliefs, memories, and experiences. In addition to the other questions listed, a simple and useful categorization that I often keep in mind when asking questions about the presenting complaint is FIDDO: frequency (how often), intensity (how loud the volume is turned up), duration (transient or enduring), developmentally appropriate, and onset (i.e., antecedents, what brings it on). It is essential that the therapist get self-reports as well as evaluations of the individual's current emotional functioning from other family members. In the case of children, the school is another valuable resource and an essential source of information that will be discussed later.

16. Use circular, reflexive questions. For examples, see Benson et al. (1991); Cecchin (1987); Fleuridas et al. (1986); Penn (1982); Tomm (1987a, 1987b, 1988).

17. Wright et al. (1996) outline how beliefs are at the heart of healing illness.

18. Penn (1985) describes future questions and maps. Also see Walsh (1995, 1998).

19. Walsh (1995, 1998).

20. *Families and Family Therapy* (Minuchin, 1974) is a classic book on structural family therapy. Minuchin defines boundary as "the rules defining who participates and how" (p. 53). He states: "For proper family functioning, the boundaries of subsystems [parental, sibling] must be clear. They must be defined enough to allow subsystem members to carry out their functions without undue interference, but they must allow contact between the members of the subsystem and others" (p. 54). He discusses the clarity of boundaries within a family and concludes: "it is a useful parameter for the evaluation of family functioning" (p. 54). Boundaries can be viewed on a continuum—disengaged (inappropriately rigid boundaries) to enmeshed (diffuse boundaries).

21. Hoffman (1981, pp. 262–263).

22. Carter & McGoldrick (1999a, 1999b) are excellent sources for reviews of family life cycle, including culture, social class, and women's issues. The family life cycle characteristically includes these stages: launching of a young adult, forming of a couple in marriage, family with young children, the family with adolescents, launching grown children—midlife stage, family in later life. Zilbach (1989, p. 65) describes the stages as follows: "early stages— forming and nesting"; "middle stages—family separation processes"; "late stages—finishing." Also see Zilbach & Gordetsky (1999). The different stages, for example, the transition to parenthood, may be challenging for a particular family; see Lewis et al. (1988).

23. See Goldner (1985, 1988) and Hare-Mustin (1987, 1991), who are outstanding contributors in the areas of gender and power issues in family therapy.

24. For example: "Plan a menu for tonight's dinner which you would all enjoy. You are allowed to have one meat dish, two vegetables, one dessert, and one drink. Try to include each person's favorite food. Remember that you must agree on the final choice of foods." (Baker et al. 1975, pp. 336–337). In addition to revealing family patterns and process, these types of activities reveal information about gender and power, conflict and conflict resolution skills, language patterns, affective reactions, and communication skills. Also see Wood et al. (2000).

25. Brown et al. (1962); Vaughn (1989). Vaughn offers an extensive review of the literature that finds a relationship between high EE in families and physiological arousal, which impacts on the course of both physical and mental illness. Wamboldt & Wamboldt (2000) note there is a burgeoning body of research linking EE to the course and outcome of major psychiatric disorders in children. They cite research by Asarnow et al. (1993), who found a predictive relationship between recovery and low EE homes, and relapse in children returning to high EE homes.

26. Steinglass et al. (1987). An aspect of family temperament is the family's usual energy level.

27. Minuchin (1974).

28. McGoldrick et al. (1999). The authors provide extensive references for use of the genogram with varied populations. Buurma (1999) has produced a manual for a family play genogram. Family members select small objects, animals, and miniature people to represent family members and then create the genogram.

29. See Buurma (1999); Gil & Sobol (2000).

30. McGoldrick et al. (1999, p. 3).

31. Mild forms of a disorder that impact on one's adjustment and well being. See Ratey & Johnson (1997).

32. Minuchin & Fishman (1981, p. 17) note: "If there is any major dysfunction within the spouse subsystem, this will reverberate throughout the family." Use observation, interview, or self-report measures, e.g., Locke & Wallace (1959). Dyadic adjustment scale (Spanier, 1976, 1988) is a quick self-report measure of relationship adjustment. Also see the Appendix, "Tools and Resources" for a listing of marriage and family assessment scales.

33. For example, Cox et al. (1989) found that when parents were in "close/confiding marriages," mothers were warmer and fathers more positive toward their infants.

34. Cummings et al. (1985) simulated angry verbal exchanges in front of toddlers and found they responded with some form of distress, as well as subsequent increases in aggression with peers; also see Cummings et al. (1989), Cummings & Smith (1993). Gottman & Katz (1989) found that peer relationships are also affected by marital conflict. Results reported by Handal et al. (1998) reveal a strong and significant relationship between husbands' and wives' perceived family conflict and child maladjustment. Isaacs et al. (1986) discuss the difficult divorce. Jouriles et al. (1988) found marital conflict was positively correlated with observations of toddler deviance and maternal reports of conduct problems; also see Jouriles et al. (1991). Kelly (2000) reviews a decade of research concerning children's adjustment in conflicted marriage and divorce. O'Brien et al. (1995) found that children's coping ability impacted on their adjustment; O'Brien et al. (1997) found aggressive marital conflict is predictive of children's feelings of low self worth; O'Brien & Bahadur (1998) found that when mothers are involved in marital aggression, it impacts on parenting behavior. Vandewater & Lansford (1998) reported that parental conflict influences children's well being regardless of family structure. Webster-Stratton & Hammond (1999) report a direct link between negative marital conflict, management style, and children's conduct problems.

35. Cummings et al. (1994); Dadds et al. (1999); Grych & Fincham (1993); Weston et al. (1998).

36. Gottman (1998, p. 189).

37. Christensen & Heavey (1999) present a review of interventions with couples. See Johnson & Lebow (2000) for an overview of the significant developments in couple therapy over the last decade. Johnson et al. (2001) discuss "attachment injury" as a way to overcome impasses in couples therapy and cite recent research (Johnson et al., 1999) that indicates emotionally focused couples therapy (see EFT, Greenberg & Johnson,

1988) has a higher success rate (70–73% of couples are no longer distressed at the end of therapy).

38. Dunn & Plomin (1990, 1991). These outstanding researchers in behavioral genetics discuss why siblings are so different. They point to nonshared environmental factors. Dunn & Plomin (1991, p. 271) state: "Siblings, who are 50% similar genetically and grow up within the same family, nevertheless differ markedly in personality and psychopathology, and most of these sibling differences cannot be explained by genetic factors. Findings from the field of behavioral genetics imply that within-family processes, called nonshared environment, that lead to sibling differences, are crucial for understanding environmental influences on individual development." Also see Pike & Plomin (1996); Plomin & Daniels (1987); Reiss et al. (2000).

39. Nichols & Schwartz (1998, p. 148).

40. See Chess & Thomas (1989); Thomas & Chess (1968, 1977, 1984). Thomas & Chess (1977) reported that children identified as less adaptable experienced the birth of a sibling as more distressing. Mash & Johnston (1983) found four times as much sibling conflict in children with highly active temperaments. Also see Kagan (1994).

41. Researchers find that siblings are affected. Lobato et al. (1988) discuss the effects of chronic disease and disability on children's sibling relationships and advocate a transactional, family systems perspective, which takes into consideration both the direct and indirect effects on the sibling relationship over time. Also see Fishman et al. (1996); Kendall (1999).

42. Differential treatment has been described in families with disabled children; see McHale & Pawletko (1992). McHale & Gamble (1989) found that child with a mentally retarded sibling reported differential treatment and negativity in the care giving from mother. Also see Seligman (1987).

43. McKeever (1983); Seligman (1987).

44. Seligman (1987).

45. Brody (1998) reviews the contributions that sibling relationships may make to cognitive and psychosocial development. Jenkins (1992) found that child symptoms often associated with marital conflict are not as frequent when sibling relationships are close as when they are not close. Also see Powell & Ogle (1985).

46. Wood (1991, 1993, 1994, 1995) and Wood et al. (2000).

47. Wood et al. (2000, p. 320). Wood includes attachment in her BBFM.

48. Wood (1995, p. 439).

49. Wood (1995, p. 439).

50. Watzlawick (1978).

51. Mattison (2000) examines four concerns of educators: absenteeism, disciplinary referrals, retention, and drop-out rates, and discusses implication for prevention and consultation.

52. Bandura (1978).

53. Levine (1994, p. 242).

54. Zins & Ponti (1990, p. 679) are authors of numerous articles on the school consultation and practices. This article, written for the school psychologist, offers useful guidelines and practices when consulting with schools.

55. There are numerous resources. Two favorites are Goldstein (1995) and Alberto & Troutman (1999).

56. Zins & Ponti (1990, p. 681). Also see Weiss & Edwards (1992) for a family-school intervention pioneered at the Ackerman Institute (Family-School Collaboration Program).

57. Weiss & Edwards (1992, p. 220) highlight the importance of collaboration when working with parents and school personnel. "Ownership of the work" by parents and school staff fosters fruitful family-school partnerships.

58. The T.E.A. approach was developed for weight loss management by registered dietician and medical writer Nadine Braunstein, MS, RD, CDE.

59. Celano & Kaslow (2000, p. 217).

60. See Bean (2001), for example, for a review of guidelines for working with Hispanic families. Falicov (1983, cited in Falicov 1995, p. 375) offers a multidimensional definition of culture: those sets of shared worldviews, meanings, and adaptive behaviors derived from simultaneous membership and participation in a multiplicity of contexts, such as rural, urban, or suburban setting; language, age, gender, cohort, family configuration, race, ethnicity, religion, nationality, socioeconomic status, employment, education, occupation, sexual orientation, political ideology; migration, and stage of acculturation. Falicov (1995) suggests that clinicians be trained to appreciate cultural sensitivity by using a multidimensional comparative framework. The key comparative parameters are as follows: "(1) Ecological context: diversity in where and how the family lives and how it fits in its environment. (2) Migration and acculturation: diversity in where the family members came from; when; how and why; how they live; and their future aspirations. (3) Family organization: diversity in the preferred forms of cultural family organization and the values connected to those family arrangements. (4) Family life cycle: diversity in how developmental stages and transitions in the family life cycle are culturally patterned" (p. 378). Also see Falicov (1998). Hardy & Laszloffy describe use of the cultural genogram as essential to training culturally competent family therapists (1995) and offer suggestions to develop the therapist's racial awareness and sensitivity (2000).

61. Celano & Kaslow (2000, p. 217). For this practice, devising culturally acceptable strategies, authors cite other researchers, for example, Falicov (1983) and McGoldrick et al. (1996).

CHAPTER 6. ZOOM IN: FOCUSING ON THE CHILD

1. Asthma is influenced by temperament (Miller & Wood, 1994) and emotional states (Miller & Wood, 1997). Wood's research (1991, 1993, 1994, 1995) highlights the influence

of family interactions in the disease process. See Wood et al. (1987, 1989) for a discussion of Chron's disease and ulcerative colitis; Zimand & Wood (1986) found that conflict increased responsivity of children with gastrointestinal disorders.

2. Children with language disorders have many struggles, such as significant social problems. See Toppelberg & Shapiro (2000) for a 10-year review of the research on language disorders. They conclude that early language disorders are "risk indicators" for present and future psychiatric problems (e.g., disruptive behavior disorders, anxiety disorders). Levine (1994) discusses the struggles of children with weaknesses in language skill: receptive, comprehension of language, and/or expressive, the ability to communicate one's ideas with words. Wren (2000) notes that these problems persist into adulthood. Also see Chapter 8 in this book.

3. It is important to consider family history. Weissman et al. (1987) report that school-age children of depressed parents have been judged to have more psychiatric diagnoses in general. Also see Beardslee et al. (1998).

4. Racusin & Kalsow (1994) offer a review of the literature concerning use of concurrent or sequential child and family sessions. Also see Carter (1987).

5. Summarized from Kuehl (1993). Kuehl notes that this enhances the child's "congruent self-expression in his or her natural environment" (p. 266). Also see Hughes & Baker (1990) for a discussion of the importance of the child's subjective experience and the benefits of the child interview.

6. Wachtel (1998, p. 18.) Also see Wachtel (1987, 1994a, 1994b).

7. See Wachtel (1987, 1994a, 1994b, 1998).

8. Kuehl (1993).

9. There are many published outlines and checklists available to use as guides for interviewing, for example, The ANSER System and STRANDS, both of which are published by Educators Publishing Service, Inc. 800-225-5750.

10. Bandura (1977, 1986); Bowlby (1969, 1973, 1988); Erikson (1963); Piaget, see Flavell (1992); Ginsburg & Opper (1969); Inhelder & Piaget (1958); Nicolopoulou (1993); Piaget (1962a, 1962b); Rubin & Pepler (1982). See Crain (2000) for reviews of theories of development. For additional theorists see: Anna Freud (1965) for a review of normality and pathology in childhood; Pine (1985); Quay (1999) for an understanding of disruptive disorders; also see Mash & Barkley (1996) on child psychopathology, and Mash & Barkley (1998) for treatment of childhood disorders.

11. Levine (1994, p. 8). Levine suggests that we employ informed observation and description of a variety of phenomena related to learning. He presents a model with six major categories of "common observable phenomena: (1) Phenomena related to weak attention controls (attention, processing, production and mental energy controls), (2) Phenomena related to reduced remembering (short and long term memory), (3) Phenomena related to chronic misunderstanding (processing problems), (4) Phenomena related to deficient output (language production, motor performance, organization, problem solving, and strategy use),

(5) Phenomena related to delayed skills acquisition (reading, spelling, writing, mathematics), (6) Phenomena related to poor adaptation (social and motivation problems)."

12. Hughes & Baker (1990, p. 29).

13. Fears and anxieties are quite common among children of all ages, Barrios & O'Dell (1998). There are differences based on age levels, Serafino (1986); gender, Ollendick et al. (1989); culture, Last & Perrin (1993); and socioeconomic status, Jersild & Holmes (1935). Vandenberg (1993) investigated the fears of normal and mentally retarded youngsters and found a distinct pattern in children classified as developmentally delayed, this group demonstrating a developmental pattern closer to their *mental-age* cohorts.

14. Children often show behaviors that fit more than one diagnostic category. Disorders have overlapping risk patterns, one perhaps creating a risk for another. See Angold et al. (1999) for a review of child and adolescent research on the prevalence, causes, and effects of diagnostic comorbidity among the following: anxiety disorders, depressive disorders, attention-deficit/hyperactivity disorders, oppositional defiant and conduct disorders, and substance abuse. Also see Angold & Costello (1993); Caron & Rutter (1991).

15. There are journals devoted to this topic, namely *Cognition and Emotion*, *Journal of Emotion and Behavioural Difficulties*, *Motivation and Emotion*, as well as books, *Handbook of Emotions*, *Emotions in the Workplace*, *The Subtlety of Emotions*, *Biocultural Approaches to Emotions*, to name a few. Also see Harter (1983, 1986).

16. For examples, see Cervantes & Callanan (1998); DeConti & Dickerson (1994); La Greca (1990). The social context in which we have been raised must also be considered, as Saarni (1999, p. 3) states: "emotional experience is developmentally embedded in social experience."

17. See Klein (1991); Perrin & Last (1992); Silverman (1991).

18. Schwab-Stone et al. (1994) found that children ages 6–11 reported fewer symptoms on the Diagnostic Interview Schedule for Children–Revised (DISC-R) than did parents.

19. Samuels & Taylor (1994).

20. Hughes & Baker (1990).

21. Hughes & Baker (1990, p. 33).

22. Vaughan (1998).

23. Sigelman et al. (1982).

24. Carey & McDevitt (1995).

25. Thomas & Chess (1968, 1977); Chess & Thomas (1989).

26. Thomas et al. (1963).

27. A wonderful book that I often recommend to professionals and parents is *The Out-of-sync Child: Recognizing and Coping With Sensory Integration Dysfunction*, Kranowitz (1998).

28. There is controversy about the use of play as an assessment. Lewis (1993) reviews different developmental models of play and highlights its distinctive worth in assessment. Sturgess (1997) provides a checklist for selecting an appropriate play assessment and in reviewing present trends, finds limitations in the instruments (they lack validity

and reliability). Farmer-Dougan & Kaszuba (1999) found positive relationships between cognitive development and social competence and higher levels of play behaviors. Eisert & Lamorey (1996) studied the association between play and other developmental areas. They suggest using play as a supplemental assessment. Child's themes in play: see Buchsbaum et al. (1992), who suggest that children's play provides clues to their witnessing or experiencing maltreatment.

29. Chethik (2000). Emotional language (p. 50); explicates major conflicts (p. 11).

30. Chethik (2000, p. 51).

31. Halperin & McKay (1998, p. 579).

32. Make a Picture Story (MAPS), available through Western Psychological Services (WPS), Los Angeles, California, 800-648-8857.

33. Gardner, The Storytelling Card Game, available through WPS, 800-648-8857.

34. E.g. Psych Corp 1-800-872-1726.

35. Freymann & Elffers (1999).

36. Roberts Apperception Test for Children (RATC), available from WPS, 800-648-8857.

37. The Family Apperception Test, available from WPS, 800-648-8857.

38. Landgarten (1981, 1984). Wilson & Ratekin (1990) present an introduction to the evaluation of children's drawings; Johnson (1990) suggests that children's drawings offer information about cognitive and psychosocial development. Also see Di Leo (1973, 1983) and Oster & Gould (1987).

39. Handler & Habenicht (1994).

40. Knoff & Prout (1985), The Kinetic Drawing System for Family and School, available from WPS, 800-648-8857.

41. Knoff & Prout (1985).

42. Play therapy: Boyd (1999); Buurma (1999); Gil (1994); Gil & Sobol (2000). Sandplay: Boik & Goodwin (2000).

43. The research literature is replete with studies associating academic underachievement and behavior problems. Hinshaw (1992) presents a broad review of externalizing problems and underachievement.

44. Halperin & McKay (1998) present a 10-year review of psychological testing. Sattler (1995) and Anastasi & Urbina (1997) are comprehensive texts. The neuropsychology assessment text by Muriel Lezak (1995) is excellent. Also see Siegel (1987) for a developmental and psychodynamic approach to psychological testing from early childhood through adolescence.

45. Siegel (1987, p. 6). The clinical utility of projective psychological tests for children has been questioned by some investigators, see Klein (1987).

46. La Greca (1990, p. 7). Also see Levine (1994).

47. Wilens (1999, p. 23).

48. Zito et al. (2000). See Riddle et al. (2001) for a review of pediatric psychopharmacology.

49. See Koplewicz (1996); Simeon (1997).

50. Biederman & Steingard (1991); Koplewicz (1996); Wilens (1999).

51. Wilens (1999) points out that because of the genetic basis of many disorders, some children don't respond to talking therapies.

52. Cognitive-behavior therapy is an effective treatment for obsessive-compulsive disorder, see March & Mulle (1998).

53. Biederman et al. (1997, p. 779).

54. Summarized from Biederman et al. (1997, p. 779).

55. I recommend a book for parents that offers "straight talk" about psychiatric medicine: see Wilens (1999).

56. Rappaport & Chubinsky (2000).

57. Beardslee et al. (1998); Weissman et al. (1987).

58. Smith (2000); Waters (2000). Also see Klein & Wender (1995) for a review of the role of methylphenidate (Ritalin) in psychiatry.

59. Zito et al. (2000).

60. Duncan et al. (2000). They state: (p. 26): "The message is seductive and it works: if these drugs were books, they would be runaway best sellers. More than 130 million prescriptions were written for them last year alone, and more than $8.58 billion was spent on them."

61. Pekkanen (2000).

62. Wurtzel (2000).

63. Breggin (1994).

64. Jensen et al. (1999) conclude that safety and efficacy studies are needed for the new generation of atypical neuroleptic medication.

65. See Abikoff & Hechtman (1996) and the study by Greenhill et al. (1999). Current evidence in studies lasting up to 24 months indicates that stimulants show efficacy and safety. Medicine along with therapy is sometimes needed for the most efficacious treatment; see Klein & Abikoff (1997) who found methylphenidate and behavior therapy resulted in significant improvement for ADHD children. Also see Bernstein et al. (2000) for treatment of school refusal using a combined approach of medication and therapy.

66. Klee & Hack (1999). Also see Koplewicz (1996); Wilens (1999).

67. Wilens (1999).

68. Freeman et al. (1997); White & Epston (1990).

69. Wynne et al. (1992, p. 3).

70. For example, solution-focused therapists. See de Shazer (1988); Walter & Peller (1992).

71. For example, Wynne et al. (1992); "problem-saturated," White & Epston (1990, p. 16).

72. Johnson (1987); Konstantareas (1989); Konstantareas & Homatidis (1989); Sloman & Konstantareas (1990).

73. Securing appropriate care is vital. This is especially important with the young child when early intervention provides the greatest impact on the developing brain. Greenspan & Wieder (1998, p. 2) point out that with intervention, numbers of children diagnosed "as having autistic spectrum disorders have become warmly related and joyful . . . many children diagnosed as mentally retarded have developed the abilities to communicate, reason, and solve problems."

74. Biology's role in ADHD, see Barkley (1998, 1999) and Castellanos (1999); autism, Tsai & Ghaziuddin (1997); schizophrenia, American Academy of Child and Adolescent Psychiatry (2000), Andreasen (1999), Campbell et al. (1997), and Malhotra (2001); learning disabilities, Lyon (1996); mood disorders, Weller & Weller (1997, pp. 336–337), who note: Neurotransmitter systems linked to depression include the "noradreneric, serotonergic, cholinergic, and dopaminergic systems"; Tourette's, Pauls et al. (1999). Also see Johnson (1987) for a discussion of biologically-based deficits.

75. Sloman & Konstantareas (1990, p. 418). See also Sloman et al. (1989) regarding the biology of family systems and mood disorders.

76. www.pastornet.net.au/jmm/ahmr/ahmr0376.htm.

77. Mel Levine (1994) recommends *demystification*, which is a process through which adults discuss with children about learning profiles, strengths, and affinities. He outlines guidelines for demystifying different phenomena related to learning that help put their struggles in a better framework.

CHAPTER 7. CHILD AND FAMILY WORK: ATTACHMENT, AFFECT REGULATION, AND THE FAMILY

1. Greenspan (1997, p. 146). This person comes into the world with a higher than average level of responsiveness, heightened sensitivity to noise and environmental stimuli, and heightened sensitivity to emotions and cues from others.

2. Problems, especially those of a chronic nature, impact on the quality of life and adjustment of family members. Gonzalez et al. (1989) talk about "finding a place for the problem and putting the problem in its place."

3. Spitz (1945) reported on the significantly high mortality of infants deprived of human contact. He coined the term *hospitalism* to describe what he observed in these "hygienic" institutions where infants were withdrawn and sickly, despite the sterile and sanitary conditions.

4. Schore (1994). Karen (1998) notes that the neonate has the ability to differentiate the smell of his mother and distinguish her voice. According to Zeanah et al. (1997, p. 166): "Early theories of development held that the human newborn was disorganized, passive, reactive, or withdrawn. Research on newborn behavior suggests a different view: biological, cognitive, communicative, emotional, and social capacities, which are functionally integrated, enable infants to seek stimulation actively and to regulate their own behavior through interactions with the environment."

5. Kaplan (1978, p. 16).

6. Schore (1994).

7. While there are many books on the subject of first relationships and how they shape one's capacity to love, Karen's (1998) is a classic. Also see Lewis et al. (2000). Bowlby (1988) discusses bonding and attachment as interconnected processes.

8. Bowlby (1973, 1988). Bowlby's early research examined the impact of physical separation from parents. His later focus was on mother/parent providing a secure base for offspring as they go out into the world.

9. Bowlby (1988). Mahler et al. (1975, p. 69) discuss how mother is a "home base" for the infant to "refuel. . . . The wilting and fatigued infant 'perks up' in the shortest time following such contact; then he quickly goes on with his explorations and once again becomes absorbed in his pleasure and functioning." Harlow (1958) experimented with infant rhesus monkeys separated from their mothers during the first few weeks of life. He used the term "contact comfort" to describe his observations of infant monkeys and their preference for cloth-covered surrogates that did not provide food over wire surrogates that provided food but no "contact comfort." He demonstrated the significant impact of social isolation and separation on the monkey's development.

10. Karen (1998, p. 204), discussing Bowlby's internal working model.

11. Stern (1985). In the first year, the infant begins to develop an internalized template for relationships, "representations of interactions that have been generalized." Infants encode experiences as interactive patterns.

12. Winnicott (1964, 1977).

13. Ainsworth (1985a, 1985b, 1989); Ainsworth et al. (1978) observed infants during a reunion after a separation from the mother. There were two groups of infants who were described as "insecure" attachments. One group of infants, whose mothers rebuffed them when the infants looked for connection, was more likely to avoid the caretaker after a short separation. This group was given the classification of avoidant. Another group of infants, who lacked consistency in their care or received intrusive care, demonstrated ambivalence, anger, and resistance upon their reunion with the mother. This group was given the classification of "ambivalent or resistant attachment."

14. Bowlby (1988, p. 121). Care by an available and responsive adult results in secure attachments as infants, which researchers note correlates with positive adjustment in life. See Fonagy & Target (1997); Goldberg et al. (1995); Main et al. (1985). Consult Siegel (1999) for a review of research regarding the assessment of adult attachment narratives from the Adult Attachment Interview (AAI). A parent's attachment history impacts on the infant, for example, Main & Hesse (1990); Hesse & Main (1999). Van Ijzendoorn et al. (1999) studied infants with disorganized attachment and suggest that this group is at risk (e.g., difficulties with stress management, increased risk of externalizing problem behavior, tendency to show dissociative behavior later in life).

15. Schore (1994, p. 78). Schore integrates research from neurobiology, sociobiology, neurochemistry, behavioral neurology, developmental psychology, infant research, and psychoanalytic theory. He presents a psychobiological model of early socioemotional

development and argues that the formation of an attachment bond is an interactive process that takes place between the primary caregiver and the infant. These nonverbal experiences result in changes in the actual structure of the brain. Also see Fleming et al. (1999), who discuss the neurobiology of mother-infant interactions during development and across generations. Suomi's (1999, 2000) research with rhesus monkeys demonstrates how relationships produce biochemical changes.

16. Schore (1994, p. 3).

17. George Lathrop, The sunshine of thine eyes. In Bartlett (1919).

18. Spitz (1958). In a reciprocal process, the baby's gaze produces the mother's gaze, and prolonged periods of engagement between the pair follow. These face-to-face transactions mediate "the dialogue between mother and child." Visual stimulation in infancy has a vital role. Preisler (1995) discusses the similarities and differences in development of communication (p. 79, described "with a focus on pre-verbal abilities, exploration of toys, social and symbolic play, communicative intent and sharing of experiences) in blind and deaf infants. There was a difference in communication in the interactions of the blind infant/sighted mother pairs and the deaf infant-hearing mother/deaf mother pairs. The blind infants in the study showed delays. Results underscore the "more critical role" of visual stimulation during infancy.

19. Beebe & Lachmann (1988); Beebe et al. (1992). The baby's excitation must be monitored in order to modulate the arousal level. What one sees in the frame-by-frame analysis is a process of engagement and disengagement as the baby goes from a neutral affect to a heightened state of positive affect. As the baby reaches this high state of arousal and excitation, it may look downward to avert the mother's gaze and in response the mother diminishes the stimulation and disengages. Also see Stern (1985). Field & Fogel (1982) note there appears to be a mirroring process between the pair and a coordination of responses. Researchers in the field of infant development found that the "attuned mother" monitors the arousal level of her baby and modulates her affect accordingly. Researchers have found that mismatches are equally important, see note 23.

20. Beebe & Lachmann (1988). This is essential for the developing brain. See Trevarthen & Aitken (2001) for a review of research on how the infant brain develops in "active engagement." The eye-to-eye messages are channels of communication in which older brains engage younger brains.

21. Schanberg (1995); Schanberg & Field (1988). Schanberg and Field discovered just how important touch is in the development of babies born prematurely. Their groundbreaking research, stressing the importance of touching and massaging preemies, literally has changed the manner in which low-birth-weight infants are handled in the hospital. Also see Tronick (1995).

22. For a discussion of how to recognize sensory integration dysfunction, see Kranowitz (1998).

23. Microanalysis of films of infant-mother interactions demonstrated that the process of matching of affects (mother attuned to the infant's emotional state) is less than imagined (only about one-third of the time). Investigators found that the infant responds to these mis-

attunements and mother corrects in approximately one-third of occurrences. Researchers emphasize the important function of misattunements and subsequent repair. Birgen et al. (1997, p. 5) discuss the positive role of "dyssynchrony, conflict, and resolution" in infant development. They argue that dyadic harmony is "better characterized by a series of microdyssynchronies and dynamic resolutions than by any metaphor of harmony or attunement." Tronick & Gianino (1986) note that infants who experience successful repair experiences are thought to develop better mechanisms for coping as well as a sense of mastery. In the case of infrequent or the absent repair experiences, the infant may develop a sense of helplessness. Also see Tronick (1989).

24. See Gilbert & Andrews (1998) for a review of different approaches and perspectives on shame. Gilbert (1998) cites H. Lewis (1986) who argues that shame experiences are associated with negative affects of anxiety ("almost a panic like quality"), and anger ("humiliated fury"). He cites other researchers who link shame to disgust. He writes about "shame-proneness" and raises a key question whether or not it has a heritable basis. Also see Schore (1998) for an excellent review of early shame experiences and infant brain development.

25. Gabbard (2000) posits that family therapy that changes the interaction between the parent and the child may be able to modify gene expression in the child.

26. Hughes (1998) writes about building bonds with poorly attached children.

27. Gonzalez et al. (1989, p. 72). These authors state (p. 70): "A psychoeducational approach aids an understanding of the impact of chronic medical conditions on family life. In particular, it uses a stress and coping paradigm rather than a psychopathology model in its attitudinal stance toward chronic-illness families, thereby establishing a group atmosphere that encourages a nonblaming review of past family coping efforts and an exploration of new strategies for tackling illness-related family issues." They cite Mullen et al. (1985) and note (p. 72): "Patient education has long been one facet of the treatment of many chronic illnesses."

28. We used the book by Webster-Stratton (1992, p. 53) who notes that the average parent gives 17 commands in a half hour. With children with behavior problems, that number increases to "an average of 40 commands" during that same time period.

29. "Shame-attacks" or "shame episodes" from Lewis (1986) cited in Gilbert (1998, p. 6). See also note 24.

30. Greene (1998, p. 25) suggests "meltdowns" often results when parent and child are inflexible. During a meltdown the "inflexible-explosive" child's behavior is likely to be destructive or abusive.

31. Sensitization might also involve the kindling model that has been applied to bipolar disorder. Papolos & Papolos (1999) state (p. 53): "Some years ago Dr. Robert Post of the National Institute of Mental Health advanced the idea that initial periods of cycling may begin with an environmental stressor, but if the cycles continue to occur unchecked, the brain becomes kindled or sensitized—pathways inside the central nervous system are reinforced, so to speak—and future episodes of depression, hypomania, or mania will occur by themselves (independently of an outside stimulus), with greater

and greater frequency." See Post & Weiss (1998) for a discussion of sensitization and kindling in mood, anxiety, and obsessive-compulsive disorders.

32. Gilbert (1998) talks about meaning, cognitions, and beliefs in shame experiences. He states (p. 29): "In cognitive theory shame-proneness would arise from the formation of early negative schema of self and others (e.g., I am unlovable, I am bad, etc.)." This would include the appraisal of someone else's nonverbal behavior, for example a reproachful look on mother's face. Carton & Carton (1998) found a relationship between nonverbal indicators of maternal warmth and a child's locus of control of reinforcement. Mothers of internally controlled children displayed more maternal warmth (smiles, hugs, pats, rubs, and gazing) than the mothers of externally controlled children. The internally controlled children engaged in less off-task behavior than externally controlled children.

33. Schore (1998, p. 60) reminds us that facial mirroring produces considerably more than outward facial changes in the mother-infant pair; "they represent a transformation of inner events." There are actual changes at the neurobiological level. An infant is biologically prepared to employ the visual pathways to stimulate the brain. Schore (1998, p. 61) cites Hofer's (1990) research, which indicates "the mother influences the neural substrates for emotion by directly regulating the levels of the catecholamines dopamine and noradrenaline in the infant's brain. Dopamine is centrally involved in arousal, elation (joy), and the anticipation of reward."

34. See Barkley (1997c), Hembree-Kigin & Bodiford McNeil (1995), Webster-Stratton (1992), and Webster-Stratton & Hancock (1998) for models to help parents play with their child.

35. See White & Epston (1990). This approach comes from narrative therapy. White and Epston (p. 38) externalize the problem: "'Externalizing' is an approach to therapy that encourages persons to objectify and, at times, to personify the problems that they experience as oppressive. In this process, the problem becomes a separate entity and thus external to the person or relationship that was ascribed as the problem." Gary named the problem "Mr. Mean and Mr. Anger."

36. These ideas come from narrative therapy. See Freeman et al. (1997); White (1989); White & Epston (1990); Zimmerman & Dickerson (1996).

37. Vostanis et al. (1994) examined maternal expressed emotion in the development of child psychopathology in children with conduct and emotional disorders. Findings suggest a relationship between the existence of negative emotional attitudes (e.g., criticism and emotional overinvolvement) and the dearth of warmth.

38. Greene (1998) talks about pathways to inflexibility-explosiveness, which may include sensory overload, language processing and expressive language difficulties, executive function deficits, and cognitive weaknesses.

39. Webster-Stratton (1992, p. 60) suggests using "when-then" commands. They inform the child beforehand of the consequences: *when* you clean your room *then* you can go out to play. A caveat: "Obviously, this kind of command should only be used if you can allow your children to decide whether or not to comply. If you need compliance to your command, then give a direct positive command."

40. The work of Gerald Patterson and his colleagues at the Oregon Social Learning Center is exemplary. See Patterson (1975, 1976); Dishion & Patterson (1996); Patterson & Forgatch (1987, 1989); Webster-Stratton (1992, 1996); Webster-Stratton & Hancock (1998). For review of different models of parent training, consult Briesmeister & Schaefer (1998). Also see Bloomquist (1996) for a review of skill training for children with behavior disorders.

41. I might use the pop-up brain model in Van der Meer & Dudink (1996). See "Tools and Resources" in the Appendix for other resources on the brain.

42. Watzlawick et al. (1988).

43. Alberto & Troutman (1999) define negative reinforcement (p. 264): the contingent removal of an aversive stimulus immediately following a response that increases the future rate and/or probability of the response."

44. Patterson (1982), a prominent social-learning theorist, proposed a coercion hypoth-esis. In the process of coercive escalation, one family member reinforces another for using coercive behavior. Physical aggression is hypothesized to be the end result of a coercive escalation spiral, and, because the aggression (temporarily) solves the problem it is rein-forced. Coercive cycles are highly predictable and become routine once they begin. Also see Patterson & Forgatch (1989); Patterson et al. (1997).

45. The aggression (coercion) develops and endures because it is rewarded (reinforced). Interactions of this nature inhibit the development and growth of positive or prosocial behav-iors. See Patterson (1982); Snyder & Patterson (1995).

46. See Coie et al. (1990) and Ladd (1999) for discussions of the consequences of peer rejection.

47. See Gresham (1981, 1986); Gresham & Elliot (1984).

48. Gresham (1986, p. 155).

CHAPTER 8. A GROUP INTERVENTION FOR CHILDREN WITH LEARNING DISABILITIES AND THEIR FAMILIES: A BIOPSYCHOSOCIAL APPROACH

1. Stern (1999). Group interventions represent a widely employed treatment modality to address a variety of problems, for example: interactive psychoeducational group therapy to reduce symptoms of posttraumatic stress disorder for traumatized women, Lubin et al. (1998); to offer support for those with irritable bowel syndrome, van Dulmen et al. (1996); group therapy working with spiritual and religious themes, Jacques (1999).

2. Family involvement is essential and has been reported to increase effectiveness, Barrett et al. (1996); Mendlowitz et al. (1999); Toren et al. (2000).

3. In Public Law 94-142 (Federal Register, 1977, p. 65083), specific learning disability is defined as "a disorder in one or more of the basic psychological processes involved in under-standing or in using language, spoken or written, which may manifest itself in an imperfect ability to listen, think, speak, write, spell or do mathematical calculations." Included are such conditions as perceptual handicaps, brain injury, minimal brain dysfunction, dyslexia, and

developmental aphasia, but not included are visual, hearing, or motor handicaps, mental retardation, or conditions resulting from environmental, cultural, or economic disadvantage. This definition was reissued under P.L. 101-476, the Individuals with Disabilities Education Act (IDEA).

4. For a review, see Kavale & Forness (1985).

5. Ysseldyke & Algozzine (1990). According to the U.S. Department of Education (1991), nearly half of all children receiving special education services are considered learning disabled.

6. Berry & Kirk (1980); Ysseldyke et al. (1982). Ames (1983), for example, takes the position that this diagnosis, learning disabled, is used too loosely and her clinical work at the Gesell Institute has led her to suggest that immaturity, and not a learning disability, is often the problem. Coplin and Morgan (1988) discuss the heterogeneity of this population and attempt to use subtypes as a means of classification.

7. Hammill (1990).

8. NJCLD Interagency Committee on Learning Disabilities (1987, p. 1).

9. For a discussion, see Levine (1993, 1994).

10. Levine (1993, p. xii) states: "Creative and effective *prescription* can emerge from careful *description*."

11. Cohen (1985). Levine (1984) asserts that there are also cumulative neurodevelopmental debts that impact on productivity in middle-late childhood.

12. Geisthardt & Munsch (1996) found differences in coping strategies regarding school stress between LD students and nonhandicapped peers. Strubbe (1989) found middle school students with learning disabilities experience significantly more stress than peers not identified as LD. Zetlin (1993) looked at the everyday stressors of Caucasian and Hispanic LD youth and found they had many concerns specifically related to learning problems. Also see Wenz-Gross & Siperstein (1998).

13. Cohen (1985, p. 292) states: "A consistent and core aspect of the youngster's *unconscious* self-representation is that of being painfully damaged, inadequate, stupid and vulnerable."

14. Yasutake & Bryan (1995).

15. Silver (1989, p. 319).

16. Levine (1993, pp. 519–520).

17. Bender et al. (1999); Huntington & Bender (1993). Researchers find this group to be at risk for severe depression and suicide.

18. Smith (1991).

19. Bachara (1976); Bryan (1998); Bryan & Bryan (1977, 1978); Bursuck (1989); Carlson (1987); Osman (1995); Vaughn & Hogan (1990).

20. LD children were more often rejected by their peers than were non-learning disabled students. See Bryan (1974, 1998); Osman (1995); Siperstein et al. (1978).

21. LD students are less able to read social cues or empathize and recognize people's emotions. See Bachara (1976); Bogas (1993); Bryan (1977); Holder & Kirkpatrick (1991).

22. They are less able to assess their social status in the group. See Bruininks (1978); La Greca & Stone (1990).

23. Oliva & La Greca (1988) report that LD students perform with less social competence and at lower developmental levels than their nondisabled peers. Pavri & Monda-Amaya (2000) found LD students in their study to be lonelier than nondisabled peers. They present strategies to increase social satisfaction in school.

24. Axelrod (1982); Silver & Young (1985); Siperstein et al. (1978).

25. Smith (1995).

26. Wren (2000, p. 1) points out that LD individuals are at risk not only because of the battle with the disability, but also because "they are misunderstood, mistaught, misdiagnosed, and mistreated not only in school but also in psychotherapy and in life." Also see Myrna Orenstein (2000); she describes the problems of adults with undiagnosed learning disabilities. Some of the emotional consequences reported are: low self-esteem, depression, tendency to shame and fragmentation states.

27. Dyson (1996) found parents of learning disabled children reported higher levels of stress when compared to parents of nondisabled children. Baker & McCal (1995) and Lardieri et al. (2000) discuss sibling and parent stress.

28. Silver (1984); Stern (1999); Wren (2000); Ziegler & Holden (1988).

29. For a discussion, see Silver (1984). Also see Osman (1979); Stern (1999).

30. The National Center for Learning Disabilities (1997/1998) reported 35% of students identified with learning disabilities drop out of high school. Also see Marder & D'Amico (1992).

31. Larson (1988) reported that LD youths are adjudicated about twice as often as their nondisabled peers and experience greater recidivism and parole failure.

32. National Center for Learning Disabilities (1997/1998); Sikorski (1991).

33. Wright & Stimmel (1984). When compared to a control group, the university students who had been diagnosed as learning disabled in childhood viewed themselves and their parents more negatively.

34. Karacostas & Fisher (1993). The authors note the presence or absence of an LD was a better predictor of classification as CD (chemically dependent) or NCD (non-chemically dependent) than were gender, ethnicity, age, SES, or family composition.

35. According to the 1992 report from the Office of the Inspector General and cited in National Center for Learning Disabilities (1997/1998).

36. Levine & Zallen (1984, p. 345). Unidentified gifted but learning disabled students often fall into this group, Baum (1990).

37. Chisenbop is a method of doing basic arithmetic using your fingers. It is an ancient technique attributed to a Korean tradition, similar to the abacus. For a tutorial, see www.klingon.cs.iupui.edu/~aharris/chis/chis.html. For a discussion of strategies and techniques to help in reading, writing, and math, see Birsh (1999).

38. Steinglass (1998).

39. McFarlane (1991).

40. McFarlane et al. (1995).

41. Gonzalez et al. (1989).

42. Gonzalez et al. (1989, p. 80) note that the family needs to take charge of deciding the role the illness will have in the family. They use the metaphor *keeping the illness in its place.*

43. McFarlane (1991).

44. Stern (1999, pp. 7–9). Hands-on simulations adapted from *How Difficult Can This Be? The F.A.T. City Workshop* by Richard Lavoie, available from WETA Videos, 1-800-343-5540.

45. Gardner (1983).

46. Levine (1994, p. 7). The Unique Minds intervention embraces Levine's point of view.

47. Gardner (1983). Also see Lazear (1994).

48. See White & Epston (1990, p. 38). " 'Externalizing' is an approach to therapy that encourages persons to objectify and, at times, to personify the problems that they experience as oppressive. In this process, the problem becomes a separate entity and thus external to the person or relationship that was ascribed as the problem."

49. See Weiss & Edwards (1992) for a family-school intervention pioneered at the Ackerman Institute (Family-School Collaboration Project). Blocking blame refocuses individuals involved back onto the problem solving.

50. Handel (1999); Weiss & Edwards (1992).

CHAPTER 9. PARTINGS AND PARTING THOUGHTS

1. Lewis & Blotcky (1997, p. 161). These authors discuss child therapy and suggest that termination can be "crucial to outcome." Patterson et al. (1998, p. 219) write about family therapy and conclude that terminations are more successful if they are thought of as a "process rather than an event."

2. Chethik (2000), in discussing termination in child therapy, suggests that the termination period should have a beginning, middle, and an end.

3. Wetchler & Ofte-Atha (1993) discuss using termination as a process to empower the family. They present techniques developed from structural and strategic approaches. Also see Patterson et al. (1998); Treacher (1989).

4. Patterson et al. (1998).

5. Patterson et al. (1998) note that most therapists work toward mutually determined termination.

6. Patterson et al. (1998). Carr (1996) also discusses the ways in which the disengagement may result in considerable loss experiences. Garcia-Lawson & Lane (1997, p. 239) discuss that in some cases the ending may be untimely and forced, such as in the unexpected death of a therapist. They note: "regardless of the type of therapy, once a patient has emotionally invested himself in the therapeutic relationship, the sudden loss of a therapist and the unplanned termination can have a significant and devastating impact on him."

7. Barker (1990, p. 142).

8. Relph (1985).

9. Chethik (2000). Barker (1990) suggests that the therapist "give notice" and mention the forthcoming ending from time to time.

10. Lewis & Blotcky (1997, p. 165).

11. Nichols & Schwartz (1998, p. 99).

12. Treacher (1989). Byrne (1997) discusses families who return for therapy for "booster sessions" and assert that the "recidivism" reinvigorates a family in a similar way that the immune status of an individual is restored by booster shots.

13. Chethik (2000) comments that the assessment should be used as a base, and termination should begin thereafter.

14. Grant (2000) discusses how families experience the end of family therapy and reports that successful outcomes were linked to a shift in thinking about family problems and resolutions: a change of focus of the problem from the index client to a family perspective, and renewed confidence in their skill to handle family relationship problems.

15. See Wilcoxon & Gladding (1985) for suggestions.

16. Patterson et al. (1998) suggest helping the client to develop a stronger social network.

17. Freeman et al. (1997). Lists, letters of reference for admission to clubs, e.g., Temper Tamers Club of America, networks, and leagues (e.g., Vancouver Anti-anorexia Anti-bulimia League); developing handbooks for others to use.

18. Dilts (2001); Ross (2000); Ryff & Singer (2000); Sperry (2000); Yamada et al. (2000). Also see McDaniel et al. (1995), medical family therapy—a systems approach to psychotherapy with patients and families experiencing a medical illness, trauma, or disability; Moltz (1993), bipolar disorder; Renfrew (1997), aggression; Wood (1993, 1994, 1995), Wood et al. (1987, 2000), Miller & Wood (1994), chronic childhood illness; Zucker (1994), alcohol.

19. Masten & Coatsworth (1995); Tiet et al. (1998); Walsh (1995, 1998).

20. Parcel & Dufur (2001, p. 32) discuss "capital" at home and school and assert: "investment at home and school can work together to promote social adjustment."

21. Hoghughi (1998, p. 1545).

22. Hoghughi & Speight (1998, p. 295).

23. Grimshaw (2000) stresses the importance of partnerships in developing parenting programs. Parents need to be active partners and "stakeholders."

24. Parental warmth is linked to a child's adjustment, see Herman & McHale (1993).

25. "Out of the mouths of babes," part 4, at www.stpaulskingsville.org/ babes4.htm.

References

Abikoff, H. B., & Hechtman, L. (1996). Multimodal therapy and stimulants in the treatment of children with attention-deficit/hyperactivity disorder. In E. D. Hibbs & P. S. Jensen (Eds.), *Psychosocial treatments for child and adolescent disorders* (pp. 341–369). Washington, DC: American Psychological Association.

Ader, R., Felten, D. L., & Cohen, N. (1990). *Psychoimmunology*. New York: Academic Press.

Ainsworth, M. D. S. (1985a). Attachments across the life span. *Bulletin of the New York Academy of Medicine, 61*, 792–812.

Ainsworth, M. D. S. (1985b). Patterns of infant-mother attachments: Antecedents and effects on development. *Bulletin of the New York Academy of Medicine, 61*, 771–791.

Ainsworth, M. D. S. (1989). Attachments beyond infancy. *American Psychologist, 44*, 709–716.

Ainsworth, M. D. S., Blehar, M. C., Waters, E., & Wall, S. (1978). *Patterns of attachment: A psychological study of the strange situation*. Hillsdale, NJ: Lawrence Erlbaum.

Alberto, P. A., & Troutman, A. C. (1999). *Applied behavior analysis for teachers* (5th ed.). Englewood Cliffs, NJ: Prentice-Hall.

American Academy of Child and Adolescent Psychiatry. (1997). AACAP Official Action: Practice parameters for the assessment and treatment of children and adolescents with bipolar disorder. *Journal of the American Academy of Child & Adolescent Psychiatry, 36*, 138–157.

American Academy of Child and Adolescent Psychiatry. (2000). Summary of the practice parameters for the assessment and treatment of children and adolescents with schizophrenia. *Journal of the American Academy of Child & Adolescent Psychiatry, 39*, 1580–1582.

American Academy of Psychiatry & the Law Task Force. (1999). Videotaping of forensic psychiatric evaluations. *Journal of the American Academy of Psychiatry & the Law, 27*, 345–358.

American Psychiatric Association. (1994). *Diagnostic and statistical manual of mental disorders* (4th ed.). Washington, DC: Author.

Ames, L. B. (1983). Learning disability: Truth or trap? *Journal of Learning Disabilities, 16*, 19–23.

Anastasi, A., & Urbina, S. (1997). *Psychological testing* (7th ed.). Upper Saddle River, NJ: Prentice Hall.

Anastopoulos, A. D., Barkley, R. A., & Shelton, T. L. (1996). Family-based treatment: Psychosocial intervention for children and adolescents with attention deficit hyperactivity disorder. In E. D. Hibbs & P. S. Jensen (Eds.), *Psychosocial treatments for child and adolescent disorders* (pp. 267–284). Washington, DC: American Psychological Association.

Anderson, R. A., & Reynolds, J. (1996). The use of play in family therapy. *TCA Journal, 24*, 15–22.

Andreasen, N. (1997). Linking mind and brain in the study of mental illness: A project for a scientific psychopathology. *Science, 275*, 1586–1593.

Andreasen, N. (1999). Understanding the causes of schizophrenia. *New England Journal of Medicine, 340*, 645–647.

Angold A., & Costello, E. J. (1993). Depressive comorbidity in children and adolescents: Empirical, theoretical, and methodological issues. *American Journal of Psychiatry, 150*, 1779–1791.

Angold A., Costello, E. J., & Erkanli, A. (1999). Comorbidity. *Journal of Child Psychology & Psychiatry & Allied Disciplines, 40*, 57–87.

Arauzo, A. C., Watson, M., & Hulgus, J. (1994). The clinical uses of video therapy in the treatment of childhood sexual trauma survivors. *Journal of Child Sexual Abuse, 3*, 37–57.

Ariel, S., Carel, C. A., & Tyano, S. (1985). Uses of children's make-believe play in family therapy: Theory and clinical examples. *Journal of Marital and Family Therapy, 11*, 47–60.

Asarnow, J. R., Goldstein, M. J., Tompson, M., & Guthrie, D. (1993). One-year outcomes of depressive disorders in child psychiatric inpatients: Evaluation of the prognostic power of a brief measure of expressed emotion. *Journal of Child Psychology & Psychiatry & Allied Disciplines, 34*, 129–137.

Atkinson, B. (1999, July-August). The emotional imperative: Psychotherapists cannot afford to ignore the primacy of the limbic brain. *Family Therapy Networker*, 22–33.

Axelrod, L. H. (1982). Social perception in learning disabled adolescents. *Journal of Learning Disabilities, 15*, 610–613.

Axline, V. M. (1947). *Play therapy*. New York: Ballantine.

Ayan, J. (1997). *Aha! 10 ways to free your creative spirit and find your great ideas*. New York: Crown.

Bachara, G. H. (1976). Empathy in learning disabled children. *Perceptual and Motor Skills, 43*, 541–542.

Baer, D. M., Wolf, M. M., & Risley, T. R. (1968). Some current dimensions of applied behavior analysis. *Journal of Applied Behavior Analysis, 1*, 91–97.

Baer, D. M., Wolf, M. M., & Risley, T. R. (1987). Some still-current dimensions of applied behavior analysis. *Journal of Applied Behavior Analysis, 20*, 313–327.

Bailey, A., Le Couteur, A., Gottesman, I., Bolton, P., Simonoff, E., Yuzda, E., & Rutter, M. (1995). Autism as a strongly genetic disorder: Evidence from a British twin study. *Psychological Medicine, 25*, 63–77.

Bailey, C. E. (Ed.). (2000). *Children in therapy: Using the family as a resource*. New York: Norton.

Baker, D. B., & McCal, K. (1995). Parenting stress in parents of children with attention-deficit hyperactivity disorder and parents of children with learning disabilities. *Journal of Child & Family Studies, 4*, 57–68.

Baker, L., Minuchin, S., Milman, L., Leibman, R., & Todd, T. (1975). Psychosomatic aspects of juvenile diabetes mellitus: A progress report. In Z. Laron (Ed.), *Modern problems in pediatrics: Vol. 12. Diabetes in juveniles: Medical and rehabilitation aspects* (pp. 332–343). New York: Karger.

Bandura, A. (1977). *Social learning theory.* Englewood Cliffs, NJ: Prentice-Hall.

Bandura, A. (1978). The self-system in reciprocal determinism. *American Psychologist, 33,* 344–358.

Bandura, A. (1986). *Social foundations of thought and action: A social cognitive theory.* Englewood Cliffs, NJ: Prentice-Hall.

Barker, P. (1990). *Clinical interviews with children and adolescents.* New York: Norton.

Barker, P. (1996). *Psychotherapeutic metaphors: A guide to theory and practice.* New York: Brunner/Mazel.

Barkley, R. A. (1996). Linkages between attention and executive functions. In G. R. Lyon & N. A. Krasnegor (Eds.), *Attention, memory, and executive function* (pp. 307–326). Baltimore: Paul H. Brookes.

Barkley, R. A. (1997a). *ADHD and the nature of self-control.* New York: Guilford.

Barkley, R. A. (1997b). Behavioral inhibition, sustained attention, and executive functions: Constructing a unifying theory of ADHD. *Psychological Bulletin, 121,* 65–94.

Barkley, R. A. (1997c). *Defiant children: A clinician's manual for assessment and parent training* (2nd ed.). New York: Guilford.

Barkley, R. A. (1998). *Attention-deficit hyperactivity disorder: A handbook for diagnosis and treatment* (2nd ed.). New York: Guilford.

Barkley, R. A. (1999). Theories of attention-deficit/hyperactivity disorder. In H. C. Quay & A. E. Hogan (Eds.), *Handbook of disruptive behavior disorders* (pp. 295–313). New York: Kluwer Academic/Plenum.

Barnet, A. B., & Barnet, R. J. (1998). *The youngest minds: Parenting and genes in the development of intellect and emotion.* New York: Touchstone.

Barragar-Dunne, P. (1997). "Catch the little fish": Therapy utilizing narrative, drama, and dramatic play with young children. In C. Smith & D. Nylund (Eds.), *Narrative therapies with children and adolescents* (pp. 71–109). New York: Guilford.

Barrett, P. M. , Rapee, R. M., Dadds, M. M., & Ryan, S. M. (1996). Family enhancement of cognitive style in anxious and aggressive children. *Journal of Abnormal Child Psychology, 24,* 187–203.

Barrios, B. A., & O'Dell, S. L. (1998). Fears and anxieties. In E. J. Mash & R. A. Barkley (Eds.), *Treatment of childhood disorders* (2nd ed.). New York: Guilford.

Barron, A. P., & Earls, F. J. (1984). The relation of temperament and social factors to behavior problems in three-year-old children. *Journal of Child Psychology & Psychiatry & Allied Disciplines, 25,* 23–33.

Bartlett, J. (Comp). (1919). *Familiar quotations* (10th ed.). Rev. & enl. by N. H. Dole. Boston: Little, Brown. Bartleby.com, 2000.

Bateson, G. (1972). *Steps to an ecology of mind.* New York: Ballantine.

Bateson, G. (1979). *Mind and nature: A necessary unity.* New York: Bantam.

Baum, A., & Posluszny, D. M. (1999). Health psychology: Mapping biobehavioral contributions to health and illness. *Annual Review of Psychology, 50,* 137–163.

Baum, S. (1990). Gifted but learning disabled: A puzzling paradox. *ERIC Digest E479* [On-line]. Available: www.ed.gov/databases/ERIC_Digests/ ed321484.html.

Baxter, L. R., Schwartz, J. M., Bergman, K. S., Szuba, M. P., Guze, B. H., Mazziotta, J. C., Alazraki, A., Selin, C. E., Fering, H. K., & Munford, P. (1992). Caudate glucose metabolic rate changes with both drug and behavior therapy for obsessive-compulsive disorder. *Archives of General Psychiatry, 49,* 681–689.

Bean, R. A. (2001). Developing culturally competent marriage and family therapists: Guidelines for working with Hispanic families. *Journal of Marital and Family Therapy, 27,* 43–54.

Beardslee, W. R., Versage, E. M., & Gladstone, T. R.G. (1998). Children of affectively ill parents: A review of the past 10 years. *Journal of the American Academy of Child & Adolescent Psychiatry, 37,* 1134–1141.

Beebe, B., Jaffe, J., & Lachmann, F. M. (1992). A dyadic systems view of communication. In N. J. Skolnick & S. C. Warshaw (Eds.), *Relational perspectives in psychoanalysis* (pp. 61–81). Hillsdale, NJ: Analytic Press.

Beebe, B., & Lachmann, F. M. (1988). Mother-infant mutual influence and precursors of psychic structure. In A. Goldberg (Ed.), *Progress in self psychology* (Vol. 3, pp. 3–25). Hillsdale, NJ: Analytic Press.

Begley, S. (1996, February 19). Your child's brain. *Newsweek,* 54–62.

Beitchman, J. H., & Young, A. R. (1997). Learning disorders with a special emphasis on reading disorders: A review of the past 10 years. *Journal of the American Academy of Child & Adolescent Psychiatry, 36,* 1020–1032.

Bender, W. N., Rosenkrans, C. B., & Crane, M. K. (1999). Stress, depression, and suicide among students with learning disabilities: Assessing the risk. *Learning Disability Quarterly, 22,* 143–156.

Benes, F. (1997). Stress and the dopamine-GABA interactions in schizophrenia. *Journal of Psychiatric Research, 31,* 257–275.

Benson, M. J., Schindler-Zimmerman, T., & Martin, D. (1991). Accessing children's perceptions of their family: Circular questioning revisited. *Journal of Marital and Family Therapy, 17,* 363–373.

Berenstein, S., & Berenstein, J. (1992). *The Berenstein bears and too much pressure.* New York: Random House.

Bernstein, G. A., Borchardt, C. M., & Perwien, A. R. (1996). Anxiety disorders in children and adolescents: A review of the past 10 years. *Journal of the American Academy of Child & Adolescent Psychiatry, 35,* 1110–1119.

Bernstein, G. A., Borchardt, C. M., Perwien, A. R., Crosby, R. D., Kushner, M. G., Thuras, P. D., & Last, C. G. (2000). Imipramine plus cognitive-behavioral therapy in the treatment of school refusal. *Journal of the American Academy of Child & Adolescent Psychiatry, 39,* 276–283.

Berry, P., & Kirk, S. (1980). Issues in specific learning disabilities: Towards a data base for decision making. *Exceptional Child, 27,* 115–125.

Biederman, J., Faraone, S. V., Keenan, K., Benjamin, J., Krifcher, B., Moore, C., Sprich, S., Ugaglia, K., Jellinek, M. S., Steingard, R., Spencer, T., Norman, D., Kolodny, R., Kraus, I., Perrin, J., Keller, M. B., & Tsuang, M. T. (1992). Further evidence for family-genetic risk factors in attention deficit hyperactivity disorder: Patterns of comorbidity in probands and relatives in psychiatrically and pediatrically referred samples. *Archives of General Psychiatry, 49,* 728–738.

Biederman, J., Faraone, S. V., Keenan, K., Knee, D., & Tsuang, M. T. (1990). Family-genetic and psychosocial risk factors in DSM-III attention deficit disorder. *Journal of the American Academy of Child & Adolescent Psychiatry, 29,* 526–533.

Biederman, J., Spencer, T., & Wilens, T. (1997). Psychopharmacology. In J. M. Wiener (Ed.), *Textbook of child & adolescent psychiatry* (2nd ed., pp. 779–812). Washington, DC: American Psychiatric Press.

Biederman, J., & Steingard, R. (1991). Pediatric psychopharmacology. In A. J. Gelenberg, E. L. Bassuk, & S. C. Schoonover (Eds.), *The practitioner's guide to psychoactive drugs* (3rd ed., pp. 341–388). New York: Plenum.

Birgen, Z., Emde, R. N., & Pipp-Siegel, S. (1997). Dyssynchrony, conflict, and resolution: Positive contributions in infant development. *American Journal of Orthopsychiatry, 67,* 4–19.

Birsh, J. R. (Ed.). (1999). *Multisensory teaching of basic language skills.* New York: Paul H. Brookes.

Bloom, F. E., & Lazerson, A. (1988). *Brain, mind, and behavior* (2nd ed.). New York: W. H. Freeman.

Bloomquist, M. L. (1996). *Skills training for children with behavior disorders: A parent and therapist guidebook.* New York: Guilford.

Bogas, S. M. (1993). An integrative treatment model for children's attentional and learning problems. *Family Systems Medicine, 11,* 385–396.

Boik, B. L., & Goodwin, E. A. (2000). *Sandplay therapy: A step-by-step manual for psychotherapists of diverse orientations.* New York: Norton.

Bond, J. T., Galinsky, E., & Swanberg, J. E. (1998). *The 1997 national study of the changing workforce.* New York: Families and Work Institute.

Borduin, C. M. (1999). Multisystemic treatment of criminality and violence in adolescents. *Journal of the American Academy of Child & Adolescent Psychiatry, 38,* 242–249.

Boscolo, L., Cecchin, G., Hoffman, L., & Penn, P. (1987). *Milan systemic family therapy: Conversations in theory and practice.* New York: Basic.

Bosworth, K., Espelage, D., DuBay, T., Daytner, G., & Karageorge, K. (2000). Preliminary evaluation of a multimedia violence prevention program for adolescents. *American Journal of Health Behavior, 24,* 268–280.

Bowen, M. (1978). *Family therapy in clinical practice.* New York: Jason Aronson.

Bowlby, J. (1969). *Attachment and loss: Vol. 1. Attachment.* New York: Basic.

Bowlby, J. (1973). *Attachment and loss: Vol. 2. Separation, anxiety and anger*. New York: Basic.

Bowlby, J. (1988). *A secure base: Parent-child attachment and healthy human development*. New York: Basic.

Boyd, N. B. (1999). *Play therapy with children in crisis*. New York: Guilford.

Boyd-Franklin, N., & Bry, B. H. (2000). *Reaching out in family therapy: Home-based, school, and community interventions*. New York: Guilford.

Brainard, M. S., & Knudsen, E. I. (1998). Brain Development, V: Experience affects brain development. *American Journal of Psychiatry, 155*, 1000.

Braswell, L., & Kendall, P. C. (2001). Cognitive-behavioral therapy with youth. In K. S. Dobson (Ed.), *Handbook of cognitive-behavioral therapies* (2nd ed., pp. 246–294). New York: Guilford.

Breggin, P. R. (1994). *Toxic psychiatry*. New York: St. Martin's Press.

Briesmeister, J. M., & Schaefer, C. E. (1998). *Handbook of parent training: Parents as co-therapists for children's behavior problems* (2nd ed.). New York: John Wiley & Sons.

Brody, G. H. (1998). Sibling relationship quality: Its causes and consequences. *Annual Review of Psychology, 49*, 1–24.

Brown, G. W., Monck, E. M., Carstairs, G. M., & Wing, J. K. (1962). Influence of family life on the course of schizophrenic illness. *British Journal of Preventive Social Medicine, 16*, 55–68.

Bruininks, V. L. (1978). Actual and perceived peer status of learning disabled students in mainstream programs. *Journal of Special Education, 12*, 51–58.

Bryan, T. H. (1974). Peer popularity of learning disabled children. *Journal of Learning Disabilities, 7*, 621–625.

Bryan, T. H. (1977). Learning disabled children's comprehension of nonverbal communication. *Journal of Learning Disabilities, 10*, 501–507.

Bryan, T. H. (1998). Social problems and learning disabilities. In B. Wong (Ed.), *Learning about learning disabilities* (2nd ed., pp. 237–275). San Diego, CA: Academic Press.

Bryan, T. H., & Bryan, J. H. (1977). The social-emotional side of learning disabilities. *Behavioral Disorders, 2*, 141–145.

Bryan, T. H., & Bryan, J. H. (1978). *Understanding learning disabilities*. Sherman Oaks, CA: Alfred.

Buchsbaum, H. K., Toth, S. L., Clyman, R. B., Cicchetti, D., & Emde, R. N. (1992). The use of a narrative story stem technique with maltreated children: Implications for theory and practice. *Developmental Psychopathology, 4*, 603–625.

Bugental, D. B., & Johnston, C. (2000). Parental cognitions in the context of the family. *Annual Review of Psychology, 51*, 315–344.

Bumpass, L. L. (1990). What's happening to the family? Interactions between demographic and institutional change. *Demography, 27*, 483–498.

Burks, H. (1978). *Imagine*. Huntington Beach, CA: Arden.

Bursuck, W. D. (1989). A comparison of students with learning disabilities to low achieving and higher achieving students on three dimensions of social competence. *Journal of Learning Disabilities, 22*, 188–194.

Butxlaff, R. L., & Hooley, J. M. (1998). Expressed emotion and psychiatric relapse: A meta-analysis. *Archives of General Psychiatry, 55*, 547–552.

Buurma, D. (1999). *The family play genogram: A guidebook.* 67 Valley View Ave., Summit, NJ 07901: Author.

Buzan, T. (1991). *Use both sides of your brain* (3rd ed.). New York: Penguin.

Byrne, N. (1997). Family therapy: Terminable and interminable. *Clinical Child Psychology & Psychiatry, 2*, 167–175.

Cadesky, E. B., Mota, V. L., & Schachar, R. J. (2000). Beyond words: How do children with ADHD and/or conduct problems process nonverbal information about affect? *Journal of the American Academy of Child & Adolescent Psychiatry, 39*, 1160–1167.

Cadoret, R. J., & Stewart, M. A. (1991). An adoption study of attention deficit/hyper-activity/aggression and their relationship to adult antisocial personality. *Comprehensive Psychiatry, 32*, 73–82.

Campbell, M., Armenteros, J. L., Spencer, K. E., Kowalik, S. C., & Erlenmeyer-Kimling, L. (1997). Schizophrenia and psychotic disorders. In J. M. Wiener (Ed.), *Textbook of child & adolescent psychiatry* (2nd ed., pp. 303–332). Washington, DC: American Psychiatric Press.

Campbell, T. L. (1998). Medical interviewing and the biopsychosocial model. *The Journal of Family Practice, 47*, 339–340.

Carey, W. B., & McDevitt, S. C. (1995). *Coping with children's temperament: A guide for professionals.* New York: Basic.

Carlier, I. V. E., Voerman, B. E., & Gersons, B. P. R. (2000). Intrusive traumatic recollections and comorbid posttraumatic stress disorder in depressed patients. *Psychosomatic Medicine, 62*, 26–32.

Carlson, C. I. (1987). Social interaction goals and strategies of children with learning disabilities. *Journal of Learning Disabilities, 20*, 306–311.

Caron, C., & Rutter, M. (1991). Comorbidity in child psychopathology: Concepts, issues, and research strategies. *Journal of Child Psychology & Psychiatry & Allied Disciplines, 3*, 1063–1080.

Carr, A. (1996). A structured approach to disengagement in family therapy with child-focused problems. *Contemporary Family Therapy, 18*, 471–487.

Carter, B., & McGoldrick, M. (Eds.). (1999a). *The expanded family life cycle: Individual, family and social perspectives* (3rd ed.). Boston: Allyn & Bacon.

Carter, B., & McGoldrick, M. (1999b). Overview of the family life cycle. In B. Carter & M. McGoldrick (Eds.), *The expanded family life cycle: Individual, family and social perspectives* (3rd ed., pp. 3–28). Boston: Allyn & Bacon.

Carter, C. A. (1987). Some indications for combining individual and family therapy. *American Journal of Family Therapy, 15*, 99–110.

Carton, J. S., & Carton, E. E. R. (1998). Nonverbal maternal warmth and children's locus of control of reinforcement. *Journal of Nonverbal Behavior, 22*, 77–86.

Castellanos, F. X. (1999). The psychobiology of attention-deficit/hyperactivity disorder. In H. C. Quay & A. E. Hogan (Eds.), *Handbook of disruptive behavior disorders* (pp. 179–198). New York: Kluwer Academic/Plenum.

Cecchin, G. (1987). Hypothesizing, circularity and neutrality revisited: An invitation to curiosity. *Family Process, 26,* 405–413.

Cederborg, A. C. (1997). Young children's participation in family therapy talk. *American Journal of Family Therapy, 25,* 28–38.

Celano, M. P., & Kaslow, N. J. (2000). Culturally competent family interventions: Review and case illustrations. *The American Journal of Family Therapy, 28,* 217–228.

Cervantes, C. A., & Callanan, M. A. (1998). Labels and explanations in mother-child emotion talk: Age and gender differentiation. *Developmental Psychology, 34,* 88–98.

Chasin, R. (1999). Interviewing families with children: Guidelines and suggestions. In C. E. Schaefer & L. J. Carey (Eds.), *Family play therapy* (pp. 57–70). Northvale, NJ: Jason Aronson.

Chasin, R., & White, T. (1989). The child in family therapy: Guidelines for active engagement across the age span. In L. Combrinck-Graham (Ed.), *Children in family contexts: Perspectives on treatment* (pp. 5–24). New York: Guilford.

Chess, S., & Thomas, A. (1989). *Temperament in clinical practice.* New York: Guilford.

Chess, S., & Thomas, A. (1991). Temperament and the concept of goodness of fit. In J. Strelau & A. Angleitner (Eds.), *Explorations in temperament: International perspectives on theory and measurement. Perspectives on individual differences* (pp. 15–28). New York: Plenum.

Chess, S., & Thomas, A. (1999). *Goodness of fit: Clinical applications from infancy through adult life.* Philadelphia: Brunner/Mazel.

Chethik, M. (1989). *Techniques of child therapy: Psychodynamic strategies.* New York: Guilford.

Chethik, M. (2000). *Techniques of child therapy: Psychodynamic strategies* (2nd ed.). New York: Guilford.

Christensen, A., & Heavey, C. L. (1999). Interventions for couples. *Annual Review of Psychology, 50,* 165–190.

Chrousos, G. P. (1998). A healthy body in a healthy mind—and vice versa—the damaging power of "uncontrollable" stress. *Journal of Clinical Endocrinology and Metabolism, 83,* 1842–1845.

Cohen, J. (1985). Learning disabilities and psychological development in childhood and adolescence. *Annals of Dyslexia, 26,* 293–294.

Cohen, J. I. (2000). Stress and mental health: A biobehavioral perspective. *Issues in Mental Health Nursing, 21,* 185–202.

Cohen, L. J. (1987). Bibliotherapy: Using literature to help children deal with difficult problems. *Journal of Psychosocial Nursing & Mental Health Services, 25,* 20–24.

Coie, J. D., Dodge, K. A., & Kupersmidt, J. B. (1990). Peer group behavior and social status. In S. R. Asher & J. D. Coie (Eds.), *Peer rejection in childhood* (pp. 17–59). Cambridge, England: Cambridge University Press.

Combrinck-Graham, L. (1989). Family models of childhood psychopathology. In L. Combrinck-Graham (Ed.), *Children in family contexts: Perspectives on treatment* (pp. 67–90). New York: Guilford.

Combs, G., & Freedman, J. (1990). *Symbol, story, & ceremony: Using metaphor in individual and family therapy.* New York: Norton.

Commoner, B. (1971). *The closing circle: Nature, man & technology.* New York: Alfred A. Knopf.

Conlan, R. (Ed.). (1999). *States of mind: New discoveries about how our brains make us who we are.* New York: John Wiley & Sons.

Cooley-Quille, M. R. , Turner, S. M., & Beidel, D. C. (1995). Emotional impact of children's exposure to community violence: A preliminary study. *Journal of the American Academy of Child & Adolescent Psychiatry, 34,* 1362–1368.

Coplin, J. W., & Morgan, S. B. (1988). Learning disabilities: A multi-dimensional perspective. *Journal of Learning Disabilities, 21,* 614–622.

Cowley, G. (2000, July 3). Generation XXL. *Newsweek,* 40–47.

Cox, M. J., Owen, M. T., Lewis, J. M., & Henderson, V. K. (1989). Marriage, adult adjustment, and early parenting. *Child Development, 60,* 1015–1024.

Coyle, J. T., & Schwarcz, R. (2000). Mind glue: Implications of glial cells biology for psychiatry. *Archives of General Psychiatry, 57,* 90–93.

Crain, W. (2000). *Theories of development: Concepts and applications* (4th ed.). Englewood Cliffs, NJ: Prentice Hall.

Crick, N. R., & Dodge, K. A. (1994). A review and reformulation of social information-processing mechanisms in children's social adjustment. *Psychological Bulletin, 115,* 74–101.

Crouter, A. C., Bumpus, M. F., Maguire, M. C., & McHale, S. M. (1999). Linking parents' work pressure and adolescents' well being: Insights into dynamics in dual earner families. *Developmental Psychology, 35,* 1453–1461.

Cummings, E. M., Davies, P. T., & Simpson, K. S. (1994). Marital conflict, gender, and children's appraisals and coping efficacy as mediators of child adjustment. *Journal of Family Psychology, 8,* 141–149.

Cummings, E. M., Ianotti, R. J., & Zahn-Waxler, C. (1985). The influence of conflict between adults on the emotions and aggression of young children. *Developmental Psychology, 21,* 495–507.

Cummings, E. M., & Smith, D. (1993). The impact of anger between adults on siblings' emotion and social behavior. *Journal of Child Psychology & Psychiatry, 34,* 1425–1433.

Cummings, J. S., Pellegrini, D. S., Notarius, C. I., & Cummings, E. M. (1989). Children's responses to angry adult behavior as a function of marital distress and history of interparent hostility. *Child Development, 60,* 1035–1045.

Curtis, J. L. (1998). *Today I feel silly.* New York: Harper Collins.

Dadds, M. R., Atkinson, E., Turner, C., Blums, G. J., & Lendich, B. (1999). Family conflict and child adjustment: Evidence for a cognitive-contextual model of intergenerational transmission. *Journal of Family Psychology, 13,* 194–208.

Davis, W. (1996). *The best of success.* Lombard, IL: Successories.

de Shazer, S. (1988). *Clues: Investigating solutions in brief therapy.* New York: Norton.

DeConti, K. A., & Dickerson, D. J. (1994). Preschool children's understanding of the situational determinants of others' emotions. *Cognition & Emotion, 8,* 453–472.

DeMaso, D. R., Gonzalez-Heydrich, J., Erickson, J. D., Grimes, V. P., & Strohecker, C. (2000). The experience journal: A computer-based intervention for families facing congenital heart disease. *Journal of the American Academy of Child & Adolescent Psychiatry, 39,* 727–734.

Denckla, M. B. (1996). A theory and model of executive function: A neuropsychological perspective. In G. R. Lyon & N. A. Krasnegor (Eds.), *Attention, memory, and executive function* (pp. 263–278). Baltimore: Paul H. Brookes.

Di Leo, J. H. (1973). *Children's drawings as diagnostic aids.* New York: Brunner/ Mazel.

Di Leo, J. H. (1983). *Interpreting children's drawings.* New York: Brunner/ Mazel.

Diamond, G. S., Serrano, A. C., Dickey, M., & Sonis, W. A. (1996). Current status of family-based outcome and process research. *Journal of the American Academy of Child & Adolescent Psychiatry, 35,* 6–16.

Diamond, M. C. (1988). *Enriching heredity: The impact of the environment on the anatomy of the brain.* New York: Free.

Diller, L. (1991, July-August). Not seen and not heard. *Family Therapy Networker,* 18–27, 66.

Dilts, S. L., Jr. (2001). *Models of the mind: A framework for biopsychosocial psychiatry.* Philadelphia: Brunner-Routledge.

Discover. (1997). Behavior—why we do what we do [Special Issue], 18.

Dishion, T. J., & Patterson, S. G. (1996). *Preventive parenting with love, encouragement, & limits: The preschool years.* Eugene, OR: Castalia.

Dixon, E. B. (1995). Impact of adult ADD on the family. In K. G. Nadeau (Ed.), *A comprehensive guide to attention deficit disorder in adults: Research, diagnosis, and treatment* (pp. 236–259). New York: Brunner/Mazel.

Drossman, D. A. (1998). Gastrointestinal illness and the biopsychosocial model. *Psychosomatic Medicine, 60,* 258–267.

Dubow, E. F., & Ippolito, M. F. (1994). Effects of poverty and quality of the home environment on changes in the academic and behavioral adjustment of elementary school-age children. *Journal of Clinical Child Psychology, 23,* 401–412.

Duhl, B. S. (1999). A personal view of action metaphor: Bringing what's inside outside. In D. J. Wiener (Ed.), *Beyond talk therapy: Using movement and expressive techniques in clinical practice* (pp. 79–96). Washington, DC: Amer-ican Psychological Association.

Duhl, F. J., Kantor, D., & Duhl, B. S. (1973). Learning space and action in family therapy: A primer of sculpture. In D. A. Bloch (Ed.), *Techniques of family psychotherapy: A primer* (pp. 47–63). New York: Grune & Stratton.

Duke, M. P., Martin, E. A., & Nowicki, S., Jr. (1996). *Teaching your child the social language of success.* Atlanta, GA: Peachtree.

Duncan, B., Miller, S., & Sparks, J. (2000, March-April). The myth of the magic pill: Exposing the mythmakers. *Family Therapy Networker,* 24–32.

Dunn, J., & Plomin, R. (1990). *Separate lives: Why are siblings so different?* New York: Basic.

Dunn, J., & Plomin, R. (1991). Why are siblings so different? The significance of differences in sibling experiences within the family. *Family Process, 30,* 271–284.

Dunn, R. (1984). Learning style: State of the science. *Theory Into Practice, 23,* 10–19.

Dunn, R., & Dunn, K. (1978). *Teaching students through their individual learning styles.* Reston, VA: Reston.

Durant, R. H., Getts, A., Cadenhead, C., Emans, S. J., & Woods, E. R. (1995). Exposure to violence and victimization and depression, hopelessness, and purpose in life among adolescents living in and around public housing. *Developmental and Behavioral Pediatrics, 16,* 233–237.

Dyson, L. L. (1996). The experiences of families of children with learning disabilities: Parental stress, family functioning and sibling self-concept. *Journal of Learning Disabilities, 29,* 280–286.

Earls, F. J. (1994). Violence and today's youth. *The Future of Children: Critical Health Issues for Children and Youth, 4,* 4–23.

Echevarria-Doan, S. (2001). Resource-based reflective consultation: Accessing client resources through interviews and dialogue. *Journal of Marital and Family Therapy, 27,* 201–212.

Eckenrode, J., Laird, M., & Doris, J. (1993). School performance and disciplinary problems among abused and neglected children. *Developmental Psychology, 29,* 53–62.

Edelman, G. M. (1987). *Neural Darwinism: The theory of neuronal group selection.* New York: Basic.

Eisenberg, L. (1998). Nature, niche, nurture: The role of social experience in transforming genotype into phenotype. *Academic Psychiatry, 22,* 213–222.

Eisenberg, L. (1999). Experience, brain, and behavior: The importance of a head start. *Pediatrics, 103,* 1031–1035.

Eisert, D., & Lamorey, S. (1996). Play as a window on child development: The relationship between play and other developmental domains. *Early Education & Development, 7,* 221–235.

Elbert, T., Panev, C., Wienbruch, C., Rockstroh, B., & Taub, E. (1995). Increased cortical representation of the fingers of the left hand in string players. *Science, 270,* 305–307.

Emberley, E. (1977). *Ed Emberley's great thumbprint drawing book.* New York: Little, Brown.

Engel, G. L. (1977). The need for a new medical model: A challenge for biomedicine. *Science, 196,* 129–136.

Engel, G. L. (1980). The clinical application of the biopsychosocial model. *American Journal of Psychiatry, 137,* 535–544.

Epker, J., & Gatchel, R. J. (2000). Coping profile differences in the biopsychosocial functioning of patients with temporomandibular disorder. *Psychosomatic Medicine, 62,* 69–75.

Epstein, L. H., Wing, R. R., & Valoski, A. (1985). Childhood obesity. *Pediatric Clinics of North America, 32*, 363–379.

Erikson, E. (1963). *Childhood and society* (Rev. ed.). New York: Norton.

Eriksson, P. S., Perfilieva, E., Bjork-Eriksson, T., Alborn, A. M., Nordborg, C., Peterson, D. A., & Gage, F. H. (1998). Neurogenesis in the adult human hippocampus. *Nature Medicine, 4*, 1313–1317.

Eslinger, P. J. (1996). Conceptualizing, describing, and measuring components of executive function: A summary. In G. R. Lyon & N. A. Krasnegor (Eds.), *Attention, memory, and executive function* (pp. 367–396). Baltimore: Paul H. Brookes.

Eslinger, P. J., Grattan, L. M., Damasio, H., & Damasio, A. R. (1992). Developmental consequences of childhood frontal lobe damage. *Archives of Neurology, 49*, 764–769.

Falicov, C. J. (1983). *Cultural perspectives in family therapy*. Rockville, MD: Aspen.

Falicov, C. J. (1995). Training to think culturally: A multidimensional comparative framework. *Family Process, 34*, 373–388.

Falicov, C. J. (1998). The cultural meaning of family triangles. In M. McGoldrick (Ed.), *Re-visioning family therapy: Race, culture, and gender in clinical practice* (pp. 37–49). New York: Guilford.

Faraone, S. V., Biederman, J., & Milberger, S. (1994). An exploratory study of ADHD among second-degree relatives of ADHD children. *Biological Psychiatry, 35*, 398–402.

Farmer-Dougan,V., & Kaszuba, T. (1999). Reliability and validity of play-based observations: Relationship between the play behaviour observation system and standardised measures of cognitive and social skills. *Educational Psychology, 19*, 429–440.

Field, T., & Fogel, A. (1982). *Emotion and early interaction*. Hillsdale, NJ: Lawrence Erlbaum.

Fisher, G. H. (1968a). Ambiguity of form: Old and new. *Perception and Psychophysics, 4*, 189–192.

Fisher, G. H. (1968b). Mother, father and daughter: A three-aspect ambiguous figure. *American Journal of Psychology, 81*, 274–277.

Fishman, S., Wolf, L., Ellison, D., Gillis, B., Freeman, T., & Szatmari, P. (1996). Risk and protective factors affecting the adjustment of siblings of children with chronic disabilities. *Journal of the American Academy of Child & Adolescent Psychiatry, 35*, 1532–1541.

Flavell, J. H. (1992). Perspectives on perspective taking. In H. Beilin & P. B. Pufall (Eds.), *Piaget's theory: Prospects and possibilities. The Jean Piaget symposium series* (pp. 107–139). Hillsdale, NJ: Lawrence Erlbaum.

Fleming, A. S., O'Day, D. H., & Kraemer, G. W. (1999). Neurobiology of mother-infant interactions: Experience and central nervous system plasticity across development and generations. *Neuroscience & Biobehavioral Reviews, 23*, 673–685.

Fleuridas, C., Nelson, T. S., & Rosenthal, D. M. (1986). The evolution of circular questions: Training family therapists. *Journal of Marital & Family Therapy, 12*, 113–127.

Fleuridas, C., Rosenthal, D. M., Leigh, G. K., & Leigh, T. E. (1990). Family goal recording: An adaptation of goal attainment scaling for enhancing family therapy and assessment. *Journal of Marital & Family Therapy, 16*, 389–406.

Fonagy, P., & Target, M. (1997). Attachment and reflective function: Their role in self-organization. *Development and Psychopathology, 9*, 679–700.

Forman, S. G. (1993). *Coping skills interventions for children and adolescents*. San Francisco: Jossey-Bass.

Fraenkel, P. (2001, March-April). Beeper in the bedroom. *Psychotherapy Networker, 25*, 22-29, 64–65.

Fraenkel, P., & Wilson, S. (2000). Clocks, calendars, and couples: Time and rhythms of relationships. In P. Papp (Ed.), *Couples on the fault line: New directions for therapists* (pp. 63–103). New York: Guilford.

Frank, E., Hlastala, S., Ritenour, A., Houck, P., Xin, M. Monk, T. H., Mallinger, A., & Kupfer, D. J. (1997). Inducing lifestyle regularity in recovering bipolar disorder patients: Results from the maintenance therapies in bipolar disorder protocol. *Biological Psychiatry, 41*, 1165–1173.

Frank, E., Kupfer, D. J., Ehlers, C. L., Monk, T. H., Cornes, C., Carter, S., & Frankel, D. (1994). Interpersonal and social rhythm therapy for bipolar disorder: Integrating interpersonal and behavioral approaches. *Behavior Therapist, 17*, 143–149.

Frank, E., Swartz, H. A., & Kupfer, D. J. (2000). Interpersonal and social rhythm therapy: Managing the chaos of bipolar disorder. *Biological Psychiatry, 48*, 593–604.

Freed, J., & Parsons, L. (1997). *Right-brained children in a left-brained world: Unlocking the potential of your ADD child*. New York: Fireside.

Freeman, J., Epston, D., & Lobovits, D. (1997). *Playful approaches to serious problems: Narrative therapy with children and their families*. New York: Norton.

Freud, A. (1965). *Normality and pathology in childhood: Assessments of development*. Madison, CT: International Universities Press.

Freymann, S., & Elffers, J. (1997). *Play with your food*. New York: Stewart, Tabori & Chang.

Freymann, S., & Elffers, J. (1999). *How are you peeling? Foods with moods*. New York: Scholastic.

Freymann, S., & Elffers, J. (2000). *The lonely seahorse*. New York: Scholastic.

Fruhbeck, G. (2000). Childhood obesity: Time for action, not complacency. Definitions are unclear, but effective interventions exist. *British Medical Journal, 320*, 328–329.

Furman, L. (1990). Video therapy: An alternative for the treatment of adolescents. *Arts in Psychotherapy, 17*, 165–169.

Gabbard, G. O. (2000). A neurobiologically informed perspective on psychotherapy. *British Journal of Psychiatry, 177*, 117–122.

Gabbard, G. O., & Goodwin, F. K. (1996). Integrating biological and psychosocial perspectives. *American Psychiatric Press Review of Psychiatry, 15*, 527–548.

Garbarino, J., Kostelny, K., & Dubrow, N. (1991). What children can tell us about living in danger. *American Psychologist, 46*, 376–383.

Garcia-Lawson, K. A., & Lane, R. C. (1997). Thoughts on termination: Practical considerations. *Psychoanalytic Psychology, 14*, 239–257.

Gardano, A. C. (1994). Creative video therapy with early adolescent girls in short-term treatment. *Journal of Child & Adolescent Group Therapy, 4*, 99–116.

Gardner, H. (1983). *Frames of mind: The theory of multiple intelligences*. New York: Basic.

Gardner, R. A. (1986). The talking, feeling, doing game. In C. E. Schaefer & S. E. Reid (Eds.), *Game play: Therapeutic use of childhood games* (pp. 41–72). New York: John Wiley & Sons.

Gardner, R. A. (1993). *Storytelling in psychotherapy with children*. Northvale, NJ: Jason Aronson.

Gazzaniga, M. S. (1972). One brain-two minds. *American Scientist, 60*, 311–317.

Geisthardt, C., & Munsch, J. (1996). Coping with school stress: A comparison of adolescents with and without learning disabilities. *Journal of Learning Disabilities, 29*, 287–296.

Geller, B., & Luby, J. (1997). Child and adolescent bipolar disorder: A review of the past 10 years. *Journal of the American Academy of Child & Adolescent Psychiatry, 36*, 1168–1176.

Getz, H. G., & Nininger, K. (1999). Videotaping as a counseling technique with families. *Family Journal: Counseling & Therapy for Couples & Families, 7*, 395–398.

Gil, E. (1994). *Play in family therapy*. New York: Guilford.

Gil, E., & Sobol, B. (2000). Engaging families in therapeutic play. In C. E. Bailey (Ed.), *Children in therapy: Using the family as a resource* (pp. 341–382). New York: Norton.

Gilbert, P. (1998). What is shame? Some core issues and controversies. In P. Gilbert & B. Andrews (Eds.), *Shame: Interpersonal behavior, psychopathology, and culture* (pp. 3–38). New York: Oxford University Press.

Gilbert, P., & Andrews, B. (1998). *Shame: Interpersonal behavior, psychopathology, and culture*. New York: Oxford University Press.

Ginsburg, H., & Opper, S. (1969). *Piaget's theory of intellectual development: An introduction*. Englewood Cliffs, NJ: Prentice-Hall.

Glodich, A. M. (1998). Traumatic exposure to violence: A comprehensive review of the child and adolescent literature. *Smith College Studies in Social Work, 68*, 321–345.

Goldberg, S., Muir, R., & Kerr, J. (1995). *Attachment theory: Social, developmental, and clinical perspectives*. London: Analytical Press.

Goldman, D. (Ed.). (1993a). *In one's bones: The clinical genius of Winnicott*. Northvale, NJ: Jason Aronson.

Goldman, D. (Ed.). (1993b). *In search of the real: The origins and originality of D. W. Winnicott*. Northvale, NJ: Jason Aronson.

Goldner, V. (1985) Feminism and family therapy. *Family Process, 24*, 31–47.

Goldner, V. (1988). Generation and gender: Normative and covert hierarchies. *Family Process, 27*, 17–31.

Goldstein, S. (1995). *Understanding and managing children's classroom behavior*. New York: John Wiley & Sons.

Gonzales, N. A., Cauce, A. M., Friedman, R. J., & Mason, C. A. (1996). Family, peer, and neighborhood influences on academic achievement among African-American adolescents: One year prospective effects. *American Journal of Community Psychology, 24*, 365–387.

Gonzalez, S., Steinglass, P., & Reiss, D. (1989). Putting the illness in its place: Discussion groups for families with chronic medical illnesses. *Family Process, 28*, 69–87.

Goodman, R., & Stevenson, J. (1989). A twin study of hyperactivity-II. The aetiological role of genes, family relationships and perinatal adversity. *Journal of Child Psychology & Psychiatry & Allied Disciplines, 30,* 691–709.

Gorman-Smith, D., & Tolan, P. (1998). The role of exposure to community violence and development among inner-city youth. *Development and Psychopathology, 10,* 101–116.

Gottman, J. (1998). Psychology and the study of marital processes. *Annual Review of Psychology, 49,* 169–197.

Gottman, J., Notarius, C., Gonso, J., & Markman, H. (1976). *A couple's guide to communication.* Champaign, IL: Research Press.

Gottman, J. M., & Katz, L. (1989). Effects of marital discord on young children's peer interaction and health. *Developmental Psychology, 25,* 373–381.

Gould, E., Tanapat, P., McEwen, B. S., Flugge, G., & Fuchs, E. (1998). Proliferation of granule cell precursors in the dentate gyrus of adult monkeys is diminished by stress. *Proceedings of the National Academy of Sciences of the United States of America, 95,* 3168–3171.

Gould, E., Tanapat, P., Rydel, T., & Hastings, N. (2000). Regulation of hippocampal neurogenesis in adulthood. *Biological Psychiatry, 48,* 715–720.

Grant, G., Jr. (2000). How families experience the end of family therapy. *Dissertation Abstracts International, A (Humanities and Social Sciences), 60(11-A).* (University Microfilms No. 4196).

Grattan, L. M., & Eslinger, P. J. (1992). Long-term psychological consequences of childhood frontal lobe lesion in patient DT. *Brain and Cognition, 20,* 185–195.

Greenberg, L. S., & Johnson, S. (1988). *Emotionally focused therapy for couples.* New York: Guilford.

Greene, R. W. (1998). *The explosive child: A new approach for understanding and parenting easily frustrated, "chronically inflexible" children.* New York: Harper Collins.

Greenfield, S. (2000). *The private life of the brain: Emotions, consciousness, and the secret of the self.* New York: John Wiley & Sons.

Greenhill, L. L., Halperin, J. M., & Abikoff, H. (1999). Stimulant medications. *Journal of the American Academy of Child & Adolescent Psychiatry, 38,* 503–512.

Greenough, W. T., Black, J. E., & Wallace, C. S. (1987). Experience and brain development. *Child Development, 58,* 539–559.

Greenspan, S. I. (1997). *The growth of the mind and the endangered origins of intelligence.* New York: Addison-Wesley.

Greenspan, S. I., & Wieder, S. (1998). *The child with special needs: Encouraging intellectual and emotional growth.* Reading, MA: Perseus.

Gresham, F. M. (1981). Social skills training with handicapped children: A review. *Review of Educational Research, 51,* 139–176.

Gresham, F. M. (1986). Conceptual issues in the assessment of social competence in children. In P. S. Strain, M. J. Guralnick, & H. M. Walker (Eds.), *Children's social behavior: Development, assessment and modification* (pp. 143–179). Orlando, Fl: Academic Press.

Gresham, F. M., & Elliot, S. T. (1984). Assessment and classification of children's social skills: A review of methods and issues. *School Psychology Review, 13*, 292–301.

Griffith, J. L., Griffith, M. E., & Slovik, L. S. (1989). Mind-body patterns of symptom generation. *Family Process, 28*, 137–152.

Grigorenko, E. L. (2001). Developmental dyslexia: An update of genes, brains, and environments. *Journal of Child Psychology & Psychiatry & Allied Disciplines, 42*, 91–125.

Grimshaw, R. (2000). Parenting programmes: The importance of partnership in research and practice. In A. Buchanan & B. Hudson (Eds.), *Promoting children's emotional well-being* (pp. 128–144). New York: Oxford University Press.

Gross, V. (1995). A child-aware approach in systemic practice. *Human Systems: The Journal of Systemic Consultation and Management, 6*, 189–200.

Groves, B. M., Zuckerman, B., Marans, S., & Cohen, D. (1993). Silent victims: Children who witness violence. *Journal of the American Medical Association, 269*, 262–64.

Grych, J., & Fincham, F. (1993). Children's appraisal of marital conflict: Initial investigations of the cognitive-contextual framework. *Child Develop-ment, 64*, 215–230.

Gurman, A. S., Kniskern, D. P., & Pinsof, W. M. (1986). Research on the process and outcome of marital and family therapy. In S. L. Garfield & A. E. Bergin (Eds.), *Handbook of psychotherapy and behavior change* (3rd ed., pp. 565–624). New York: John Wiley & Sons.

Halfon, N., & Newacheck, P. W. (1999). Prevalence and impact of parent-reported disabling mental health conditions among U.S. children. *Journal of the American Academy of Child & Adolescent Psychiatry, 38*, 600–609.

Halperin, J. M., & McKay, K. E. (1998). Psychological testing for child and adolescent psychiatrists: A review of the past 10 years. *Journal of the American Academy of Child & Adolescent Psychiatry, 37*, 575–584.

Hamer, D., & Copeland, P. (1998). *Living with our genes*. New York: Anchor.

Hammill, D. (1990). On defining learning disabilities: An emerging consensus. *Journal of Learning Disabilities, 23*, 74–85.

Handal, P. J., Tschannen, T., & Searight, H. R. (1998). The relationship of child adjustment to husbands' and wives' marital distress, perceived family conflict, and mothers' occupational status. *Child Psychiatry & Human Development, 29*, 113–126.

Handel, P. D. (1999). Family relationships and perceived competence in students with learning disabilities. *Dissertation Abstracts International, A (Humanities and Social Sciences), 60(3-A)*, 0647.

Handler, L., & Habenicht, D. (1994). The kinetic family drawing technique: A review of the literature. *Journal of Personality Assessment, 62*, 440–464.

Hannaford, C. (1995). *Smart moves: Why learning is not all in your head*. Arlington, VA: Great Ocean.

Harary, K., & Weintraub, P. (1991). *Right-brain learning in 30 days: The whole mind program*. New York: St. Martin's.

Hardy, K. V., & Laszloffy, T. A. (1995). The cultural genogram: Key to training culturally competent family therapists. *Journal of Marital & Family Therapy, 21*, 227–237.

Hardy, K. V., & Laszloffy, T. A. (2000). Uncommon strategies for a common problem: Addressing racism in family therapy. *Family Process, 39,* 35–50.

Hare-Mustin, R. T. (1987). The problem of gender in family therapy theory. *Family Process, 26,* 15–27.

Hare-Mustin, R. T. (1991). Sex, lies, and headaches: The problem is power. In T. G. Goodrich (Ed.), *Women and power: Perspectives for family therapy* (pp. 63–86). New York: Norton.

Harlow, H. F. (1958). The nature of love. *American Psychologist, 13,* 673–685.

Hart, B., & Risley, T. R. (1999). *The social world of children learning to talk.* Baltimore: Paul H. Brookes.

Harter, S. (1983). Children's understanding of multiple emotions: A cognitive-developmental approach. In W. F. Overton (Ed.), *The relationship between social and cognitive development* (pp. 147–194). Hillsdale, NJ: Lawrence Erlbaum.

Harter, S. (1986). Cognitive-developmental processes in the integration of concepts about emotions and the self. *Social Cognition, 4,* 119–151.

Harvey, S. (1990). Dynamic play therapy: An integrative expressive arts approach to the family therapy of young children. *Arts in Psychotherapy, 17,* 239–246.

Hayghe, H. V. (1997, September). Developments in women's labor force participation. *Monthly Labor Review,* 41–46.

Healy, J. M. (1990). *Endangered minds: Why children don't think—and what we can do about it.* New York: Simon & Schuster.

Healy, J. M. (1994). *Your child's growing mind: A practical guide to brain development and learning from birth to adolescence* (Rev. ed.). New York: Mainstreet.

Healy, J. M. (1998). *Failure to connect: How computers affect our children's minds—and what we can do about it.* New York: Simon & Schuster.

Hebb, D. O. (1949). *The organization of behavior: A neuropsychological theory.* New York: John Wiley & Sons.

Hembree-Kigin, T. L., & Bodiford McNeil, C. (1995). *Parent-child interaction therapy.* New York: Plenum.

Henggeler, S. W., Schoenwald, S. K., Borduin, C. M., Rowland, M. D., & Cunningham, P. B. (1998). *Multisystemic treatment of antisocial behavior in children and adolescents.* New York: Guilford.

Henker, B., & Whalen, C. K. (1999). The child with attention-deficit/hyperactivity disorder in school and peer settings. In H. C. Quay & A. E. Hogan (Eds.), *Handbook of disruptive behavior disorders* (pp. 157–178). New York: Kluwer Academic/Plenum.

Herman, M. A., & McHale, S. M. (1993). Coping with parental negativity: Links with parental warmth and child adjustment. *Journal of Applied Developmental Psychology, 14,* 121–136.

Hernandez, S. L. (1998). The emotional thermometer: Using family sculpting for emotional assessment. *Family Therapy, 25,* 121–128.

Herrmann, N. (1995). *The creative brain.* Lake Lure, NC: Ned Herrmann Group.

Hershorn, M., & Rosenbaum, A. (1985). Children of marital violence: A closer look at the unintended victims. *American Journal of Orthopsychiatry, 55*, 260–266.

Hesse, E., & Main, M. (1999). Second-generation effects of unresolved trauma in non-maltreating parents: Dissociated, frightened, and threatening parental behavior. *Psychoanalytic Inquiry, 19*, 481–540.

Hinshaw, S. P. (1992). Externalizing behavior problems and academic underachievement in childhood and adolescence: Causal relationships and underlying mechanisms. *Psychological Bulletin, 111*, 127–155.

Hockfield, S., & Lombroso, P. J. (1998a). Development of the cerebral cortex: IX. Cortical development and experience: I. *Journal of the American Academy of Child & Adolescent Psychiatry, 37*, 992–993.

Hockfield, S., & Lombroso, P. J. (1998b). Development of the cerebral cortex: X. Cortical development and experience: II. *Journal of the American Academy of Child & Adolescent Psychiatry, 37*, 1103–1105.

Hoes, M. (1997). Adverse life events and psychosomatic disease. *Current Opinion in Psychiatry, 10*, 462–465.

Hofer, M. A. (1990). Early symbiotic processes: Hard evidence from a soft place. In R. A. Glick & S. Bone (Eds.), *Pleasure beyond the pleasure principle* (pp. 55–78). New Haven: Yale University Press.

Hoffman, L. (1981). *Foundations of family therapy: A conceptual framework for systems change*. New York: Basic.

Hoghughi, M. (1998). The importance of parenting in child health: Doctors as well as the government should do more to support parents. *British Medical Journal, 316*, 1545.

Hoghughi, M., & Speight, A. N. P. (1998). Good enough parenting for all children—a strategy for a healthier society. *Archives of Disease in Childhood, 78*, 293–296.

Holder, H. B., & Kirkpatrick, S. W. (1991). Interpretation of emotion from facial expressions in children with and without learning disabilities. *Journal of Learning Disabilities, 24*, 170–177.

Hubel, D. H., & Wiesel, T. N. (1965). Receptive fields and functional architecture in the two nonstriate visual areas (18 and 19) of the cat. *Journal of Neurophysiology, 28*, 289–299.

Hughes, C., Dunn, J., & White, A. (1998). Trick or treat? Uneven understanding of mind and emotion and executive dysfunction in "hard-to-manage" preschoolers. *Journal of Child Psychology & Psychiatry, 39*, 981–994.

Hughes, D. A. (1998). *Building the bonds of attachment: Awakening love in deeply troubled children*. Northvale, NJ: Jason Aronson.

Hughes, J. N., & Baker, D. B. (1990). *The clinical child interview*. New York: Guilford.

Huntington, D. D., & Bender, W. N. (1993). Adolescents with learning disabilities at risk? Emotional well-being, depression, suicide. *Journal of Learning Disabilities, 26*, 159–166.

Hyman, S. (1999). Susceptibility and "second hits." In R. Conlan (Ed.), *States of mind: New discoveries about how our brains make us who we are* (pp. 9–28). New York: John Wiley & Sons.

Imber-Black, E. (2000). The new triangle: Couples and technology. In P. Papp (Ed.), *Couples on the fault line: New directions for therapists* (pp. 48–62). New York: Guilford.

Imber-Black, E., Roberts, J., & Whiting, R. A. (Eds). (1988). *Rituals in families and family therapy*. New York: Norton.

Inhelder, B., & Piaget, J. (1958). *The growth of logical thinking from childhood to adolescence: An essay on the construction of formal operational structures*. New York: Basic.

Isaacs, M. B., Monatalvo, B., & Abelsohn, D. (1986). *The difficult divorce: Therapy for children and families*. New York: Basic.

Jacques, J. R. (1999). Working with spiritual and religious themes in group therapy. *Year Book of Psychiatry & Applied Mental Health, 2*, 92–93.

Jenkins, J. (1992). Sibling relationships in disharmonious homes: Potential difficulties and protective effects. In F. Boer & J. Dunn (Eds.), *Children's sibling relationships: Developmental and clinical issues* (pp. 125–138). Hillsdale, NJ: Lawrence Erlbaum.

Jensen, P. S., Bhatara, V. S., Vitiello, B., Hoagwood, K., Feil, M., & Burke, L. (1999). Psychoactive medication practices for US children: Gaps between research and clinical practice. *Journal of the American Academy of Child & Adolescent Psychiatry, 38*, 557–565.

Jersild, A. T., & Holmes, F. (Eds.). (1935). *Children's fears (Child Development Monograph No. 20)*. New York: Columbia University Press.

Johnson, B. H. (1990). Children's drawings as a projective technique. *Pediatric Nursing, 16*, 11–17.

Johnson, H. C. (1987). Biologically based deficit in the identified patient: Indications for psychoeducational strategies. *Journal of Marital and Family Therapy, 13*, 337–348.

Johnson, L., & Volker, T. (1999). Influences on the inclusion of children in family therapy. *Journal of Marriage & Family Counseling, 25*, 117–123.

Johnson, S. L., Greenhouse, W., & Bauer, M. (2000). Psychosocial approaches to the treatment of bipolar disorder. *Current Opinion in Psychiatry, 13*, 69–72.

Johnson, S. M., Hunsley, J., Greenberg, L. S., & Schindler, D. (1999). Emotionally focused couples therapy: Status and challenges. *Clinical Psychology: Science and Practice, 6*, 67–79.

Johnson, S. M., & Lebow, J. (2000). The "coming of age" of couple therapy: A decade review. *Journal of Marriage & Family Counseling, 26*, 23–38.

Johnson, S. M., Makinen, J. A., & Millikin, J. W. (2001). Attachment injuries in couple relationships: A new perspective on impasses in couples therapy. *Journal of Marital and Family Therapy, 27*, 145–155.

Jouriles, E. N., Murphy, C. M., Farris, A. M., Smith, D. A., & Richters, J. E. (1991). Marital adjustment, parental disagreements about child-rearing, and behavior problems in boys: Increasing the specificity of the marital assessment. *Child Development, 62*, 1424–1433.

Jouriles, E. N., Pfiffner, L. J., & O'Leary, S. G. (1988). Marital conflict, parenting, and toddler conduct problems. *Journal of Abnormal Child Psychology, 16*, 197–206.

Joyce, B. M., Rockwood, K. J., & Mate-Kole, C. C. (1994). Use of goal attainment scaling in brain injury in a rehabilitation hospital. *American Journal of Physical Medicine and Rehabilitation, 73*, 10–14.

Kaduson, H. G., Cangelosi, D., & Schaefer, C. (Eds.). (1997). *The playing cure: Individualized play therapy for specific childhood problems*. Northvale, NJ: Jason Aronson.

Kaduson, H. G., & Schaefer, C. (Eds.). (1997). *101 favorite play therapy techniques*. Northvale, NJ: Jason Aronson.

Kagan, J. (1994). *Galen's prophecy: Temperament in human nature*. New York: Basic.

Kandel, E. R. (1998). A new intellectual framework for psychiatry. *American Journal of Psychiatry, 155*, 457–469.

Kandel, E. R. (1999). Of learning, memory, and genetic switches. In R. Conlan (Ed.), *States of mind: New discoveries about how our brains make us who we are* (pp. 151–178). New York: John Wiley & Sons.

Kandel, E. R., & Squire, L. R. (2000, November 10). Neuroscience: Breaking down scientific barriers to the study of brain and mind. *Science Magazine, 290*, 1113–1120.

Kanter, J., Lamb, H. R., & Loeper, C. (1987). Expressed emotion in families: A critical review. *Hospital and Community Psychiatry, 38*, 374–380.

Kaplan, L. (1978). *Oneness and separateness: From infant to individual*. New York: Simon & Schuster.

Karacostas, D. D., & Fisher, G. L. (1993). Chemical dependency in students with and without learning disabilities. *Journal of Learning Disabilities, 26*, 491–495.

Karen, R. (1998). *Becoming attached: First relationships and how they shape our capacity to love*. New York: Oxford University Press.

Kavale, K. A., & Forness, S. R. (1985). Learning disability and the history of science: Paradigm or paradox? *Remedial and Special Education, 6*, 12–23.

Kazak, A. E, Simms, S., Barakat, L., Hobbie, W., Foley, B., Golomb, V., & Best, M. (1999). Surviving cancer competently intervention program (SCCIP): A cognitive-behavioral and family therapy intervention for adolescent survivors of childhood cancer and their families. *Family Process, 38*, 175–191.

Kazdin, A. E. (2000a). Developing a research agenda for child and adolescent psychotherapy. *Archives of General Psychiatry, 57*, 829–835.

Kazdin, A. E. (2000b). *Psychotherapy for children and adolescents*. New York: Oxford University Press.

Keith, D. V., & Whitaker, C. A. (1981). Play therapy: A paradigm for work with families. *Journal of Marital and Family Therapy, 7*, 243–251.

Kelleher, K. J., Childs, G. E., Wasserman, R. C., McInerny, T. K., Nutting, P. A., & Gardner, W. P. (1997). Insurance status and recognition of psychosocial problems: A report from PROS and ASPN. *Archives of Pediatric Adolescent Medicine, 151*, 1109–1115.

Kelly, J. B. (2000). Children's adjustment in conflicted marriage and divorce: A decade review of research. *Journal of the American Academy of Child & Adolescent Psychiatry, 39*, 963–973.

Kempermann, G., & Gage, F. H. (1999). Experienced-dependent regulation of adult hippocampal neurogenesis: Effects of long-term stimulation and stimulus withdrawal. *Hippocampus, 9,* 321–332.

Kempermann, G., Kuhn, H. G., & Gage, F. H. (1997). More hippocampal neurons in adult mice living in an enriched environment. *Nature, 386,* 493–495.

Kendall, J. (1999). Sibling accounts of attention deficit hyperactivity disorder (ADHD). *Family Process, 38,* 117–136.

Kendall, P. C., & Braswell, L. (1993). *Cognitive-behavior therapy for impulsive children* (2nd ed.). New York: Guilford.

Kendall, P. C., & Chambless, D. L. (1998). Empirically supported psychological therapies. *Journal of Consulting and Clinical Psychology, 66,* 3–167.

Kendall, P. C., & Panichelli-Mindel, S. M. (1995). Cognitive-behavioral treatments. *Journal of Abnormal Child Psychology, 23,* 107–124.

Kendler, K. S., Kessler, R. C., & Neale, M. C. (1995). Stressful life events, genetic liability, and onset of major depression in women. *American Journal of Psychiatry, 152,* 833–842.

Kendler, K. S., Thornton, L. M., & Gardner, C. O. (2000). Stressful life events and previous episodes in the etiology of major depression in women: An evaluation of the "kindling" hypothesis. *American Journal of Psychiatry, 157,* 1243–1251.

Kerr, M. E., & Bowen, M. (1988). *Family evaluation: An approach based on Bowen theory.* New York: Norton.

King, N. J., & Bernstein, G. A. (2001). School refusal in children and adolescents: A review of the past 10 years. *Journal of the American Academy of Child & Adolescent Psychiatry, 40,* 197–205.

King-Storm, A., Engi, S., & Poulos, S. T. (1998). Using the internet to assist family therapy. *British Journal of Guidance and Counselling, 26,* 43–52.

Kiresuk, T. J., & Sherman, R. E. (1968). Goal attainment scaling: A general method for evaluating community mental health programs. *Community Mental Health Journal, 4,* 443–453.

Kiresuk, T. J., Smith, A., & Cardillo, J. E. (Eds.). (1994). *Goal attainment scaling: Applications, theory, and measurement.* Hillsdale, NJ: Lawrence Erlbaum.

Klee, B., & Hack, S. (1999). Child and adolescent psychopharmacology at a glance. *NYU Child Study Center Letter, 3*(4).

Klein, M. (1975). *The psycho-analysis of children.* New York: Free Press.

Klein, R. G. (1987). Questioning the clinical usefulness of projective psychological tests for children. *Annual Progress in Child Psychiatry & Child Development, 1987,* 451–461.

Klein, R. G. (1991). Parent-child agreement in clinical assessment of anxiety and other psychopathology: A review. *Journal of Anxiety Disorders, 5,* 187–198.

Klein, R. G., & Abikoff, H. (1997). Behavior therapy and methylphenidate in the treatment of children with ADHD. *Journal of Attention Disorders, 2,* 89–114.

Klein, R. G., & Wender, P. (1995). The role of methylphenidate in psychiatry. *Archives of General Psychiatry, 52,* 429–433.

Knoff, H. M., & Prout, H. T. (1985). The kinetic drawing system: A review and integration of the kinetic family and drawing techniques. *Psychology in the Schools, 22,* 50–59.

Knudsen, E. (1998). Capacity for plasticity in the adult owl auditory system expanded by juvenile experience. *Science, 279,* 1531–1533.

Kolb, B., & Whishaw, I.Q. (1998). Brain plasticity and behavior. *Annual Review of Psychology, 49,* 43–64.

Konstantareas, M. M. (1989). After diagnosis what? Some of the possible problems around diagnostic assessments. *Canadian Journal of Psychiatry, 34,* 549–553.

Konstantareas, M. M., & Homatidis, S. (1989) Assessing child symptom severity and stress in parents of autistic children. *Journal of Child Psychology & Psychiatry & Allied Disciplines, 30,* 459–470.

Koplewicz, H. S. (1996). *It's nobody's fault: New hope and help for difficult children and their parents.* New York: Random House.

Korner, S. (1988). Family therapists and children: A case of neglect. *Psychotherapy in Private Practice, 6,* 101–113.

Korner, S., & Brown, G. (1990). Exclusion of children from family psychotherapy: Family therapists' beliefs and practices. *Journal of Family Psychology, 4,* 420–430.

Kotulak, R. (1993, May 2). How early stimulus boosts the brain to maximum power. *The Chicago Tribune,* p. B6.

Kotulak, R. (1996). *Inside the brain: Revolutionary discoveries of how the mind works.* Kansas City, MO: Andrew and McMeel.

Kranowitz, C. S. (1998). *The out-of-sync child: Recognizing and coping with sensory integration dysfunction.* New York: Skylight.

Krickeberg, S. K. (1991). Away from Walton Mountain: Bibliographies for today's troubled youth. *School Counselor, 39,* 52–56.

Kuehl, B. P. (1993) Child and family therapy: A collaborative approach. *American Journal of Family Therapy, 21,* 260–266.

Kuntsi, J., & Stevenson, J. (2000). Hyperactivity in children: A focus on genetic research and psychological theories. *Clinical Child & Family Psychology Review, 3,* 1–23.

La Greca, A. M. (1990). *Through the eyes of the child: Obtaining self-reports from children and adolescents.* Needham Heights, MA: Allyn & Bacon.

La Greca, A. M., & Stone, W. L. (1990). LD status and achievement: Confounding variables in the study of children's social status, self-esteem, and behavioral functioning. *Journal of Learning Disabilities. 23,* 483–490.

Ladd, G. W. (1999). Peer relationships and social competence during early and middle childhood. *Annual Review of Psychology, 50,* 333–359.

Laird, M., & Doris, J. (1993). School performance and disciplinary problems among abused and neglected children. *Developmental Psychology, 29,* 53–62.

Lamorey, S., Robinson, B. E., Rowland, B. H., & Coleman, M. (1998). *Latchkey kids: Unlocking doors for children and their families* (2nd ed.). Thousand Oaks, CA: Sage.

Landgarten, H. B. (1981). *Clinical art therapy*. New York: Brunner/Mazel.

Landgarten, H. B. (1994). *Magazine photo collage: A multicultural assessment and treatment technique*. New York: Brunner/Mazel.

Lardieri, L. A., Blacher, J., & Swanson, H. L. (2000). Sibling relationships and parent stress in families of children with and without learning disabilities. *Learning Disability Quarterly, 23*, 105–116.

Larson, K. A. (1988). A research review and alternative hypothesis explaining the link between learning disability and delinquency. *Journal of Learning Disabilities, 21*, 357–363.

Last, C. G., & Perrin, S. (1993). Anxiety disorders in African-American and white children. *Journal of Abnormal Child Psychology, 21*, 153–164.

Lazear, D. (1991). *Seven ways of teaching: The artistry of teaching with multiple intelligences*. Palatine, IL: IRI/Skylight.

Lazear, D. (1994). *Seven pathways of learning: Teaching students and parents about multiple intelligences*. Tucson, AZ: Zephyr.

Lebow, J. (2000). What does the research tell us about couple and family therapies? *Journal of Clinical Psychology, 56*, 1083–1094.

LeDoux, J. (1996). *The emotional brain*. New York: Simon & Schuster.

Lenkowsky, R. S. (1987). Bibliotherapy: A review and analysis of the literature. *Journal of Special Education, 21*, 123–132.

Lesage-Higgins, S. A. (1999). Family sculpting in premarital counseling. *Family Therapy, 26*, 31–38.

Levine, M. D. (1984). Cumulative neurodevelopmental debts: Their impact on productivity in late middle childhood. In M. D. Levine & P. Satz (Eds.), *Middle childhood: Development and dysfunction* (pp. 227–243). Baltimore: University Park Press.

Levine, M. D. (1993). *Developmental variation and learning disorders*. Cambridge, MA: Educators Publishing Service.

Levine, M. D. (1994). *Educational care: A system for understanding and helping children with learning problems at home and at school*. Cambridge, MA: Educators Publishing Service.

Levine, M. D., & Zallen, B. G. (1984). The learning disorders of adolescence: Organic and non-organic failure to strive. *Pediatric Clinics of North America, 31*, 345–369.

Lewandowski, L. M., Gebing, T. A., Anthony, J. L., & O'Brien, W. H. (1997). Meta-analysis of cognitive-behavioral treatment studies for bulimia. *Clinical Psychology Review, 17*, 703–718.

Lewis, H. B. (1986). The role of shame in depression. In M. Rutter, C. E. Izard, & P. B. Read (Eds.), *Depression in young people: Developmental and clinical perspectives* (pp. 325–339). New York: Guilford.

Lewis, J. M. (1993). Childhood play in normality, pathology, and therapy. *American Journal of Orthopsychiatry, 63*, 6–15.

Lewis, J. M. (2000). Repairing the bond in important relationships: A dynamic for personality maturation. *American Journal of Psychiatry, 157*, 1375–1378.

Lewis, J. M., & Blotcky, M. J. (1997). *Child therapy: Concepts, strategies, and decision making*. Bristol, PA: Brunner/Mazel.

Lewis, J. M., Owen, M. T., & Cox, M. J. (1988). The transition to parenthood: III. Incorporation of the child into the family. *Family Process, 27*, 411–421.

Lewis, T., Amini, F., & Lannon, R. (2000). *A general theory of love.* New York: Random House.

Lezak, M. D. (1995). *Neuropsychological assessment* (3rd ed.). New York: Oxford University Press.

Light, K. (1997). Stress in employed women: A woman's work is never done if she's a working mom. *Psychosomatic Medicine, 59*, 360–361.

Linesch, D. (1999). Art making in family therapy. In D. J. Wiener (Ed.), *Beyond talk therapy: Using movement and expressive techniques in clinical practice* (pp. 263–286). Washington, DC: American Psychological Association.

Lobato, D., Faust, D., & Spirito, A. (1988). Examining the effects of chronic disease and disability on children's sibling relationships. *Journal of Pediatric Psychology, 13*, 389–407.

Locke, H. J., & Wallace, K. M. (1959). Short-term marital adjustment and prediction tests: Their reliability and validity. *Journal of Marriage and Family Living, 21*, 251–255.

Loeber, R., Burke, J. D., Lahey, B. B., Winters, A., & Zera, M. (2000). Oppositional defiant and conduct disorder: A review of the past 10 years, Part I. *Journal of the American Academy of Child & Adolescent Psychiatry, 39*, 1468–1484.

Lombroso, P. J., Pauls, D. L., & Leckman, J. F. (1994). Genetic mechanisms in childhood psychiatric disorders. *Journal of the American Academy of Child & Adolescent Psychiatry, 33*, 921–938.

Lowenstein, D. H., & Parent, J. M. (1999). Brain heal thyself. *Science, 283*, 1126–1127.

Lubin, H., Loris, M., Burt, J., & Johnson D. R. (1998). Efficacy of psychoeducational group therapy in reducing symptoms of posttraumatic stress disorder among multiply traumatized women. *American Journal of Psychiatry, 155*, 1172–1177.

Luthar, S. S. (1999). *Poverty and children's adjustment.* Thousand Oaks, CA: Sage.

Lyon, G. R. (1996). Learning disabilities. In E. J. Mash & R. A. Barkley (Eds.), *Child psychopathology* (pp. 390–435). New York: Guilford.

Lyon, G. R., & Krasnegor, N. A. (Eds.). (1996). *Attention, memory, and executive function.* Baltimore: Paul H. Brookes.

MacKay, G., Somerville, W., & Lundie, J. (1996). Reflections on goal attainment scaling (GAS): Cautionary notes and proposals for development. *Educational Research, 38*, 161–172.

MacLean, P. D. (1970). The triune brain, emotion and scientific basis. In F. O. Schmitt & F. G. Worden (Eds.), *The neurosciences: Third study program* (pp. 263–286). Cambridge, MA: MIT Press.

MacLean, P. D. (1990). *The triune brain in evolution: Role in paleocerebral functions.* New York: Plenum.

Mahler, M., Pine, F., & Bergman, A. (1975). *The psychological birth of the human infant.* New York: Basic.

Main, C. J., Richards, H. L., & Fortune, D. G. (2000). Why put new wine in old bottles: The need for a biopsychosocial approach to the assessment, treatment, and understanding of unexplained and explained symptoms in medicine. *Journal of Psychosomatic Research, 48*, 511–514.

Main, M., & Hesse, E. (1990). Parents' unresolved traumatic experiences are related to infant disorganized status: Is frightened and/or frightening parental behavior the linking mechanism? In M. T. Greenberg, D. Cicchetti, & E. M. Cummings (Eds.), *Attachment in the preschool years: Theory, research, and intervention* (pp. 161–182). Chicago: University of Chicago Press.

Main, M., Kaplan, N., & Cassidy, J. (1985). Security in infancy, childhood, and adulthood: A move to the level of representation. *Monographs of the Society for Research in Child Development, 50*, 66–104.

Malec, J. F. (1999). Goal attainment scaling in rehabilitation. *Neuropsychological Rehabilitation, 9*, 253–275.

Malec, J. F., Smigielski, J. S., & De Pompolo, R. W. (1991). Goal attainment scaling and outcome measurement in postacute brain injury rehabilitation. *Archives of Physical Medicine and Rehabilitation, 72*, 138–143.

Malhotra, A. K. (2001). The genetics of schizophrenia. *Current Opinion in Psychiatry, 14*, 3–7.

Manning, D. T. (1987). Books as therapy for children of alcoholics. *Child Welfare, 66*, 35–43.

March, J. S. (1995). *Anxiety disorders in children and adolescents.* New York: Guilford.

March, J. S., & Mulle, K. (1998). *OCD in children and adolescents: A cognitive-behavioral treatment manual.* New York: Guilford.

Marder, C., & D'Amico, R. (1992). *How well are youth with disabilities really doing? A comparison of youth with disabilities and youth in general.* (SRI International, Contract 300-87-0054). Washington, DC: U.S. Department of Education, Office of Special Education Programs. (ERIC Document Reproduction Service No. 369 233)

Margolin, G., & Gordis, E. B. (2000). The effects of family and community violence on children. *Annual Review of Psychology, 51*, 445–479.

Marguiles, N. (1997). *Inside Brian's brain.* Tuscon, AZ: Zephyr.

Martin, G. (1984). Metaphor: Complete or incomplete. *Australian Journal of Family Therapy, 5*, 125–140.

Martin, S. B., & Thompson, C. L. (1995). Reality therapy and goal attainment scaling: A program for freshman student athletes. *Journal of Reality Therapy, 14*, 45–54.

Martin, T. C., & Bumpass, L. (1989). Recent trends in marital disruption. *Demography, 26*, 37–51.

Mash, E. J., & Barkley, R. A. (Eds.). (1996). *Child psychopathology.* New York: Guilford.

Mash, E. J., & Barkley, R. A. (Eds.). (1998). *Treatment of childhood disorders* (2nd ed.). New York: Guilford.

Mash, E. J., & Johnston, C. (1983). Parental perceptions of child behavior problems, parenting self-esteem, and mothers' reported stress in younger and older hyperactive and normal children. *Journal of Consulting & Clinical Psychology, 51*, 86–99.

Masten, A., & Coatsworth, J. D. (1995). Competence, resilience, and psychopathology. In D. Cicchetti & D. J. Cohen (Eds.), *Developmental psychopathology, Vol. 2: Risk, disorder, and adaptation* (pp. 715–752). New York: John Wiley & Sons.

Masten, A. S., Sesma, A., Jr., Si-Asar, R., Lawrence, C., Miliotis, D., & Dionne, J. A. (1997). Educational risks for children experiencing homelessness. *Journal of School Psychology, 35,* 27–46.

Mattison, R. E. (2000). School consultation: A review of research on issues unique to the school environment. *Journal of the American Academy of Child & Adolescent Psychiatry, 39,* 402–413.

McAdam, E. (1995). Tuning into the voice of influence: The social construction of therapy with children. *Human Systems: The Journal of Systemic Consultation and Management, 6,* 171–188.

McCloskey, L. A., Figueredo, A. J., & Koss, M. P. (1995). The effects of systemic family violence on children's mental health. *Child Development, 66,* 1239–1261.

McCloskey, L. A., & Stuewig, J. (2001). The quality of peer relationships among children exposed to family violence. *Development and Psychopathology, 13,* 83–96.

McConatha, J. T., McConatha, D., Deaner, S. L., & Dermigny, R. (1995). A computer-based intervention for the education and therapy of institutionalized older adults. *Educational Gerontology, 21,* 129–138.

McDaniel, S. H., Hepworth, J., & Doherty, W. J. (1995). Medical family therapy with somaticizing patients: The co-creation of therapeutic stories. *Family Process, 34,* 349–361.

McEwen, B. S. (1999). Development of the cerebral cortex: XIII. Stress and brain development: II. *Journal of the American Academy of Child & Adolescent Psychiatry, 38,* 101–103.

McEwen, B. S. (2000). The neurobiology of stress: From serendipity to clinical relevance. *Brain Research, 886,* 172–189.

McEwen, B. S., & Sapolsky, R. M. (1995). Stress and cognitive function. *Current Opinion in Neurobiology, 5,* 205–216.

McFarlane, W. R. (1991). Family psychoeducational treatment. In A. S. Gurman & D. P. Kniskern (Eds.), *Handbook of family therapy* (Vol. 2, pp. 363–395). New York: Brunner/Mazel.

McFarlane, W. R., Lukens, E., Link, B., Dushay, R., Deakins, S. A., Newmark, M., Dunne, E. J., Horen, B., & Toran, J. (1995). Multiple-family groups and psychoeducation in the treatment of schizophrenia. *Archives of General Psychiatry, 52,* 679–687.

McGoldrick, M., Gerson, R., & Shellenberger, S. (1999). *Genograms: Assessment and intervention* (2nd ed.). New York: Norton.

McGoldrick, M., Pearce, J. K., & Giordano, J. (Eds.). (1996). *Ethnicity and family therapy* (2nd ed.) New York: Guilford.

McHale, S., & Gamble, W. C. (1989). Sibling relationships of children with disabled and nondisabled brothers and sisters. *Developmental Psychology, 25,* 421–429.

McHale, S., & Pawletko, T. (1992). Differential treatment of siblings in two family contexts. *Child Development, 63,* 68–81.

McIntosh, I I. (1998). Neuroimaging tools offer new ways to study autism. *APA Monitor, 29,* 15.

McKeever, P. (1983). Siblings of chronically ill children: A literature review with implications for research and practice. *American Journal of Orthopsychiatry, 53,* 209–218.

McLoyd, V. C. (1998). Socioeconomic disadvantage and child development. *American Psychologist, 53,* 185–204.

Mendlowitz, S. L., Manassis, K., Bradley, S., Scapillato, D., Miezitis, S., & Shaw, B. (1999). Cognitive-behavioral group treatments in childhood anxiety disorders: The role of parental involvement. *Journal of the American Academy of Child & Adolescent Psychiatry, 38,* 1223–1229.

Miklowitz, D. J., & Goldstein, M. J. (1997). *Bipolar disorder: A family-focused treatment approach.* New York: Guilford.

Miklowitz, D. J., Goldstein, M. J., Nuechterlein, K. H., Snyder, K. S., & Mintz, J. (1988). Family factors and the course of bipolar disorder. *Archives of General Psychiatry, 45,* 225–231.

Miller, B. D., & Wood, B. L. (1994). Psychophysiologic reactivity in asthmatic children: A cholinergically mediated confluence of pathways. *Journal of the American Academy of Child & Adolescent Psychiatry, 33,* 1236–1245.

Miller, B. D., & Wood, B. L. (1997). Influence of specific emotional states on autonomic reactivity and pulmonary function in asthmatic children. *Journal of the American Academy of Child & Adolescent Psychiatry, 36,* 669–677.

Miller, L. S., Wasserman, G. A., Neugebauer, R., Gorman-Smith, D., & Kamboukos, D. (1999). Witnessed community violence and antisocial behavior in high-risk, urban boys. *Journal of Clinical Child Psychology, 28,* 2–11.

Mills, J. C., & Crowley, R. J. (1986). *Therapeutic metaphors for children and the child within.* New York: Brunner/Mazel.

Minuchin, P., Colapinto, J., & Minuchin S. (1998). *Working with families of the poor.* New York: Guilford.

Minuchin, S. (1974). *Families and family therapy.* Cambridge, MA: Harvard University Press.

Minuchin, S., & Fishman, H. C. (1981). *Techniques of family therapy.* Cambridge, MA: Harvard University Press.

Moats, L. C., & Farrell, M. L. (1999). Multisensory instruction. In J. R. Birsh (Ed.), *Multisensory teaching of basic language skills* (pp. 1–17). New York: Paul H. Brookes.

Moltz, D. A. (1993). Bipolar disorder and the family: An integrative model. *Family Process, 32,* 409–423.

Morrison, J. R., & Stewart, M. A. (1973). The psychiatric status of the legal families of adopted hyperactive children. *Archives of General Psychiatry, 28,* 888–891.

Moustaka, C. (1996). *The child's discovery of himself.* New York: Ballantine.

Mullen, P., Green, L., & Persinger, G. (1985). Clinical trials of patient education for chronic conditions: A comparative meta-analysis of intervention types. *Preventive Medicine, 14,* 753–781.

Nash, J. M. (1997, February 3). Fertile minds. *Time*, *149*, 48–56.

National Center for Health Statistics. (1988, November). *National health interview survey*. Hyattsville, MD: Author.

National Center for Learning Disabilities. (1997/1998). Facts on learning disabilities. *Their World*, inside cover. New York: Author.

National Coalition for the Homeless. (1999, February). *How many people experience homelessness? National Coalition for the Homeless Fact Sheet #2* [On-line]. Available: nch.ari.net/numbers.html

National Coalition for the Homeless. (1999, June). *Why are people homeless? National Coalition for the Homeless Fact Sheet #1* [On-line]. Available: nch.ari.net/causes.html

National Institutes of Health. (2000). National Institutes of Health consensus development conference statement: Diagnosis and treatment of attention-deficit/hyperactivity disorder (ADHD). *Journal of the American Academy of Child & Adolescent Psychiatry*, *39*, 182–193.

Negrao, A. B., Deuster, P. A., Gold, P. W., Singh, A., & Chrousos, G. P. (2000). Individual reactivity and physiology of the stress response. *Biomedicine and Pharmacology*, *54*, 122–128.

Nelson, C. A., & Carver, L. J. (1998). The effects of stress and trauma on brain and memory: A view from developmental cognitive neuroscience. *Development & Psychopathology*, *10*, 793–809.

Nichols, M. P., & Fellenberg, S. (2000). The effective use of enactments in family therapy: A discovery-oriented process study. *Journal of Marriage & Family Counseling*, *26*, 143–152.

Nichols, M. P., & Schwartz, R. C. (Eds.). (1998). *Family therapy: Concepts and methods* (4th ed.). Boston: Allyn & Bacon.

Nickerson, E. T. (1986). Integrating the child into family therapy: The remaking of a for-adults-only orientation. *International Journal of Family Psychiatry*, *7*, 59–69.

Nicolopoulou, A. (1993). Play, cognitive development, and the social world: Piaget, Vygotsky, and beyond. *Human Development*, *36*, 1–23.

NJCLD Interagency Committee on Learning Disabilities. (1987). *Learning disabilities: A report to the US Congress*. Bethesda, MD: National Institutes of Health.

Norman, P. E., & Gorman, J. M. (1998). *Treatments that work*. New York: Oxford University Press.

O'Brien, M., & Bahadur, M. A. (1998). Marital aggression, mother's problem-solving behavior with children, and children's emotional and behavioral problems. *Journal of Social & Clinical Psychology*, *17*, 249–272.

O'Brien, M., Bahadur, M. A., Gee, C., & Balto, K. (1997). Child exposure to marital conflict and child coping responses as predictors of child adjustment. *Cognitive Therapy & Research*, *21*, 39–59.

O'Brien, M., Margolin, G., & John, R. S. (1995). Relation among marital conflict, child coping, and child adjustment. *Journal of Clinical Child Psychology*, *24*, 346–361.

Oliva, A. H., & La Greca, A. M. (1988). Children with learning disabilities: Social goals and strategies. *Journal of Learning Disabilities*, *21*, 301–306.

Ollendick, T. H., King, N. J., & Frary, R. B. (1989). Fears in children and adolescents: Reliability and generalizability across gender, age, and nationality. *Behaviour Research and Therapy, 27,* 19–26.

Orenstein, M. (2000). Picking up the clues: Understanding undiagnosed learning disabilities, shame, and imprisoned intelligence. *Journal of College Student Psychotherapy, 15,* 35–46.

Osman, B. B. (1979). *Learning disabilities: A family affair.* New York: Warner.

Osman, B. B. (1995). *No one to play with: Social problems of LD and ADD children* (Rev. ed.). Novato, CA: Academic Therapy.

Osofsky, J. D. (1995). The effects of exposure to violence on young children. *American Psychologist, 50,* 782–788.

Oster, G. D., & Gould, P. (1987). *Using drawings in assessment and therapy: A guide for mental health professionals.* New York: Brunner/Mazel.

Ottenbacher, K. J., & Cusick, A. (1990). Goal attainment scaling as a method of clinical service evaluation. *American Journal of Occupational Therapy, 44,* 521–524.

Ottenbacher, K. J., & Cusick, A. (1993). Discriminative versus evaluative assessment: Some observations on goal attainment scaling. *American Journal of Occupational Therapy, 47,* 349–352.

Pagani, L., Boulerice, B., Vitaro, F., & Tramblay, R. E. (1999). Effects of poverty on academic failure and delinquency in boys: A change and process model approach. *Journal of Child Psychology & Psychiatry & Allied Disciplines, 40,* 1209–1219.

Papolos, D., & Papolos, J. (1999). *The bipolar child: The definitive and reassuring guide to childhood's most misunderstood disorder.* New York: Broadway.

Papp, P. (1976). Family choreography. In P. J. Guerin, Jr. (Ed.), *Family therapy: Theory and practice* (pp. 465–479). New York: Gardner.

Papp, P., Silverstein, O., & Center, E. (1973). Family sculpting in preventive work with well families. *Family Process, 12,* 197–212.

Parcel, T. L., & Dufur, M. J. (2001). Capital at home and at school: Effects on child social adjustment. *Journal of Marriage and the Family, 63,* 32–47.

Pardeck, J. T. (1989). Bibliotherapy and the blended family. *Family Therapy, 16,* 215–226.

Pardeck, J. T., & Markward, M. J. (1995). Bibliotherapy: Using books to help children deal with problems. *Early Child Development and Care, 106,* 75–90.

Pardeck, J. T., & Pardeck, J. A. (1997). Recommended books for helping young children deal with social and development problems. *Early Child Development and Care, 136,* 57–63.

Paris, J., Zelkowitz, P., Guzder, J., Joseph, S., & Feldman, R. (1999). Neuropsychological factors associated with borderline pathology in children. *Journal of the American Academy of Child & Adolescent Psychiatry, 38,* 770–774.

Patterson, G. R. (1975). *Families: Application of social learning to family life.* Eugene, OR: Castalia.

Patterson, G. R. (1976). *Living with children: New methods for parents and teachers* (Rev. ed.). Champaign, IL: Research Press.

Patterson, G. R. (1982). *A social learning approach: III. Coercive family process*. Eugene, OR: Castalia.

Patterson, G. R., DeBaryshe, B. D., & Ramsey, E. (1989). A developmental perspective on antisocial behavior. *American Psychologist, 44*, 329–335.

Patterson, G. R., & Forgatch, M. (1987). *Parents and adolescents living together, Part 1: The basics*. Eugene, OR: Castalia.

Patterson, G. R., & Forgatch, M. (1989). *Parents and adolescents living together, Part 2: Family problem solving*. Eugene, OR: Castalia.

Patterson, G. R., Reid, J. B., & Dishion, T. J. (1997). *Antisocial boys: Vol. 4. A social interactional approach*. Eugene, OR: Castalia.

Patterson, J., Williams, L., Grauf-Grounds, C., & Chamow, L. (1998). *Essential skills in family therapy: From the first interview to termination*. New York: Guilford.

Pauls, D. L., Alsobrook, J. P., Gelernter, J., & Leckman, J. F. (1999). Genetic vulnerability. In J. F. Leckman & D. J. Cohen (Eds.), *Tourette's syndrome—tics, obsessions, compulsions: Developmental psychopathology and clinical care* (pp. 194–212). New York: John Wiley & Sons.

Pavri, S., & Monda-Amaya, L. (2000). Loneliness and students with learning disabilities in inclusive classrooms: Self-perceptions, coping strategies, and preferred interventions. *Learning Disabilities Research & Practice, 15*, 22–33.

Pekkanen, J. (2000, January). Making sense of Ritalin. *Reader's Digest*, 152–158.

Penn, P. (1982). Circular questioning. *Family Process, 21*, 267–281.

Penn, P. (1985). Feed-forward: Future questions, future maps. *Family Process, 24*, 299–310.

Penn, P. (1991). Letters to ourselves. *Family Therapy Networker, 15(5)*, 43–45.

Penn, P., & Frankfurt, M., (1994). Creating a participant context: Writing, multiple voices, narrative multiplicity. *Family Process, 33*, 217–231.

Pennington, B. F., Bennetto, L., McAleer, O., & Roberts, R. J., Jr. (1996). Executive functions and working memory: Theoretical and measurement issues. In G. R. Lyon & N. A. Krasnegor (Eds.), *Attention, memory, and executive function* (pp. 327–348). Baltimore: Paul H. Brookes.

Pennington, B. F., & Ozonoff, S. (1996). Executive functions and developmental psychopathology. *Journal of Child Psychology & Psychiatry & Allied Disciplines, 37*, 51–87.

Perrin, S., & Last, C. G. (1992). Do childhood anxiety measures measure anxiety? *Journal of Abnormal Child Psychology, 20*, 567–578.

Perry, A., Tarrier, N., Morriss, R., McCarthy, E., & Limb, K. (1999). Randomised controlled trial of efficacy of teaching patients with bipolar disorder to identify early symptoms of relapse and obtain treatment. *British Medical Journal, 318*, 149–153.

Perry, B. D., Pollard, R. A., Blakley, T. L., Baker, W. L., & Vigilante, D. (1995). Childhood trauma, the neurobiology of adaptation, and "use-dependent" development of the brain: How "states" become "traits." *Infant Mental Health Journal, 16*, 271–291.

Perry-Jenkins, M., Repetti, R. L., & Crouter, A. C. (2000). Work and family in the 1990s. *Journal of Marriage & the Family, 62*, 981–998.

Piaget, J. (1962a). *The moral judgment of the child*. London: Kegan Paul.

Piaget, J. (1962b). *Play, dreams and imitation in childhood*. New York: Norton.

Piercy, F. P., Sprenkle, D. H., & Wetchler, J. L. (1996). *Family therapy sourcebook* (2nd ed.). New York: Guilford.

Pike, A., & Plomin, R. (1996). Importance of nonshared environmental factors for childhood and adolescent psychopathology. *Journal of the American Academy of Child & Adolescent Psychiatry, 35*, 560–570.

Pine, F. (1985). *Developmental theory and clinical process*. New Haven, CT: Yale University Press.

Pinker, S. (1997). *How the mind works*. New York: Norton.

Plomin, R., & Daniels, D. (1987). Why are children in the same family so different from one another? *Behavioral and Brain Sciences, 10*, 1–16.

Plomin, R., Owen, M. J., & McGuffin, P. (1994). The genetic basis of complex human behaviors. *Sciences, 264*, 1733–1739.

Post, R. M., & Weiss, S. R. B. (1998). Sensitization and kindling phenomena in mood, anxiety, and obsessive-compulsive disorders: The role of serotonergic mechanisms in illness progression. *Biological Psychiatry, 44*, 193–206.

Powell, T. H., & Ogle, P. A. (1985). *Brothers and sisters: A special part of exceptional families*. Baltimore: Paul H. Brookes.

Preisler, G. M. (1995). The development of communication in blind and in deaf infants: Similarities and differences. *Child: Care, Health and Development, 21*, 79–110.

Presser, H. B. (1995). Job, family, and gender: Determinants of nonstandard work schedules among employed Americans in 1991. *Demography, 32*, 577–598.

Presser, H. B. (2000). Nonstandard work schedules and marital instability. *Journal of Marriage & the Family, 62*, 93–110.

Public Law 94-142. (1977). Federal Register, Washington, DC.

Pynoos, R. S. (1994). Traumatic stress and developmental psychopathology in children and adolescents. In R. S. Pynoos (Ed.), *Posttraumatic stress disorder: A clinical review* (pp. 65–98). Lutherville, MD: Sidran.

Quay, H. C., & Hogan, A. E. (Eds.). (1999). *Handbook of disruptive behavior disorders*. New York: Kluwer Academic.

Racusin, G. R., & Kalsow, N. J. (1994). Child and family therapy combined: Indications and implications. *American Journal of Family Therapy, 22*, 237–246.

Rappaport, N., & Chubinsky, P. (2000). The meaning of psychotropic medications for children, adolescents, and their families. *Journal of the American Academy of Child & Adolescent Psychiatry, 39*, 1198–1200.

Ratey, J. J., Hallowell, E. M., & Miller, A. C., (1995). Relationship dilemmas for adults with ADD: The biology of intimacy. In K. G. Nadeau (Ed.), *A comprehensive guide to attention-deficit disorder in adults* (pp. 218–235). New York: Brunner/Mazel.

Ratey, J. J., & Johnson, C. (1997). *Shadow syndromes*. New York: Pantheon.

Rauch, S. L., Whalen, P. J., Shin, L. M., McInerney, S. C., Macklin, M. L., Lasko, N. B., Orr, S. P., & Pitman, R. K. (2000). Exaggerated amygdala response to masked facial stimuli in posttraumatic stress disorder: A functional MRI study. *Biological Psychiatry, 47*, 769–76.

Reiss, D., Neiderhiser, J. M., Hetherington, E. M., & Plomin, R. (2000). *The relationship code: Deciphering genetic and social influences on adolescent development*. Cambridge, MA: Harvard University Press.

Relph, A. (1985). The last time: A metaphor for leaving. *Australian & New Zealand Journal of Family Therapy, 6*, 123–127.

Renfrew, J. W. (1997). *Aggression and its causes: A biopsychosocial approach*. New York: Oxford University Press.

Renner, M., & Rosenzweig, M. (1987). *Enriched and impoverished environments: Effects on brain and behavior*. New York: Springer Verlag.

Restak, R. (1995). *Brainscapes: An introduction to what neuroscience has learned about the structure, function, and abilities of the brain*. New York: Hyperion.

Riddle, M. A., Kastelic, E. A., & Frosch, E. (2001). Pediatric psychopharmacology. *Journal of Child Psychology & Psychiatry, 42*, 73-90.

Rief, S. F. (1993). *How to reach and teach ADD/ADHD children: Practical techniques, strategies, and interventions for helping children with attention problems and hyperactivity*. New York: Center for Applied Research in Education.

Rogers, C. (1995). What understanding and acceptance mean to me. *Journal of Humanistic Psychology, 35*, 7–22.

Ross, D. E. (2000). A method for developing a biopsychosocial formulation. *Journal of Child and Family Studies, 9*, 1–6.

Ross, F. L. (1992). The use of computers in occupational therapy for visual-scanning training. *American Journal of Occupational Therapy, 46*, 314–322.

Rotter, J. C., & Bush, M. V. (2000). Play and family therapy. *Counseling & Therapy for Couples & Families, 8*, 172–176.

Rourke, B. P. (1989). *Nonverbal learning disabilities: The syndrome and the model*. New York: Guilford.

Rourke, B. P. (1995). Treatment program for children with NLD. In B. P. Rourke (Ed.), *Syndrome of nonverbal learning disabilities: Neurodevelopmental manifestations* (pp. 497–508). New York: Guilford.

Rourke, B. P., & Fuerst, D. R. (1991). *Learning disabilities and psychosocial functioning: A neuropsychological perspective*. New York: Guilford.

Rowe, D. C. (1994). *The limits of family influence: Genes, experience, and behavior*. New York: Guilford.

Rubin, K. H., & Pepler, D. J. (1982). Children's play: Piaget's views reconsidered. *Contemporary Educational Psychology, 7*, 289–299.

Ruble, N. C. (1999). The voices of therapists and children regarding the inclusion of children in family therapy: A systemic research synthesis. *Contemporary Family Therapy, 21*, 485–503.

Rudolph, S. M., & Epstein, M. H. (2000). Empowering children and families through strength-based assessment. *Reclaiming Children and Youth, 8*(4), 207–209.

Rutter, M., Dunn, J., Plomin, R., & Simonoff, E. (1997). Integrating nature and nurture: Implications of person-environment correlations and interactions for developmental psychopathology. *Development & Psychopathology, 9*, 335–364.

Rutter, M., Silberg, J., O'Connor, T., & Simonoff, E. (1999). Genetics and child psychiatry: II. Empirical research findings. *Journal of Child Psychology & Psychiatry & Allied Disciplines*, 40, 19–55.

Ryff, C. D., & Singer, B. H. (2000). Biopsychosocial challenges of the new millennium. *Psychotherapy and Psychosomatics*, 69, 170–177.

Rymer, R. (1993). *Genie: An abused child's flight from silence*. New York: Harper Collins.

Saarni, C. (1999). *The development of emotional competence*. New York: Guilford.

Sabbath, J. C. (1969). The suicidal adolescent: The expendable child. *Journal of the American Academy of Child Psychiatry*, 8, 272–285.

Samuels, A., & Taylor, M. (1994). Children's ability to distinguish fantasy events from real-life events. *British Journal of Developmental Psychology*, 12, 417-427.

Sapolsky, R. M. (1996). Why stress is bad for your brain. *Science*, 273, 749–750.

Satir, V. (1972). *Peoplemaking*. Palo Alto, CA: Science and Behavior Books.

Satterfield, J. M. (1999). Adjunctive cognitive-behavioral therapy for rapid-cycling bipolar disorder: An empirical case study. *Psychiatry*, 62, 357–369.

Sattler, J. M. (1995). *Assessment of children* (3rd ed.). San Diego, CA: Author.

Schaefer, C. E., & Carey, L. J. (Eds.). (1994). *Family play therapy*. Northvale, NJ: Jason Aronson.

Schaefer, C. E., & Reid, S. E. (Eds.). (1986). *Game play: Therapeutic use of childhood games*. New York: John Wiley & Sons.

Schanberg, S. M. (1995). The genetic basis for touch effects. In T. M. Field (Ed.), *Touch in early development* (pp. 67–79). Mahwah, NJ: Lawrence Erlbaum.

Schanberg, S. M., & Field, T. M. (1988). Maternal deprivation and supplemental stimulation. In T. M. Field, P. M. McCabe, & N. Schneiderman (Eds.), *Stress and coping across development* (pp. 3–25). Hillsdale, NJ: Lawrence Erlbaum.

Scharff, D. E., & Scharff, J. S. (1987). *Object relations therapy*. Northvale, NJ: Jason Aronson.

Scharff, J. S. (1999). Play with young children in family therapy: An extension of the therapist's holding capacity. In C. E. Schaefer & L. J. Carey (Eds.), *Family play therapy* (pp. 87–98). Northvale, NJ: Jason Aronson.

Schinke, S. P., Orlandi, M. A., Gordon, A. N., & Weston, R. E. (1989). AIDS prevention via computer-based intervention. *Computers in Human Sciences*, 5, 147–156.

Schor, J. (1991). *The overworked American*. New York: Basic.

Schore, A. N. (1994). *Affect regulation and the origin of the self: The neurobiology of emotional development*. Hillsdale, NJ: Lawrence Erlbaum.

Schore, A. N. (1997). Interdisciplinary developmental research as a source of clinical models. In M. Moskowitz, C. Monk, C. Kaye, & S. Ellman (Eds.), *The neurobiological and developmental basis for psychotherapeutic intervention* (pp. 1–71). Northvale, NJ: Jason Aronson.

Schore, A. N. (1998). Early shame experiences and infant brain development. In P. Gilbert & B. Andrews (Eds.), *Shame: Interpersonal behavior, psychopathology, and culture* (pp. 57–77). New York: Oxford University Press.

Schreiber, J. L., Breier, A., & Pickar, D. (1995). Expressed emotion: Trait or state? *British Journal of Psychiatry, 166*, 647–649.

Schwab-Stone, M. E., Ayers, T. S., Kasprow, W., Voyce, C., Barone, C., Shriver, T., & Weissberg, R. P. (1995). No safe haven: A study of violence exposure in an urban community. *Journal of the American Academy of Child & Adolescent Psychiatry, 10*, 1343–52.

Schwab-Stone, M. E., Fallon, T., Briggs, M., & Crowther, B. (1994). Reliability of diagnostic reporting for children aged 6–11 years: A test-retest study of the diagnostic interview schedule for children-revised. *American Journal of Psychiatry, 151*, 1048–1054.

Science Magazine. (2001, February 16). Human genome special issue [On-line serial], *291*. Available: www.sciencemag.org/content/vol291/issue5507

Scientific American. (1996). Mysteries of the mind: New and updated explorations of how we think, how we behave, and how we feel [Special Issue], *7*.

Scieszka, J. (1989). *The true story of the 3 little pigs!* New York: Puffin.

Seccombe, K. (2000). Families in poverty in the 1990s: Trends, causes, consequences, and lessons learned. *Journal of Marriage & the Family, 62*, 1094–1113.

Seligman, M. (1987). Adaptation of children to a chronically ill or mentally handicapped sibling. *Canadian Medical Association Journal, 136*, 1249–1252.

Selman, R. L. (1981). The development of interpersonal competence: The role of understanding in conduct. *Developmental Review, 1*, 401–422.

Selye, H. (1975). *The stress of life.* New York: McGraw Hill.

Selye, H. (1978). *Stress without distress.* New York: Dutton.

Sensky, T., Turkington, D., Kingdon, D., Scott, J. L., Scott, J., Siddle, R., O'Carroll, M., & Barnes, T. R. E. (2000). A randomized controlled trial of cognitive-behavioral therapy for persistent symptoms in schizophrenia resistant to medication. *Archives of General Psychiatry, 57*, 165–172.

Serafino, E. P. (1986). *The fears of childhood.* New York: Human Sciences Press.

Shin, L. M., McNally, R. J., Kosslyn, S. M., Thompson, W. L., Rauch, S. L., Alpert, N. M., Metzger, L. J., Lasko, N. B., Orr, S. P., & Pitman, R. K. (1997). A positron emission tomographic study of symptom provocation in PTSD. *Annals of the New York Academy of Sciences, 821*, 521–523.

Shore, R. (1997). *Rethinking the brain: New insights into early development.* New York: Families and Work Institute.

Shrier, D. K. (1997). Severe stress and mental disturbance in children. *Journal of the American Academy of Child & Adolescent Psychiatry, 36*, 1154–1155.

Siegel, D. J. (1999). *The developing mind: Toward a neurobiology of interpersonal experience.* New York: Guilford.

Siegel, M. G. (1987). *Psychological testing from early childhood through adolescence.* Madison, CT: International Universities Press.

Sigelman, C. K., Budd, E. C., Winer, J. L., Schoenrock, C. J., & Martin, P. W. (1982). Evaluating alternative techniques of questioning mentally retarded persons. *American Journal of Mental Deficiency, 86*, 511–518.

Sikorski, J. (1991). Learning disorders and the juvenile justice system. *Psychiatric Annals, 21,* 742–747.

Silva, R. R., Alpert, M., Munoz, D. M., Singh, S., Matzner, F., & Dummit, S. (2000). Stress and vulnerability to posttraumatic stress disorder in children and adolescents. *American Journal of Psychiatry, 157,* 1229–1235.

Silver, D. S., & Young, R. D. (1985). Interpersonal problem solving abilities, peer status, and behavioral adjustment in learning disabled and non-learning disabled adolescents. *Advances in Learning and Behavioral Disabilities, 4,* 201–223.

Silver, L. B. (1984). *The misunderstood child: A guide for parents of learning disabled children.* New York: McGraw-Hill.

Silver, L. B. (1989). Psychological and family problems associated with learning disabilities: Assessment and intervention. *Journal of the American Academy of Child & Adolescent Psychiatry, 28,* 319–325.

Silverman, W. K. (1991). Diagnostic reliability of anxiety disorders in children using structured interviews. *Journal of Anxiety Disorders, 5,* 105–124.

Simeon, J. G. (1997). Challenges to pediatric psychopharmacology. *Journal of Psychiatry & Neuroscience, 22,* 15–17.

Simeonsson, R. J., Baily, D. B., Jr., Huntington, G. S., & Brandon, L. (1991). Scaling and attainment of goals in family-focused early intervention. *Community Mental Health Journal, 27,* 77–83.

Simon, R. (1972). Sculpting the family. *Family Process, 11,* 49–59.

Singh, N. N., Curtis, W. J., Ellis, C. R., Wechsler, H. A., Best, A. M., & Cohen, R. (1997). Empowerment status of families whose children have serious emotional disturbance and attention-deficit/hyperactivity disorder. *Journal of Emotional & Behavioral Disorders, 5,* 223–229.

Siperstein, G. N., Bopp, M. J., & Bak, J. J. (1978). Social status of learning disabled children. *Journal of Learning Disabilities, 11,* 49–53.

Slade, J. (1987). Bibliotherapy with siblings of handicapped children. *TACD Journal, 15,* 133–137.

Sloman, L., Gardner, R., & Price, J. (1989). Biology of family systems and mood disorders. *Family Process, 28,* 387–398.

Sloman, L., & Konstantareas, M. M. (1990). Why families of children with biological deficits require a systems approach. *Family Process, 29,* 417–429.

Smith, C. W., & Renter, S. G. (1997). The play is the thing: Using self-constructed board games in family therapy. *Journal of Family Psychotherapy, 8,* 67–72.

Smith, I. K. (2000, March 6). Ritalin for toddlers. *Time,* 84.

Smith, S. L. (1991). *Succeeding against the odds: How the learning-disabled can realize their promise.* Los Angeles: J. P. Tarcher.

Smith, S. L. (1995). *No easy answers: The learning disabled child at home and at school* (Rev. ed.). New York: Bantam.

Snyder, J. J., & Patterson, G. R. (1995). Individual differences in social aggression: A test of a reinforcement model of socialization in the natural environment. *Behavior Therapy, 26,* 371–391.

Snyder, S. H., & Ferris, C.D. (2000). Novel neurotransmitters and their neuropsychiatric relevance. *American Journal of Psychiatry, 157*, 1738–1751.

Sokol, R. J. (2000). The chronic disease of childhood obesity: The sleeping giant has awakened. *Journal of Pediatrics, 136*, 711–713.

Spanier, G. B. (1976). Measuring marital adjustment: New scales for assessing the quality of marriage and similar dyads. *Journal of Marriage and the Family, 38*, 15–28.

Spanier, G. B. (1988). Assessing the strengths of the dyadic adjustment scale. *Journal of Family Psychology, 2*, 92–94.

Sperry, L. (2000). Biopsychosocial therapy: Essential strategies and tactics. In J. Carlson & L. Sperry (Eds.), *Brief therapy with individuals and couples* (pp. 535–563). Phoenix, AZ: Zeig, Tucker & Theisen.

Sperry, R. (1974). Lateral specialization in the surgically separated hemispheres. In F. O. Schmitt & F. G. Worden (Eds.), *The neurosciences: Third study program*. Cambridge, MA: MIT Press.

Spitz, R. A. (1945). Hospitalism: An inquiry into the genesis of psychiatric conditions in early childhood. *Psychoanalytic Study of the Child, 1*, 53–74.

Spitz, R. A. (1958). On the genesis of superego components. *Psychoanalytic Study of the Child, 13*, 375–404.

Sroufe, L. A. (1995). *Emotional development: The organization of emotional life in the early years*. New York: Cambridge University Press.

State, M. W., Lombroso, P. J., Pauls, D. L., & Leckman, J. F. (2000). The genetics of childhood psychiatric disorders: A decade of progress. *Journal of the American Academy of Child & Adolescent Psychiatry, 39*, 946–962.

Steen, R. G. (1996). *DNA & destiny: Nature & nurture in human behavior*. New York: Plenum.

Steffenburg, S., Gillberg, C., Hellgren, L., & Andersson, L. (1989). A twin study of autism in Denmark, Finland, Iceland, Norway and Sweden. *Journal of Child Psychology & Psychiatry & Allied Disciplines, 30*, 405–416.

Steinglass, P. (1998). Multiple family discussion groups for patients with chronic medical illness. *Families, Systems, & Health, 16*, 55–70.

Steinglass, P., Bennett, L. A., Wolin, S. J., & Reiss, D. (1987). *The alcoholic family*. New York: Basic.

Stern, D. N. (1985). *The interpersonal world of the infant*. New York: Basic.

Stern, M. (1999). *Unique minds program for children with learning disabilities and their families*. New York: Unique Minds Foundation.

Stern, M., & Walker, G. (2001). Children's Emotional and Learning Problems: A family systems perspective. NYU *Child Study Center Letter, 5*(3).

Sternberg, E. M., & Gold, P. W. (1997). The mind-body interaction in disease [Special Issue]. *Scientific American*, 8–15.

Sterr, A., Muller, M. M., Elbert, T., Rockstroh, B., Pantev, C., & Taub, E. (1998). Changed perceptions in braille readers. *Nature, 391*, 134–135.

Stokes, T. F., & Baer, D. M. (1977). An implicit technology of generalization. *Journal of Applied Behavior Analysis, 10,* 349–367.

Stolee, P., Zaza, C., Pedlar, A., & Myers, A. M. (1999). Clinical experience with goal attainment scaling in geriatric care. *Journal of Aging & Health, 11,* 96–124.

Stratton, P. (1995a). Editorial. *Human Systems: The Journal of Systemic Consultation and Management, 6,* 167–169.

Stratton, P. (1995b). Hearing the voice of the child [Special issue]. *Human Systems: The Journal of Systemic Consultation and Management.*

Straus, M. B. (1994). *Violence in the lives of adolescents.* New York: Norton.

Strober, M., Morrell, W., Lampert, C., & Burroughs, J. (1990). Relapse following discontinuation of lithium maintenance therapy in adolescents with bipolar illness: A naturalistic study. *American Journal of Psychiatry, 147,* 457–461.

Strober, M., Schmidt-Lackner, S., Freeman, R., Bower, S., Lampert, C., & DeAntonio, M. (1995). Recovery and relapse in adolescents with bipolar affective illness: A five-year naturalistic, prospective follow-up. *Journal of the American Academy of Child & Adolescent Psychiatry, 34,* 724–731.

Strubbe, M. A. (1989). *An assessment of early adolescent stress factors.* Columbus, OH: National Middle School Association. (ERIC Document Reproduction Service No. ED 318 086)

Sturgess, J. L. (1997). Current trends in assessing children's play. *British Journal of Occupational Therapy, 60,* 410–414.

Suomi, S. J. (1999). Developmental trajectories, early experiences, and community consequences: Lessons from studies with rhesus monkeys. In D. P. Keating & C. Hertzman (Eds.), *Developmental health and the wealth of nations: Social, biological, and educational dynamics* (pp. 185–200). New York: Guilford.

Suomi, S. J. (2000). A biobehavioral perspective on developmental psychopathology: Excessive aggression and serotonergic dysfunction in monkeys. In A. J. Sameroff, M. Lewis, & S. M. Miller (Eds.), *Handbook of developmental psychopathology* (pp. 237–256). New York: Kluwer Academic.

Sweeney, T. J. (1998). *Adlerian counseling: A practitioner's approach* (4th ed.). Philadelphia: Taylor & Francis.

Szmukler, G., & Dare, C. (1996). Family therapy. *Current Opinion in Psychiatry, 9,* 198–203.

Taylor, B. A., Levin, L., & Jasper, S. (1999). Increasing play-related statements in children with autism toward their siblings: Effects of video modeling. *Journal of Developmental and Physical Disabilities, 11,* 253–264.

Taylor, T. K., & Biglan, A. (1998). Behavioral family interventions for improving child-rearing: A review of the literature for clinicians and policy makers. *Clinical Child and Family Psychology Review, 1,* 41–60.

Teachman, J. D., Tedrow, L. M., & Crowder, K. D. (2000). The changing demography of America's families. *Journal of Marriage and the Family, 62,* 1234–1246.

Thase, M. E., Fasiczka, A. L., Berman, S. R., Simons, A. D., & Reynolds, C. F., III. (1998). Electroencephalographic sleep profiles before and after cognitive behavior therapy of depression. *Archives of General Psychiatry, 55,* 138–144.

Thomas, A., & Chess, S. (1968). *Temperament and behavior disorders in children.* New York: International Universities Press.

Thomas, A., & Chess, S. (1977). *Temperament and development.* New York: Brunner/Mazel.

Thomas, A., & Chess, S. (1984). Genesis and evolution of behavior disorders: From infancy to early adult life. *American Journal of Psychiatry, 141,* 1–9.

Thomas, A., Chess, S., Birch, H. G., Hertzig, M. E., & Korn, S. (1963). *Behavioral individuality in early childhood.* New York: New York University Press.

Tiet, Q. Q., Bird, H. R., Davies, M., Hoven, C., Cohen, P., Jensen, P. S., & Goodman, S. (1998). Adverse life events and resilience. *Journal of the American Academy of Child & Adolescent Psychiatry, 37,* 1191–1200.

Tomm, K. (1987a). Interventive interviewing: Part I. Strategizing as a fourth guideline for the therapist. *Family Process, 26,* 3–13.

Tomm, K. (1987b). Interventive interviewing: Part II. Reflexive questioning as a means to enable self healing. *Family Process, 26,* 167–183.

Tomm, K. (1988). Interventive interviewing: Part III. Intending to ask lineal, circular, strategic and reflexive questions. *Family Process, 27,* 1–15.

Toppelberg, C. O., & Shapiro, T. (2000). Language disorders: A 10-year research update review. *Journal of the American Academy of Child & Adolescent Psychiatry, 39,* 143–152.

Toren, P., Wolmer, L., Rosental, B., Eldar, S., Koren, S., Lask, M., Weizman, R., & Laor, N. (2000). Case series: Brief parent-child group therapy for childhood anxiety disorders using a manual-based cognitive-behavioral technique. *Journal of the American Academy of Child & Adolescent Psychiatry, 39,* 1309–1312.

Treacher, A. (1989). Termination in family therapy: Developing a structural approach. *Journal of Family Therapy, 11,* 135–147.

Trevarthen, C., & Aitken, K. J. (2001) Infant intersubjectivity: Research, theory, and clinical applications. *Journal of Child Psychology & Psychiatry & Allied Disciplines, 42,* 3–48.

Tronick, E. Z. (1989). Emotions and emotional communication in infants. *American Psychologist, 44,* 112–119.

Tronick, E. Z. (1995). Touch in mother-infant interaction. In T. M. Field (Ed.), *Touch in early development* (pp. 53–65). Mahwah, NJ: Lawrence Erlbaum.

Tronick, E. Z., & Gianino, A. (1986). Interactive mismatch and repair: Challenges to the coping infant. *Zero to Three: Bulletin of the National Center for Clinical Infant Programs, 6,* 1–6.

Tsai, L. Y., & Ghaziuddin, M. (1997). Autistic disorder. In J. M. Wiener (Ed.), *Textbook of child & adolescent psychiatry* (2nd ed., pp. 219–254). Washington, DC: American Psychiatric Press.

Turkington, D., & Kindon, D. (2000). Cognitive-behavioural techniques for general psychiatrists in the management of patients with psychoses. *British Journal of Psychiatry, 177*, 101–106.

U.S. Department of Education. (1991). *Thirteenth annual report to Congress on the implementation of the education of the handicapped act.* Washington, DC: U.S. Government Printing Office.

U.S. Department of Education. (1996). *Implementation of the individuals with disabilities education act: Eighteenth annual report to Congress.* Washington, DC: Education Publications Center.

U.S. Department of Education. (1997). *Violence and discipline problems in U.S. public schools: 1996–97* (NCES Publication No. 98030). Washington, DC: National Center for Education Statistics.

U.S. Department of Health and Human Services. (2001). *Youth violence: A report of the Surgeon General.* Rockville, MD: U.S. Department of Health and Human Services, Centers for Disease Control and Prevention, National Center for Injury Prevention and Control; Substance Abuse and Mental Health Services Administration, Center for Mental Health Services; and National Institutes of Health, National Institute of Mental Health.

Van der Meer, R., & Dudink, A. (1996). *The brain pack.* Philadelphia: Running Press.

van Dulmen, A. M., Fennis, J. F. M., & Bleijenberg, G. (1996). Cognitive-behavioral group therapy for irritable bowel syndrome: Effects and long-term follow-up. *Psychosomatic Medicine, 58*, 508–514.

van Goozen, S. H. M., Matthys, W., Cohen-Kettenis, P. T., Buitelaar, J. K., & van Engeland, H. (2000). Hypothalamic-pituitary-adrenal axis and autonomic nervous system activity in disruptive children and matched controls. *Journal of the American Academy of Child & Adolescent Psychiatry, 39*, 1438–1445.

van Ijzendoorn, M. H., Schuengel, C., & Bakermans-Kranenburg, M. J. (1999). Disorganized attachment in early childhood: Meta-analysis of precursors, concomitants, and sequelae. *Development & Psychopathology, 11*, 225–249.

Vandenberg, B. (1993). Fears of normal and retarded children. *Psychological Reports, 72*, 473–474.

Vandewater, E. A., & Lansford, J. E. (1998). Influences of family structure and parental conflict on children's well-being. *Family Relations: Interdisciplinary Journal of Applied Family Studies, 47*, 323–330.

Vaughan, S. C. (1998). *The talking cure: The science behind psychotherapy.* New York: Henry Holt.

Vaughn, C. E. (1989). Annotation: Expressed emotion in family relationships. *Journal of Child Psychology & Psychiatry, 30*, 13–22.

Vaughn, S., & Hogan, A. (1990). Social competence and learning disabilities: A prospective study. In H. L. Swanson & B. K. Keogh (Eds.), *Learning disabilities: Theoretical and research issues* (pp. 175–191). Hillsdale, NJ: Lawrence Erlbaum.

Velting, O. N., & Albano, A. M. (2001). Current trends in the understanding and treatment of social phobia in youth. *Journal of Child Psychology & Psychiatry & Allied Disciplines*, *42*, 127–140.

Villeneuve, C. (1979). The specific participation of the child in family therapy. *Journal of the American Academy of Child Psychiatry, 18*, 44–53.

Villeneuve, C., & LaRoche, C. (1993). The child's participation in family therapy: A review and a model. *Contemporary Family Therapy, 15*, 105–119.

von Bertalanffy, L. (1962). General system theory: A critical review. *General Systems, 7*, 1–20.

von Bertalanffy, L. (1968). *General system theory*. New York: George Braziller.

Vostanis, P., Nicholls, J., & Harrington, R. (1994). Maternal expressed emotion in conduct and emotional disorders of childhood. *Journal of Child Psychology & Psychiatry & Allied Disciplines, 35*, 365–376.

Wachtel, E. F. (1987). Family systems and the individual child. *Journal of Marital and Family Therapy, 13*, 15–25.

Wachtel, E. F. (1994a). An integrative approach to working with troubled children and their families. In C. E. Schaefer & L. J. Carey (Eds.), *Family play therapy* (pp. 147–164). Northvale, NJ: Jason Aronson.

Wachtel, E. F. (1994b). *Treating troubled children and their families*. New York: Guilford.

Wachtel, E. F. (1998). Fostering resiliency through child-in-family therapy. *American Family Therapy Academy Newsletter, 72*, 18–20.

Wade, N. (1997a, April 24). Scientists discover role of 2 genes in breast cancer in families. *The New York Times*, p. A20.

Wade, N. (1997b, November 14). Discovery of gene offers clues on deafness. *The New York Times*, p. A28.

Wade, N. (1997c, December 30). 2 gene discoveries help explain the misfires of epilepsy in the brain. *The New York Times*, p. F3.

Wade, N. (1998, March 10). The struggle to decipher human genes. *The New York Times*, p. F1.

Wade, N. (1999, April 20). Tailoring drugs to fit the genes. *The New York Times*, p. F9.

Wade, N. (2000, September 27). Researchers find gene for type 2 diabetes. *The New York Times*, p. A14.

Wade, N. (2001, February 13). Reading the book of life; Genome's riddle: Few genes, much complexity. *The New York Times*, p. F1.

Walker, G., & Shimmerlik, S. (1994, May-June). The invisible battlefield. *Family Therapy Networker*, 50–60.

Walker, G., Stern, M., & Shimmerlik, S. (1999, July-August). Restoring the bond: The brain's role in nurturing family. *Family Therapy Networker*, 34–56.

Walsh, F. (1995). From family damage to family challenge. In R. H. Mikesell, D. D. Lusterman, & S. H. McDaniel (Eds.), *Integrating family therapy: Handbook of family psychology and systems theory* (pp. 587–606). Washington, DC: American Psychological Association.

Walsh, F. (1998). *Strengthening family resilience*. New York: Guilford.

Walter, J. L., & Peller, J. E. (1992). *Becoming solution-focused in brief therapy*. New York: Brunner/Mazel.

Wamboldt, M. A., & Wamboldt, F.S. (2000). Role of the family in the onset and outcome of childhood disorders: Selected research findings. *Journal of the American Academy of Child & Adolescent Psychiatry, 39*, 1212–1219.

Wark, L., & Scheidegger, T. (1996). Engaging children in therapeutic enactments with the use of a videocamera. *Journal of Family Psychotherapy, 7*, 63–67.

Waters, R. (2000, March-April). Generation Rx. *Family Therapy Networker, 34–43*.

Watzlawick, P. (1978). *The language of change: Elements of therapeutic communication*. New York: Norton.

Watzlawick, P., Weakland, J. H., & Fisch, R. (1988). *Change: Principles of problem formation and problem resolution*. New York: W. W. Norton.

Webb, N. B. (1999). *Play therapy with children in crisis: Individual, group, and family treatment* (2nd ed.). New York: Guilford.

Weber, T., & Levine, F. (1995). Engaging the family: An integrative approach. In R. H. Mikesell, D. D. Lusterman, & S. H. McDaniel (Eds.), *Integrating family therapy: Handbook of family psychology and systems theory* (pp. 45–71). Washington, DC: American Psychological Association.

Webster-Stratton, C. (1992). *The incredible years*. Toronto, Ontario: Umbrella Press.

Webster-Stratton, C. (1996). Early intervention with videotape modeling: Programs for families of children with oppositional defiant disorder or conduct disorder. In E. D. Hibbs & P. S. Jensen (Eds.), *Psychosocial treatments for child and adolescent disorders* (pp. 435–474). Washington, DC: American Psychological Association.

Webster-Stratton, C., & Hammond, M. (1999). Marital conflict management skills, parenting style, and early-onset conduct problems: Processes and pathways. *Journal of Child Psychology & Psychiatry & Allied Disciplines, 40*, 917–927.

Webster-Stratton, C., & Hancock, L. (1998). Training for parents of young children with conduct problems: Content, methods, and therapeutic processes. In J. M. Briesmeister & C. E. Schaefer (Eds.), *Handbook of parent training: Parents as co-therapists for children's behavior problems* (2nd ed., pp. 98–152). New York: John Wiley & Sons.

Webster-Stratton, C., & Lindsay, D. W. (1999). Social competence and conduct problems in young children: Issues in assessment. *Journal of Clinical Child Psychology, 28*, 25–43.

Weintraub, P., & Wamboldt, M. Z. (1996). Expressed emotion in child psychiatry: A risk factor for psychopathology and treatment resistance? *Current Opinion in Psychiatry, 9*, 241–246.

Weiss, H., & Edwards, M. (1992). The family-school collaboration project: Systemic interventions for school improvement. In S. L. Christenson & J. C. Conoley (Eds.), *Home-school collaboration: Enhancing children's academic and social competence* (pp. 215–243). Silver Spring, MD: National Association of School Psychologists.

Weiss, M. J. S., & Wagner, S. H. (1998). What explains the negative consequences of adverse childhood experiences on adult health? Insights from cognitive and neuroscience research. *American Journal of Preventive Medicine, 14,* 356–360.

Weissman, J. S., Stern, R. S., & Epstein, A. M. (1994). The impact of patient socioeconomic status and other social factors on readmission: A prospective study in four Massachusetts hospitals. *Inquiry, 31,* 163–172.

Weissman, M. M., Gammon, G. D., John, K., Merikangas, K. R., Warner, V., Prusoff, B., & Sholomskas, D. (1987). Children of depressed parents: Increased psychopathology and early onset of major depression. *Archives of General Psychiatry, 44,* 847–853.

Weller, E. B., & Weller, R. A. (1997). In J. M. Wiener (Ed.), *Textbook of Child & Adolescent Psychiatry* (2nd ed., pp. 333–342). Washington, DC: American Psychiatric Press.

Wenz-Gross, M., & Siperstein, G. N. (1998). Students with learning problems at risk in middle school: Stress, social support, and adjustment. *Exceptional Children, 65,* 91–100.

Weston, H. E., Boxer, P., & Heatherington, L. (1998). Children's attributions about family arguments: Implications for family therapy. *Family Process, 37,* 35–49.

Wetchler, J. L., & Ofte-Atha, G. R. (1993). Empowering families at termination: A structural/strategic orientation. *Journal of Family Psychotherapy, 4,* 33–44.

Whalen, C. K., & Henker, B. (1999). The child with attention-deficit/hyperactivity disorder in family contexts. In H. C. Quay & A. E. Hogan (Eds.), *Handbook of disruptive behavior disorders* (pp. 139–155). New York: Kluwer Academic/Plenum.

White, M. (1989). *Selected papers.* Adelaide, South Australia: Dulwich Centre.

White, M., & Epston, D. (1990). *Narrative means to therapeutic ends.* New York: Norton.

Wiener, D. J. (Ed.). (1999). *Beyond talk therapy: Using movement and expressive techniques in clinical practice.* Washington, DC: American Psychological Association.

Wiesel, T. N., & Hubel, D. H. (1965). Extent of recovery from the effects of visual deprivation in kittens. *Journal of Neurophysiology, 28,* 1060–1072.

Wilcoxon, S. A., & Gladding, S. T. (1985). Engagement and termination in marital and familial therapy: Special ethical issues. *American Journal of Family Therapy, 13,* 65–71.

Wilens, T. E. (1999). *Straight talk about psychiatric medications for kids.* New York: Guilford.

Wilson, D., & Ratekin, C. (1990). An introduction to using children's drawings as an assessment tool. *Nurse Practitioner, 15,* 23–24, 27, 30–35.

Winnicott, D. W. (1964). *The child, the family, and the outside world.* Baltimore: Penguin.

Winnicott, D. W. (1965). *The maturational process and the facilitating environment.* New York: International Universities Press.

Winnicott, D. W. (1977). *Therapeutic consultation in child psychiatry.* New York: Basic.

Witkin, G. (1999). *Kid Stress: Effective strategies parents can teach their kids for school, family, peers, the world—and everything.* New York: Penguin Putnam.

Wolfe, L. A., & Collins-Wolfe, J. A. (1983). Action techniques for therapy with families with young children. *Family Relations: Journal of Applied Family & Child Studies, 32,* 81–87.

Wood, B. L. (1991). Biopsychosocial care. In W. A. Walker, P. R. Durie, J. R. Hamilton, J. A. Walker-Smith, & J. B. Watkins (Eds.), *Pediatric gastrointestinal disease: Pathophysiology, diagnosis, management* (pp. 1747–1758). Philadelphia: B. C. Decker.

Wood, B. L. (1993). Beyond the "psychosomatic family": A Biobehavioral family model of pediatric illness. *Family Process, 32,* 261–278.

Wood, B. L. (1994). One articulation of the structural family therapy model: A biobehavioral family model of chronic illness in children. *Journal of Family Therapy, 16,* 53–72.

Wood, B. L. (1995). A developmental biopsychosocial approach to the treatment of chronic illness in children and adolescents. In R. H. Mikesell, D. D. Lusterman, & S. H. McDaniel (Eds.), *Integrating family therapy: Handbook of family psychology and systems theory* (pp. 437–455). Washington, DC: American Psychological Association.

Wood, B. L., Klebba, K. B., & Miller, B. D. (2000). Evolving the biobehavioral family model: The fit of attachment. *Family Process, 39,* 319–344.

Wood, B. L., Watkins, J. B., Boyle, J. T., Nogueira, J., Zimand, E., & Carroll, L. (1987). Psychological functioning in children with Crohn's disease and ulcerative colitis: Implications for models of psychobiological interaction. *Journal of the American Academy of Child & Adolescent Psychiatry, 26,* 774–781.

Wood, B. L., Watkins, J. B., Boyle, J. T., Nogueira, J., Zimand, E., & Carroll, L., (1989) The "psychosomatic family": An empirical and theoretical analysis. *Family Process, 28,* 399–417.

Woodward, C. A., Santa-Barbara, J., Levin, S., & Epstein, N. B. (1978). The role of goal attainment scaling in evaluating family therapy outcome. *American Journal of Orthopsychiatry, 48,* 464–476.

Wren, C. (2000). *Hanging by a twig: Understanding and counseling adults with learning disabilities and ADD.* New York: Norton.

Wride, N. (1999, August 9). Children learn to say, "buy, buy." *The Los Angeles Times, Home Edition,* p. 1.

Wright, K. (1997, October). Babies, bonds, and brains. *Discover, 18,* 74–78.

Wright, L. M., Watson, W. L., & Bell, J. M. (1996). *Beliefs: The heart of healing in families and illness.* New York: Basic.

Wright, L. S., & Stimmel, T. (1984). Perceptions of parents and self among college students reporting learning disabilities. *Exceptional Child, 31,* 203–208.

Wurtzel, E. (2000, April 1). Adventures in Ritalin. *The New York Times,* p. A15.

Wynne, L. C., Shields, C. G., & Sirkin, M. I. (1992). Illness, family theory, and family therapy: I. Conceptual issues. *Family Process, 31,* 3–18.

Yamada, S., Greene, G., Bauman, K., & Maskarinec, G. (2000). A biopsychosocial approach to finding common ground in the clinical encounter. *Academic Medicine, 75,* 643–648.

Yasutake, D., & Bryan, T. (1995). The influence of affect on the achievement and behavior of students with learning disabilities. *Journal of Learning Disabilities, 28,* 329–334.

Young, A., & Chesson, R. (1997). Goal attainment scaling as a method of measuring clinical outcome for children with learning disabilities. *British Journal of Occupational Therapy*, 60, 111–114.

Ysseldyke, J., & Algozzine, B. (1990). *Introduction to special education*. Boston: Houghton Mifflin.

Ysseldyke, J., Algozzine, B., Richey, L., & Graden, J. (1982). Declaring students eligible for learning disabilities services: Why bother with the data? *Learning Disabilities Quarterly*, 5, 37–43.

Zeanah, C. H., Boris, N. W., & Larrieu, J. A. (1997). Infant development and developmental risk: A review of the past 10 years. *Journal of the American Academy of Child & Adolescent Psychiatry*, 36, 165–178.

Zeki, S. (1993). *A vision of the brain*. Oxford, England: Blackwell Scientific.

Zelenko, M., & Benham, A. (2000). Videotaping as a therapeutic tool in psychodynamic infant-parent therapy. *Infant Mental Health Journal*, 21, 192–203.

Zetlin, A. G. (1993). Everyday stressors in the lives of Anglo and Hispanic learning handicapped adolescents. *Journal of Youth Adolescence*, 22, 327–336.

Ziegler, R., & Holden, L. (1988). Family therapy for learning disabled and attention-deficit disordered children. *American Journal of Orthopsychiatry*, 58, 196–210.

Zilbach, J. J. (1986). *Young children in family therapy*. New York: Brunner/Mazel.

Zilbach, J. J. (1989). The family life cycle: A framework for understanding children in family therapy. In L. Combrinck-Graham (Ed.), *Children in family contexts: Perspectives on treatment* (pp. 46–66). New York: Guilford.

Zilbach, J., & Gordetsky, S. (1999). The family life cycle: A framework for understanding family development and play in family therapy. In C. E. Schaefer & L. J. Carey (Eds.). *Family play therapy* (pp. 165–183). Northvale, NJ: Jason Aronson.

Zimand, E., & Wood, B. L. (1986). Implications of contrasting patterns of divorce in families of children with gastrointestinal disorders. *Family Systems Medicine*, 4, 385–397.

Zimmerman, J. L., & Dickerson, V. C. (1996). *If problems talked: Narrative therapy in action*. New York: Guilford.

Zins, J. E., & Ponti, C. R. (1990). Best practices in school-based consultation. In A. Thomas & J. Grimes (Eds.), *Best practices in school psychology-II* (pp. 673–693). Washington, DC: National Association of School Psychologists.

Zito, J. M., Safer, D. J., dosReis, S., Gardner, J. F., Boles, M., & Lynch, F. (2000). Trends in the prescribing of psychotropic medications to preschoolers. *Journal of the American Medical Association*, 283, 1025–1030.

Zucker, R. A. (1994). Pathways to alcohol problems and alcoholism: A developmental account of the evidence for multiple alcoholisms and for contextual contributions to risk. In R. A. Zucker, G. Boyd, & J. Howard (Eds.), *The development of alcohol problems: Exploring the biopsychosocial matrix of risk* (pp. 255–289). Rockville, MD: U.S. Department of Health and Human Services.

Appendix

Tools for Information Gathering

BIOPSYCHOSOCIAL VARIABLES

	Individual	Family	School/Peers/ Community	Resources/ Strengths	Treatment Targets & Planning
Biological and/or health,					
Psychological					
Social spiritual, cultural					

Overall functioning: + + (excellent), + (above average), + − (average), − (below average), − − (very below)

Symptoms: ① transient, ② acute, ③ chronic

Treatment Targets: ↑ increase, ↓ decrease

FAMILY STRENGTHS INVENTORY

Family Member's Name	Interests, Talents, Hobbies	School or Academic Strengths	Social Strengths	Other*

* Artistic, Athletic, Cooking, Joke-Telling, Fun-loving . . . etc.

TAKING INVENTORY

Make a list of what is going well, fair, or yucky. You can write a word or draw a picture. Include school, homework, family relationships, friends, sports, health, and leisure time.

WELL	FAIR	YUCKY

A PIECE OF THE PIE

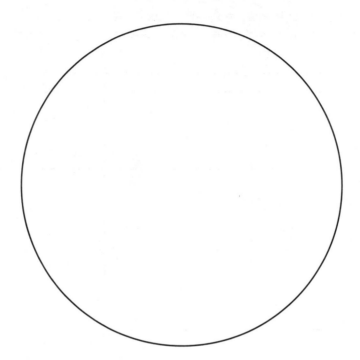

1. Make a list of any area(s) of difficulty for the child or any reasons that you might observe (e.g., slow copying from the board, can't follow directions, is distractible) that could be keeping the child from getting to her/his goal.

2. Look over your list.

   • What do you think causes the most trouble for her/him? Place a number 1 next to that item.

   • What is the item on your list that has the second largest impact? Place a number 2 next to that item, etc.

3. Make a pie chart. Divide the circle into "slices" that show what "piece of the pie" you believe each area represents (e.g., $\frac{1}{4}$ of the pie—"slow copying from the board," $\frac{1}{2}$ of the pie—"is distractible," etc.).

RECORDING TESTING RESULTS

Skills, Competencies, and Abilities	– – Very Below	– Below Average	+ – Average	+ Above Average	+ + Excellent
intelligence (overall, verbal, performance)					
reading (word attack skills, oral reading, comprehension)					
math (calculation, applied problems)					
writing (informal sample, grammar)					
spelling					
speech (articulation)					
language (receptive, expressive)					
perceptual discrimination (auditory, visual)					
attention and concentration					
memory (short-term, long-term)					
motor skills (fine and gross)					
acuity (visual, auditory)					
personality assessment					

TEACHER INTERVIEW

1. What are the child's strengths? What does s/he *like* to do (look forward to, enjoy)? What does s/he seem to have the hardest time with?

2. What concerns you most about the child?

3. In general, how does the child do academically?

4. How does s/he function throughout the day?

5. What time of day does the child do the best work? Does s/he start the day fine, then run out of "steam"? Does s/he finish a task? Complete homework? Complete long-range assignments and reports? Work independently?

6. How is the child's attention span? How restless does s/he seem to be?

7. Does the child seem impulsive? Does s/he interrupt? Wait his/her turn?

8. Is the child an active class participant? A cooperative member of the class? Does s/he follow class routines?

9. How does the child cope in class? What happens when the child gets frustrated? What is his/her temper like? Does s/he seem nervous or worried? Does s/he seem happy or sad in school? How do you think the child feels about him/herself? What does the child do or say that lets you know this (e.g., "I'm stupid, I can't do that")?

10. In general, how does the child do in school socially? Are there any concerns about social functioning? Does the child get along with others during recess? in the class? What is the quality of friendships? Is s/he an accepted, sought-after youngster or an isolated child?

11. Please estimate the child's skill levels: (grade levels; standardized testing)
Math_____ Reading _____ Written language _____
Expressing him/herself _____ Understanding what others say
_____.

12. What are the child's weaknesses in school? Is there a discrepancy between his/her perceived ability and actual performance?

13. Does the child receive any extra or special help (home or school tutoring, remedial or resource room services, speech/language/occupational/physical therapy services)? What do the others involved tell you?

14. What strategies have you found helpful when you work with the child? What helps the child function best?

15. What do you like best about the child?

16. Is there anything else you think I should know about him/her?

This is not an inclusive list of questions; the points presented here are meant to serve as guidelines for teacher interviews.

SUGGESTIONS FOR INTERVIEWING CHILDREN
ABOUT LEARNING AND ATTENTION

Think about the physical environment.

- Sit at the same eye level as the child.
- Be comfortable (e.g., use pillows).

Remember to interview, not interrogate.

- An interview has an ebb and flow; questions are woven through.
- Use what happens in the session (e.g., if a child says she had difficulty with homework, take the opportunity to ask what's difficult about it).

Make session interactive, fun.

- Incorporate toys, games.
- Use humor.
- Be ready to use jokes and riddles.

Be prepared to deal with the range of problematic behaviors.

- Have behavioral interventions on hand.
- Use "Tools to Get and Stay on Track" found in this Appendix.

Set and maintain the tone.

- Show respect (e.g., ask permission before you look in a child's notebook).
- View the family as an expert and yourself as coresearcher, codetective.
- Move toward the child (but not so near as to invade space, which could be especially upsetting to a child with ADHD).
- Be sensitive to the child's cognitive level.

Begin with strengths. Ask:

- "What are you good at? What do you like doing?"
- "What are your favorite TV shows, movies, and games?" (From the child's descriptions, you can get a sense of sequencing, storytelling, memory, language.)

Be a skilled observer.

- Consult a clinical observation checklist. (See, for example, Table 6.1, p. 127.)
- Use what is happening in the session. For example, if the child asks "what?" and needs repetition, try to understand why. (Is the child distracted? Does the child have receptive language problems?)

Think about physiology and brain-behavior connections. The problems that plague children every day may be *uninvited guests* in the session. These might include:

- Fidgeting, high level of motor activity
- Distractibility, difficulty sustaining attention
- Inability to organize information, tasks, and activities
- Impulsivity, blurting out answers, touching everything, not waiting turn
- Inability to control anger (e.g., "makes a mountain out of a molehill")
- Insatiability

Consider language ability.

- Listen for language and match yours accordingly.
- If the child doesn't understand a question, as evidenced by a quizzical look or no answer, say: "Sometimes I may not do a good job of asking a question in a way that you can understand. Did you understand my question? I'll try to do a better job this time."
- If the child has a language disability, speak in small bytes; don't give many instructions.
- Use visual images (e.g., picture books).
- Prompting is sometimes helpful. Try either/or questions, or multiple-choice questions, rather than yes/no questions.
- Ask different kinds of questions. Instead of asking, "Do you have difficulty sitting still and paying attention?" you might ask: "Some children say that sitting still and paying attention is a hard thing for them. What about you?" "Can you tell me a time when it is difficult for you to sit and pay attention?" "Can you tell me a time when it is easy for you to sit and pay attention?"
- Give different choices. For example: "Some children tell me reading is difficult because they can't figure out what sounds the letters make, or because they don't understand the words. Which one sounds like you?"

Is the child bored? Ask:

- "Are you going to have to fight against boredom?"
- "Do you get bored when adults talk?"
- "Can you hang onto your boredom for a while?"
- "How many questions can I ask?"

Ask about what's working.

- Are there problem-free times?
- What about successes?

Build on unique outcomes. For example, if a child who generally blurts things out waits her turn in the session, acknowledge the "birth" of a new behavior. Ask:

- "If you keep this up, what might be different for you with your friends, brother, sister, teacher, mother, father?"
- "Is there anybody who would be surprised about this new behavior?"
- "How can you invite it to be a part of your life?"

Listen to language. Ask questions like these:

- "When you try to explain things, is it easy or is it hard to find the words?"
- "When people are talking to you, do you have to ask them to repeat themselves? Do you need people to say things over again?"
- As you listen to the child's response, watch for the parent's reactions. Then ask the parent if they have noticed the same things.

Ask questions that tap into memory.

- "When is your birthday? What year were you born?"
- "Please tell me your address and telephone number."
- "Tell me the months of the year. What month comes before March? after November?"
- "What season are we in now? What are the other seasons of the year?"
- "Do you find that you learn something and then in the morning (next day, next week) you forget it?"
- Ask the parents: "Do you find you teach your child things, then a couple of days later she or he doesn't remember the information?"

Assess abstract reasoning.

- "How are a table and chair alike?"
- "How are a fork and a spoon alike?"

Ask the child to draw.

- Picture of a person (you can use this as a gross measure of intellect. Keep in mind, however, that fine motor or graphomotor problems will affect a child's ability to draw).
- Shapes (draw them, name them).
- Look at the way the child holds the pencil.
- Ask, "When you write, does your hand get tired?" If so, inquire further.

Ask questions about attention. Note: Some children have trouble concentrating because of things going on inside of them, fantasy, imagination, anxieties, and worries. Sometimes children are distracted because they are unable to filter extraneous auditory or visual stimuli.

- "When you are in school, and someone is talking, do you start thinking about something else?"
- "Do you have the kind of brain that has a lot of ideas all the time?"
- "Is it hard or easy to keep your mind on work?"
- "Is working on something you like easier than working on something you don't like?"
- "When you aren't paying attention in class, what are you thinking about?"
- "Do you find it difficult to sit still?"
- "Do you have trouble starting things? Finishing them?"
- If you suspect ADHD or ADD, you can employ some paper and pencil screening tools (see "Tools and Resources" in this Appendix for various scales).
- When in doubt, ask for help from a person experienced in working with LD/ADHD/ADD.

Ask about academics.

- What's easy? difficult?
- What subject does the child like best? least?

Informally evaluate reading and math skills.

- Ask, "How is reading for you?"
- You can have the child read aloud from his notebook. See if he can read back what he wrote.
- Have on hand some reading passages from different grades.
- Ask, "When you don't know a word, how do you figure it out?"
- Ask what sounds some words begin with.
- Ask, "How is math for you?" If the child is above fourth grade, ask about multiplication tables, borrowing, carrying, and other skills.

Ask about how the child studies for a test.

- "If you were to going to have a spelling (science, math) test tomorrow, how would you study?"

Use pictorial representation of topics.

- Circle (fill in how difficult it is to pay attention)
- Thermometer

Draw upon fantasies, wishes.

- "If my pen were a magic wand and I could give you any three wishes, what would you wish for most in the world?"
- "If I could wave my magic wand and change anything about you, what would you want to change?"
- "If you were to go to a desert island (if the child doesn't know what a desert island is, be sure to describe it) and could take one person along, who would you take with you? Who would you take second? Third?" Children often choose the person closest to them; this can give you a window into relationships.

Some additional thoughts:

- Informally screen and assess over time.
- Keep track of your findings.
- Check them out with the child, the family, and the teacher.
- Speak to and consult with others as needed.

- Is a referral for a full evaluation of learning and/or attention needed? If so help pave the way and don't forget to share your thoughts and findings with the person to whom you are making the referral. Complete the "Piece of the Pie" worksheet found in this section of the Appendix together with the child and the family.
- Is the problem chronic?
- If you suspect ADD or ADHD, remember early onset (before age 7).
- Consult the *Diagnostic and Statistical Manual of Mental Disorders* (4th ed.).

Tools to Get and
Stay on Track

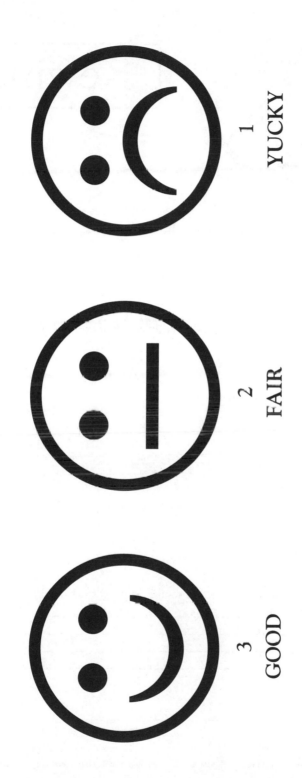

SELF-MONITORING FACES

1
YUCKY

2
FAIR

3
GOOD

Rewinds

1. "Rewind the tape" and take another look at what happened.

2. Write or draw the steps.

3. Review what happened.

4. Think about how you could do it differently if you did it again.

5. Come up with a new plan.

6. Write or draw your new plan.

I rewind the tape and look back at what happened.

1.

2.

3.

4.

I think about what happened. If I could do it again, I would do it differently. Here is my new plan. _____

_____

_____

_____

Signed: _____

How Am I Doing?

YUCKY 1

OKAY 2

VERY GOOD 3

GREAT 4

Don't Agree/Agree

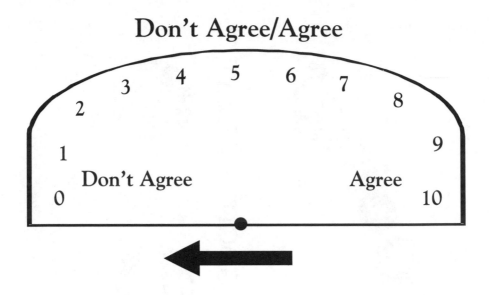

How Much?

KEEPING TRACK OF MY GOALS

Name:_____ Date: _____

Level of Attainment	Goal 1:							Goal 2:						
	M	T	W	Th	F	S	Su	M	T	W	Th	F	S	Su
Lots better than expected +2 ☺														
A little better than expected +1 ☺														
Just what was expected 0 😐														
A little less than expected −1 ☹														
A lot less than expected −2 ☹														
Designated Completion Time for Goal Attainment														

This page from *Child-Friendly Therapy* © Marcia B. Stern (W.W. Norton & Company, 800-233-4830) may be reproduced.

Tools to Talk and
Send Therapy Home

ABCs OF GAME-MAKING

Materials Needed

- colored construction paper, large posterboard, magazines to cut up, index cards, stickers
- pens, pencils, colored markers, and crayons
- glue, scissors, ruler
- art materials (cloth, string, glitter, buttons, ribbon, yarn, pipe cleaners)
- game tokens, dice, spinners, egg timer, hourglass, play money

Planning the Game

Step 1

- **Assess.** Before you use this tool, it is important to assess the child and family as a whole. You will need a general idea of the developmental stage of the child, in terms of gross and fine motor skills, visual motor skills, and cognitive abilities, such as memory and language development.
- **Be prepared.** The making of the game should not begin before one or more sessions have occurred.
- **Commit.** In order for the game construction to be a success you need to establish a rapport with the family and child. This works best when you gain a commitment from all of the participants.

Step 2

- **Ask.** Ask the child and family what the game should be about. Use whatever is of interest to the child; Sesame Street characters, Pokemon, Harry Potter, football players, and baseball figures can all be used.
- **Brainstorm.** Facilitate the collection of all ideas. Let the child take the lead in this process. Come up with a few ideas to pick from.
- **Combine.** Choose one theme of interest for your game and combine it with the therapeutic targets for that child and family. The goal of the game should be in tune with a desired therapeutic outcome.

Step 3

- **Agree** on a format for the game. Ask questions such as:

    Will there be a winner? What must you accomplish in order to win? In some cases, I prefer making games that don't have a competitive aspect. This helps keep the focus on the content and process of the game rather than on the outcome. However, I often use tokens or money to enhance the child's motivation for responding. For example, use play money and give the largest coin denomination for a complete answer, and smaller denominations for a one- or two-word answer. If a story is required, it must have a beginning, middle, and an end to get the most money or tokens.

    How will the game be played? How many players are allowed? Who goes first? Will there be a roll of dice or a spin of a wheel? Will there be time constraints? This is the time to negotiate the rules. Everyone gets to discuss the rules they think should be included or discarded. Let the child take the lead in developing the rules.

    What ages are appropriate for this game? Gear the rules and procedures to the youngest member participating, but make sure the interest level is high enough for the older players.

- **Balance** having fun with achieving your goal. Use all stages of game-making to work toward your therapeutic goal, but also remember that fun is important. A lot can be accomplished in a stimulating, fun, and rewarding setting.

- **Collaborate** with the family. In order for the game construction to be a success, you have to establish a rapport with the family and child. Teach the family to use this activity as a communication tool.

Creating the Game

Step 1

- **Allow** as much freedom as possible for the family and child to create an individualized and special game. Let the children contribute their input and participate in decision-making.

- **Begin** to construct the game. During this phase the family will engage in behaviors that will demonstrate how they cooperate, problem-solve, listen to one another, and make choices.

- **Create, Color, Cut.** The family will choose the playing board from among different blank boards (such as the one in this Appendix). Observe and coach the family members while they draw figures on the board and decide what each figure means. As a therapist, your job is to help the family by making suggestions that are in line with your therapeutic goals. You may notice the perfectionist trying to draw perfect figures of the same shape and size. Another child will start off with an idea, change his or her mind, make a mistake, and end up with something entirely different. Decorate the board with colors, stickers, and construction paper, using the theme you have chosen. If the game involves drawing from a pile of cards, use the index cards to write special instructions, penalties, and bonus rewards. A good way to link sessions is to give the family the cards as a homework assignment.

Step 2

- **Assist** each child in contributing to the activity. By doing this, the therapist can provide a model of behavior for the parents. As they observe the therapist interacting with the child, the parents can learn new ways to communicate with their son or daughter.
- **Be perceptive.** The therapist should observe how different family members perceive rules, communicate ideas, and participate in the game's construction. This can be a valuable time for the therapist to watch the family dynamics in action and observe how members work together.
- **Complete** the making of the game. It will take three to four sessions to complete the game, depending on the speed and abilities of the child and on the situations that may arise during the session that need to be dealt with and discussed. It is best not to start playing immediately after you have completed the game. Put it aside until the next session. This will give the family time to think about their work and anticipate playing with it. Finally, play the game with the family several times. They can then take the game home and play it or modify it as situations evolve.

Where to Order Supplies for Making Games

In order to make your individualized board game you will need different kinds of materials. Add your own creative touches and surprise families and children with an array of special supplies. Your local office supply store will often have the basic materials you need.

For additional ideas and supplies, here are a few useful sources.

For colored paper, posters, construction paper, fancy cards, and stationery:
  www.rediform.com
  www.paperdirect.com
  www.ampad.com
  www.mcgpaper.com

For crafts and art supplies at affordable prices:
  www.cut-ratepreschoolsupplies.com

For spinners, overhead spinners and templates:
  Creative Publications, Inc
  5005 West 110th Street
  Oak Lawn, IL 60453
  1-800-624-0822
  www.creativepublications.com

For stickers, flash cards, wipe-off books, award certificates, incentives, diplomas:
  Trend Enterprises, Inc.
  PO Box 64073
  St. Paul, MN 55164
  1-800-328-5540
  www.trendenterprises.com

For Velcro® circles with sticky backs and many more Velcro® products:
  Fastech of Jacksonville, Inc.
  PO Box 11838
  Jacksonville, FL 32239
  1-800-940-6934
  www.hookandloop.com

For game boards, paper play money, award badges:
  Instructional Fair TS Denison
  www.edumart.com/fair/

For educational products used to make games:
  Creative Teaching Press
  www.creativeteaching.com

Novel notes, fun shaped note pads, homework books:
  Carson-Dellosa Publishing
  www.carson-dellosa.com

PUPPETS

Buying Puppets

A resource for manufactured puppets of all shapes and sizes is:
> The Puppet Petting Zoo
> 213 Crystal Lake Road
> Tolland, CT 06084
> 1-860-872-6899

The following Web sites are also useful:

Puppet manufacturer:
> www.folkmanis.com

To purchase finger, wrap-around, and full-body hand puppets, and puppet stages:
> www.puppetgallery.com

The "puppet-everything place":
> www.legendsandlore.com/puppet_store.html

Making Puppets

For information on making your own puppets, including instructions and where to obtain supplies—also an excellent Internet site for any information devoted to puppetry:
> www.sagecraft.com/puppetry/

For patterns and suggestions for making stick, sock, paper bag, and tube finger puppets:
> www.pbs.org/totstv/english/puppets.html

A source for specialty puppet patterns and e-patterns you can receive electronically:
> www.puppetpatterns.com

For foam rubber in 1/2-inch thickness, if you use patterns to make your own puppets:
> www.foamrubber.com

To learn the basics of making sack and sock puppets, writing puppet plays, puppet scripts:
> www.legendsandlore.com/puppet-resource.html

Some Easy Puppets to Make

There are many ways to make hand puppets, depending on the time and effort you allot for the project.

Stick-and-Paper Puppets

Materials needed

- popsicle sticks or tongue depressors from a craft or medical supply store
- magic markers or crayons
- 8 1/2" x 11" paper
- scissors
- stapler, paste, or tape

Take pieces of paper and cut out large circles or outlines of boys or girls. Draw a face or paste a picture of people or animals, found in magazines or coloring books, on each circle, or decorate each outline (color it in, draw buttons, etc.). Then paste the pictures onto popsicle sticks or tongue depressors. Alternatively, roll pieces of paper lengthwise and staple or paste the pictures directly onto them.

Paper-Bag Puppets

Materials needed

- magic markers or crayons
- paper
- paper bags (sandwich size)
- scissors
- paste

Draw a face on a piece of paper. Then take a flattened paper bag and turn it so that the flap is at the top. Paste the face you have drawn onto the flap. You can draw details such as clothing on the front of the bag, or paste on buttons or decorations. Then place your hand in the bag, bending your fingers to fit into the flap. Move the flap to make the puppet "talk."

Sock Puppets

Materials needed

- socks
- magic markers

- paper
- felt
- yarn
- scissors
- paste
- styrofoam packing (peanuts)

Stuff a sock with styrofoam peanuts or pieces of fabric. Draw a face with magic marker or create one with felt. Use yarn for hair.

Additional materials for creative touches:

- Velcro® circles
- ink pads (washable ink) to make thumbprints
- glitter and glitter glue
- funny sticky (googly) eyes that move
- fabric and wallpaper scraps, pipe cleaners, sequins, beads, buttons, and colorful material for accessories and clothing
- fabric crayons, markers, and paints
- foam, sponges
- hot-glue gun, fabric glue

Felt, Iron-On Transfer Puppets

Materials needed

- computer
- color printer
- scanner (optional)
- 8 1/2 inches x 11 inches pieces of felt
- iron-on transfers (available at www.hanes2u.com, PrintPaks 1-800-774-6860, www.mcgpaper.com)
- sewing supplies
- hot-glue gun, fabric glue

One of my favorites, because it allows children to actually create their own puppets. Fold felt into 5 1/2" x 11" pieces, with the fold to the left. Sew (or glue) across the top and down the right side, so that the piece is closed on three sides. Turn the felt inside out with the seams inside. Have the child draw a picture that you scan into your computer. Follow the instructions to turn the child's scanned picture into the image that is then printed onto the iron-on transfer paper. (If you do not have access to a scanner, use any accessible design or picture.) Send the felt and the transfer home for the child to complete the puppet.

Edible Puppets*

- lollipop: use gummy-rings for eyes, candy corn for fangs; use icing to attach candies
- vegetable: use vegetables for bodies, cream cheese as glue, nuts for facial features
- cookie: (a sugar cookie recipe is available at this site), use candies to decorate the cookie; attach the cookie to a lollipop stick

Wooden Spoon Puppets**

Materials needed

- wooden spoon
- nonbleeding colored markers (Woodcraft brand works well)
- pipe cleaners
- rubber bands
- pieces of fabric
- ribbon

Draw facial features on the front and back of a wooden spoon. For fun, give each face a different expression (such as happy, surprised, sleepy). Add hair by bending a pipe cleaner around the edge of the bowl and gluing it in place. (Stretch rubber bands around the spoon to hold the hair until the glue dries.) Dress the puppet by loosely wrapping a piece of fabric around the spoon handle, gathering the cloth at the base of the bowl and tying a ribbon around the cloth to secure the dress at the neck.

Books about Making Puppets

Allison, D., & Devet, D. (1997). *The foam book: An easy guide to building polyfoam puppets*. Charlotte, NC: Grey Seal Puppets Inc.
Buetter, N. (1998). *Simple puppets from everyday materials*. Winnipeg, Manitoba, Canada: Tamos Books.

*Familyfun.com (to search, type in "edible puppets")
**Familyfun.com (to search, type in "wooden spoon puppets")

Henson, C. (1994). *The Muppets make puppets!/Book and puppet kit: How to make puppets out of all kinds of stuff around your house.* NY: Workman.

Moss, L. (1990). *Hand puppets: How to make and use them* (rev. ed.). Mineola, NY: Dover Publications.

ADDITIONAL TOOLS TO TALK & HELP SEND THERAPY HOME

Create and send home unique messages, family mottos, and motivators (I Can Do It, Yes I Can!). These activities are great fun for individual children or for the family. On the computer, design a personalized logo or slogan. After the words, sentences, pictures, or designs are created, follow the product instructions to add them to keychains, mousepads, posters, etc.

Decals, Stickers, Tattoos, Magnets, and the Like

Materials needed

- computer (scanner optional)
- color printer
- Microsoft® Word, Microsoft® Works, Microsoft® Publisher, Corel® WordPerfect, or any software, such as Broderbund Print Shop®, Sierra™ Print Artist™ used for art projects
- banner and poster paper*
- body sticker tattoos
- bumper stickers (download free template from www.Nashua.com/tmplts.html and/or www.ibmezprint.com)
- software for designing stickers (Printertainment™ Software Kit available from Avery Dennison, www.avery.com and/or KidLabel, Alston Software Labs)
- holographic stickers (kids love these; available from Southworth Company, www.southworth.com)
- clear decal paper (great for decorating windows or mirrors)
- magnet kit with templates (clip art available at www.ibmezprint.com; magnetic sheets available through Southworth Company, www.southworth. com)
- mousepad, photo calendar, and puzzle kits

*Most of the following supplies are available at office supply stores or at www. clubinventit.com. Kits include software. Prink Paks (1-800-774-6860) has software for calendar kits, jewlery, kits, window art, pinwheels, pop-up books, and craft projects.

- raffle and event tickets (download free template from www.Nashua.com/ tmplts.html)
- door hangers (download free template from www.Nashua.com/ tmplts.html, and/or Microsoft® Publisher)
- snap-together mug (available at www.joann.com)

Transfers and Logos

Materials needed

- computer (scanner optional)
- color printer
- white or solid-color cotton T-shirts, calendars, aprons, totes
- T-shirt maker software (available at www.hanes2u.com or 1-800-426-3728, PrintMaster T-shirt Design Shop™; templates available www.ibmezprint. com)
- easy-peel iron-on transfer paper (available at www.hanes2u.com, PrintPaks 1-800-774-6860, www.mcgpaper.com)
- iron

Fun to Make and Fun to Play: Recipes for Parents and Children to Use at Home

Play Dough

Materials needed

- 2 cups flour
- 1 cup salt
- 2 cups water
- 2 tablespoons baby oil
- 2 tablespoons cream of tartar
- food coloring (add last)
- lemon or orange oil (for fragrance, optional)

Combine dry ingredients. Add liquids. Stir well. Microwave on high 4 to 5 minutes. Stir. Microwave an additional 1 minute. Repeat until it is the consistency of mashed potatoes. Cool enough to touch. Knead. Store in air-tight container or resealable bag. Makes several cups.

Additional recipes for play dough and clay are available at www.teachnet.com/lesson/art/playdough061699.html. Edible play dough recipes are available at www.childfun.com/menus/playdough.shtml.

Finger Paint

Materials needed

- liquid starch
- water
- 1 teaspoon powdered tempera paint

Pour a small amount of liquid starch on piece of paper. Sprinkle a teaspoon of paint into starch. Add water as needed, mixing with hands while painting.

Silly Putty

Materials needed

- Elmer's or any white glue
- liquid starch
- food coloring

Mix equal parts of glue and liquid starch. Stir with a spoon, then with hands. Add more starch if the mixture is too sticky.

Bubbles

Materials needed

- 3/4 cup liquid soap
- 1/4 cup glycerin
- 2 quarts tap water

Combine all ingredients and mix well.

Papier-Mâché

Materials needed

- liquid starch (or wallpaper paste)
- water
- newspaper strips

Mix equal parts liquid starch and water and stir until starch is dissolved. Dip newspaper strips in liquid mixture one at a time and apply one strip at a time to form a shape (or use a mold).

BOOKS

Arts and crafts, and games

Fernandez, E., & Green, M. (1996). *Peg solitaire: 23 all-on-your-own games*. Palo Alto, CA: Klutz Press.

Green, M. (1999). *Beaded bobby pins*. Palo Alto, CA: Klutz Press.

Klutz Press. (1990). *The book of classic board games*. Palo Alto, CA: Author.

Klutz Press. (2000). *A book of artrageous projects*. Palo Alto, CA: Author.

MacColl, G. (1992). *The book of cards for kids*. New York: Workman.

Torres, L., & Sherman, M. (1997). *Pipe cleaners gone crazy: A complete guide to bending fuzzy sticks*. Palo Alto, CA: Klutz Press.

Caricatures

Blitz, B. (1999). *The fun book of cartoon people*. Philadelphia, PA: Running Press.

Emberley, E. (1977). *Ed Emberley's great thumbprint drawing book*. New York: Little Brown.

Dance & Drama Activities

Bany-Winters, L. (2000). *Show time: Music, dance, and drama activities for kids*. Chicago, IL: Chicago Review.

Rooyackers, P. (1996). *101 dance games for children: Fun and creativity with movement*. Alameda, CA: Hunter House.

Rooyackers, P. (1997). *101 drama games for children: Fun and learning with acting and make-believe*. Alameda, CA: Hunter House.

Storms, J. (2001). *101 More music games for children: New fun and learning with rhythm and song*. Alameda, CA: Hunter House.

Humor

Archbold, T. (1999). *Ha! Ha! Ha!: Over 400 very funny jokes*. New York: Larousse Kingfisher Chambers.

Barry, S. A. (Ed.). (1994). *Kids' funniest jokes*. New York: Sterling.

Kids are punny: Jokes sent by kids to the Rosie O'Donnell Show. (1997). New York: Warner.

Kids are punny 2: More jokes sent by kids to the Rosie O'Donnell Show. (1998). New York: Warner.

Marzollo, J. (1999). *I spy treasure hunt: A book of picture riddles.* New York: Scholastic.

Rovin, J. (1990). *500 hilarious jokes for kids.* New York: New American Library.

Music Books & Audio

Gindick, J. (1984). *Country & blues harmonica for the musically hopeless.* Palo Alto, CA: Klutz Press.

Lande, A., Wiz, B., & Hickman, L. (2000). *Songames for sensory integration.* Boulder, CO: Belle Curve Records.

Turner, J. B. (1997). *Smartstart guitar: A fun, easy approach to beginning guitar.* Milwaukee, WI: Hal Leonard.

Paper Crafts

Klutz Press. (1998). *The best paper airplanes you'll ever fly.* Palo Alto, CA: Author.

Klutz Press. (2000). *Fold real money into real cool origami.* Palo Alto, CA: Author.

Point-of-View Story Books

Granowsky, A. (1994). *Cinderella/That awful Cinderella: A classic tale.* Austin, TX: Raintree/Steck-Vaughn.

Granowsky, A. (1994). *Snow White/The unfairest of them all: A classic tale.* Austin, TX: Raintree/Steck-Vaughn.

Granowsky, A. (1995). *Goldilocks and the three bears: Bears should share!* Austin, TX: Raintree/Steck-Vaughn.

Granowsky, A. (1996). *Giants have feelings, too/Jack and the beanstalk.* Austin, TX: Raintree/Steck-Vaughn.

Science

Barbor, M. (1999). *The human brain.* Philadelphia, PA: Running Press.

Cromwell, S. (1998). *How do I know it's yucky? and other questions about the senses.* Des Plaines, IL: Reed Educational & Professional Publishing.

Klutz Press. (2000). *Bedroom astronomy.* Palo Alto, CA: Author.

Tricks and Magic

Finnigan, D. (1991). *The complete juggler book: All the steps from beginner to professional*. Palo Alto, CA: Klutz Press.

Fulves, K. (1985). *Self-working paper magic: 81 foolproof tricks*. New York: Dover.

Stroud, M., & Cassidy, J. (1989). *The klutz book of magic*. Palo Alto, CA: Klutz Press.

SOFTWARE

Creating stories

Storybook Weaver® Deluxe by The Learning Company® 1-800-395-0277

Orly's Draw-a-Story (for young children, 4–5 years old) Broderbund 1-800-395-0277

The Amazing Writing Machine by Broderbund 1-800-395-0277

Kid Pix® Deluxe 3 by The Learning Company 1-800-395-0277

Print Master® by Broderbund 1-800-395-0277

Stanley Sticker Stories by Harcourt Brace (available at edmark.com)

Visual Learning Tools

Kidspiration by Inspiration Software (available at inspiration.com)

Inspiration 6 by Inspiration Software (available at inspiration.com)

Just for Fun

Crayola Print Factory by IBM Multimedia1-800-426-7235

Awesome Animated Monster Maker, Ultra Edition by Houghton Mifflin Interactive 1-800-225-3362

Web Sites for Software and Reviews

Children's software & new media revue™ online reviews children's interactive media and articles. This site provides LittleClickers™ column, Safe web explorations for children 6–12. Fee for subscription.
www.childrenssoftware.com

This excellent site has articles, games, software reviews and free downloads, useful links, craft projects, newsletter, and jokes for children and grownups.
www.kidsdomain.com

Source for unbiased information about children's educational software. Free newsletter.
www.superkids.com

Reviews of educational software, games, toys, books and audio.
www.school.discovery.com/parents/reviewcorner

For reviews, computer books, software, tech toys.
www.thereviewzone.com

Purchase software for preschoolers to adults. Free downloads, creative print materials, crafts, card designs, web designs.
www.learningco.com

For interactive learning products for pre-kindergarten–12 and special needs students. Free downloads.
www.edmark.com

Web sites to Learn and Talk about the Brain

This home page has links to teaching tools, resources, information about the nervous system, on-line and off-line books and articles. One can also subscribe to an informative newsletter, the Neuroscience Newsletter for Kids, delivered by e-mail each month. Dr. Eric H. Chudler (chudler@u.washington.edu) developed and maintains this excellent resource. It highlights recent research about the brain.
http://faculty.washington.edu/chudler/neurok.html

Offers pictures of both the whole human brain and cross-sections of it.
http://faculty.washington.edu/chudler/flash/brainfly.html

Provides an index of neuroscience resources available on the Internet.
www.neuroguide.com

Health, science, technology animation and educational site for kids.
www.brainpop.com

Sources for Ordering Brain-related Products: Models, Charts, Software

Einstein's Emporium
Phone   1-800-522-8281

Brain Mart
Web site   Brain-mart.com

Medical Multimedia Systems
90 Knollwood Drive, Cherry Hill, New Jersey 08002
Phone   1-800-769-7799
Source for Brainiac! A computerized interactive neuroanatomy atlas.

Zephyr Press
Phone   1-800-232-2187
Web site   www.zephyrpress.com
Materials on multiple intelligences, learning, and the brain.

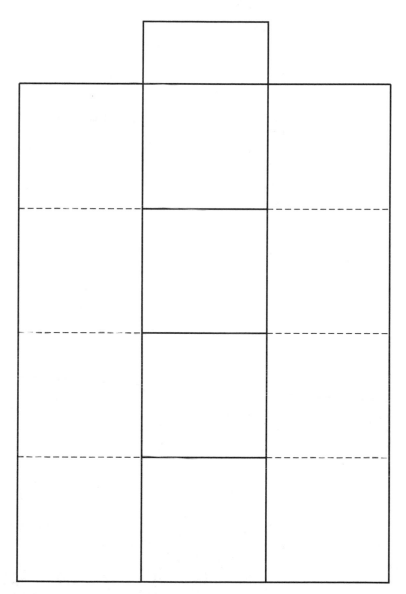

Blank Die

Choose 6 feeling words (e.g. angry, happy, sad). Write one of the words in each of the three boxes across the top of the blank and write the remaining words in the three boxes down the middle of the blank.

Cut the blank along the dotted lines. Then fold along the solid lines, and form a cube.

To Play: Throw the die. See what feeling it lands on and then tell about a time this week you felt that way.

Tools and Resources

MEDICATION GUIDE*

Medication+	Class	Benefits	Side Effects
Ritalin (methylphenidate) Concerta (methylphenidate) Dexedrine (dextroamphetamine) Cylert (pemoline) Adderall (dextroamphetamine and amphetamine neutral salts)	Stimulants	Treatment for ADHD symptoms of inattention, hyperactivity, and impulsivity with proven efficacy. Most studied medication in child psychiatry.	Decreased appetite, GI upset, headaches, insomnia, decreased growth, tics
Catapres (clonidine) Tenex (guanfacine)	Alpha agonists	Useful for ADHD, tics, and aggression.	Sedation, hypotension, nightmares, EKG changes, depression
Prozac (fluoxetine) Zoloft (sertraline) Paxil (paroxetine) Luvox (fluvoxamine) Celexa (citalopram)	Selective serotonin reuptake inhibitors (SSRI)	Useful in treatment of depression, anxiety, and pervasive developmental disorders. Generally well tolerated.	GI upset, insomnia or sedation, activation, headaches, sexual dysfunction in adolescents
Tofranil (imipramine) Norpramin (desipramine) Elavil (amitriptyline) Pamelor (nortriptyline) Anafranil (clomipramine)	Tricyclic antidepressants	Useful in treatment of depression, anxiety, ADHD, enuresis. Anafranil useful in obsessive-compulsive disorder.	Sedation, headache, dry mouth, GI upset, constipation, orthostatic hypotension, blurry vision, urinary retention, EKG changes
Wellbutrin (bupropion) Effexor (venlafaxine) Serzone (nefazodone) Remeron (mirtazapine)	Other antidepressants	Useful for depression and ADHD. New medications considered for use in anxiety and depression. Little data with children.	Sleep disturbance, GI upset, hypertension (Effexor only)

continued on p. 350

MEDICATION GUIDE* continued

Medication[+]	Class	Benefits	Side Effects
Haldol (haloperidol) Orap (pimozide) Prolixin (fluphenazine) Mellaril (thioridazine)	Standard antipsychotic medications	Useful in treatment of psychosis, tics, PDD, aggression, and bipolar disorder.	Sedation, movement disorders (may be lasting), weight gain, orthostatic hypotension, neuroleptic malignant syndrome, cognitive blunting, Parkinsons-like symptoms, decreased seizure threshold
Clozapine (clozaril) Risperdal (risperidone) Zyprexa (olanzapine) Serloquel (quetiapine)	Atypical antipsychotic medications (newer medications believed to carry less risk of Parkinsons-like symptoms and movement disorders)	Useful in treatment of psychosis, tics, PDD, aggression, and bipolar disorder.	Sedation, movement disorders (may be lasting), weight gain, orthostatic hypotension, neuroleptic malignant syndrome, cognitive blunting, Parkinsons-like symptoms, agranulocytosis (decrease in white blood cells), seizures (Clozapine only), fatty liver, EKG changes (Risperdal only)
Ativan (lorazepam) Klonopin (clonazepam) Xanax (alprazolam)	Anxiolytics	Useful in treatment of anxiety disorders and sleep problems. Provides immediate symptom relief.	Sedation, cognitive blunting, dizziness, potential for addiction
Lithium Depakote (valproic acid) Tegretol (carbamazepine) Neurontin (gabapentin)	Mood stabilizers	Useful in bipolar disorder and aggression. Lithium can augment other medications.	GI upset, dizziness, weight gain, enuresis, tremor, sedation, acne, polyuria, polydipsia, thyroid dysfunction (Lithium only), polycystic ovary disease (Depakote only)

[+]Medications are referred to by brand name, followed by generic name in parentheses.
*Reprinted with permission from NYU Child Study Center. See their Web site, www.aboutourkids.com, for more information.

COMMON PSYCHOMETRIC TESTS AND RATING SCALES

Achievement Tests

- Kaufman Test of Educational Academics (KTEA)
- Wide Range Achievement Test Revised (WRAT3)

Adaptive Behavior Measures

- AAMR Adaptive Behavior Scale (ABS)
- Scales of Independent Behavior (SIB)
- Vineland Adaptive Behavior Scales (VABS)
    Classroom edition
    Interview edition

Attention/Concentration Rating Scales

- ADD-H Comprehensive Teachers Rating Scale (ACTeRS)
- Conners' Parent Rating Scales (CPRS-R) and Conners' Teacher Rating Scales (CTRS-R)
- Brown Attention Deficit-Disorder Scales for Adolescents and Adults
- Brown Attention Deficit-Disorder Scales for Children

Autism Measures

- Autism Diagnostic Observation Schedule (ADOS)
- Childhood Autism Rating Scale (CARS)

Behavioral Rating Scales

- Achenbach Child Behavior Checklist System
    Parent Form (CBCL)
    Teacher Report Form (TRF)

- Behavior Assessment System for Children (BASC)
    - Parent Rating Scale (PRS)
    - Teacher Rating Scale (TRS)
- Carey Temperament Scales (CTS)
- Comprehensive Behavior Rating Scale for Children (CBRSC)-Teacher scale
- Walker Problem Behavior Identification Checklist (WPBIC)

Intelligence Tests

- Kaufman Assessment Battery for Children (K-ABC)
- Wechsler Intelligence Scale for Children—third edition (WISCIII-R)

Interview Instruments & Questionnaires

- Achenbach Child Behavior Checklist System (CBCL)
- Aggregate Neurobehavioral Student Health and Education Review (The ANSER System is a series of questionnaires for parents, clinicians, and children themselves, from age 3 through adolescence. It is a comprehensive method for gathering information.)
- Behavior Assessment System for Children (BASC)
- Brief Symptom Inventory (BSI)
- Children's Inventory of Anger (ChIA)
- Diagnostic Interview for Children and Adolescents (DICA–IV)
- Schedule for Affective Disorders and Schizophrenia for School-Aged Children (K-SADS)
- Semistructured Clinical Interview for Children
- Structured Developmental History
- Structured Interview for the Diagnostic Assessment of Children (SIDAC)
- The Survey of Teenage Readiness and Neurodevelopmental Status (STRANDS has two parts: Student Interview and Student Questionnaire; available from Educators Publishing Service)

Learning Styles

- Dunn, R., Dunn, K., & Price, G. (1985). Manual: Learning style inventory. Lawrence, KS: Price Systems
- Learning Styles Inventory (available from Western Psychological Services)
- Perrin, J. (1981). Primary version: Learning style inventory. Jamaica, NY: Learning Style Network, St. John's University.
- The Learning Style Inventory (LSI) for youth in grades 3–12 is a 104-item self-report questionnaire that identifies 22 elements relating to the environmental, emotional, sociological, physical, and psychological preferences of the individual.
- The Learning Style Inventory–Primary Version for children in kindergarten through grade 2 is a pictorial questionnaire.

Marriage and Family

- Dyadic Adjustment Scale (DAS)
- Family Apperception Test
- Family Assessment Measure III
- Marital Satisfaction Inventory Revised (MSI-R)
- Parent-Child Relationship Inventory (PCRI)
- Parenting Alliance Measure (PAM)
- Parenting Report Card (Kid's view of parenting skills)
- Parenting Satisfaction Scale (PSS)
- Parenting Stress Index (PSI) Third Edition
- Stress Index for Parents of Adolescents (SIPA)

Perceptual (Visual/Motor) Tests

- Bender-Gestalt Test
- Developmental Test of Visual/Motor Integration (VMI)

Projective Measures

- Children's Apperception Test (CAT)
- Draw A Person: Screening Procedure for Emotional Disturbance (DAP:SPED)
- House-Tree-Person (HTP)
- Kinetic Family Drawing (KFD)
- Roberts Apperception Test for Children (RATC)
- Rotter Incomplete Sentence Blank
- Tell Me A Story (TEMAS)
- Thematic Apperception Test (TAT)

Self-report Measures

- Achenbach Child Behavior Checklist System (CBCL)
    Youth Self-Report
- Behavior Assessment System for Children (BASC)
    Self-Report of Personality
- Children's Depression Inventory (CDI)
- Children's Personality Questionnaire (CPQ)
- Coopersmith Self-Esteem Inventories
- Harter and Pike Pictorial Scale of Perceived Competence and Acceptance/ Self-Perception Profiles
- Personality Inventory for Youth (PIY)
- Piers-Harris Children's Self-Concept Scale (PHCSCS)
- Revised Children's Manifest Anxiety Scale (RCMAS)
- Reynolds Adolescent Depression Scale (RADS)
- Reynolds Children's Depression Scale (RCDS)
- Social Phobia and Anxiety Inventory for Children (SPAIC)
- Social Skills Rating System (SSRS) - Student Form
- Suicide Probability Scale (SPS)

Social Skills Rating Scales

- Social Skills Rating System (SSRS)
    Teacher Form
    Parent Form

Useful References

Achenbach, T. M. (1991). *Manual for the child behavior checklist/4–18 and 1991 profile*. Burlington: University of Vermont Department of Psychiatry.

Achenbach, T. M. (1991). *Manual for the teacher's report form and 1991 profile*. Burlington: University of Vermont Department of Psychiatry.

Anastasi, A., & Urbina, S. (1997). *Psychological testing* (7th ed.). Upper Saddle River, NJ: Prentice Hall.

Dana, R. H. (1993). *Multicultural assessment perspectives for professional psychology*. Boston, MA: Allyn & Bacon.

Kamphaus, R.W., & Frick, P. J. (1996). *Clinical assessment of child and adolescent personality and behavior*. Boston, MA: Allyn & Bacon.

Reynolds, C. R., & Kamphaus, R. W. (1992). *Behavior assessment system for children manual*. Circle Pines, MN: American Guidance Service.

Sattler, J. M. (1995). *Assessment of children* (3rd ed.). San Diego, CA: Author.

Siegel, M. G. (1987). *Psychological testing from early childhood through adolescence*. Madison, CT: International Universities Press.

Selected List of Web Sites and Catalogues for Ordering Assessment Tools

http://www2.hawaii.edu/~psyasses/Topics.htm
Link for psychological assessment references of published articles by topic.

Educators Publishing Service, Inc.

Phone   1-800-435-7728

Web site   www.epsbooks.com

Provides assessment materials and materials for students with varying learning styles.

MHS, Inc.

Phone   1-800-456-3003

Web site   www.mhs.com

Develops and markets standardized and integrated assessment and diagnostic products.

Pro-Ed

Phone   1-800-897-3202

Web site   www.proedinc.com

Publishes the Journal of Learning Disabilities, Remedial and Special Education, Journal of Special Education, and assessment tools.

The Psychological Corporation

Phone   1-800-872-1726

Web site   www.psychcorp.com

Publishes a wide range of assessment tools and online assessment center.

Riverside Publishing

Phone   1-800-323-9540

Web site   www.riversidepublishing.com

Publishes educational assessment tools, college and career guidance, and online assessments.

Western Psychological Services

Phone   1-800-648-8857

Web site   www.wpspublish.com

Publishes assessment and therapy tools, and games.

BOOKS FOR PARENTS

Brett, D. (1986). *Annie stories*. New York: Workman.

Brett, D. (1992). *More Annie stories*. New York: Workman.

Chernofsky, B., & Gage, D. (1996). *Change your child's behavior by changing yours: Thirteen new tricks to get kids to cooperate*. New York: Three Rivers.

Clark, L. (1985). *SOS! Help for parents*. Bowling Green, KY: Parents Press.

Davis, R. D. (1997). *The gift of dyslexia: Why some of the smartest people can't read . . . and how they can learn*. New York: Perigee.

Duke, M. P., Martin, E. A., & Nowicki, S., Jr. (1996). *Teaching your child the social language of success*. Atlanta, GA: Peachtree.

Forehand, R., & Long, N. (1996). *Parenting: The strong-willed child*. Lincolnwood, IL: Contemporary.

Freed, J., & Parsons, L. (1997). *Right-brained children in a left-brained world: Unlocking the potential of your ADD child*. New York: Fireside.

Greene, R. W. (1998). *The explosive child: A new approach for understanding and parenting easily frustrated, "chronically inflexible" children*. New York: HarperCollins.

Hallowell, E. (1996). *When you worry about the child you love: Emotional and learning problems in children*. New York: Simon & Schuster.

Healy, J. M. (1990). *Endangered minds: Why children don't think—and what we can do about it.* New York: Simon & Schuster.

Healy, J. M. (1994). *Your child's growing mind: A practical guide to brain development and learning from birth to adolescence* (Rev. ed.). New York: Mainstreet.

Healy, J. M. (1998). *Failure to connect: How computers affect our children's minds—and what we can do about it.* New York: Simon & Schuster.

Hipp, E. (1995). *Fighting invisible tigers: A stress management guide for teens* (Rev. ed.). Minneapolis, MN: Free Spirit.

Koplewicz, H. S. (1996). *It's nobody's fault: New hope and help for difficult children and their parents.* New York: Random House.

Kranowitz, C. S. (1998). *The out-of-sync child: Recognizing and coping with sensory integration dysfunction.* New York: Skylight.

Levine, M. D. (1990). *Keeping a head in school: A student's book about learning abilities and learning disorders.* Cambridge, MA: Educators Publishing Service.

Levine, M. D. (1993). *All kinds of minds.* Cambridge, MA: Educators Publishing Service.

Levine, M. D. (1994). *Educational care: A system for understanding and helping children with learning problems at home and at school.* Cambridge, MA: Educators Publishing Service.

MacKenzie, R. J. (1998). *Setting limits* (2nd ed.). Rocklin, CA: Prima.

Michelli, J. (1998). *Humor, play & laughter: Stress-proofing life with your kids.* Golden, CO: Love & Logic.

Newman, S. (1999). *Small steps forward: Using games and activities to help your pre-school child with special needs.* UK: Jessica Kingsley

Osman, B. B. (1995). *No one to play with: Social problems of LD and ADD children* (Rev. ed.). Novato, CA: Academic Therapy.

Rapee, R., Spence, S. H., Cobham, V., & Wignall, A. (2000). *Helping your anxious child: A step-by-step guide for parents.* Oakland, CA: New Harbinger Publications.

Ricker, A., & Crowder, C. (1998). *Backtalk: Steps to ending rude behavior in your kids.* New York: Simon & Schuster.

Schachter, R., & MaCauley, C. S. (1988). *When your child is afraid.* New York: Simon & Schuster.

Schaefer, C. E., & DiGeronimo, T. F. (1989). *Toilet training without tears.* New York: Signet.

Singer, D. G., & Singer, J. L. (2001). *Make-Believe: Games & activities for imaginative play.* Washington, DC: Magination

Turecki, S. (1985). *The difficult child.* New York: Bantam.

Ziegler, R. G. (1992). *Homemade books to help kids cope: An easy-to-learn technique for parents & professionals.* New York: Magination.

BOOKS TO HELP IN SCHOOL

Brennan, J. (1998). *Study skills to the rescue!* Cypress, CA: Creative Teaching.

Flynn, K. (1995). *Graphic organizers . . . helping children think visually.* Cypress, CA: Creative Teaching.

Forte, I., & Schurr, S. (1996). *Graphic organizers & planning outlines for authentic instruction and assessment.* Nashville, TN: Incentive.

Schneiderman, R., & Werby, S. (1996). *Homework improvement: A parent's guide to developing successful study habits in children before it's too late.* Glenview, IL: GoodYear Books

ADDITIONAL SOURCES AND RESOURCES

Games, Counseling Aids

Childswork/Childsplay

Phone   1-800-962-1141

Web site   www.childswork.com

Source for games, books, workbooks, counseling aids to address social and emotional needs of children and adolescents.

A.D.D. Warehouse

Phone   1-800-233-9273

Web site   www.addwarehouse.com

Specializes in products for attention-deficit/hyperactivity and related problems; books, videos, games, assessment products.

Free Spirit Publishing

Phone   1-800-735-7323

Web site   www.freespirit.com

Books on parenting, teaching, emotion, social concerns.

PLS Bookstore (division of Performance Learning Systems, Inc.)

Phone   1-800-506-9996

Web site   www.plsbookstore.com

Books on multiple intelligences in the classroom, learning styles, diverse learners, games, puzzles.

Western Psychological Services Creative Therapy Store

Phone   1-800-648-8857

Web site   www.wpspublish.com
Therapeutic toys, games, books, and activities for use by counselors, therapists, teachers, parents, and children.

Paperbacks for Educators
426 West Front Street
Washington, MO 63090
Web site   www.any-book-in-print.com
Publishes a comprehensive bibliotherapy catalog.

National Organizations

Center for Mental Health Services
5600 Fishers Lane, Rockville, MD 20857
Web site   www.mentalhealth.org
Includes "KEN" (Knowledge Exchange Network), an excellent site for information on mental health publication links.

National Institute on Drug Abuse
Web site   www.nida.nih.gov
Information about drugs and drug education.

National Institute of Mental Health
NIMH Public Inquiries
6001 Executive Boulevard, Room 8184, MSC 9663, Bethesda, MD 20892-9663
Phone   1-301-443-4513
Web site   www.nimh.nih.gov

Substance Abuse and Mental Health Services Administration
5600 Fishers Lane, Rockville, MD 20857
Web site   www.samhsa.gov

Surgeon General
Web site   www.surgeongeneral.gov
Featuring the new mental health report, the report on youth violence, and great links for children, parents, and teachers.

Special Needs Organizations

American Speech-Language-Hearing Association (ASHA)
10801 Rockville Pike, Rockville, MD 20852
Phone   1-800-638-8255 or 1-301-897-5700
Web site   www.asha.org

ERIC Clearinghouse on Disabilities and Gifted Education (ERIC/CEC)
The Council for Exceptional Children, 110 North Glebe Road, Suite 300, Arlington, VA 22201
Phone   1-888-232-7733
Web site   www.ericec.org

Federation for Children with Special Needs
1135 Tremont Street, Suite 420, Boston, MA 02120
Phone   1-617-236-7210
Web site   www.fcsn.org

International Dyslexia Association (IDA) (formerly the Orton Dyslexia Society)
Chester Building, Suite 382, 8600 La Salle Road, Baltimore, MD 21286-2044
Phone   1-410-296-0232 or 1-800-222-3123
Web site   www.interdys.org

Learning Disabilities Association of America (LDA)
4156 Library Road, Pittsburgh, PA 15234
Phone   1-412-341-1515
Web site   www.ldanatl.org

National Center for Learning Disabilities (NCLD)
381 Park Avenue South, Suite 1401, New York, NY 10016
Phone   1-212-545-7510 or 1-888-575-7373
Web site   www.ncld.org
A resource for referrals, information, educational programs, legislation, for children and adults with learning disabilities.

National Information Center for Children and Youth with Disabilities (NICHCY)

PO Box 1492, Washington, DC 20013-1492

Phone   1-800-695-0285 or 1-202-884-8200

Web site   www.nichcy.org

Recordings for the Blind and Dyslexic

20 Roszel Road, Princeton, NJ 08540

Phone   1-609-452-0606

Web site   www.rfbd.org

LD Online Site

Web site   www.ldonline.org

Center for the Study of Autism

Web site   www.autism.org

The Center provides information about autism to parents and professionals, and conducts research on the efficacy of various therapeutic interventions. Many links and resources including information about Pervasive Developmental Disorders and Asperger Syndrome.

Children and Adults with Attention-Deficit Disorder (CHADD)

8181 Professional Place, Suite 201, Landover, MD 20785

Phone   1-800-233-4050

Web site   www.chadd.org

The Attention-Deficit Information Network, Inc. (AD-IN)

475 Hillside Avenue, Needham, MA 02194

Phone   1-781-455-9895

Web site   www.addinfonetwork.com

The National Attention-Deficit Disorder Association (ADDA)

1788 Second Street, Suite 200, Highland Park, IL 60035

Phone   1-847-432-2332

Web site   www.add.org

Obsessive-Compulsive Foundation, Inc.

Web site   www.ocfoundation.org

Research updates, treatment options, resources.

The Child and Adolescent Bipolar Foundation
Web site   www.bpkids.org
Articles, information and many links for resources.

NAMI (The National Alliance for the Mentally Ill)
200 N. Glebe Road, Suite 1015, Arlington, VA 22203 1-800-950-NAMI
Web site   www.nami.org
Information on mental illness with many links to information concerning children and adolescents.

Library Resources

American Library Association
Web site   www.ala.org

Internet Public Library
Web site   www.ipl.org
Provide library services to Internet users. Activities include: finding, evaluating, selecting, organizing, describing, and creating information resources; also provide direct assistance to individuals.

Internet School Library Media Center
Web site   www.falcon.jmu.edu/~ramseyil/index.html
Links to 25 sources of information for kindergarten through high school.

New York City Public Library
Web site   www.webpac.nypl.org/leo.html
Online library entrance.

School and Education

The Center for Effective Collaboration & Practice
1000 Thomas Jefferson Street NW, Suite 400, Washington, DC 20007
Phone   1-888-457-1551
Web site   www.air-dc.org/cecp

Dedicated to a policy of collaboration at federal, state, and local levels that contributes to and facilitates the production, exchange, and use of knowledge about effective practices.

National Center for Educational Statistics
Web site   www.nces.ed.gov

U.S. Department of Education
400 Maryland Avenue SW, Washington, DC 20202
Phone   1-800-872-5327 (1-800-USA-LEARN)
Web site   www.ed.gov

Parenting and Family Resources

www.talkingwithkids.org
Provides information about HIV, sex, violence, terrorism, and helpful ideas for talking with kids about tough issues.

www.familyeducation.com
Parenting advice, child development information

www.npin.org
Research-based information about the process of parenting, and about family involvement in education.

www.childrenspartnership.org
Dedicated to building a constituency for needs of children. Provides information for parents about children and technology, children and health reform, with excellent links to online resources.

www.family.com
Parenting advice, family fun and craft activities, recipes.

www.positiveparenting.com
Provides parenting resources, newsletter, and books.

www.parentsoup.com
Parenting information covering a wide range of topics, free newsletter.

www.kidsource.com
Includes information on newborns, toddlers, gifted children, health, learning disabilities, and safety.

Bereavement: Compassionate Friends

PO Box 3696, Oak Brook, IL 60522-3696

Phone   1-877-969-0010

Web site   www.compassionatefriends.org

Help for those who have lost a child.

Help With Homework

www.kidsclick.org

www.startribune.com/education/homework.shtml

Homework help with a response in 24 hours; games, quizzes, drills, modified news articles, web links.

www.school.discovery.com/homeworkhelp/bjpinchbeck

Links for homework help and over 700 links to educational sites on the Internet

www.bigchalk.com

An excellent site that provides homework help and a wide range of educational Internet services for educators and families.

Children's Health

Web site   www.kidshealth.org

Provides information about kids' health.

The American Academy of Pediatrics

Web site   www.aap.org

American Medical Association

515 N. State Street, Chicago, Il 60610

Phone   312-464-5000

Web site   www.ama-assn.org

Provides timely information about health issues.

Educators

www.eduhoundschoolsontheweb.com

Provides links to educational sites, free newsletter with educational resources, a pre-screened directory of more than 20,000 links in over 50 categories

www.eduplace.com
Resources for elementary-school teachers, students, and parents.

www.discoveryschool.com/schrockguide
Kathy Schrock's Guide for Educators. Excellent Internet site for teachers.

Download Worksheets for Students
www.freeworksheets.com
www.quia.com
Provides easy-to-use templates specifically designed for educators at all levels to create online learning activities, exercises, and quizzes, as well as informational Web pages.

Psychology-Miscellaneous

American Psychological Association: Prevention & Treatment Journal
Web site   www.apa.org/prevention

American Psychiatric Association
Web site   www.psych.org

American Academy of Child and Adolescent Psychiatry
Web site   www.aacap.org

National Association of School Psychologists
4340 East West Highway, Suite 402, Bethesda, MD 20814
Phone   1-301-657-0270
Web sites   www.nasponline.org
                  www.nasponline.org/information/main_links.html
Alphabetical listing of excellent online directories, resources, and sources.

New York University Child Study Center
550 First Avenue, New York, NY 10016
Phone   1-212-263-6622
Web site   www.aboutourkids.org
Excellent resource for information concerning child and adolescent mental health.

Index

SPECIAL OFFER

UNIQUE MINDS™ PROGRAM
FOR CHILDREN WITH LEARNING DISABILITIES
AND THEIR FAMILIES

Marcia Stern, Psy.D.

In Collaboration with the Unique Minds™ Project
of the Ackerman Institute for the Family

- Used by educators, guidance counselors, mental health professionals, and educational therapists
- Includes action-oriented activities, games, and simulations adaptable for use in the classroom, educational therapy, and individual or family counseling
- Helps families work together to defeat the common enemies of children who learn differently
- Increases motivation for success and provides tools for increasing self-esteem

"Unique Minds is an innovative program that helps children with learning disabilities recognize their strengths. The program works with families in a fun and supportive way, giving them new understanding and hope."
—Harold Koplewicz, M.D.
New York University School of Medicine

"What is unique is that Marcia Stern illuminates complex theories of learning using simple language, clever analogies, role playing, and dramatizations."
—Claire Wurtzel, M.S.
Director of General and Special Education Initiatives in Schools
Bank Street College

The Unique Minds Project was founded in 1991 at the Ackerman Institute for the Family in New York City and creates interventions for families in which a child has LD, ADHD, or other neurobiological variations. Project members are family therapists, learning disabilities specialists, and psychologists.

Manual and 2-hour videotape: 0-967-33050-5 • SPECIAL 50% DISCOUNT: $150.00
(list price: $300.00)

Ordering Information

To order a copy of this program, and receive a 50% discount, please call our warehouse at 1-800-233-4830. Mention Code **OUM 595** for the 50% discount!